Shakespeare's Life

Backgrounds to Shakespeare

Culture and Society in Shakespeare's Day
Literature and the Theater in Shakespeare's Day
Shakespeare's Life

Shakespeare's Life

Brett Foster

CHELSEA HOUSE
An Infobase Learning Company

Chelsea House
An imprint of Infobase Publishing
132 West 31st Street
New York, NY 10001

Library of Congress Cataloging-in-Publication Data
Foster, Brett, 1973–
    Shakespeare's life / Brett Foster.
        p. cm. — (Backgrounds to Shakespeare)
    Includes bibliographical references and index.
    ISBN 978-1-60413-522-0 (acid-free paper)
1. Shakespeare, William, 1564–1616. 2. Dramatists, English—Early modern,
1500–1700—Biography. I. Title.
    PR2894.F58 2012
    822.3'3—dc23
    [B]
                                                              2011045049

Chelsea House books are available at special discounts when purchased in bulk quantities for businesses, associations, institutions, or sales promotions. Please call our Special Sales Department in New York at (212) 967-8800 or (800) 322-8755.

You can find Chelsea House on the World Wide Web at
http://www.chelseahouse.com

Series design and composition by Erika K. Arroyo
Cover designed by Takeshi Takahashi
Cover printed by Yurchak Printing, Landisville, Pa.
Book printed and bound by Yurchak Printing, Landisville, Pa.
Date printed: April 2012
Printed in the United States of America

This book is printed on acid-free paper.

CONTENTS

SHAKESPEARE'S BIRTH AND ADOLESCENCE

William Shakespeare's first great accomplishment in life was not writing *Hamlet*, which he did around 1600 at roughly the age of thirty-five, or, centuries later, being voted the "Man of the Millennium" by the British Broadcasting Company in 2000. No, his first accomplishment was simple enough—Shakespeare lived. In the English market village of Stratford-upon-Avon (that is, the town situated along the River Avon), merely surviving was no easy task in the year of Shakespeare's birth, 1564. As many as fifteen percent of Stratford's population of approximately two thousand residents perished that year. What made Stratford so deadly?

An entry in the parish register at Stratford's Holy Trinity Church reads: "1564, Apr. 26. C. Gulielmus filius Johannes Shakspere." This may be a little mystifying at first glance, but the meaning becomes clear when we take into account its Latin words, abbreviations, and loose spellings, which differ from common spellings today. It simply means: "April 26, 1564, christened, William, son of John Shakespeare." It's curious to think that William Shakespeare's first appearance in print, so to speak, features his name in Latin—"Gulielmus." It is one modest sign of how far back in time Shakespeare and his age stands from our own. His was an age still shaped by Latin Christendom, whereas ours is defined by twenty-first-century modernity. We must make committed strides to encounter that earlier era again, as if face to face.

SHAKESPEARE'S HOMETOWN: STRATFORD-UPON-AVON

When we encounter that church register's page and scan down it, we see that many of the following entries suddenly begin to appear with the letter "B," which stands for "burial." Shortly after Shakespeare's birth, then, Stratford's parishioners started dying at an unusually fast pace. Twenty deaths in the first half of 1564 spiked to two hundred in the second half. This death rate equals one in seven people, a number that should make anyone shudder. A note in the margin of the parish register explains everything—*hic incepit pestis*—that is, "here begins the plague." Shakespeare entered the world at a site of epidemic. Nor was this the only time the bubonic plague would

William Shakespeare's home and birthplace, Stratford-upon-Avon in Warwickshire, England. This photograph was taken in August of 2005. *(Photographed by Stuart Yeates; used under a Creative Commons license)*

affect Shakespeare's life: it is generally thought that Shakespeare wrote many of his sonnets during a time away from London, when plague there in 1593–94 caused the closing of the city's theaters. The threat may still have been on Shakespeare's mind a year or two later, when Mercutio cries out in *Romeo and Juliet*, "A plague o'er both your houses." Moreover, the tragic miscommunication occurs between the lovers after Romeo fails to receive a letter from Friar Laurence—a letter that is held up because its messenger, Friar John, is detained by fears of plague infection.

The plague was an acutely dangerous outbreak, but it also grimly symbolizes the perilous times people confronted, and had to endure, during the English Renaissance. During the decade of Shakespeare's birth, only one in three children would live long enough to become an adult citizen of Stratford, and the historian Keith Thomas has concluded that life expectancy during this era was only in the mid-thirties. Various maladies such as tuberculosis and typhus also threatened, and everybody was vulnerable: two years before Shakespeare's birth, even Queen Elizabeth I nearly died of smallpox, and four years before that, influenza had swept through Stratford, killing many. A survey of town history during Shakespeare's life reveals a wide range of dangers and trials. In 1597, rainy conditions fermented another epidemic, and in destroying the crops, also led to a severe food shortage. Sometimes riots erupted in the village's streets as a result, or due to immigrant or vagrant tensions relating to these reeling social pressures. Fires were also a grave concern, especially since many of the houses were timber-framed and could quickly be engulfed in flames. Such conflagrations in Stratford in the mid-1590s ruined a significant portion of the town's homes.

Still, we must refrain from thinking of Stratford as constantly on the verge of apocalypse. On the contrary, it was a robust early-modern English community. Nor should we imagine a rural back-water town from which any bright, lively young man such as Shakespeare was dying to escape as soon as he came of age. Admittedly, compared with the booming capital of London, Stratford was a quiet village. Shakespeare's hometown is far removed from London, about eighty-five miles to the northwest—roughly a four-day walk or a two-day horse ride, with a stopover in the great university town of Oxford a common itinerary. (Even today, Oxford likes to claim its part of Shakespearean history by associating the author with the Crown pub and inn, and with the baptismal font at St. Michael's church, at the site of the former north gate, where Shakespeare may have stood as godfather to an Oxford friend's child.)

Stratford's region is known as Warwickshire or the Midlands, and its site as a river crossing made it a key town. A commercial wool route from Wales to London passed through Stratford, crossing the River Avon at Clopton Bridge. The prosperous citizen Hugh Clopton had rebuilt the sometimes-washed-away wooden bridge as a more lasting stone structure in the 1490s, ensuring that this commercial traffic could move regularly through the town. Stratford was founded centuries earlier, around 1200, and its central axis was along Wood Street/Bridge Street (as they are named today).

"Stratford will help you to understand Shakespeare," wrote the influential scholar F. J. Furnivall in 1875, and with this promise in mind, let us take a brief tour of the town, the circuit of which takes about twenty minutes to walk. At the west end of Wood Street, there was an open space that served as a cattle market, called Rother Market. Today, the railway station is located a little beyond this spot. From Bridge Street, Henley Street ran to the northwest and featured various shops, including John Shakespeare's glover's shop. Another main shopping area was High Street, running due south from the intersection of Wood and Bridge streets, at Market Cross. High Street led into

THE ROYAL SHAKESPEARE COMPANY IN STRATFORD

Stratford-upon-Avon is almost always crowded with international tourists visiting the town's various Shakespeare landmarks—the Birthplace on Henley Street; Holy Trinity Church, where the writer was baptized and where he is buried; the family cottage of his wife, Anne Hathaway, just outside of town. The most fitting tribute to Stratford's most famous hometown hero, however, is surely the theaters that mark the town. In these spaces, Shakespeare's plays continue to live year by year, and to be reinterpreted and restaged freshly for each new generation.

Grandly inhabiting the bank along the River Avon, just north of Holy Trinity Church, sits the red-brick Royal Shakespeare Theatre, which reopened in late 2010 after undergoing major renovations. The theater originated in 1879 as the Shakespeare Memorial Theatre. Like Shakespeare's original Globe playhouse, this theater unfortunately burned down, in 1926, and for a while shows were performed in a local Stratford cinema. An open competition led to the rebuilding of the theater in Art Deco style, and it reopened on Shakespeare's birthday, April 23, 1932. The Memorial Theatre housed there officially became the Royal Shakespeare Company on March 20, 1961, under the leadership of renowned director Peter Hall. Other changes involved a shift from festival scheduling to year-round performances, the creation of a permanent company, and a second theater in London (the Aldwych, the Place, the Barbican, and the Pit, in turn).

The year 1974 saw the opening of the Other Place, a smaller, alternative theater whose name wittily alludes to a line by Hamlet. The director Trevor Nunn staged a *Macbeth* production there in 1976, featuring the highly esteemed actors Ian McKellen and Judi Dench. (Dench's performance was subsequently judged the best acting in the history of the Royal Shakespeare Theatre.) The Swan Theatre opened in 1986, on the other side of the main Royal Theatre. It features a thrust stage and galleried seating for approximately four hundred spectators.

The RSC experienced some rocky, turbulent times in the 1990s, but the turn of the century has brought renewed opportunities and fresh achievements to the company. It hosted a Complete Works of Shakespeare Festival beginning in 2006, and in the following year began work on needed updates. The main theater was closed for interior renovations, with the temporary Courtyard Theatre opening in the heart of Stratford.

The company has enjoyed some illustrious productions and memorable moments in English stage history over the past few decades. Peter Brook directed Paul Scofield in *King Lear* in 1962 and, even more iconically, *A Midsummer Night's Dream* in 1970. Likewise, Peter Hall was hailed for shows that included *The Wars of the Roses* and *Hamlet*. The director John Barton was responsible for many still-praised productions, and actors who have garnered much attention and acclaim have included Ben Kingsley, Derek Jacobi, Sinéad Cusack, Kenneth Branagh, and Ralph Fiennes. The RSC has also staged modern shows, including world premieres of plays by eminent English playwrights such as Tom Stoppard and the Nobel laureate Harold Pinter. Recent hits have included Ian McKellen in Trevor Nunn's production of *King Lear*, as well as a *Hamlet* featuring David Tennant in the title role and Patrick Stewart as the villain Claudius.

SEE ALSO:

Adler, Steven. *Rough Magic: Making Theatre at the Royal Shakespeare Company.* Carbondale: Southern Illinois University Press, 2001.
Chambers, Colin. *Inside the Royal Shakespeare Company: Creativity and the Institution.* New York: Routledge, 2004.

Chapel Street and Church Street as it continued south. This route would pass by the Town Hall, the Guild Chapel, and the grammar school. As the road wound around and became Old Town

Street, the lovely Holy Trinity Church would soon appear. This area would have felt slightly separate from the town proper, and around the church only a few large houses, occupied by the well-to-do gentry of the town, marked the area as the original village. The environs outside the main commercial areas were quiet, with barns standing on the side streets. However, as a central market town, Stratford would also be bustling when residents within a five-mile radius traveled there for seasonal fairs and weekly markets, where they would trade produce and products and services. Thus, both of William Shakespeare's grandfathers, Richard Shakespeare of Snitterfield and Robert Arden of Wilmcote, would have visited Stratford often and known the town well.

SHAKESPEARE'S FAMILY

Shakespeare's family was not immune to Stratford's occasionally lethal conditions described above. As we begin this biographical tale composed largely of Shakespeare's frequent successes—his many literary and theatrical triumphs; the agile, pleasant impression that many had of his personality (at least as it developed in legend); and the enduring power and global recognition of his cultural after-life—we would do well to keep in mind that Shakespeare, from childhood on, knew death well and suffered tragic family losses. Of the Shakespeares' eight children—four girls and four boys, of whom William was the first son—only one daughter, Joan, lived beyond infancy or early childhood. Both of William's parents died during the first decade of the seventeenth century. One brother, Edmund, a fellow actor, died in 1607 (when William was forty-three) in London, and two other brothers died in Stratford, in successive years, during the last five years of William's own life. Perhaps most devastatingly, Shakespeare lost his only son, named Hamnet, when the boy was eleven years old.

William himself was to die in 1616, on the very day of his birthday, April 23. This "same birthday/

death date" notion relies on Shakespeare's baptism record in the Stratford parish register as April 26. As the argument goes, it was natural for baptism to occur three days after birth. That would mean William Shakespeare was beginning his fifty-third year on April 23, 1616, the last day of his life. (This may be why his monument in Stratford says "Aetatis 53," or "53 years.") That story is nicely tidy, but it should be added that April 23 is also St. George's Day, named for England's patron saint. Therefore patriotism, or a simple desire for symmetry to symbolize a famous life well lived and completed, may also contribute to the general agreement on the April 23 birth date. In any case, that is when we celebrate it, and celebrate it we do: last year, April 23 saw a variety of festivities and observances in both Stratford and London, and worldwide as well, if from a geographical distance.

That first birth record of Shakespeare identifies him as the "son of John," and we are lucky to know a good deal about Shakespeare's ancestry on both his father's and his mother's side of the family. Shakespeare's father hailed from the village of Snitterfield, four miles northeast of Stratford. His own father, Richard, William's grandfather, farmed there, leasing land from one Robert Arden, who blossoms in the writer's family tree as well. You see, John Shakespeare married Mary Arden, the youngest of Robert Arden's eight daughters. Arden's powerful, wealthy family resided in Wilmcote, four miles west of Snitterfield. It is reasonable to imagine that John Shakespeare arrived in Stratford around 1545 and commenced with a seven-year apprenticeship. By 1552, he was a glover in the town. We know this from a fine levied against him, preserved in civic records, for allowing a muckheap or dunghill to accumulate near his home in Henley Street.

This may sound merely unsightly and unneighborly today, but it also caused a serious threat of infection. Remember, the prospect of plague was always looming, and early-modern town or city life was already a dirty affair. Unlike today's sewers, those in Stratford or London were in open ditches. City leaders were clearly concerned by John Shakespeare's practice, and they had a right to be. We should refrain, however, from reacting to this dung-heap fine with snickers at Shakespeare's "country bumpkin" father. Keep in mind that he was a young glover or whittawer—someone who cured and prepared white or soft leather—and the business of preparing animal hides for sale had its unpleasant, unclean aspects. Glovers took goat and pig skins and soaked them in salt solutions, followed by the application of egg-yolk and flower mixtures. It is not surprising that some early biographers spoke of Shakespeare's father as a "butcher," considering the carcass materials he worked with. In discarding this refuse just outside his home, Shakespeare's father may very well have been trying to make his new business more efficient and financially viable.

In the early years of his business, Shakespeare's father, John, leased one of two houses now preserved as the Shakespeare Birthplace Trust, a popular museum, archive, research center, and tourist attraction today. (There is also an excellent Shakespeare-themed bookshop located just across the street.) Students of American history may enjoy knowing that two early U.S. presidents, John Adams and Thomas Jefferson, made a literary pilgrimage to Shakespeare's birthplace in 1786. John Shakespeare would not purchase this house for several years, but in 1556 he expanded his domain and bought the house to the east, perhaps in preparation for the arrival of his bride, Mary Arden, in 1557.

Upon their marriage, the Shakespeares would have benefited from Mary's dowry, which included a valuable estate outside of town that included another house and a good amount of acreage. The Ardens sprung from a Warwickshire noble family, and as such they assumed

An 1896 engraving of Mary Arden's Cottage in Stratford-upon-Avon *(Engraving by Stas Walery & Co.)*

the name Arden after the geographical identity of their property—the Forest of Arden was to the north of Stratford, where cattle farming was common, whereas the more open region of Feldon lay to the south, where crops were more typically grown. Stratford was also long famous for "malting," which is the roasting of grain for the making of beer. As we will see, the adult William Shakespeare seems himself to have been involved in this town activity, and controversially so. The property John Shakespeare acquired through his marriage to Mary may explain why early biographers also speak of him as a wool dealer, though generally he is better known for his business in town. "He was a glover's son," wrote Thomas Plume about Shakespeare the writer in 1660, and relates a story about another who once visited the family's Henley Street shop. John is described as a "merry cheeked old man," who said of his son that "Will was a good honest fellow."

WILLIAM SHAKESPEARE, STRATFORD SCHOOLBOY

Can we know anything about that "good honest fellow" William Shakespeare in his youth? Nothing that we may safely call evidence exists, yet perhaps we can infer something from the general increase of the family's fortunes during the writer's early years. First, it is worth noting that John and Mary were married at the dawn of a new age in England—in the year before Henry VIII's daughter Elizabeth Tudor assumed the throne as Elizabeth I. The first decades of her reign were tumultuous, and no one could have envisioned the glorious half-century this shrewd ruler would see. Yet it was the beginning of a Golden Age in English culture and literature, all the same. More locally, Shakespeare's father had timed well his arrival and establishment in Stratford, and he had also married well: the Ardens were far higher in social standing than were the Shakespeares. In 1553, the year after John was fined, Stratford

was granted a charter of incorporation, officially creating a town council made up of aldermen and burgesses. Members were not elected to this group, but rather chosen by nomination, and came to include the town's main tradesmen. John's good standing in town may be seen in his nomination to the council in 1557, the same year as his marriage. He rose through the ranks and eventually served as high bailiff—Stratford's equivalent to mayor—in 1568. Records indicate that his fortunes in town soon changed, as we shall see.

One of the town council's new responsibilities was the operating of a grammar school and almshouses for the poor. These had been under the jurisdiction of the Guild of the Holy Cross, a medieval religious foundation, but one of the many social changes during the English Reformation was to shift these religious properties and activities to secular, civic organizations. These changes equated with a shift from the Roman Catholic identity of the medieval church and its various para-church foundations to the newer Protestant sympathies of the national, or Anglican, church. The possessions of the foundations generally were confiscated and delivered to town governments, noble families, or to the monarch himself. Therefore, we have evidence of town-approved dramatic performances in the Guildhall, and although no records exist to prove his attendance, it is almost certain that young William Shakespeare would have attended the grammar school overseen by the council, soon renamed the King's New School. The Guildhall, chapel, almshouses, and school all still survive and can be visited in Stratford today. In 1553, the school was moved to the upper floor of the Guildhall, so this is where Shakespeare would have commenced his studies, most likely after spending some time at a "petty" school where young students first learned to read and write. Shakespeare captures this figure memorably in *As You Like It*: "Then, the whining schoolboy, with his satchel / And shining morning face, creeping like snail / Unwillingly to school . . . " Often these first schools were not run by trained teachers, but by shopkeepers, tailors, weavers, or others willing to do it. The pupils would make use of hornbooks, that is, a small plank for writing attached to a wooden handle and protected by a thin slice of transparent horn. On this sheet appeared a printed alphabet and possibly a short prayer in different typefaces.

The young Shakespeare soon would have been ready for grammar school. Although he appears never to have attended college or university, Shakespeare came of age at a felicitous time, for despite how modest it sounds—a grammar school in a provincial Warwickshire town—the King's New School was impressive in various ways. First, the town paid the schoolmaster a £20 salary, which was a substantial amount. The Warwick schoolmaster received only slightly more than half this amount, and it was greater than an average fellowship at Oxford or Cambridge universities. Now, there is some debate as to whether or not John Shakespeare was illiterate. He signed his name with a simple mark, an X or cross or even a compass, but it seems clear, based on his civic responsibilities and successes, that he was able to read documents effectively. Perhaps he could also write ably, despite the insinuations of his simple signature. Whatever the case, one thing is absolutely clear—his son William was anything but illiterate. In fact, he experienced during his stint at the Stratford grammar school an intensive humanist curriculum developed just a few decades earlier by European intellectual luminaries such as Erasmus of Rotterdam and Juan Luis Vives and, closer to home, the great educator and Dean of St. Paul's Cathedral, John Colet. Students in grammar school were there not to learn English, which was a given at this level, but to master the Latin language, often carried out through a rigorous process called "double translation," moving with increasing fluency back and forth between English and Latin. The atmosphere of these schools would make many modern students gasp: students—*male* students only, that is—worked for long hours, often from early in the morning till early in the evening, with few breaks. Some contemporary woodcuts feature stern schoolmasters whipping the bare backsides of vainly objecting pupils with birch rods.

It has been argued that the average Renaissance grammar-school student would have obtained the level of Latin proficiency reserved mainly for advanced college students today. The comparison notwithstanding, Shakespeare and his fellow students would have moved swiftly from the English primers of their early school days to a popular Latin grammar by William Lilly and onward to an array of classics from Latin literature. Their textbooks would have included Aesop's *Fables*, *The Distichs of Cato*, the speeches of Cicero, historical passages from Julius Caesar, Tacitus, and Sallust, and lyric, epic, and mythological poetry by Horace, Virgil (the great poet of imperial Rome), and Ovid, whose various and frequent influences throughout Shakespeare's works make many believe he was our English writer's favorite poet. Shakespeare's schoolmasters were Thomas Jenkins and Simon Hunt, and it is possible that Shakespeare later recalls them fondly in a few scenes in his plays. For example, in *The Merry Wives of Windsor*, a Welsh schoolmaster named Hugh Evans, with a penchant for comic mispronunciation, takes his pupil, aptly named William, through his Latin parts of speech. Funny English-Latin wordplay prevails ("pulcher" and "polecats," for example), and further talk of the Latin word "hang-hog" and the "focative" case add to the hilarity. "That's a good William," says the schoolmaster. Elsewhere, in the early play *Love's Labour's Lost*, the pedant Holofernes suggests memories of Shakespeare's school days. "Old Mantuan, old Mantuan!" he declares. "Who understandeth thee not, loves thee not." Holofernes sounds learned enough, but for many in the London audience, the joke would have been on him: he is quoting from the *Adulescentia*, or pastoral poems for young readers by the Neo-Latin poet Baptista Mantuanus. It would rather be like a sophisticated literary type today name-dropping Benjamin Franklin, or a children's author, even, such as Beverly Cleary or Judy Blume.

The goal of these grammar schools, it should be emphasized once again, was not simply to make English students mere understanders of the Latin language, but to make them supremely able and versatile imitators of Latin style, or literary excellence. Thus the boys also read works such as Erasmus's *Colloquies* (or dialogues) and his *De Copia*, which aimed to equip students with a copiousness or fullness of skill in Latin usage. One often-quoted example from this work teaches students how to say "thank you" in Latin in sixty different ways. More substantively, though, this work was a catalog of rhetorical practices, namely schemes and tropes. Schemes were the surface patterns that could make poetry dazzling linguistically and highly emotive in expression. Affects of repetition and paralleling and antithesis are common in these cases. Tropes involved anything that "turned" (as the Greek word means) from the factual or straightforward into the imaginative realms of the figurative, or primarily metaphorical. Metaphors, many Renaissance poets felt, following Aristotle, were the building blocks for great poetry writing. What resulted was often an ostentatious, "oily" kind of dense poetry, as in this famous speech by Valentine, from the early comedy *The Two Gentlemen of Verona*:

> What light is light if Sylvia be not seen?
> What joy is joy if Sylvia be not by?—
> Unless it be to think that she is by
> And feed upon the shadow of perfection.

It is a wise critic who recently described the development of Shakespeare's aesthetic sensibility in paradoxical terms: throughout his career, the playwright learned to subtly conceal the considerable rhetorical and poetic talents he had developed as a boy and young man. Shakespeare's reading during this time also would have provided him with an imaginative world of Greek and Roman stories and characters, and ways of mentally grouping them and their circumstances. Think of that night scene in Belmont, late in *The Merchant of Venice*, where the lovers Lorenzo and Jessica recall to each other that "On such as night as this" diverse classical figures experienced their own doomed love or romantic betrayal. Their own quickness with these examples arguably does not bode well for their future happiness together. The richest resource for many stories such as these would have been found in the long poem by Ovid, the *Metamorphoses*.

SHAKESPEARE THE TEENAGER

Usually boys finished grammar school at fifteen or sixteen and were prepared to proceed to university. This was not the path followed by Shakespeare; in fact, there is a real possibility that he was not able to finish the full course of grammar school, due to the flagging fortunes of his father. After serving as bailiff in 1568 and then as justice of the peace in 1571, John Shakespeare experienced professional, legal, and civic setbacks throughout the 1570s and 1580s. It was not a precipitous fall from grace, but rather a momentum-building pattern of altercation, financial straits, loss of property (mainly belonging originally to his in-laws), and negligence of town leadership still expected of him. Debt went unpaid or was contested, John was involved in lawsuits as both plaintiff and defendant, and he was hit with substantial fines in some cases and excused from paying levies in others, a sign of considerably reduced fiscal means. His attendance at town meetings dropped dramatically after 1577, and by 1587 the council appointed a new alderman to replace him, for "Mr. Shaxpere doth not come to the halls . . . nor hath not done of long time." In 1592, the council made a list of those citizens, including John, who were failing to come to church. This fact has led to some speculation about the true religious sympathies and allegiances of Shakespeare's father, but other circumstances suggest he was most likely hiding out and lying low for fear of being arrested for his debt.

His father's fall may also explain a detail included in the first biography of Shakespeare in 1709. There Nicholas Rowe reports that Shakespeare had attended Stratford's free school till his father withdrew him because of the "narrowness of his circumstances, and the want of his assistance at home." Simply paraphrased, it sounds like a struggling John Shakespeare needed his growing, increasingly educated son to shift his focus and help with the family business. And who knows? Maybe these "narrow" circumstances were ultimately to benefit the young man, giving him some early experience in Stratford's mercantile world in addition to the education received within the four walls of the Guildhall schoolroom. The scholar David Bevington nicely points out that the children in Shakespeare's plays are an "odd lot generally. They are precocious; they speak like little adults." One thinks of the princes in *Richard III*, who make wise with their uncle Gloucester before they are sent to the Tower to meet their fates. Perhaps this was Shakespeare's attitude in school as well, and maybe it was all for the better when his father required him to move on, to leave the grammar school behind and begin to assist him.

At least a pair of late-seventeenth-century anecdotes speak of William following in his father's footsteps, but with a certain oratorical flair probably gained at school: "when he killed a calf, he would do it in a high style, and make a speech," says John Aubrey in his *Lives*. We may

This 1904 print depicts the Stratford schoolroom known traditionally as the place Shakespeare was taught. *(A.C. Wyatt)*

infer from this odd mix of skinning and declaiming a particular aspect of Shakespeare's Latin training, which involved student productions of Latin comedies by the playwrights Plautus and Terence. The influence of these classical Roman plays can be seen most evidently in Shakespeare's own early comedy of misplaced twins, *The Comedy of Errors*. However indebted to its source, though, Shakespeare's play has its own signature of the confident young virtuoso writer: he took the twins plot from Plautus and *doubled* it, creating twin gentlemen and servants, all of whom are separated. The result is massive confusion, and maximum fun. And these classical Roman influences were just the beginning. For all the mysteries that still surround Shakespeare, many signs of his being a wide-reaching, voluminous reader are apparent throughout his career, a habit likely developed during these school years. His other major sources would include the Bible, medieval works such as Geoffrey Chaucer's *The Canterbury Tales* and John Gower's *Confessio Amantis*, large compilations of history such as Raphael Holinshed's *Chronicles*, and Italian and English prose romances.

So Shakespeare may have had to quit school early in order to assist his father at home. Even so, when we think of a rich boyhood, be it our own or others', surely we think of far more than those many hours spent in school, or helping one's parents, or even the reading of favorite books during free time. Although, once again, we have nothing like a contemporary description of the young Shakespeare exploring the streets of Stratford and the surrounding areas around the town, it is nonetheless hard to imagine an active boy, even one busy with school and family responsibilities, not roving in this way. So let us indulge for a minute and imagine Shakespeare the Stratford boy playing on Henley Street, in the garden or out the back gate. Picture him interacting with his family's neighbors—George Badger on the other side of a wall, the Hornsbys on the other end of the house, the Quineys across the street, and the Johnsons' and the Smiths' barns nearby. Picture him playing beneath the elm trees at the church yard in front of Holy Trinity Church, or skipping stones from the banks of the Avon, or running a little recklessly in and out of the archery butts beside Clopton Bridge and near the road to Warwick.

The American author Anna Quindlen captures well this hard-to-define aspect—let's call it the essential uneventfulness of childhood—in an essay called "Summer Coming." First, she notices some of the tell-tale signs of late May:

> …An old remembered glee rises inside me. Summer is coming. Uniform skirts in mothballs. Pencils with their points left broken. Open windows. Day trips to the beach. Pickup games. Hanging out.
>
> How boring it was.
>
> Of course, it was the making of me, as a human being and a writer. Downtime is where we become ourselves, looking into the middle distance, kicking at the curb, lying on the grass or sitting on the stoop and staring into the tedious blue of the summer sky.

The unexciting, unrecorded days of youth in a small market town may feel like boredom to the young person experiencing them, but they are in fact essential for any creative productions that lie in the future. These slow, familiar days are in reality "the quiet moving of the wheels inside that fuel creativity." The poet Donald Justice likewise captures those sweet do-nothing days, days that are profoundly formative, and how they affect an impressionable boy in his "Sonnet: The Poet at Seven":

> And on the porch, across the upturned
>   chair,
> The boy would spread a dingy counterpane
> Against the length and majesty of the rain,
> And on all fours crawl under it like a bear
> To lick his wounds in secret, in his lair;
> And afterwards, in the windy yard again,
> One hand cocked back, release his paper
>   plane
> Frail as a mayfly to the faithless air. …

Justice's verses, with their young protagonist stretching his imagination and play-acting like a bear on a summer evening, could apply to Shakespeare especially well.

Park Honan, one of Shakespeare's major biographers of the past two decades, argues that biographies are prone to falsify history because they tend to look backward into life, as if everything that eventually occurred were somehow certain, and known by the subject, in his earliest days. Better, he says, to capture that "unknown future ahead of him." The more successful biographies, he continues, "should give a continual sense of a whole verifiable present unfolding before us. Or a sense of time as it was lived through, and with an unknown future problematically ahead." William Shakespeare, as he grew up and studied and worked and played during the 1570s and early 1580s, could not know what to expect in the coming years. It is the uncertainty we all face, after all, but it does seem that he flourished in these present days, perhaps receiving special parental care, as Honan posits, because he had been a newborn who survived the plague. So his childhood appears to have been normal and happy, though he couldn't yet know then what lay ahead—a wife and children and regional travels, with an eventual arrival in London. And in between those first things and that last thing? Well, we have very little clue.

Sources and Further Reading

Bearman, Robert, ed. *The History of an English Borough: Stratford-upon-Avon 1196–1996.* Stroud, Gloucestershire: Sutton, 1997.

Fripp, Edgar I. *Shakespeare's Stratford.* London: Oxford University Press, 1928

Furness, Alexander (photographs) and H. J. Massingham (introduction). *The Shakespeare Country including the Peak and the Cotswolds.* London: Allen and Unwin, 1951.

Holderness, Graham. *Cultural Shakespeare: Essays in the Shakespeare Myth.* Hatfield, U.K.: University of Hertfordshire Press, 2001.

Miola, Robert. *Shakespeare's Reading.* New York: Oxford University Press, 2000.

Ward, H. Snowden and Catharine Weed Ward. *Shakespeare's Town and Times.* London: Sampson Low, Marston & Co. Ltd, 1905.

SHAKESPEARE THE YOUNG MAN

As a young man in his mid-teens, William Shakespeare's apparently normal and uneventful home life may have begun to feel more turbulent, less certain, around 1578. His father, John, had withdrawn abruptly from public life the year before, and in 1578 the family was forced to sell some of his wife's estates, brought to the marriage as dowry, to one of her brothers-in-law. John tried to regain the property in 1580, but the brother-in-law refused to receive payment in exchange for the property, on account of another debt John owed that he feared would go unpaid. Awkward legal wrangling between the families ensued for the next several years. John was also fined repeatedly during these years, in part because of bad money-lending investments that others defaulted on, leaving him fiscally responsible. Money-lending was a dubious enterprise, as was John's involvement in wool-trading, with which his son William may also have helped, though secretly (the Shakespeares were not licensed wool dealers, and thus their activities in this area were illegal). John was also called before the Queen's Bench, a major court in Westminster (a legal and royal hub next to London), and was demanded to keep the queen's peace. It is possible that John Shakespeare may have intentionally distanced himself from some of his properties because he feared being fined for religious nonconformity. This issue, regarding Shakespeare and his family both, will be explored in more detail shortly.

William probably had to quit his studies at the King's New School at the age of fourteen or fifteen, in 1578–79, and was likely helping his father with his gloving business in the following years: "He exercised his father's trade," writes John Aubrey late in the seventeenth century, and Nicholas Rowe early in the next century added that "upon his leaving school he seems to have gone entirely into that way of living which his father had proposed him." Working beside his father may have been tense at times, since John must have been regularly vexed and distracted by the aforementioned financial and legal problems. His father also had enemies in Stratford: one man, Ralph Chaldrey, had to vow in a legal con-

Portrait of John Aubrey, a seventeenth century Shakespeare biographer, published by Edward Evans in the early nineteenth century.

text that he would not assault John Shakespeare! The Shakespeare family experienced both sad and joyous changes during this time. William's eight-year-old sister Anne died during the following year, but 1580 brought the birth of his brother Edmund. Eventually, like his older brother, he, too, would be an actor on London's stages.

As a more recent biographer has imagined it, William spent these teenaged days "engrossed with the mysteries of skins and wool, tan-bark and timber, looking after the farm-land that his father owned or occupied, and giving an eye to the cutters in the shop, and the glove sewers who worked at their homes." William's father's shop was right in a front room of the family home on Henley Street, with a storefront or window facing the street. Fortunately, their street was a key thoroughfare in Stratford and guaranteed a lot of foot traffic. (Visitors today can still get a sense of its importance from the very width of the street.) He probably interacted regularly with many of Stratford's citizens, being more or less a young businessman-in-training. The Shambles, or slaughterhouse, from which his father obtained his hides, was quite nearby in Middle Row, and William probably knew this place, and its smells and sounds, very well. Many of the materials from the tanning trade appear in his writing—neat's oil, greasy fells, bowgets, cowgut—and sometimes leather products lent themselves as fitting metaphors. For example, one character has the "wit of cheveril," which was flexible, easily stretchable baby lamb's skin, and another has a "soft cheveril conscience." In *Romeo and Juliet*, Romeo, upon beholding Juliet at her balcony, exclaims, "O, that I were a glove upon that hand / That I might touch that cheek!"

One of the Shakespeare family's customers may have been Alexander Aspinall, who became schoolmaster at the King's New School in 1582. Although not verifiable, one seventeenth-century commonplace book (something like a personal notebook or diary) contains verses sent by Aspinall to a woman who interested him: "The gift is small, the will is all. Alexander Aspinall." The entry in the commonplace books says: "Shaxpaire upon a pair of gloves that master send to his mistress." The scholar Stephen Greenblatt imagines Shakespeare as a young "writer of personalized jingles," into which, in this case at least, he may have mischievously inserted his own name. In a couple of sonnets, Shakespeare would pun on his name "Will," which incidentally was also a word with sexual connotations.

SHAKESPEARE'S EARLY PLAYGOING

Shakespeare, however, could not have worked all the time, and biographers have almost always been interested in contemplating how this particular grammar-school student and then teen-aged employee from Stratford first developed an interest in the theater. Soon enough, he would revolutionize the medium and make it enduringly interesting. We have seen already that as a student, William would have encountered the texts of Latin plays by Plautus and Terence. It was a common practice for classes in these schools to perform plays as well. (Students at Stratford's school still do so to this day.) Perhaps those lively, sometimes bawdy Roman comedies first caught William's interest and charged his imagination. Think about something that you yourself are passionate about—some sport, or pastime, or object avidly collected. Now remember your first encounter with that thing, beginning with curiosity, then the thrill of discovery, followed by an intense wish to know the ins and outs of the thing. And the overall impression? A deep, rewarding feeling of rightness. We must realize that we have no basis in reality as we try to imagine the young Shakespeare discovering the power—and the fun and excitement—of reading and acting in dramatic works. Nevertheless, we can allow ourselves to visualize that moment when a still developing genius first experienced his eventual calling.

In the community at large, the town of Stratford hosted its share of theatrical events. In fact, when he was bailiff in 1569, William's father himself approved payments to two traveling theater companies, the Queen's players and the Earl of Worcester's players, for their official performances in the town Guildhall. Theater troupes had to obtain the patronage, or sponsorship, of powerful figures such as the queen or her noblemen or courtiers—otherwise, the actors were considered too sketchy to be entertained; they were merely vagabonds or "masterless men." For this 1569 performance, in effect John Shakespeare would have served as the sponsor: the troupe's first performance was known as the "Mayor's Play" and was free for everyone. We have no record of what play was performed in 1569, but morality plays were popular during this time. These plays often featured "Everyman" figures who are tempted by personified vice characters or face various trials, and some of the surviving plays of this sort feature titles such as *The Interlude of Youth* and *The Castle of Perseverance*. These companies and several others made appearances in Stratford throughout the 1570s and 1580s, suggesting that Shakespeare had many occasions, right in his hometown, to witness professional theater.

Stratford also hosted amateur theater productions, in which Shakespeare may have participated. They were often connected with church holidays or feast days, and should be placed in the context of a robust tradition of medieval mystery plays. This earlier phase of English drama featured productions sponsored by various professional guilds in English towns. These shows involved the re-creation of biblical episodes, often acted upon a stage-topped wagon that moved from point to point through the streets. Annual pageants were often held in late spring, around the time of the Corpus Christi holiday. There is a Stratford record of a production in 1583 on Whitsuntide, and a later record, in 1602, states that "there shall be no plays or interludes played in the chamber, the Guildhall." This comment suggests that performances had been going on just prior to this ban—hence the need for it to be made formally. The ban itself may reflect a growing influence of Puritans, who were hostile toward theater, by this time in Stratford. Nevertheless, some dramatic displays, associated with folksier, earthier, more mirthful holidays, persisted; these included May Day as well as mummers' plays at Christmastime.

William and his family may have also attended even more eventful dramatic displays, although this hypothesis is necessarily more speculative. This last kind of spectacle we may call "theater of state"—that is, pageant and ceremony associated with monarchs or other political leaders, in this case Queen Elizabeth I and her court. One version of this political drama was simply a royal progress, whereby the queen and her extensive retinue of servants, courtiers, and councilors traveled through the various realms of England. They proceeded in self-conscious, highly opulent fashion, aware that (in an age before mass communication) these sorts of processions were how the queen best connected, in person and with majestic appearance, with common citizens in diverse towns and villages. Elizabeth traveled through Shakespeare's region, Warwickshire or the Midlands, in 1566, 1572, and 1575. And then there were the truly awe-inspiring occasions, such as the powerful Earl of Leicester's historically elaborate hosting of the queen in 1575, at Kenilworth Castle, just twelve miles to the northeast of Stratford. The place was transformed into a fantastical site for diverse forms of entertainment, and they had to please the queen and hold her interest for nineteen days, at the conclusion of her latest progress. If the eleven-year-old Shakespeare were in the audience, he would have seen mythical figures such as Hercules greet the arriving queen, fireworks going off overhead, acrobats, bears fighting, and multiple plays performed, on both land and water. One of the most memorable spectacles featured a mechanical dolphin rising from the nearby lake, from which an actor, identified with Arion, sang and recited his oratorical lines.

Some critics have pointed out the comparison in the comedy *Twelfth Night*, "Like Arion on the dolphin's back," and wondered in print if a well-known image from *A Midsummer Night's Dream* also has this historical performance behind it. The fairy king Oberon asks his assistant Puck if he remembers:

> Since once I sat upon a promontory
> And heard a mermaid on a dolphin's back
> Uttering such dulcet and harmonius breath
> That the rude sea grew civil at her song
> And certain stars shot madly from their
>   spheres
> To hear the sea maid's music?

These exquisitely lyrical lines capture well the composed elegance and refined beauty of the High Renaissance, and they possibly may have been inspired by the memorable pageant at Kenilworth in the middle of Elizabeth's long reign. That said, we should also take note of that other, opposite vision of theatrical activity we see in Shakespeare's great play—the amateur, if enthusiastic, efforts to stage a play by common citizens such as Peter Quince, Nick Bottom, and the "rude mechanicals." In the play's fictional world, this group of citizen actors hails from Athens, but they may have been modeled on some of the Shakespeare family's neighbors and fellow townspeople in Stratford.

SHAKESPEARE IN LOVE

Sometime in 1582, perhaps just before William Shakespeare turned eighteen in late April, he began seeing a young woman named Anne Hathaway, the daughter of an established yeoman or farming family. They lived in the nearby village of Shottery, about a mile to the west of Stratford. From his home, William would have walked south, past Rother Market, passing Scholars Lane and Pools Close on the left, and taking a right at Two Elms. Probably by that summer he was walking the skinny footpath out of town on a regular basis, passing the fields and eventually arriving at a cluster of farmhouses, one of which is called Anne Hathaway's Cottage today. Of course, it wasn't called that then. First of all, her family spoke of their home as Hewlands, and second, words such as "cottage" or even "farmhouse" belie what an impressive, scenic site this was, settled at the edge of the Forest of Arden. The Hathaway home had twelve rooms and a carefully trimmed thatched roof, timber-framed walls with the wattle-and-daub plaster common to Tudor buildings, open ceilings, a large stove, latticed windows with jasmine upon the walls, and, surrounding the house, gardens, meadows in which sheep grazed, and orchards with apple trees. It remains a lovely place to visit today, although the tourists' coach buses in the street beside the house and the general suburban growth along the path from Stratford to Shottery have somewhat dampened the rural, pastoral charm experienced centuries ago. For those touring the cottage today, its rooms will also feel small by modern standards, but make no mistake: this was an impressive family dwelling.

It is hard to resist romanticizing the romance between William and Anne, who, despite being a young woman, was nevertheless unusually old for the eighteen-year-old William—she was twenty-six, eight years his senior. Because Stratford birth records only began to be kept in 1558, we do not have a record of her baptism, as we do for William. Instead, we know her approximate age based on an engraving at her tomb in Stratford's church. The pair may have known each other

An 1896 engraving of the interior of Anne Hathaway's Cottage in Stratford-upon-Avon. The cottage was acquired and made into a museum by the Shakespeare Birthplace Trust in the late nineteenth century. *(Engraving by Stas Walery & Co.)*

for some time because Anne's father, Richard, sometimes had financial business with William's father, John. We have so many questions as we imagine their first meetings. Were they attracted to each other instantly, or did their interest in and fondness for each other develop slowly? Was the younger Shakespeare intimidated by Anne Hathaway as the "older woman"? Or was she a more reticent sort, secretly charmed by a brash, witty young man who had a way with words? Of course, this is romanticizing as well. Maybe they were both retiring, she quietly modest and he a little embarrassed and deeply thoughtful. Again, we can never really know, but must settle for filling in the matter with the few details we do know, or might know.

Shakespeare may have been a source of consolation for Anne, whose father had died just

a few years earlier. He speaks of being "sick in body" in his will in 1581, in which he left a nice sum of money for Anne's dowry. This was presumably for Anne; her name does not appear in the will, but she is probably the "Agnes" mentioned there. The name was pronounced "Ann-es" and was often interchangeable with Anne's name. Yet the image of Anne does not fit our usual way of thinking about the couple's courtship. We can only imagine the growing romance between them: what was it like? Shy outwardly, but intensely shared? Fun and easy-going, whereby the pair exchanged laughs and witty banter, rather like Beatrice and Benedick in Shakespeare's later comedy *Much Ado About Nothing*? Or torrid and passionate, involving secret meetings and snatched moments of privacy dotted with kisses? We have only a few pieces of evidence, if we can even call it evidence. One clue is Shakespeare's sonnet 145, which was published only in 1609, but which scholars today think may be one of the earliest samples of Shakespeare's writing that we have, dating from this time of courtship.

> Those lips that Love's own hand did make
> Breathed forth the sound that said "I hate"
> To me that languish'd for her sake;
> But when she saw my woeful state,
> Straight in her heart did mercy come,
> Chiding that tongue that ever sweet
> Was used in giving gentle doom,
> And taught it thus anew to greet:
> "I hate" she alter'd with an end,
> That follow'd it as gentle day
> Doth follow night, who like a fiend
> From heaven to hell is flown away;
> "I hate" from hate away she threw,
> And saved my life, saying "not you."

The scholar Andrew Gurr first pointed out (in 1971—surprisingly recently, all things considered) the possible pun in the second-to-last line, as in "'I hate' from *Hathaway* she threw," and subsequent scholars, wanting in on the detective-like fun, have also heard a pun in the last line: "*Anne* saved my life . . ." This may be so, but it is hardly strong evidence. Even setting aside the puns for a minute, we should keep in mind that sonnets are dramatizing literary works, and in this particular case, many remain puzzled as to why this early "apprentice sonnet" appears late in Shakespeare's collection, incongruously amid those poems that constitute the "Dark Lady" section. Finally, if one reads the poem carefully, it is hardly an effusive expression of desire that one might understandably expect to find in a love sonnet, especially one arguably written by an infatuated young man. The beloved is finally able to say, only, "I hate not you." For any wooing fellow, that is a start, I guess.

The next detail really is a substantive piece of evidence, though it requires some backdating to apply to William's and Anne's relationship. One major development emerged from their involvement together in 1582, whatever the nature, pace, or pastimes of their romance. In the baptismal register in Stratford's Holy Trinity Church, there is the following entry: *1583 May 26 Susanna, daughter of William Shakespere*. That is, by late the following spring, a first child was born to William and Anne. This arrival means (if one quietly and discreetly does the math) that William and Anne had been intimate at least once in the late summer of 1582. The poet and novelist Ron Koertge has a charming poem called "My Students," who first can imagine only the canonical, institutional Bard. Without pulse or blood, totally unrelatable, they picture only "the domed / busy in Senior English plus puffy pants / and sissy shoes." But eventually they can see him in their mind's eye sitting thoughtfully at a window, with the Avon rolling by, and then

> Along the banks, young people kissing
> with their mouths open, grappling with
> the other's odd clothes,
> all that stuff that doesn't make you famous
> but that's a lot more fun than poetry.

No doubt Koertge has in mind that eventful late-summer day, of dramatic conception of a different, more bodily sort. It may have been one of many days like it, and the poem imagines it, in a rather idealized, romantic-movie-set way, occuring on the river's banks amid the peaceful, private sedge and reeds. In any case, this pregnancy likely explains some of the mysterious details surrounding the couple's pending marriage.

THE SHAKESPEARES' BETROTHAL AND WEDDING

The wedding of William Shakespeare and Anne Hathaway was unusual for a few reasons. First,

ANNE HATHAWAY

You may have heard the following comments, or ones like them: "anonymous" early literature means it was written by a woman, or behind every good male author is a great wife. In other words, women sometimes face difficulties in the literary world, or when married to a writer. This was especially true in earlier times—ones less intent on, or unable to conceive of, gender equity. Through the centuries, Shakespeare's wife, Anne Hathaway, and her posthumous reputation have faced their own challenges. She has been denigrated as a manipulator of a younger man, as a shrew, as old and unattractive, as a burden upon her creative-genius husband, and as responsible for a loveless marriage (although any evidence for that last claim is very tenuous indeed).

The very fact that we rarely refer to her as "Anne Shakespeare," but rather by her maiden name of Hathaway, may reflect a traditional critical resistance to thinking of Anne as a true lover and partner of the great writer who just happened to be her husband. If we know her best as Anne Hathaway, then to some degree she always remains an outsider, always from another Stratford family instead of the family she formed with William Shakespeare. Her children certainly thought of her as a central part of her family: a Latin epigraph, on a brass plate near her gravestone in the chancel of Stratford's Holy Trinity Church, addresses her with an elegiac voice as "O mother, milk and life thou didst give."

That said, there are worse slights. For example, the most famous woman associated with Shakespeare is arguably not Anne at all: since Shakespeare immortalized her in his *Sonnets*, the mysterious Dark Lady probably comes to mind most quickly. It is she we think of, as well as the Young Man in earlier sonnets, when we imagine Shakespeare as passionately in love or involved in intense romantic relationships. Never mind that the *Sonnets* are lyrical poems, and not necessarily biographical at all; they may be little fourteen-line dramas, but there is a tone of authenticity in these love poems that irresistibly makes readers connect their professions and

A nineteenth-century painting of William Shakespeare and Anne Hathaway.

the groom was only eighteen years old, and therefore required his parents' approval to be wedded. His bride was considerably older, and would soon begin to show with their first child. She was three months pregnant when they sought a marriage license, in late November. Although the license itself does not exist, we have a record for its issuing from the Bishop of Worcester, dated November 27: "there went out a license [for marriage] between Wm Shaxpere and Anne Whateley of Temple Grafton." A bond dated the next day also exists, also from Worcester, that calls for a sub-

circumstances with their author. These sonnets conveniently fill a biographical void—for unfortunately we have no letters or other personal effects exchanged between William and Anne.

Despite this absence of evidence, or maybe because of it, novelists regularly take up the challenge of speaking for this woman in imagined ways, this wife of the most famous writer who ever lived, and to find a voice that can finally tell her side of the story. In the process, these authors just as often take pleasure in shedding light—if strictly fanciful, hypothetical light—on many of the mysterious obscurities surrounding William's life. For example, Robert Nye, in *Mrs. Shakespeare: The Complete Works*, builds upon a comment made by the eighteenth-century scholar Edmund Malone, that William and Anne "lived very happy" and that after he found success as a playwright, he "fetched her to London." Just so, Nye imagines Anne arriving in London to give her husband a birthday present of a lambskin jacket. It is an intimate, tender scene between spouses, but elsewhere Nye's Anne says, "I believe I deserved better treatment," and she calls herself "the detested wife."

There also is a sonnet by Britain's poet laureate Carol Ann Duffy spoken in Anne's voice. Anne remembers her dead husband fondly: "My living laughing love— / I hold him in the casket of my widow's head / as he held me upon that next best bed." In that last line, Duffy takes on a longstanding biographical controversy—whether or not Shakespeare was dismissing his wife in leaving her in his will "my second best bed." Duffy's version of Anne solves that mystery on a happy note of marital concord.

Fortunately, things have been looking up lately for Anne Hathaway-Shakespeare in the scholarly world as well. Germaine Greer's book *Shakespeare's Wife* defends Anne's reputation against a list of detractors. She laments the abuse Anne has received through the centuries, but points out that wives of intellectuals have been slandered for a long, long time (see Socrates's Xanthippe or Aristotle's Phyllis). She adds that literature In Shakespeare's day was seen as a "particularly laddish enterprise," one best pursued by men, single men. Conversely, Greer goes so far as to suggest that Anne may have been highly involved in her husband's artistic life, including the years after his death, when the First Folio of his plays was being prepared and printed by some of his fellow actors. Anne, Greer argues, may have used some of the family Income to underwrite the initial printing of this impressively large Folio volume. Less eventfully, Greer claims that Anne faithfully honored her husband throughout their marriage by "doing the right thing," which in Shakespeare's day meant "remaining silent and invisible." In an earlier study, Greer refers to Anne likewise as "that invisible woman"—but fortunately she is less so today, in both scholarly and literary eyes.

SEE ALSO:

Duffy, Carol Ann. "Anne Hathaway," *The World's Wife*. New York: Faber and Faber, 1999.

Greer, Germaine. *Shakespeare's Wife* London: Bloomsbury, 2007.

Nye, Robert. *Mrs. Shakespeare: The Complete Works*. London: Arcade Publishing, 1993.

Ryan, Arliss. *The Secret Confessions of Anne Shakespeare*. New York: New American Library, 2010.

stantial sum of money to be put up more or less to protect the bishop if the marriage he was approving, under hasty circumstances it seems, turned out for any reason to be invalid—one of the parties was already married, there was "consanguinity" or a kin relationship between them, and so on. The bond was witnessed by two friends of the Hathaway family, including the executor named in Anne's father's will. There is no record of William's family in attendance or even the groom himself being present in Worcester, which has led some scholars darkly to infer coercion on the part of Anne's family. Perhaps, they conjecture, Shakespeare's family did not even know about this marriage. Or, embarrassed by their unmarried daughter's pregnancy, was her family pressuring the Shakespeares, and the offending young man in particular, to make the situation right through lawful marriage? It seems likely that both families would have dealt with different kinds of uncertainty and anxiety during much of the fall of 1582. One uncertainty may have involved the effects upon their reputation in a small market town such as Stratford. The great Shakespeare biographer Samuel Schoenbaum points out that Anne is decorously called a "maiden" in the bond, rather than the less decorous and suggestive "single woman."

Others have attempted to make light of these implications of a "shotgun marriage," pointing out that William and Anne may have already been married, if not by official religious sanction, then in the eyes of their fellow Elizabethans. This argument involves the formal betrothal between young people, or "troth plight," a taking of hands that could indeed signal a valid marriage in this era. Typically, though, the church was involved, and there is present in these circumstances a sense of urgency and overcoming of obstacles that make it likely that William and Anne were concerned about a formal, church-recognized marriage. First, a marriage license was not typically necessary, although our couple obtained one. Usually a marriage could go ahead with three readings of the banns during a Sunday church service, which involved the preacher asking the congregation publically if there were any reasons, or impediments, why the man and woman in question should not be married. Unfortunately for our couple, they waited too late into the fall to undertake this normal process smoothly. The banns were forbidden to be read during the upcoming Advent and Christmas seasons, and it

seems that, instead of waiting till the new year for the required third reading of the banns, the couple and their families were willing to undertake special pains—the twenty-mile trip to Worcester, the significant cost of the bond—to circumvent this requirement and obtain an exception for the sake of a more timely wedding. It is also suggestive that there is no record of the wedding in Stratford, and certain smaller parishes around Stratford have been mentioned as possible wedding sites—Bishopton, Luddington, or Temple Grafton, which is mysteriously mentioned in the record of the license. Perhaps Anne was living in Temple Grafton, five miles outside Stratford, at this time?

Many a mystery buzzes around this important event in the young Shakespeare's life. Some have argued that the couple went to a small parish to benefit from an unsuspicious priest or one who looked upon these questionable arrangements with latitude. Perhaps, some add, he was a Roman Catholic priest, who would marry the couple despite their pregnancy. However, once William and Anne had successfully obtained the license, any priest could lawfully marry them. It has also been argued, as suggested above, that the young William was more or less hijacked by Anne, her hostile parents, and their intimidating friends. There is really no reason to suspect this, except for the dramatic pleasures of the heart-pounding story itself. The pair found themselves in a delicate situation, and seem to have taken the proper if demanding steps to make the best of it, as husband and wife.

There has also swirled around this incident the specter of a tragic love triangle, centering on the curious name in the license record, "Anne Whateley of Temple Grafton." As this story goes, Anne Whateley and Anne Hathaway are two different women, and Shakespeare was involved with them both. The two records of the marriage in fact tell a story of a dramatic turn of events, and of allegiances. In the license record, William is attempting to marry Anne Whateley, his true love, but the Hathways intercept him and force him to marry Anne, since she is carrying his baby. Anthony Burgess, in his wonderful novelization of Shakespeare's life, *Nothing Like the Sun*, narrates this version of events with great gusto. In his dramatic imagined landscape, Anne Hathaway proved that she "hath a way," as he puts it. And very recently Karen Harper has written the what-if novel *Mistress Shakespeare*, whose heroine Anne Whateley remains in Shakespeare's life and joins him in the theaters in London! It is a terrific story, but it is also entirely likely that what we have in this discrepancy between the names is sheer carelessness on the part of the scribe who recorded the names for the license. For example, a number of names recorded many times here are not spelled alike at all—"Barber" becomes "Baker," and "Darby" turns into "Bradley." With the transposition or mistaken placement of a few letters, "Whateley" and "Hathaway" actually do not seem that far apart.

In any case, the records indicate that William and Anne were duly married, with only two readings of the banns required by the license. "If any of you know cause, or just impediment, why these two persons should not be joined together in holy Matrimony, ye are to declare it," reads "The Solemnization of Matrimony" section in the *Book of Common Prayer*, which would have been the order of service for the wedding. We hear echoes of this passage, and of the language of the bond William and Anne had to put forward, in Shakespeare's famous sonnet 116: "Let me not to the marriage of true minds / Admit impediments; love is not love /

Which alters when it alteration finds . . . " "Alteration" means a change of circumstances or fortune, and the couple certainly experienced that in 1582. Their love did alter, in fact—it had to, but it was, one hopes for all involved, a change for the better.

SHAKESPEARE'S FAMILY

The parish register in Stratford's church has already shown us that William and Anne welcomed their first daughter, Susanna, into the world in May 1583. Their family's size grew quickly, for before Susanna was two years old, another entry was made in the baptismal register: *1584* [actually, 1585] *February 2 Hamnet and Judeth, son and daughter to William Shakspere.* The family now had twins! Shakespeare's life must have felt very different, and very quickly so. In less than three years, and at an unusually early age, he went from being a single young man, and not officially an adult yet, to a husband and father of three young children. His concerns must have risen greatly, especially when considering the high mortality rate previously mentioned. His joys must have broadened and deepened as well, along with his firsthand awareness, his felt

Shakespeare's Family Circle, ca. 1890 *(Artist unknown)*

knowledge of one of the most common of human experiences—that partnering with another in life, and that shift from being a child to being a parent. As with everything in Shakespeare's life, we wish we knew more about his wife, Anne, and about their three children. Unsurprisingly, many imaginative efforts have been made to answer that intriguing question—what in the world would it have been like to be married to the world's greatest writer, or to have such a man as a father? I especially recommend Grace Tiffany's charming book *My Father Had a Daughter: Judith Shakespeare's Tale*, but there are many others. And of course the plays must offer their own quiet clues to Shakespeare's experiences as father—how many of them feature strong, memorable heroines, or stories of relational breakdown or reconciliation. And in most of them, these characters are splendidly dramatized daughters, growing up and setting out upon the edge of life.

Sources and Further Reading

Brooke, Tucker. *Shakespeare of Stratford: A Handbook for Students*. New Haven: Yale University Press, 1926.

Burgess, Anthony. *Nothing Like the Sun*. New York: W.W. Norton, 1964.

Harper, Karen. *Mistress Shakespeare*. New York: G.P. Putnam's Sons, 2009.

Ortiz, Michael J. *Swan Town: The Secret Journal of Susanna Shakespeare*. New York: HarperCollins, 2006.

Schoenbaum, Samuel. *William Shakespeare: A Compact Documentary Life*. New York: Oxford University Press, 1977.

Tiffany, Grace. *My Father Had a Daughter: Judith Shakespeare's Tale*. New York: Berkley Books, 2003.

SHAKESPEARE'S "LOST YEARS"

After the Stratford church record of William and Anne Shakespeare's second and third children—the twins Judith and Hamnet, baptized on February 2, 1585—no reliable record involving our author appears again till 1592. At that point the irritated writer Robert Greene attacks William as an actor who, like an "upstart crow," is now trying to write plays like his university-trained betters. Henceforth, Shakespeare is more or less traceable through the procession of plays he writes for London's theaters, and particularly from 1594 onward, when he becomes an official partner in the new, quickly successful company known as the Lord Chamberlain's Men. The years in between these records, however, are frustrating insofar as they offer no documentary proof as to where Shakespeare was or what he was doing. Well, that is not entirely true: we do have a 1589 legal document with William's name therein. He is mentioned as the son of John Shakespeare, and the document relates to one of Will's father's countless lawsuits over disputed property. This is thin stuff for substantive biography.

More interesting are various stories and anecdotes, more legend than historical fact, that give us some possible ideas about Shakespeare's life during this critical time of young adulthood, when he was a new husband and parent. He was likely concerned about making a living and perhaps just a little restless and imagining "making it big" in the big city of London. For good reason, then, these years between 1585 and 1592 have become known as the "Lost Years," and scholarly ingenuity and folly have been tireless in trying to fill the void of this period with possible, if sometimes improbable, theories about Shakespeare's days. They may be veiled to us today, but these years were fully lived by him, full of family joys, present-day cares, and perhaps dreams for a still unknown future.

SHAKESPEARE'S FAMILY IN COMMUNITY

The very names of William and Anne Shakespeare's twins may give us some idea as to how involved the family was in Stratford community life, how known and friendly they were with neighbors. In a small market village such as Stratford, this participation in town social life would have been the norm. Perhaps the young Shakespeare family spent time with Thomas Russell and his wife; Russell was a country gentleman and eventually the executor of Shakespeare's will in 1616.

Most people with even a general awareness of Shakespeare's achievements in literature may do a double-take when they notice the name of Shakespeare's son, Hamnet. This sounds awfully like—doesn't it?—the name of Shakespeare's great prince of Denmark, the namesake protagonist in his tragedy *Hamlet*. However, there were altogether more local possibilities for inspiration. For example, a woman named Katherine Hamlet drowned in the River Avon in nearby Tiddington in 1579. Her name lends itself to Shakespeare's hero, while her fate suggests that of the tragic heroine of *Hamlet*, Ophelia. More likely namesakes for the twins, however, are found among the neighbors, longtime friends of the Shakespeares and the children's godparents—Hamnet and Judith Sadler, who lived nearby at the corner of High and Sheep streets, near the Corn Market. (The couple would reciprocate in 1598, by naming their son William.)

Doubtless the couple remained in close touch with Anne's family, including her brother Bartholomew, who leased a house nearby on Ely Street. In 1601, Thomas Whittington, who had long ago served as shepherd to Anne's deceased father, Richard, left in his will "unto the poor people of Stratford 40 shillings that is in the hand of Anne Shaxspere, wife unto William Shaxspere." The will also announced a debt owed him by Anne's father, as well as an expectation that her husband, William, would now pay Whittington's executor that sum. This document suggests that William remained close to his in-laws and involved in their—and in Whittington's case, their employees'—lives. It is even safer to imagine that the young family remained close to William's parents and siblings. William and Anne did not purchase their own house for more than ten years, so it is very likely that they were housemates of the older Shakespeares, occupying part of the family home on Henley Street. The son may have been a source of comfort when the father was officially removed from the Stratford Corporation in 1587, after being absent from meetings for a decade. And as we shall see, William certainly remained involved in his father's legal wranglings and his efforts to obtain a gentleman's arms. Moreover, even at the height of his theatrical success in London, Shakespeare was increasingly active in purchasing properties in Stratford and conducting various other sorts of business there. Like father, like son, as they say.

SHAKESPEARE'S ALLEGED CAREERS

Shakespeare found himself, by the age of twenty-one, a husband and father of three small children, and he was himself a grown child still living in his parents' home. Naturally he needed to make a living. He may have simply continued working for his father, John, in the family tanning business. Related to that, early biographers' mistaking of John for a butcher may have something to do with another story, recorded by a Mr. Dowdall when he visited Shakespeare's monument in Holy Trinity Church in 1693. The church's sexton and clerk showed the visitor around, and told him that

> this Shakespear was formerly in this town bound apprentice to a butcher; but that he run from his master to London, and there was received into the playhouse as a serviture, and by this means had an opportunity to be what he afterwards proved.

There is something charming about that ending understatement, perhaps born of a feeling of civic pride in an accomplished fellow townsman. Yet no other piece of evidence corroborates this particular claim about Shakespeare's early career. That clerk was William Castle, and he seems to have specifically fancied himself as Shakespeare's unofficial biographer. He relayed another story (to a different visitor) about the young writer composing the ghost scene in *Hamlet* "in a Charnel house in the midst of night," presumably the one attached to Stratford's church. However, since Castle was born in 1614, just two years before Shakespeare's death and long after the writing of *Hamlet*, his testimony must be considered dubious, if rather colorfully so.

Another legend about Shakespeare's days as a young father presents him as a teacher. John Aubrey in his notes mentions the quip by Shakespeare's fellow playwright Ben Jonson, that William had "but little Latin and less Greek," but Aubrey begs to differ, saying "he understood Latin pretty well: for he had been in his younger years a schoolmaster in the country." It is worth noting that Aubrey, whom some find generally unreliable, attributes this information to William Beeston, an in-the-know actor in his own day, but more importantly the son of Christopher Beeston, who performed with Shakespeare in the Lord Chamberlain's Men. So there just might be something to this claim. Skeptics point out that Stratford's schoolmasters during Shakespeare's days were all university-trained men, and this requirement argues against Shakespeare's employment. That said, Shakespeare may have worked in a schoolhouse outside of Stratford, where training for instructors was not as great, or perhaps he even served the Stratford schoolmaster in the more modest role of usher or abecedarius (think teaching assistant or grader). Finally, Shakespeare may have been privately employed by a wealthy English family, thereby becoming a tutor in a manor-house setting. We certainly see such scenes between tutor and pupil in his plays, although when we consider his schoolmaster characters—Holofernes, Evans, and even Prospero—there does not seem to be a genuine identification with these figures; put more precisely, sympathy in these scenes always resides with the students' perspective.

Yet here again, we risk determining too much about Shakespeare's work experiences from what are, after all, imagined characters, constructed out of blank-verse poetry and dramatic prose. Likewise, we should be sensitive about how the general view of Shakespeare as a young provincial man either confirms this shadowy schoolmaster story—"Aha! Shakespeare served as an underappreciated rural schoolmaster before becoming a famous writer in London!"—or, if this rags-to-riches narrative is not a primary focus, makes the story seem untenable—"No way! Shakespeare was not educated enough himself to teach others within a demanding, Latin-based Tudor curriculum." This latter view, of Shakespeare as an unlearned, "natural" writer, has influenced some of the most formidable of Shakespeare's critics

The "Chandos" portrait of William Shakespeare, ca. 1610. Its authenticity is in dispute. *(Attributed to John Taylor)*

and biographers, including Richard Farmer in the eighteenth century and E. K. Chambers in the twentieth.

Others have imagined different jobs for the young Shakespeare on even less evidence, usually based on personal experience. For example, Edmund Malone remains one of the greatest Shakespeare scholars ever, but he nevertheless indulged in a personal, feel-good hunch when he, an English lawyer himself, concluded that his favorite writer once worked as a clerk in a Stratford law office. In 1973, another scholar recycled this idea but with a London setting, imagining Shakespeare at the Inns of Court there. Other jobs connected with Shakespeare have included apothecary, or something in medicine generally, and apprentice to a printer. This latter idea had at least one possibility going for it—Richard Field, the London printer of Shakespeare's first books (the poems *Venus and Adonis* and *The Rape of Lucrece*) was a Stratford man, too. He may have given his fellow citizen his first big writing break—by publishing his verse, obviously, but perhaps also by hiring him as an apprentice. A nineteenth-century antiquarian claimed that Shakespeare had been a soldier, based on his name appearing in the muster rolls in Rowington in 1605. It was an exciting find, no doubt, but this name refers almost certainly to a different fellow. Behind all of these vocational speculations lies an incredulousness about Shakespeare's art—namely, that he must have had these professional experiences because he seems to include the activities and terminologies of these jobs with such effortless accuracy. The skill and persuasion of his lines make us demand some professional experience to supplement his fiction making.

SHAKESPEARE'S ALLEGED TRAVELS

If you imagine Shakespeare's county or shire, Warwickshire, as a diamond-shaped region in the English Midlands, then the town of Stratford is in the southwest corner. Aside from his certain walks to and from the Hathaway home in Shottery, there are other signs in the area that suggest, even if fancifully, that Shakespeare explored the surrounding region. A little outside Stratford, in Bidford, there stood for a long while a crab tree called Shakespeare's Canopy, and a 1762 article reported that Shakespeare had once visited Bidford to "take a cup" with its residents, whom he heard were "deep drinkers and merry fellows." Another tradition claims that the poet was in residence in Dursley and throughout the southern area of the Cotswolds region close by Stratford. Maybe the young man traveled around on behalf of his father's business interests. "We are entitled to assume a roving and apperceptive mind, conversant in some way with many men and man-

ners, and gifted with that felicity in the selection and application of varied knowledge, which is one of the secrets of genius," writes one Shakespeare biographer, E. K. Chambers, admiringly. Naturally, we equate a roving mind with roving itself—for how else did Shakespeare come by, in Chambers's words, "a ready touch over a wide space of human experience"?

Some of Shakespeare's plays do indeed feature noticeable traces of local knowledge. For example, in the opening Induction scenes of *The Taming of the Shrew*, we meet the tinker and beggar Christopher Sly, "old Sly's son of Burton Heath," and he soon says, "Ask Marian Hacket, the fat alewife of Wincot, if she know me or not." Shakespeare in fact had family in Barton on the Heath, fifteen miles south of Stratford, and Wincot was only five miles to the southwest. An Oxford librarian visited in the eighteenth century and heard a longstanding tale of Shakespeare's time there. Of course, this "local color" in his creative works does not imply residence in these places or reveal specific incidents that happened to Shakespeare there, but it does reflect a young Warwickshire writer who knew his region well, one having some fun by including his hometown area in plays performed on London's stages.

Some readers are convinced that Shakespeare must have traveled farther afield as a young man, either across England or even to more exotic destinations in continental Europe. These ideas are motivated by a general feeling that Shakespeare must have been more refined than any simple Stratford kid, and thus must have experienced other cultures and even foreign court life. One popular, traditional notion places the young Shakespeare in the ocher-colored squares and among the marble monuments of Renaissance Italy, either during these "Lost Years" or, as it has also been argued, during his hiatus from the London stages during a plague outbreak in 1592–93.

One can understand why this seems reasonable—like his English contemporaries, Shakespeare as a writer was greatly influenced by the poems and literary styles of the Italian Renaissance. Some Italian stories provide plots for Shakespeare's plays, many of which, especially the comedies, feature fairly accurate Italian settings and familiar Italian names. He seems to have known the Italian language, since some of his sources were not yet translated into English, but then again, someone with solid Latin training would not find it too difficult to learn and read Italian.

Another exotic hypothesis has Shakespeare sailing the high seas during the golden age of English Renaissance exploration. One version even puts him on the *Golden Hind*, the ship of the English hero-explorer Francis Drake. (A model of the ship can still be visited in Bankside, just downriver, and a few docks down, from the restored Globe Theatre.) Drake famously circumnavigated the globe in 1577, but Shakespeare would have been a young sailor, or even cabin-boy, at thirteen years of age. Defenders of this theory behind Shakespeare's early career claim that his writing is full of sea imagery—Hamlet's famous "To be or not to be" soliloquy on taking arms "against a sea of troubles," for example, or sea wrecks in plays such as *The Comedy of Errors*, *Twelfth Night*, *Pericles*, and *The Tempest*. In *As You Like It*, Jacques remarks that Touchstone's brain is "as dry as the remainder biscuit after a voyage," and this real-life detail (Drake's sailors had to survive on such biscuits) has fueled speculation that young Shakespeare was a mariner. In any case, these notions have endured through the ages, but they remain flimsy theories, lacking evidence. In other words, there is no proof that Shakespeare ever left England, ever sailed at all. On the other hand, he does have certain characters, especially in the early comedies, express a youthful restlessness that he himself may have felt. In *The Two Gentlemen of Verona*, Antonio says of the young gentleman Proteus,

> I have considered well his loss of time,
> And how he cannot be a perfect man,
> Not being tried and tutored in the world.
> Then, tell me, whither were I best to send
> him . . . ?

Similarly, Petruchio explains his arrival in Padua thus in *The Taming of the Shrew*: "Such wind as scatters young men through the world / To seek their fortunes farther than at home, / Where small experience grows."

If Shakespeare traveled much during this mysterious period, it is perhaps most likely that he did so with a traveling theater company, and mainly around the English countryside, from town to town, any place willing to sponsor the company's performances. The documentary maker Michael Wood believes he was recruited by the Queen's Men when that troupe visited Stratford in 1587. Several companies passed through Stratford, so there may have been other opportunities as well. However, there is no record of companies making a habit of recruiting novice actors while touring. If he did undertake this early acting work, would he have visited some of the places in England that show up in his plays, such as the Gloucestershire landscape in *Richard II*, or the Dover cliffs powerfully evoked for their elemental presence in *King Lear*? And what about Milford Haven, that important arrival point in *Cymbeline* and the closest port to Stratford? Did he visit the more popular port of Plymouth, or East Anglia on the other side of England? Alternately, perhaps like his Italian locations, his English landmarks and locales were written products of a fertile, curious imagination only, and not based on personal sightseeing experience.

(continues on page 30)

SHAKESPEARE'S 1580s WRITINGS?

No one really knows when exactly William Shakespeare arrived in London as a young actor and an aspiring playwright, intent on succeeding in the intense, highly competitive world of Elizabethan drama in the public playhouses. Nor do we know when exactly Shakespeare began his writing career. His professional life in London and his more active writing life certainly go chronologically hand in hand, but it is important to see these two questions—about this arrival in the capital city and how early he began to write—as ultimately two separate questions. A traditional city-country bias has often led biographers to assume that Shakespeare hardly would have had literary interests in a small, provincial, unsophisticated town such as Stratford, and that it would take the excitement and artistic opportunities of London to open Shakespeare's eyes to his calling and to stimulate his career. This notion that Shakespeare appeared on the London scene as a novice, who almost immediately managed to write great, commercially successful plays and wow his more experienced and formally trained contemporaries, also nourishes our cherished legend of the writer as a "native genius," one who could write poetry and assemble a play with miraculous ease.

As satisfying as those assumptions are, in a rags-to-riches, bright-lights-big-city, country-boy-makes-good kind of way, there is probably more to the story than that.

We have already seen how many scholars today identify Shakespeare's sonnet 145 as perhaps his earliest piece of writing that we still possess. If that poem is indeed related to William's courtship of Anne Hathaway (with the poem's pun on "hate away"), then its composition would date roughly to 1582. Since we do not have any record of or reaction to Shakespeare as a writer till almost a decade later—in a theater manager's recording of a "Henry VI" play (likely Shakespeare's) at the Rose Theatre in 1591 and in Robert Greene's attack on him the following year—this sonnet would be an early example of Shakespeare's writing indeed, if it in fact was composed in the early 1580s.

Of course Shakespeare, who was almost certainly a student at Stratford's grammar school, would have spent many of his young days immersed in texts and poetry, including difficult, artistically complex works of classical literature in Latin. He also likely acted in Roman dramas in this academic setting. A few stories have come down to us that hint at Shakespeare's early activity in poetry and drama, although unfortunately these anecdotes are best approached with a caution befitting legendary stories. We have seen how John Aubrey described Shakespeare as a boy working for his father's trade. Aubrey mistakenly thought John Shakespeare was a butcher, and, he writes, when Shakespeare "killed a calf, he would do it in a high style, & make a speech." The boy's odd dramatic flair is heightened by eagle-eyed scholars' connection with Aubrey's story and a play called "Killing a Calf" listed in the repertoire of traveling actors of the day. Did Aubrey mistakenly literalize the detail? And through the story's mistiness, can we glimpse a young man rehearsing a speech? Another interpretation, which holds that "killing the calf" is merely a figurative phrase to describe high-style oratorical display, only complicates this story.

Additionally, according to another tale that has proven varyingly convincing to scholars, Shakespeare was caught up in a deer-stealing controversy, from which emerged another example of his writing. After narrating William's possible imprisonment and punishment by Sir Thomas Lucy of Charlecote, the early-eighteenth-century biographer Nicholas Rowe reports that William

in order to revenge that ill Usage, he made a Ballad upon him [that is, against Sir Thomas] . . . it is said to have been so very bitter, that it redoubled the Prosecution against him to that degree, that he was obliged to leave his Business and Family in Warwickshire, for some time, an to shelter himself.

This ballad was, according to Rowe, "probably the first Essay [that is, attempt] of his Poetry," and another version of this legend adds that Shakespeare boldly attached the ballad to the gentleman's gate. Whatever the true details, it was already lost, alas, by the time of Rowe's writing. Versions of the ballad have appeared in the centuries following Shakespeare and Rowe, but none has earned distinction as a genuine candidate for the young writer's historical verses. The existence of such an acrimonious ballad, however, gains some support by the clear talents in satirical writing shown by Shakespeare later in

Portrait of Nicholas Rowe, often credited as Shakespeare's first editor, by an unknown artist.

his career—the character Thersites in the mid-career play Troilus and Cressida, for example.

Recently the scholar Eric Sams has made a case for Shakespeare as present and "learning on the job," as it were, in London's theater industry much earlier than is usually suggested. The most prominent Shakespeareans, he argues, accept too passively that Shakespeare, after leaving grammar school, "wrote nothing for the next twelve years" (the so-called "Lost Years"). Consequently, these critics overlook thousands of Shakespeare's early lines of poetry "together with at least a decade of his career." He believes, against conventional wisdom, that by the late 1580s Shakespeare had composed first versions of *Pericles*, *Titus Andronicus*, *Hamlet*, *The Taming of the Shrew*, and *King John*. A few of these works exist as plays generally thought to have influenced Shakespeare but written by others—*The Taming of a Shrew*, *The Troublesome Reign of King John*—while others are presumably lost, and we have only the single familiar play associated with a later stage in the writer's career.

Mysteries about Shakespeare's earliest writing will continue to challenge scholars, but in any case, one thing is certain. By the early 1590s, the young playwright hit the ground running with accomplished plays in diverse genres: *The Comedy of Errors* in comedy, *Titus Andronicus* in tragedy, and, among history plays, the three *Henry VI* plays. Shakespeare had arrived and would quickly make a name for himself; he would rule the stage for the next twenty years—a time considered the Golden Age of English drama and literature.

SEE ALSO:

Fraser, Russell A. *Young Shakespeare*. New York: Columbia University Press, 1988.

Gurr, Andrew. "Shakespeare's First Poem: Sonnet 145," *Essays in Criticism* 21 (1971): 427-29.

Sams, Eric. *The Real Shakespeare: Retrieving the Early Years, 1564-1594*. New Haven: Yale University Press, 1995.

(continued from page 27)

He may have been on the road even earlier. John Ward, a new vicar in Stratford in 1661–62, included in a memorandum that Shakespeare was a "natural wit" who "frequented the plays all his younger time, but in his elder days lived in Stratford." Ward's title is intriguing because it mentions his intention to see "Mrs. Queeny," that is, Judith Quiney, Shakespeare's younger daughter, who was seventy-seven at the time. If they met, one wishes that Ward would have obtained more specific information from this family member. For example, does "frequented the plays" mean the pageants and performances he may have seen as a boy, in Stratford and Coventry nearby, or does it mean that he was active as a young father and husband touring with a theater company? Considering that his "younger time" is contrasted with "his elder days lived in Stratford," meaning his return in retirement, this phrase ceases to look like a helpful clue and seems a mere paraphrase for the obvious—that Shakespeare spent his career acting and writing plays in London. It may be that the writer was in London for much of the 1580s, but no trace about him appears during this time. We have already seen how one Mr. Dowdall reported that he had abandoned his butcher's apprenticeship by going to London, and John Aubrey writes that he "came to London, I guesse about 18." This would be considerably early—in 1582, when he was courting Anne Hathaway. We may need to emphasize Aubrey's appropriate "I guess" and allow a few years' flexibility there. A few scholars, masters of the obvious, have pointed out that a traveling Shakespeare must have been present for the conception of his and Anne's first child, but he may have already been on the road the following year. Can we assume he was there for her birth, at least? With the "Lost Years," it is really not advisable to assume anything.

TWO ALLEGED INCIDENTS FROM THE "LOST YEARS"

Another theory about Shakespeare's travels has become more popular in recent years, and it loosely refers to a possible "Lancastrian" phase, that is, a time in Shakespeare's young adulthood when he traveled roughly one hundred miles north of Stratford to the county known as Lancashire. More specifically, he may have lived and worked there for a stint, although the proposed time line would have made him quite young, either fourteen or fifteen years old. The theory emerges from the enigmatic name "William Shakeshafte" listed in the household accounts of a powerful Catholic landowner in Lancashire, Alexander Hoghton of Lea Hall. In his will of August 1581, Hoghton also requested that his half-brother Thomas "be friendly unto Foke Gyllome and William Shakeshafte, now dwelling with me, and either take them unto his service or else help them to some good master." Just beforehand, this Thomas was also granted "all my instruments belonging to musics, and all manner of play-clothes, if he be minded to keep and do keep players." Otherwise these items are to go to his brother-in-law, Sir Thomas Hesketh of Rufford, ten miles away. The details are enigmatic: could this "Shakeshafte" be William Shakespeare? If so, why is his name altered? There may be cleverness behind the change, since "shaft" and "spear" share something in common, but was he more seriously in need of an alias? And are "play-clothes" related to the musical instruments in the will, and thus musicians' outfits, or does this talk of "players" also involve a group of actors who perhaps performed at Hoghton's manor?

Supporters of this theory thus imagine Shakespeare as a young tutor, or even assistant to a tutor, who also gained early theater experience within the household. Further leads beckon if Shakespeare became involved with the Hesketh family. (The Sherlockian scholar Leslie Hotson discovered that one of Shakespeare's co-signers for the Globe Theatre's lease was the London goldsmith Thomas Savage, related by marriage to the Heskeths.) This family entertained players as well, and were friends with the Stanleys, one of northern England's most prominent families. The Stanleys were also patrons of Derby's Men and Strange's Men, two of the most active theater companies in the 1580s. Records indicate that Shakespeare was likely involved with these troupes as a young playwright. E. A. J. Honigmann, in his influential book *Shakespeare: The "Lost Years,"* is responsible for giving this theory a wider audience. (Earlier Shakespeareans had been aware of it since at least the 1930s, but it proved to be, as Honigmann says, "so much more intricate" than first expected.) Yet he also proposed reasons for doubting this identification. Although the name sounds unusual to us, there were actually several "Shakeshafte" families in Lancashire, and the bequest that this Shakeshafte receives in the will seems too high; Shakespeare could not have been in residence at the Hoghtons for very long, given his young age in 1581, and he seems to have received more in the will than senior servants.

A more celebrated incident from this mysterious period involves William's relationship with another powerful Englishman—this one named Sir Thomas Lucy, who resided in Charlecote, quite near Stratford, rather than to the north in Lancashire. Lucy was also a strong Protestant and active on Elizabeth I's behalf, whereas the previous Lancashire gentleman, Alexander Hoghton, was a Catholic in a staunchly Roman Catholic, old-faith region of England. This account, in which the young Shakespeare is apprehended and punished for poaching in Sir Thomas's deer-park, appears in some of the earliest biographies of the writer. Richard Davies, a village rector from the nearby Cotswolds, wrote in 1700 that Shakespeare was "much given to all unluckinesse in stealing venison & Rabbits particularly from Sr Lucy who had him oft whipt & sometimes Imprisoned & at last made Him fly his Native Country to his great Advancement." Less than a decade later, Nicholas Rowe, in his more thorough biography, expands on some of the details: the newly married Shakespeare was "settled" for some time, "till an Extravagance that he was guilty of, forc'd him both out of his Country and that way of Living which he had taken up." What does Rowe mean by "Extravagance" or "that way of Living," and why is he speaking so, well, delicately? Fortunately he soon explains himself. Shakespeare had, he writes,

> by a Misfortune common enough to young Fellows, fallen into ill Company; and amongst them, some that made a frequent practice of Deer-stealing, engag'd him with them more than once in robbing a Park that belong'd to Sir Thomas Lucy . . . For this he was prosecuted by that Gentleman, as he thought, somewhat too severely.

Rowe may have heard of this story from the actor Thomas Betterton, who recently had visited Stratford to seek out information on his hero Shakespeare. In any case, it is important to note that Rowe's and Davies's tales, largely consistent with each other, were arrived at separately.

Notice that Rowe presents his story somewhat apologetically—that is, Shakespeare was basically running with the wrong crowd. Many illustrations celebrating this incident in the following centuries show a young, virile Shakespeare, defiant as he is arrested by two bailiffs. Such illustrations effectively present Shakespeare as a Warwickshire wild child. This image conforms nicely with that early critical emphasis on Shakespeare's native, self-taught character and rougher, less polished style compared with writ-

An 1861 mezzotint of Shakespeare before Thomas Lucy. *(Thomas Brooks)*

ers who came after him, composing in ages more self-conscious about rules of drama, matters of style, and so on. If Shakespeare were caught stealing deer, it may be that he was trying to obtain additional food for his young family, but this gives the legendary scene a defensive, ennobling quality—"He only did it for the sake of his family." This tone is similar to the one subtly heard in Rowe's account when he says, in effect, that Shakespeare was corrupted by bad company. It should be added that some historians have raised one major objection to this incident, or at least to the detail of Sir Thomas's involvement or the location of the incident: his manor at Charlecote did not have a deer-park till the seventeenth century, decades after this conflict supposedly occurred.

But for the sake of argument, let us focus on the stories once more. Both early accounts of this famous deer-stealing scene share two important

details. First, both discuss this incident as a catalyst for Shakespeare's departure from Stratford and eventual arrival in London, where he would soon find professional success and literary fame. Second, both accounts feature William's revenge against the severity of punishment on Sir Thomas's part. However, these individual moments differ. Rowe claims that Shakespeare got back at Sir Thomas by writing a ballad against him that "was so very bitter" that it renewed the gentleman's vengeance; this poem, Rowe claims, was the reason Shakespeare was "obliged to leave his Business and Family in Warwickshire, for some time, and shelter himself in London."

Davies says that Shakespeare later got revenge when he comically immortalized Lucy as Justice Clodpate—this is actually a character from a play, not very old when Davies was writing in 1700, by Thomas Shadwell, yet further details make it clear that he has in mind Shakespeare's Justice

Shallow, who in *The Merry Wives of Windsor* attacks the play's comic hero, Falstaff: "you have beaten my men, killed my deer, and broke open my lodge." The character Slender then defends Shallow's upper-crust background: "all his ancestors, that come after him . . . they give the dozen white luces in their coat," to which Shallow obnoxiously adds, "It is an old coat." He means, of course, his family's esteemed coat of arms, but the Welsh character Evans next takes the meaning differently—"The dozen white louses do become an old coad well." This is typical Renaissance wordplay, and the kind of which Shakespeare was particularly fond. In reality, the coat of arms of Sir Thomas Lucy featured, in the same punning spirit, three luces, which are fish better known as pike. The playwright, then, may just be sending up his pretentious, overbearing adversary from his earlier days in Stratford. The Lucy/luce/louse puns, and even a possible quip on coad/cod/coat/Charlecote, invite these winking—or *coded*—readings of the passage. This legend only grew and grew. Eventually it was said that Elizabeth I herself saved Shakespeare from Sir Thomas's prosecution, which is truly ridiculous, or the Earl of Leicester. This last argument further adds that Shakespeare dedicated *The Merry Wives of Windsor* to this nobleman as a show of gratitude for being freed.

RELIGIOUS STRIFE AND THE 1580S

One final, more important element—that of religious division—may also be present in both of these debated incidents above, and scholars today are more inclined to notice this presence. It must always be remembered that the Renaissance England in which Shakespeare grew up, worked, and presumably worshipped frequently convulsed with religious conflict. The period's strife makes our own age's "culture wars" look tame indeed.

Henry VIII, Elizabeth I's father, had formally dismantled in 1534 the ancient connection between England and the Roman Catholic Church, which from the early years of Christianity had been the unified church of Europe, if not all Christendom. Henry was to some degree influenced by the reformer Martin Luther in Germany, who attacked the vice and worldliness of the Catholic Church beginning in 1517. However, the English king, in seeking a divorce from Catherine of Aragon that the pope would not

Portrait of Queen Elizabeth I in her coronation robes, early seventeenth century *(Artist unknown)*

grant, also had political reasons for severing his allegiance with Roman Catholicism, and he went about forming in its place a national, "Anglican" church, the Church of England, in whose services all citizens were expected to participate. Henry declared himself the "Supreme Governor" of the English church, thereby entwining politics and religion in ways that would later be highly problematic for some families.

One can find no better clue to this tumultuous age than by looking at the sharp religious changes, back and forth, under subsequent monarchs: Henry's son Edward VI was the most Protestant of England's Renaissance monarchs, being deeply influenced by Continental reformers. However, he died young, so this "Protestant hightide" was short-lived as well. Mary I next assumed the throne and immediately restored Catholicism

SHAKESPEARE'S BELIEFS

Shakespeare's true beliefs and feelings, tastes and preferences, have remained famously elusive to generations of readers, and they are difficult to isolate and identify in his writings. In part, this lack of declaration results because he wrote not letters or treatises (at least none that we have), but rather imaginative works such as plays and poems. Does a comment anywhere in these works truly belong to him? In one sense, yes, for Shakespeare wrote them, usually in a highly memorable way. However, attempts to ascribe any such comment as a genuine belief or position of the writer should be undertaken with extreme critical caution. A character's and an author's beliefs are not the same thing, and in Shakespeare's life as in his works, reticence reigns. For this reason, the Romantic poet John Keats ascribed to Shakespeare that power of "negative capability," which involved both an unusual resistance to a writer's typical need to declare beliefs, values, and certainties, and a chameleon-like ability to give voice to an almost inconceivable range and diversity of characters, as if each one were that single personality most truly reflective of the author.

Despite these considerable obstacles, the question of Shakespeare's true beliefs remains one of abiding interest. Often one's own preoccupations seem to blend into the figure one is trying to understand. For example, those who focus most on Shakespeare the literary genius may prioritize artistic destiny, even to a deterministic degree, as Shakespeare's guiding rule

for decision, action, and conduct. Thus the sensitive biographer Peter Alexander writes,

His business of life, which a man of genius is in some ways less free to choose than his less gifted fellows, is an adequate answer as to questions about what took Shakespeare to London.

On the other hand, M. C. Bradbrook seems sensible in the following comment: "I have assumed that for him, in common with the rest of his age, family and religion were governing features of his inner as his outer life," and she is likewise sensitive in adding that neither influence "is likely to be as powerful today." This is not to shortchange either family or religion in twenty-first-century life, but it does helpfully remind us that there are many contrasting beliefs and emphases between our contemporary culture and Shakespeare's early-modern Tudor and Stuart culture. The importance of Shakespeare's family experiences on his personality and beliefs should certainly not be discounted, for they must have shaped many things about his life, from his country upbringing and formative moments to his ongoing allegiances and anxieties. Shakespeare's loss of a son, his life-long marriage to Anne, and his eventual return to Stratford are all telling details that validly contribute to our sense of this complex man.

throughout the realm. Her marrying the Spanish king Philip and burning at the stake roughly three hundred Protestant martyrs ensured that a significant number of Englishmen would never return to the Catholic fold—it became a matter of national pride, and not just religious confession or ecclesiastical allegiance. When Elizabeth I became queen in 1558, she was determined to find a *via media*, or middle course, between these two extremes, and broadly conceived, she did just that, avoiding religious wars (as France did not), assassination by Catholics, and rebellion by Puritans until her long reign ended in 1603.

Elizabeth did not wish, as she famously said, to "make windows into men's souls," but she did assert her supremacy over the church, and demanded uniformity of worship from her citizens.

It is also true that religion must have shaped Shakespeare's beliefs. As one critic has said, no one of any intelligence could have avoided thinking deeply about religious truth, tradition, and conviction during this turbulent time of great religious divisiveness following the Protestant Reformation. It is easy to claim Shakespeare, or rather certain convenient passages from his life story or his writings, for this or that "side" in the great Renaissance struggle between Protestants and Catholics, but it may be more important to acknowledge the strong presence and influence that religion in general enjoyed during this era. Whatever position one held personally, religious beliefs in general and a Christian outlook in particular helped to define the mental universe and the habits of thought of people from all backgrounds in Renaissance England. As the intellectual historian Charles Taylor recently argued, our own secular age today involves ideas about life and reality that in a very real way were simply not conceivable as legitimate intellectual choices by most people in the Renaissance, or really in any age before the middle of the nineteenth century.

Recently the Shakespearean critic David Bevington, who has devoted his long, distinguished career to Shakespeare and to Renaissance drama and culture generally, has tried to say more, or at least more that is reliable, by saying less. Bevington cautions against seeing Shakespeare (as some have) as a great moral philosopher, pointing out the restraint required of a dramatist. That said, Bevington does credit Shakespeare with being a "natural philosopher,"

one "innately gifted and wisely self-taught." He believes that Shakespeare, by the time he reached his fiftieth year, would have shared the following pieces of advice strongly and freely: be generous; honor your father and mother (especially your father!); forgive the unforgiveable, since you are remembered for kindness; there is a kind of immortality in writing, but theater cannot change the world, nor can religion; churchgoing is generally a good thing; mankind does seem to suffer from and must learn to endure and accept a fallen nature; it is possible to believe and still feel skeptical about some matters; some sort of providence seems to govern human lives and history; and prize self-knowledge, sane survival, fairness and compassion in domestic life, and the preciousness of friendships. That final group of especially important beliefs may explain why Shakespeare, most sane and humane of writers, continues to reward our repeated reading of his works, where so many of the above themes are so memorably expressed.

SEE ALSO:

Alexander, Peter. *Shakespeare.* New York: Oxford University Press, 1964.

Bevington, David. *Shakespeare's Ideas.* Malden, Mass.: Blackwell Pub., 2008.

Bradbrook, M. C. *Shakespeare: The Poet in His World.* New York: Columbia University Press, 1978.

Cox, John. *Seeming Knowledge: Shakespeare and Skeptical Faith.* Waco, Tex.: Baylor University Press, 2007.

Unfortunately, Elizabethans did not have the benefit of this long view or reassurance of a happy ending to their own era. Moreover, the 1580s, the time of Shakespeare's "Lost Years," were especially critical, marked by new tensions, increased uncertainty, and strong (some would even say panicked) reactions from the government. The entire religious balance changed dramatically in England in 1580, when some of the nation's young Catholic exiles, educated in seminaries in France and Rome, began to return to minister to English families for whom Catholic forms of worship, especially the mass, were outlawed. Elizabeth's Protestant regime, however, saw it differently. It considered these returning priests to be spies and para-military agents aligned with Spain. After all, the pope in 1570 had "excommunicated" Elizabeth, more or less relieving true Catholic believers from loyalty to her. These arriving priests were more sophisticated, more militant kinds of Catholics, trained in the atmosphere of renewed devotion and sacrifice in the Catholic Counter-Reformation. Two men in particular, Edmund Campion and Robert Persons, created a great stir when they returned to England in 1580 at the vanguard of a "Jesuit mission." (Jesuits were a special order of priest, formed earlier in the century by Ignatius Loyola.) Campion would eventually be captured and then executed early in 1582, but beforehand he and other priests moved secretly from Catholic household to household through Warwickshire and into Lancashire.

RELIGIOUS LIFE AND THE SHAKESPEARE FAMILY

Some biographers have posited a direct connection between the charismatic Jesuit Campion and the sixteen-year-old Shakespeare, but there is no proof of their meeting. However, the Jesuit Mission and the corresponding English crackdown was on everyone's minds, and there was one figure in Shakespeare's life who provides a direct connection with this Catholic network of priests. One of his Stratford schoolmasters, John Cottom, had a brother who was captured, tortured, and executed along with Campion, in 1582. This schoolmaster soon returned to his family property in Lancashire—less than ten miles from the Hoghton manor. Might he have been a conduit by which Shakespeare took up residence in this Catholic family's Lancashire manor house? Motivation for this journey remains mysterious, but there is a rough consensus now that Shakespeare's family likely retained, or at least remained sympathetic to, the old Catholic faith. Therefore, the notion that Shakespeare resided in Lancashire amid resistant Catholics fits the overall inclination toward the Shakespeare family nicely.

Stratford was certainly a scene of religious conflict in its own right, and John Shakespeare as a public official would have been in the middle of these battles. We have seen how he was fined at various times from the late 1570s through the 1590s, and it was also recorded that he was absent from required church attendance. Some critics have seen these records in the context of religious "recusancy," or refusal—that is, he was not present at Stratford's church because of religious principles. Devout Catholic believers thought the Anglican services were heretical and abysmal. It is true that stiff fines for Catholics refusing to attend Anglican services rose sharply in the 1580s, as the government grew concerned about the Jesuit Mission's influence. However, one record also makes it clear that John's erratic attendance, his "lying low" as we might say, was as likely to be related to his financial troubles. In one anti-recusant report, he is not grouped with Stratford's prominent Roman Catholics, but within a second group—"It is said that these last nine come not to Church for fear of process of Debt." The two reasons, of course, need not be mutually exclusive, but government officials made this distinction, and it should not be overlooked. The discovery of a Counter-Reformation "Spiritual Testament" in 1757—featuring John Shakespeare's name and discovered in the attic of the Birthplace home—contributed further, if more mysteriously, to arguments for the Shakespeare family's Catholicism. Perhaps the book was hidden because the home had been searched by government officials; it was in fact a book that the priests of the Jesuit Mission may have distributed through England. Finally, the brief report of clergyman Davies above ends with a note of clarity rare in Shakespeare studies—"He died a papist" (that is, a Roman Catholic), he says of the famous writer.

On the other hand, William Shakespeare's father was among Stratford's leadership when the town conformed to government efforts to advance the Reformation in England. For example, reformers halted an annual pageant in Stratford involving St. George, England's patron saint—the event was thought to be too superstitious, redolent of the excesses of the old faith. Better known is the whitewashing of the Last Judgment chapel fresco in the Guildhall, which was done in the year of William's birth, 1564. This action was an iconoclastic one, another Protestant effort to eliminate what they considered the Catholic vice of idolatry from the town. John Shakespeare was borough chamberlain at the time. In this environment, Catholic families had much to fear—their religious loyalty could easily be seen as treason against their Protestant queen, and events throughout the decade heightened this tension. The Babington Plot against Elizabeth in 1586 implicated the Catholics' great hope for Elizabeth's successor, Mary Queen of Scots (she was executed the next year), and most monumentally, the Spanish Armada menaced England in 1588—a storm, which Englishmen saw as providential, kept the Spanish fleet from an outright invasion of the beleaguered Protestant nation. During this time, the Elizabethan government

An 1861 painting of Mary Queen of Scots being led to her execution. *(Scipione Vannutelli)*

reacted aggressively, developing spy networks and retaining loyal Protestants to ferret out and punish Catholic holdouts.

Sir Thomas Lucy, from the deer-poaching incident above, was just such a powerful agent, and he even confiscated the property of one Catholic family. His effigy can be seen in Charlecote's church. He looks intimidating—thick nostrils, broad forehead, short beard, cropped hair. A battle between him and anyone, Shakespeare included, would have been a heated encounter, and all the more so if intensified by opposed religious beliefs. Behind the legendary standoff over stolen deer and rabbits, can we begin to make out a confessional quarrel? Did Sir Thomas's animosity toward Shakespeare reflect a Protestant reaction against Catholics in Stratford? Perhaps, but this theory, too, is just that, and is far from substantiated.

Shakespeare's personal presence within this legend only makes it more shadowy. The scholar Richard Wilson describes Shakespeare as "the most secret writer of his age," and this fact should give pause to anyone wanting to claim Shakespeare as a spokesperson for this or that side of Renaissance England's confessional divide. He never blows the trumpet of his personal faith anywhere in his writings, as did so many other writers of this period, be they historians such as John Foxe or poets such as John Donne. The ventriloquist nature of drama writing partially explains Shakespeare's secrecy, but it cannot be the only answer. Some plays were indeed strikingly Protestant, whereas Shakespeare is never an openly confessional poet. Scholars such as Wilson and Jeffrey Knapp see in this reticence not an indifference or disinterest in religious belief, but rather a Catholic's fearful perspective in speaking out at all. If Shakespeare did grow up in a Catholic family and if he retained those beliefs to any degree, then he must have become familiar at an early age to play-acting in certain ways, and to keeping sensitive religious matters to himself, or so this argument goes. He may have felt himself as Beatrice says about Benedick in *Much Ado About Nothing*—"He wears his faith but as the fashion of his hat, it ever changes with the next block."

We will not solve these complicated matters here, but it may be enough to point out that the role of religion in Shakespeare's biography is as fascinating, and timely, as ever. At the end of 2009, the vice-rector of the Venerable English College in Rome, where young Catholic exiles trained during the time of Shakespeare's "Lost Years," claimed that it may have been Shakespeare who signed the college's guest book in 1585 as (in Latin) "William the Clerk from Stratford." If this were conclusive (it is not), it would tell us at least one place where Shakespeare was. Perhaps we must simply feel grateful to be able to state with confidence where Shakespeare was at the end of the "Lost Years"—in London, where his acting and writing and business careers were about to take off, in ways unparalleled before or since.

Sources and Further Reading

Chambers, E. K. and Charles Williams. *A Short Life of Shakespeare*. Oxford, U.K.: The Clarendon Press, 1933.

Eccles, Mark. *Shakespeare In Warwickshire*. Madison: University of Wisconsin Press, 1961.

Honigmann, E. A. J. *Shakespeare: The 'Lost Years'*. Manchester, U.K.: Manchester University Press, 1985.

Knight, W. Nicholas. *Shakespeare's Hidden Life: Shakespeare at the Law, 1585-1595*. New York: Mason & Lipscomb, 1973.

Wilson, Richard. *Secret Shakespeare: Studies in Theatre, Religion, and Resistance*. Manchester, U.K.: Manchester University Press, 2004.

Wood, Michael. *Shakespeare* [based on Wood's *In Search of Shakespeare* BBC2 television series]. London: BBC, 2003.

SHAKESPEARE THE YOUNG ACTOR AND WRITER

On some fateful day, Shakespeare must have set out from his hometown of Stratford, from his wife and children and parents and home, and traveled on his way to the city of London. There, within its young but rapidly developing world of public theaters and acting companies, he would reveal the lasting powers of his imagination, his "quick forge and working-house of thought" (as he describes it in *Henry V*). His plays and poems that we still read and attend today would emerge from this vibrant, energetic scene—the site of Renaissance urban entertainment.

If one sets out from the Shakespeare Birthplace House today, proceeding down Henley Street and into Bridge Street, one will find at the foot of that street a Tourist Information Center. Bancroft Gardens sits across the road, and there beside the River Avon stands a Shakespeare Monument presented to the town in 1888. An older bronzed Shakespeare, pensive and seated, is surrounded by some of his most famous characters—Prince Hal, who would become the renowned Henry V; the irrepressible and round Falstaff; Hamlet pondering the skull of Yorick; and Lady Macbeth obsessing on the blood of Duncan. Of course, this monument to Shakespeare and his stage creations was not there when the young writer passed this way on that day; instead, he would have seen a pastureland for cattle and for practicing archery. He next crossed the river and walked onward in the direction of Banbury. Many like to romanticize this trip, one of the most consequential decisions in literary history, and imagine Shakespeare leaving on a whim. Yet it is more likely that he left—whether with a theater company or not—determined to become an actor in London. He may not have traveled there immediately, especially if he had joined a group of actors in the middle of a tour, but we know that he arrived there soon enough. Legendary stories exist about Shakespeare's first humble jobs at a London theater, or his apprentice work acting and writing for the theater, but all we really know is that he was noticed and accepted into that world no later than the early 1590s, and perhaps much earlier.

THROUGH OXFORD TO LONDON

Two main itineraries led from Stratford to London. The road through Banbury continued on to Buckingham and Aylesbury. John Aubrey, in his late-seventeenth-century profile of Shakespeare, says the writer encountered along this route, in the village of Grendon, the comically misspeaking constable who inspired the stage equivalent of Dogberry in *Much Ado About Nothing*. (Aubrey oddly associates the character with *A Midsummer Night's Dream*, and dubiously says Shakespeare must have encountered this Grendon man on midsummer's night.) The real-life constable was still alive in 1642, Aubrey affirms. The more direct route, roughly a four-day journey, passed through Shipston and Long Compton and over gently rolling hills toward Woodstock and Oxford. Various anecdotes place Shakespeare in this or that Oxford tavern, and it seems very likely that he passed through the university town often, at least once a year and possibly much more frequently as he traveled, or even "commuted," between working life in London and his Stratford home. Although no records of his attendance exist, critics still debate the possibility that Shakespeare for a time studied at Oxford University, possibly before Anne Hathaway became pregnant. The retired scholar Robert F. Fleissner, in a letter entitled "Shakespeare at Oxford?" (which appeared recently in the journal of the Modern Language Association), points to Richard Ledes's Latin play, *Caesar Interfectus*, performed in Oxford in 1582, as a possible source for Shakespeare's later play on Julius Caesar. He may also have encountered there John Florio, an Italian tutor whose translation of the French essayist Montaigne is echoed in *Hamlet* and *The Tempest*. Florio, at this time, was instructing at Oxford the young Earl of Southampton, whom we will encounter again soon. On the other hand, other scholars, emphasizing Shakespeare's broad intelligence naturally obtained, argue against formal university enrollment—our writer may have soaked up the atmosphere, but in Frank Kermode's words, "it seems unlikely that he went into Bodley to read," meaning here Oxford's Bodleian Library.

Eventually the two itineraries from Stratford merged, at Uxbridge, and continued through Shepherd's Bush and Tyburn (notorious site of the gallows, for the executing of traitors) and onto Oxford Road, where today London's major department stores stand. In Shakespeare's day, these areas were still wooded areas, and villages at best. We hear traces of this rural past in the parish name of St. Giles-in-the-Fields, now at the heart of London's theater district along Shaftsbury Avenue. From there, the route led to Holburn and at last to Newgate, one of the seven main gates through the ancient wall surrounding the city of London proper—Newgate and Ludgate were on the west side, with Cripplegate, Moorgate, Bishopsgate, and Aldersgate on the north, and Aldgate facing east. The public theaters where Shakespeare soon worked were, significantly, located outside of London itself, to the north of the city walls in Shoreditch and to the south, across the River Thames, in the suburb of Southwark, also known as Bankside.

What was the city, one of Europe's great Renaissance capitals, like back then, and what did Shakespeare encounter? Let us imagine his first walk through the city, although it should be said that there was another popular way to travel—by waterway. London was a uniquely riverside city, in ways visitors today cannot fully appreciate. Fashionable mansions lined the bend of the Thames, connecting the city proper to adjacent Westminster to the southwest. Westminster, site of a famous abbey and hall, was a long-established site for legal and court activities. River traffic was quite heavy—with only London Bridge at the eastern edge of the city, boats constantly shuttled people from bank to bank and up and down the river, with shouts of "Westward Ho!" or "Eastward Ho!" to signal their direction. Before the tour, a few facts: first, Shakespeare found himself in a booming metropolis, a place differing considerably from the relatively sleepy market town of Stratford. London, from the beginning to the end of the sixteenth century, exploded in population, from roughly fifty thousand people to nearly two hundred thousand. As the center of government and site of international trade, London was constantly circulating with new inhabitants. As an increasingly dominant urban area, it also attracted a considerable number of citizens from the countryside, including young men serving as apprentices among London's tradesmen. They could be a rowdy bunch, and fears of their rebelling often concerned the Lord Mayor and his aldermen, or civic leaders.

The city fathers and London's many preachers also warned against pickpockets or con men, what they called "coney-catchers" and "cozeners," as well as the shiftless drifters comprising the urban underworld—prostitutes and whoremongers and vagrants and "masterless" men and horse-stealers and traitors and various others committing their various sins in the bawdy houses (brothels), gambling dens, and other places of ill repute. (These very terms were used by Lord Mayor William Fleetwood in a concerned note sent to the Privy Council, Queen Elizabeth's main cabinet, in 1597.) These "red-light" areas associated with diverse vices usually developed just outside the city walls, in an area suggestively called the "liberties." And as it has been said, these were the precise locations of Renaissance London's public theaters.

The word "suburb," then, had a much different connotation than today, and the suburban entertainment of theater was unhesitatingly grouped with what, to many, are more obvious criminal or at least unsavory activities. In one well-known syllogism, a preacher proclaimed that plays were sinful and sins brought about God's condemnation in the form of plague—therefore, the city's theaters caused the plague. More practically, the theaters also encouraged the spread of plague because they concentrated so many citizens into one crowded place, and many were sketchy citizens to boot, who encouraged ungodly idleness and lasciviousness (this group formed a "rabble" that led London's rulers to fear an anarchic uprising as well). Shakespeare would soon make this controversial pastime and gathering place more popular and successful than ever.

A TOUR OF WESTERN LONDON

Entering London at Newgate on the western side of the city, Shakespeare and other travelers in the late 1580s had much to see and take note of in this cauldron of urban energy and moral temptation. To the right and downriver stood Ludgate, which was next to the Fleet Prison and the young, urbane sophisticates of the Inns of Court, England's main site for the training of law students. The Bel Savage Inn was also nearby, one of several inns whose yards were a suitable, popular place for plays to be staged. Also close by was Blackfriars, where in a few years Shakespeare's company would be performing plays as well.

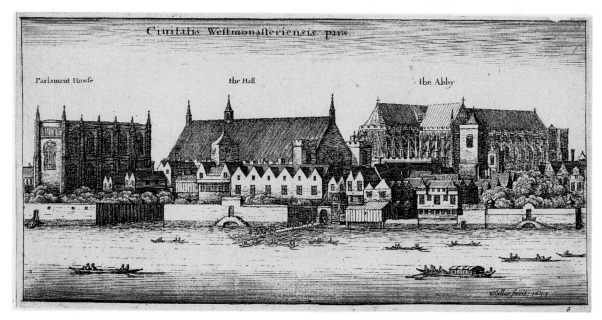

Cuitatis Weltmonasteriensis pars

Parliament House　　　　the Hall　　　　the Abby

This 1647 engraving shows Westminster as seen from across the Thames. The Abbey, Hall, and Parliament House are labeled. *(Wenceslaus Hollar)*

Proceeding from Newgate or Ludgate, newcomers soon encountered London's main western landmark—the cathedral of St. Paul's, not yet sporting its seventeenth-century dome that makes it so iconic today. (Moreover, a lightning strike in 1561 had destroyed its old wooden steeple, giving it for many years a half-finished look.) Citizens of course attended the divine service at the cathedral and numerous other parish churches throughout London. Many heard the linguistic elegance and powerful cadences of the *Book of Common Prayer* on a daily basis in morning and evening services. And as rituals, these formal services constituted, as well, their own kind of visual theater. Other activities occurred in or around the cathedral. Though hard to imagine, the wide space within St. Paul's was a gathering place of sorts, a place to see and be seen and a site for transactions of various sorts—hiring, consulting with clients, and the like. The pillared middle aisle became known as "Paul's Walk."

Just outside the church itself, on the northwest side, was Paul's Cross, an outdoor pulpit where popular preachers spoke, often drawing large crowds. We might compare this place of cultural exchange and news proclamation to the digitized, ever-running ticker screens that flash today's headlines in New York's Times Square. Paul's Churchyard and Paternoster Row were located just to the north of the Cathedral. The area was populated by stationers and printers and the stalls of booksellers, and thus must have been a very important place for Shakespeare and his fellow writers and actors. Browsing the published books, he likely found inspiration in earlier plays already printed, as well as in history books such as Holinshed's *Chronicles*, prose romances from which he borrowed plots, and in diverse classical works, often in translation—books by Plutarch on famous Greeks and Romans, as well as his school favorite, Ovid's *Metamorphoses*. Playing compa-

nies often eked out slightly more profit by selling to publishers the plays from their repertories, especially once a production's popularity waned. At that point, audiences at performances were dwindling, and so publication would not undermine the playhouses' revenues at the door.

CENTRAL LONDON AND ITS THEATER SCENE

From St. Paul's, a visitor would proceed west on High Street, through a central commercial area known as Cheapside and the impressive merchants' houses along Goldsmiths' Row. Cheap Street was London's central east-west artery, passing St. Mary Le Bow, whose tolling bell Shakespeare must have often heard. The street soon broke into three paths at the Royal Exchange, an opulent market hall that stood as testament to Elizabethan England's mercantile powers and colonial expansion. The hall, fairly new in Shakespeare's day, would be crowded with international merchants and traders. The southern fork of Cornhill led on a short walk to Gracious Street, or Gracechurch Street today, a major north-south thoroughfare.

If Shakespeare went left, or north, he would soon arrive at St. Helen's Bishopsgate, a still vibrant church, where, thanks to tax records, we know that our writer was for a while a parishioner. Onward through the city walls, he would arrive eventually at the less developed area of Shoreditch, a half mile or so farther. The fields of this area soon held the wooden octagonal structures of the new public theaters, primarily the Theatre and the Curtain. James Burbage, a carpenter and one of the most important figures in English theater history, first built the Theatre in the spring of 1576 near Holywell Lane, although audiences had to cross sometimes muddy lands to arrive there. Beyond the theater stood Finsbury Fields. The Curtain opened the following year, just south of Burbage's building and across the lane. John Stow's popular survey of the city features a marginal note for this area that reads, "Theatre and Curten for comedies and other shows," and city preachers began to condemn the place as one where vices were tempting citizens by their concentration and free indulgence.

One foreign visitor, Thomas Platter, recalls a 1599 visit there in appreciative (and appreciated) detail. He reports that plays began around two in the afternoon, and are meant to "make people merry." Groundlings, or those standing in front of the stage, pay only a penny, and they often had food and drink as well. (There are stories of early audiences throwing apples and nuts at the less successful actors.) The actors themselves "are dressed most exquisitely and elegantly," Platter says, and they concluded their shows with a dance, "very gracefully." Hardly the city center, there were no signs here of the bright lights and star-struck tourists of a big-time theater scene. Visitors were more likely to see rubbish, tenements (we know there were some near the Theatre), and even carcasses of animals, left in the fields from the nearby slaughterhouses. This soon would be Shakespeare's neighborhood.

The biographer Aubrey speaks of Shakespeare as a "natural wit" who "lived in Shoreditch." A few decades later, Robert Shiels put it this way, in a more elaborate story that has all the imagination—and no verification—of legend:

Concerning Shakespeare's first appearance in the playhouse. When he came to London, he was without money and friends, and being a stranger he knew not to whom to apply, nor by what means to support himself. At that time coaches not being in use, and as gentlemen were accustomed to ride to the playhouse, Shakespeare, driven by the last necessity, went to the playhouse door, and picked up a little money by taking care of the gentlemen's horses who came to the play; he became eminent in that profession, and was taken notice of for his diligence and skill in it . . . Some of the players accidentally conversing with him, found him so acute, and master of so fine a conversation, that struck therewith they recommended him to the house.

Thus was born the legend of Shakespeare's earliest work in London, and even fastidious critics such as Samuel Johnson found the image of the eloquent country boy, just waiting for his genius to be discovered, too irresistible. Johnson, in 1765, embellished the story even further, envisioning for Shakespeare great prosperity even at menial tasks outside the theater: "Shakespeare finding more horses put into his hand than he could hold, hired boys to wait under his inspection, who when *Will Shakespeare* was summoned, were immediately to present themselves, *I am Shakespeare's boy, sir.*" Shakespeare would soon find "higher employment," but even this modest start, as Johnson memorably says, "was the first dawn of better fortune." This story was later altered slightly, by the time of the great editor Edmund Malone at the end of the eighteenth century, so as to feature Shakespeare first working at least inside the theater. He was not yet an actor, in this version anyway, but a prompter's manager. In this role he would have served as a production assistant, more or less, helping the players with lines, ensuring they were placed for their entrances, and helping with costume changes. Some modern scholars find this whole nexus of stories dubious, although details about horses do suggest the setting of these first public theaters, just outside London's northern walls.

Returning to Gracechurch Street, that area was theatrically alive as well, featuring a number of inns in whose courtyards plays had been performed since the 1550s or 1560s: the Bell Inn and

THE COMMERCIAL THEATERS OF LONDON

Arriving in London in the late 1580s or early 1590s, the young actor and playwright William Shakespeare showed up in the middle of the development of the English Renaissance theater scene. In terms of cultural influence, artistic achievement, and a budding entertainment industry, the London theaters have hardly been paralleled.

William Burbage was responsible for opening the first public theater in London in 1576—a wooden structure straightforwardly called the Theatre. Burbage chose as a neighborhood the area known as Shoreditch, just north of London proper and the city walls. This location outside of the city limits was not by accident—London's mayor and aldermen, in fact, were highly hostile toward questionable practices like playgoing, thus enterprising theater companies had to set up shop outside of the jurisidiction of these powerful, disapproving civic leaders. For this reason, these areas around the city walls—such as Shoreditch to the north and Bankside to the south, on the other side of the River Thames—were known as the "liberties" and were also the homes of other disreputable pursuits such as gambling, bordellos, and rings for bear-baiting, which were violent confrontations between bears and mastiff hounds. Spectators today would be repulsed by these sorts of cruel pastimes, but for Elizabethans, this was popular entertainment that competed with theatrical performances.

The year 1576, then, is a significant year in European theater history, and some critics have even argued that the Elizabethan playhouses were the first public, commercial spaces for theater since the times of ancient Greek tragedy, some twenty centuries earlier. The public theaters created some significant advantages for an acting company. First, a public theater ensured that the company had its own space, and did not need to rely on churches (for sacred dramas) or inn yards, a common site for an earlier generation of English drama. Theaters expressly established for dramatic performances meant that companies no longer needed to travel the English countryside in search of venues (though in reality they would still take tours as another form of revenue), and it also kept them from relying on a willing bailiff or mayor in a small town, or on the generosity of spectators who were just happening to be standing around when a hat was passed for tips or payment. Companies in public theaters could now charge a regular admission fee, and the theater also enabled them to perform shows on a daily basis—and not only for town fairs or for religious feasts, as with the early mystery plays. These troupes sometimes even performed on sabbath Sundays, which infuriated some of the more pious city fathers and preachers in London.

Many other theaters followed the creation of the Theatre. The Rose Theatre in Bankside, or Southwark, was the famous (or infamous) stage for many of Christopher Marlowe's plays in the late 1580s and 1590s. Today, scholars know a good deal about dramatic activity at the Rose thanks to the existence of diaries by Philip Henslowe, the theater manager there. For example, we know how much he paid playwrights, the relative popularity of this or that play based on income recorded for different performances, and the frequency of performances of certain plays. The Theatre was eventually disassembled and its timber transported through the city and across the river, to Bankside quite near the Rose Theatre. The new building that arose in 1599 was called the Globe, famously associated with many of Shakespeare's greatest plays. The Swan was also in this neighborhood (a contemporary drawing of its stage exists), and early in

Cross Keys Inn on Gracechurch, the Bull on nearby Bishopsgate Street, and, a little farther off, the Red Lion and Boar's Head in White Chapel. And let's not forget the colorfully named Saracen's Head. If Shakespeare, newly arrived from Stratford and first walking through London, now turned right

The interior of the rebuilt Globe Theatre in London. This photograph was taken in August of 2007. *(Used under a Creative Commons license)*

the next century a square-shaped theater, the Fortune, opened as well. These were the best known of several theaters throughout London. Unfortunately, the Globe burned down in 1613, due to cannon fire related to Shakespeare's history play Henry VIII. It was later rebuilt to slightly different specifications. All of the playhouses were closed in 1642, during the Puritan rule following the English Civil War. They would reopen during the Restoration nearly twenty years later, but the golden age of Renaissance drama in London was by then forever gone.

SEE ALSO:

Gurr, Andrew. *The Shakespearean Stage,* 3rd ed. Cambridge: Cambridge University Press, 2009.

Gurr, Andrew. *Playgoing in Shakespeare's London.* New York: Cambridge University Press, 2005

Henslowe, Philip. *Henslowe's Diary.* Ed. R. A. Foakes. London: Cambridge University Press, 1961.

Sullivan Jr., Garrett A., ed. *Early Modern English Drama: A Critical Companion.* New York: Oxford University Press, 2006.

Womack, Peter. *English Renaissance Drama.* Malden, Mass.: Blackwell, 2006.

onto Gracechurch Street (rather than left or north toward Bishopsgate and Shoreditch), he would have descended southward to the bank of the Thames. Near there stood the Tower of London, a Norman stronghold since the time of William the Conqueror. The Tower was a massive fortress, with its moats and crenellations and the turrets of the White Tower. Shakespeare in one play speaks of "Julius Caesar's ill-erected Tower," and the doomed princes describe it forebodingly in *Richard III*.

The place was so ominous because it was a site notorious for imprisonment, torture, and execution. One tower was the Bloody Tower, and the many unfortunate inhabitants entered by Traitors' Gate by the wharf. A scaffold stood on adjacent Tower Hill. If Shakespeare avoided the Tower area—and one did well to do just that—Gracious Street eventually led into London Bridge, a city landmark and the single bridge connecting the city across the Thames to Southwark, or Bankside. The bridge itself had many stately arches rising from the river, atop which were supported rows of shops and houses, three or four stories tall, on each side. Tourists often remarked on its grandeur. If Shakespeare crossed the bridge and turned to the right, now reversing direction on the other, southern side of the river, he likely would have noticed traitors' heads stuck on poles above the bridge's southern façade. These may have made an impression upon a young actor who was soon working, or already at work, on a trilogy of history plays about England's own bloody civil wars, full of betrayals and executions.

MORE THEATERS: THE COLORFUL WORLD OF SOUTHWARK

Farther down Gracious Street, on the southern side of London Bridge, visitors can still take a left into a seemingly unpromising alleyway and soon marvel at the George Inn. It is the last survivor among the several galleried inns that once lined this long street. Next, Shakespeare would have passed Southwark's cathedral, St. Mary Overy as it was called, where one of the writer's brothers, also an actor, would be laid to rest early in the seventeenth century. Shakespeare could not have known of that upcoming grief, fortunately. Moving along, he would have soon appreciated, or steeled himself against, the wayward, freewheeling character of this "liberty" area, which like Shoreditch was outside the city's jurisdiction. Thus brothels and gaming houses were plentiful, as were, of course, rowdy taverns. (The Anchor remains there today, just downriver from the present Globe playhouse.) The Clink Prison was a stinking, dangerous site in this neighborhood.

The area also had bull- and bear-baiting rings, a brutal pastime that involved mastiff hounds being set upon those larger animals. Such activity would rightfully be decried as a savagery today (think of the controversy surrounding the subculture of dog-fighting), but Elizabethan spectators often liked their entertainment bloody, whether attending actual executions or witnessing staged versions in tragedies or history plays. As it turns out, our culture is not terribly different, if one considers the popularity of film director Quentin Tarantino and horror- or action-oriented diversions. Some bears, such as Harry Hunks, became town celebrities. Harry's turf, the Beargardens, is gone now, but a trace still survives in the street name there.

Around the block are the foundations of the Rose Theatre, which tour groups can still visit today. (The foundations were excavated fairly recently.) The Rose is a rich location in English Renaissance theater history. Philip Henslowe, an opportunistic pawnbroker and shrewd businessman, built the Rose in 1587, and so most likely it was new when Shakespeare first visited Southwark. Twelve years later, the most famous English theater of all time would open just around the corner and down the street—the Globe Theatre, home of Shakespeare, his company the Lord Chamberlain's Men, and his timeless tragedies and high comedies. Taken together, these details and landmarks throughout Southwark may give an impression of a crowded urban environment. However, despite the boom in London's population and expansion of its metropolitan area, it should be remembered that Southwark, like Shoreditch to the north, was on the city's periphery. For example, contemporary maps such as Jan Visscher's "Long View of London" feature an engraving of that future playhouse, the Globe; there are a few playgoers outside its doors, as if waiting to gain entrance to the day's performance, but what is more noticeable are all the trees and bushes on three sides of the building. The far side, the only one that looks remotely like a city scene (more like a modest town), contains one or two rows of houses, and then the River Thames beyond. A broader view further reveals the less developed, if not entirely wooded, character of Southwark; one sees a lot of homes and buildings all along the river front, but very quickly manmade evidence gives way to trees and woods that stretch off toward the south.

Historians have theater owner Philip Henslowe to thank for a detailed diary in which he recorded plays performed at the Rose, along with their earnings and how frequently they were performed. We also get a sense from his diary of writing practices and the low status of playwrights during this era. First, Henslowe used his pawn-broking skills in making loans to broke writers, who often wrote plays as a desperate means to pay back Henslowe or extend their credit. It is also clear that many plays were highly collaborative, since Henslowe sometimes lists a handful of writers as receiving payment for a single play. Shakespeare may have had collaborators on some plays that are ascribed to him alone, including some early plays and more certainly a few of the quite late ones. However, critics today are increasingly confident in crediting him as a main author even early in his writing career, and not viewing him merely as a collaborator or, as

was a popular theory for a while, a novice getting his start via "patchwork"—that is, by rewriting or updating existing plays. Regarding the practices and realities recorded in Henslowe's diary, we can even more confidently point out one exception in Shakespeare's career: he not only avoided the financial ruin or near ruin that hounded many writers (justly called the "Elizabethan Prodigals" by one critic), but he also soon found himself in a singularly advantageous commercial situation. After a few years, he became the "house writer," as well as actor and owner and sharer in profits, for a new theater company that enjoyed quick success. They were playing regularly at Elizabeth's court by the mid-1590s, while Henslowe's Rose had become famous as the playhouse where some of the greatest works of the English Renaissance were performed—the bold new plays by Shakespeare's contemporary Christopher Marlowe.

Unlike Shakespeare's, Marlowe's career was dashing, controversial, and meteoric, although in several ways their plays resembled each other's work. Marlowe's early influence on Shakespeare's first plays is completely apparent. Christopher Marlowe was a cobbler's son from Canterbury who was educated at Cambridge University. Thus his humble, provincial origins were Shakespeare's, too, but Marlowe could rely on—and he made full use of—a university education in classical literature and theology that in all likelihood Shakespeare never experienced. Marlowe soon charged onto London's stages with all of the fiery self-confidence of a recent graduate. His first play, *Tamburlaine*, about a Scythian shepherd of humble origins (the biographical parallel is often noted) who conquers the world, seemingly with impunity, revolutionized the language and spectacle of Renaissance theater upon its appearance in 1587. The very prologue dismisses the "jigging veins of rhyming mother wits," that is, the trotting, sing-song verses of the morality plays and earlier, simpler plays such as *Cambyses* and *The Famous Victories of Henry V.*

Instead, the prologue of *Tamburlaine* promises "high astounding terms," a reference to Marlowe's appealing refinement and versatile deployment of strongly accented, five-beat-per-line, unrhymed poetry lines, called blank verse. This would soon be the form of Shakespeare's own poetic language in his plays, and blank verse would provide the rhythms of thought and emotion for all of his characters' most famous soliloquies. Marlowe soon had many imitators who also wrote, in the words of fellow Cambridge writer and likely collaborator Thomas Nashe, with the "swelling bombast of a bragging blank verse." The young writer Shakespeare was as impressionable as anyone else, as his first plays will reveal. Yet his writing soon matured. One of the greatest insights into his artistic development over two decades is that of David Bevington, who said that, compared with Marlowe's ostentatious, rhetorical style, Shakespeare continued to develop his literary art by learning variously how to conceal that art. The seasoned, mid-career writer seems to say as much in *Hamlet* (1600–01), when Hamlet gives advice to the visiting players:

> . . . for in the very torrent, tempest, and as I may say, whirlwind of your passion, you must acquire and beget a temperance that may give it smoothness. O it offends me to the soul to hear a robustious, peri-wig pated fellow tear a passion to tatters, to very rags, to split the ears of the groundlings. I would have such a fellow whipped for overdoing . . .

Here the writer, through the mouth of one of his greatest creations, seems to ponder an earlier theatrical era—style-wise, a time of breathless, energized innovations onstage with larger-than-life characters and highly emotional, even melodramatic, outbursts. From the sound of it, he seems happier to be a writer now, although it also sounds as if this abuse of this or that speech was an ongoing problem between sensitive authors and intense actors.

This less impassioned kind of theater lay in the future, then, but few wanted subtlety or concealment in the late 1580s. This was the time of the Armada threat, and Marlowe's superman protagonist and his martial exploits resonated with an increasingly patriotic English nation, preparing for possible war with Spain. There were also radically different themes in Marlowe's dramatic universe—ones of self-definition, self-determination, a wild veering toward freedom with which this provocative playwright confronted audiences: " . . . Then applaud his fortunes as you please," says the prologue of *Tamburlaine*. Make of it what you will. Try to make sense of this intimidating, unpredictable moral universe, where power and persuasion seem to reign. This was very different fare from the town mystery plays, with their familiar biblical stories, or the morality plays, with their stark good-and-bad outcomes. Even a few lines give a taste of Marlowe's appealing effects, as in this soliloquy by Tamburlaine as he ponders his imperial ambitions:

> Nature, that framed us of four elements
> Warring within our breasts for regiment,
> Doth teach us all to have aspiring minds.
> Our souls, whose faculties can comprehend
> The wondrous architecture of the world
> And measure every wand'ring planet's
>   course,
> Still climbing after knowledge infinite
> And always moving as the restless spheres,
> Wills us to wear ourselves and never rest
> Until we reach the ripest fruit of all,
> That perfect bliss and sole felicity,
> The sweet fruition of an earthly crown.

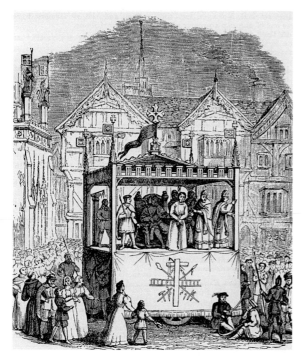

Illustration of a mystery play from Robert Chambers's *Book of Days*, ca. nineteenth century.

Critics have spoken of a new secular spirit during this phase of Renaissance drama, and of Marlowe's iconoclastic spirit in particular. Both words are partially correct. More encompassing, there is something in Marlowe's writing that mixes the idealistic and inspiring with the edgy and subversive, and it remains deeply recognizable. As F. E. Halliday notes, with Marlowe "the modern English drama is born." *Tamburlaine* was so popular that a sequel soon appeared, and Marlowe had additional theatrical successes, mainly at Henslowe's Rose Theatre. His *Doctor Faustus*, for instance, remains one of the great tragedies of western drama. It influenced Shakespeare in various scenes throughout his career, from a conjuring scene in an early history play to his late great magician character, Prospero, in *The Tempest*.

SHAKESPEARE'S ACTING AND EARLY WRITING

John Aubrey says simply that Shakespeare "came to London, I guesse about 18; and he was an Actor at one of the Play-houses, and did act exceedingly well." He soon adds that his "Plays took well," too. Some critics point to quotations by fellow writers—Shakespeare's contemporary Ben Jonson and the Restoration poet John Dryden, respectively—to claim that as early as the 1580s, Shakespeare had written his first tragedy, *Titus Andronicus*, and an early version of *Pericles*, typically now considered a later romance. Some lost version of *Hamlet* is another possibly very early play by Shakespeare, although others attribute this inferred first version to another young writer, Thomas Kyd.

More certainly, Kyd's shocking revenge play *The Spanish Tragedy* was, like the plays of Marlowe, deeply influential on this generation of writers. It, too, enjoyed an ongoing popularity. Kyd himself drew upon the Roman tragedies of Seneca, which were read at the universities and which were popularized in English translations throughout the 1580s. Shakespeare's *Hamlet* (the one we know of, the famous one) clearly borrows aspects of both Seneca's and Kyd's models—the revenger's feigned madness, the play within a play, the supernatural presences, and the classical inclusions. However, it is that aforementioned first tragedy, *Titus Andronicus*, probably written as early as 1589–90, that seems most inspired by Kyd's bloody revenge play. Once thought to be a mere collaboration, *Titus Andronicus* today receives greater credit as one of Shakespeare's first plays, and one with noticeable dramatic strengths. It excelled among many plays of its time in poetry and scenic plotting, for example. Conversely, successful modern productions, often playing up the exaggerated language and violence in ritualistic, stylized fashion, have proven that *Titus* is not simply a period piece, but speaks powerfully and brutally to later ages as well:

> What stern, ungentle hands
> Hath lopped and hewed and made thy body
>   bare
> Of her two branches—those sweet
>   ornaments
> Whose circling shadows kings have longed
>   to sleep in?

Shakespeare has transported Kyd's revenge scenario to ancient Rome, and here an uncle addresses a mutilated Lavinia, the daughter of the title character, a victorious general. The sons of a vanquished queen have raped Lavinia and cut off her hands as well as her tongue, so that she may not report their outrages. Shakespeare obviously borrowed this narrative from the Philomel story in Ovid's *Metamorphoses*—the play makes reference to the story, and Ovid's book itself (a schoolbook dear to Shakespeare) appears in a crucial scene. The book, in fact, becomes an instrument by which Titus will learn of his family's tragedy and enact his revenge, which involves murder and cannibalism. Shakespeare's first effort at tragedy, it is safe to say, was not for the squeamish or faint of heart. But it did reflect the tastes of the Elizabethan theater, as did the bear-baiting houses mentioned earlier.

Shakespeare, therefore, began soon enough to find success as a writer of plays, though we are probably safe in imagining a longer initiation period for this second profession, for which he would soon be best known. He must have had, to some degree, that personal presence and charisma possessed by so many actors. Aubrey describes Shakespeare the new Londoner as a "handsome, well-shaped man: very good company, and of a very ready and pleasant smooth Wit." The professional theater companies in London were intensive and highly demanding of their actors, even those who, as Shakespeare surely was at first, a minor player, one for hire, and not among the main ensemble of investors or "sharers." Each actor had to memorize various roles, sometimes multiple characters per play, and with the theaters' repertory format, the companies had to prepare and perform new plays at what would be considered a breakneck pace by today's standards. Physical prowess and agility, for fight scenes and for moving quickly from one area of the theater to another, would also have been highly valuable. And this was only the beginning, as Gary O'Connor points out in a biography popular with actors and theater students:

> The unknown actor could walk in a jig, make water in a cinque pace, entune a song through his nose, extemporize a melody on the viol-de-gamboys. His eyes scoured dance manuals, he hummed from popular song sheets, he culled jokes from everything—simple and crude, or highly sophisticated, the level did not matter much—and invented puns from basic body functions to the most sophisticated use of foreign tongues.

As O'Connor summarizes, "Acting was serious, heavy work," and as an actor Shakespeare likely rehearsed in the morning, performed in productions in the afternoon, and perhaps reserved time in the early evening for early efforts at writing his own plays, or possibly sonnets or a pair of longer narrative poems soon to see the light of day in print. We should not yet imagine him too much of a writer and hardly an actor. He seems to have acted fully and for a long time, if his being called by one contemporary an "old player" is to be taken seriously. Critics today suspect he spent his early days as an actor and first days as stage writer working with the Queen's Men or with the related companies of Strange's and

Derby's Men. He had at least some connection with Pembroke's Men as well.

E. K. Chambers has argued for a punning reference, and a satisfied playwright's homage, to Shakespeare the actor in the following line from George Peele's *Edward I*: "Shake thy speares in honour of his name, / Under whose royalty thou wear the same." If it does pay homage to Shakespeare, there is certainly a swaggering quality to it, as with his spear-Shaking surname. In this spirit, it may be easy to imagine him living a little recklessly, as a young husband and father free of common responsibilities and newly arrived in an exciting capital city, not to mention within the roguish theater neighborhoods of Shoreditch and Bankside. Jess Winfield's recent book, *My Name is Will: A Novel of Sex, Drugs, and Shakespeare*, features a Catholic (and thus outlaw) writer and celebrates this vision. Yet Aubrey presents it otherwise: "He was not a company keeper, lived in Shoreditch, wouldn't be debauched, & if invited to write, he was in pain." It is a curious portrait, particularly in light of other anecdotes that Shakespeare was rather friendly and social and capable of practical jokes, and in light of written testimony that he wrote with a striking smoothness and ease.

GREENE'S ATTACK AND SHAKESPEARE'S *HENRY VI* PLAYS

Shakespeare must have kept some company, and London's playing companies were clearly buying, keeping, and performing his plays, for in the fall of 1592 the young writer's name suddenly reemerges, in a highly hostile context, back into print records. Robert Greene will live forever as the first person to speak of William Shakespeare as a writer, but at the time, he was far, far from happy about this person in question. Well, more precisely, at the very time these words were printed, Robert Greene was already dead. A Norwich man, Greene was yet another author who attended Cambridge University; he was also the informal head of a group known as the University Wits. He wrote a series of successful plays for the Queen's Men (and may very well have first met Shakespeare in the context of this playing company), as well as various prose texts. By all accounts, including his own, he led a drunken, shifty, dissipated life, abandoning his young family, taking up with thieves and cutthroats, and in one case selling the same play to two different theater companies. His self-described "sickness, riot, incontinence" all took its toll eventually, and he died in August 1592. There appeared in the months following his death two posthumous pamphlets, *The Repentance of Robert Greene* and *Greene's Groatsworth of Wit, bought with a Million of Repentance*, a sort of deathbed confession.

These sensational texts were presumably by Greene, though perhaps by another in ventriloquist's fashion. In the latter work, he offers advice for the wise living he himself was incapable of, and reserves a special warning for his "fellow scholars about this city":

> Base-minded men all three of you, if by my misery you be not warned: for unto none of you (like me) sought those burrs to cleave: those puppets (I mean) that spake from our mouths, those antics garnished in our colours. Is it not strange, that I, to whom they all have been beholding, shall (were ye in that case as I am now) be both at once of them forsaken? Yes, trust them not: for there is an upstart crow, beautified with our feathers, that with his *tiger's heart wrapped in a player's hide* supposes he is as well able to bombast out a blank verse as the best of you; and, being an absolute *Johannes Factotum*, is in his own conceit the best Shake-scene in a country.

(continues on page 54)

SHAKESPEARE'S STAGE

We have now identified the various theaters that arose in London, or more precisely, those to the north of London in Shoreditch and to the south of the city in Southwark, otherwise known as Bankside. The Theatre, the Curtain, the Rose, the Swan, the Hope—they all differed somewhat in terms of size and design, but a few general characteristics were universal. Contemporary illustrations of these theaters show a circular or polygonal building, usually made with timber and sealed with daub or plaster. They typically featured a thatched roof. The one major exception to this rule was Henslowe's later theater, the Fortune, which was square in shape and featured exterior staircases. These playhouses were roughly, by today's standards, three or four stories tall.

But what were the interiors like? Can we easily imagine the stages where Shakespeare's and his contemporaries' plays came to life during the Renaissance? Existent contracts for the building of the Fortune and Swan playhouses provide us with some information, but the single most valuable piece of evidence is a drawing—or rather a copy of an original sketch—that shows us a play or rehearsal occurring on a Renaissance London stage, all from the perspective of an audience member, one sitting front and center and possibly from a higher seat in a gallery, directly across from the stage. The original recorder was a Dutch priest named Johannes de Witt, who visited London in 1596 and sketched the Swan Theatre while there. His drawing accompanied his "London Observations," but alas, this original document has not survived. Fortunately, his friend Arend van Buchell copied de Witt's words and sketch in a commonplace book, or personal journal, and this volume was discovered in Amsterdam in 1880. This stage illustration gives us many good ideas about the interior spaces of the theater and how playwrights and actors commonly made use of the space. Scholars have supplemented or sought to verify these ideas by inferring further information from the stage directions often included in texts of plays.

The de Witt drawing (as it is often called) displays an actor downstage, near the front of the stage's edge. He holds a stick or crook and is possibly a shepherd. Center stage, two ladies (they would have been male actors dressed as women) surround a long bench. The large thrust stage is a square floor space raised a few feet off the ground, around three sides of which the groundlings, or standing audience members, could look up to watch the dramatic action taking place just a few feet away. For spectators willing to pay a little more, there were three levels of galleries that made up the outer ring of the theater's circular edifice. In the drawing, a set of stairs leads up to the ground-level gallery. The stages, extending about halfway into the yard (the open space in the middle of the theater), generally would have been about forty feet across. Farther upstage, two pillars, sometimes painted (as they were at the Swan) to appear as marble, thus evoking the ancient Roman amphitheaters, held aloft a tiled canopy or roof, which would protect the actors from the weather. All performances, remember, were technically outdoor performances, since the diameter of the theaters was uncovered. On the other hand, the stage and the galleries did have roofs.

This canopy would also hold a mechanical device—a suspension system, basically—from which actors could descend to or ascend from the main stage, as plays' actions called for this "special effect." This upper area was known as the heavens, and correspondingly the area below the stage was called hell. A trapdoor on the main stage allowed for quick movement between the central and lower spaces, and often demons or ghosts or gravediggers (as in *Hamlet*) made sudden appearances from below. At the back of the stage area, behind the pillars, is a wall with two doors for entrances and exits. Certain plays indicate that a scene is "discovered" or dramatically revealed, leading some theater historians to hypothesize about a "discovery space"—possibly an inner playing area upstage which could be easily concealed with a curtain running between the pillars. The pillars could be simple props as well, behind which hiding or eavesdropping characters could stand, obvious to the audience but invisible to onstage characters. This back wall was actually the front façade of the "tiring house," or place for the attiring of actors. Today, we would call this area "backstage"—the place where actors put on costumes and prepare for their entrances or rest between scenes.

In de Witt's drawing, the second floor of the tiring-house façade is a deck area in which several people stand. Are these actors or audience members? We cannot tell from the drawing, but stage directions in plays do indicate that some actions took place on a higher plane, signifying a city wall or even the heavens. Texts of plays speak of such actions occurring "above" or "aloft" or even "on the walls." Think of the famous balcony scene in *Romeo and Juliet*; that scene likely required an upper-story playing space. It may sound improbable for those several people to be audience members, since they appear to be behind the action on stage. However, this was not only a possible space for viewing but also a coveted one, sometimes called the "lord's room" or gentlemen's room—apparently these better-off spectators appreciated such a prominent space within the theater where they, like the actors, could be widely seen by many. Finally, atop this deck space is a thatched hut, in which musicians may have played before or during performances. In the drawing, there is a flag atop this structure, whose color would indicate to passersby what sort of play was to be presented that afternoon—comedy or tragedy. There is also the lone figure of trumpeter stepping out of this hut, beckoning London's playgoers.

In his "London Observations," written originally in Latin, de Witt speaks of "four amphitheatres in London of notable beauty," and he privileges the two in Bankside, namely the Rose and the Swan, as the "more magnificent." Moreover, he says that the "largest and most magnificent" is the Swan, which can accommodate three thousand people. He informs us that it is built with "a mass of flint stones," which are plentiful in England, and is supported by wooden columns, meaning the pillars on stage.

Romeo (William Faversham) calls up to Juliet (Maude Adams) in Act 2, Scene 2 of *Romeo and Juliet,* in this photograph (published by the Byron Company) of an 1899 production by Charles Frohman at the Empire Theatre.

SEE ALSO:

Fox, Levi. *The Shakespeare Handbook.* Boston, Mass.: G.K. Hall, 1987.

Gurr, Andrew and Mariko Ichikawa. *Staging in Shakespeare's Theaters.* New York: Oxford University Press, 2000.

Gurr, Andrew. *The Shakespearean Stage, 1574-1642.* Cambridge: Cambridge University Press, 2009.

Gurr, Andrew. *Playgoing in Shakespeare's London.* New York: Cambridge University Press, 1987.

Hattaway, Michael. *Elizabethan Popular Theatre: Plays in Performance.* Boston: Routledge & Kegan Paul, 1982.

Taylor, Gary. "Shakespeare Plays on Renaissance Stages," *Cambridge Companion to Shakespeare on Stage,* ed. Stanley Wells and Sarah Stanton. New York: Cambridge University Press, 2002.

Thomson, Peter. *Shakespeare's Theatre.* New York: Routledge, 1992.

(continued from page 51)

Shakespeare has long been identified as the object of Greene's attack. "Shake-scene" is an obvious clue, but so is the misquoted line, "tiger's heart wrapped in a player's hide," which parodies a highly rhetorical attack in one of Shakespeare's first history plays. This play is known as *3 Henry VI* from the First Folio collection (1623), but was possibly first performed as *The True Tragedy of Richard Duke of York*. A play by this name appeared in print in 1595, following the publication of *The First Part of the Contention betwixt the two famous Houses of York and Lancaster* (1594), which equates with Shakespeare's *2 Henry VI*. Generations of scholars once thought these printed plays were originals from which the young Shakespeare, as play-patcher, revised and developed his *Henry VI* plays, but now it is thought that these less-known plays are rough versions, likely based on actors' memories, subsequent to Shakespeare's initial texts.

In the passage Greene echoes, Queen Margaret has imprisoned the Duke of York and torments him with a fake crown and a handkerchief dipped in his dead son's blood. He responds,

> O tiger's heart wrapped in a woman's hide!
> How couldst thou drain the life-blood of
>   the child,
> To bid the father wipe his eyes withal,
> And yet be seen to bear a woman's face?
> Women are soft, mild, pitiful and flexible;
> Thou stern, obdurate, flinty, rough,
>   remorseless.

Greene, then, not only is angry with Shakespeare, but also suggests that as a fellow writer he may have even been cruel. What was Shakespeare's crime? It is true that a number of curious connections exist between plays performed by the Queen's Men and later plays of Shakespeare's, such as *Two Gentlemen of Verona*, *Richard III*, *King John*, *Henry V*, and *King Lear*. Was Greene accusing him of stealing or plagiarizing outright, or perhaps revising Greene's own writing if the *Henry VI* plays, as long thought, were collaborative? These are both possible scenarios, but it is also possible, and parts of Greene's attack suggest it, that he was simply furious at Shakespeare for writing at all. He shows here the kind of resentment born of class sensitivity and educational arrogance. Remember, Greene is addressing three fellow writers, and in particular ones trained at university—most likely Christopher Marlowe, Thomas Nashe, and George Peele. He warns them that he as a writer has suffered professionally at the hands of actors, called "puppets" and "antics" here. This persecution is ironic, and thus more bitter to Greene, for as a writer he has supplied them with the very words they speak. Trust them not, he warns his companions, and watch out especially for the "upstart crow" Shakespeare, a mere actor who is "beautified with our feathers"—that is, wrongly and disingenuously assuming the rhetorical trappings that belong to playwrights and university men: blank-verse poetry like Marlowe's, extended metaphors or conceits, and the rest. This Shakespeare is a jack-of-all-trades, who neither appreciates the training required to write well nor respects his fellow writers; he thinks of himself as the only one who writes for the stage.

Greene was not particularly kind to anyone in this deathbed confession; aside from the attack on Shakespeare, he seems to accuse Marlowe of atheism and Machiavellian behavior, and Nashe for being too stinging and satirical. It caused fallout that Greene's printer, fellow writer, and perhaps ghost writer Henry Chettle soon tried to contain. Nashe issued a public denial of authorship, and later, in 1592, Chettle in *Kind-Hartes Dreame* also denied writing the Greene pamphlet. However, Chettle did issue an apology that he had not "moderated the heat" of Greene's vitriol. Or rather it is a semi-apology: he seems to blow off Marlowe, saying he cares never to meet him. He regrets having offended Shakespeare, however, "because myself have seen his demeanor no less civil than he excellent in the quality he professes: besides divers of worship have reported, his uprightness of dealing, which argues his honesty, and his facetious grace in writing, that approves his art." These words are high praise, of both Shakespeare's disposition and his professionalism—as a writer he is both reliable and trustworthy.

Finally, the Greene-Chettle literary flare-up more importantly establishes that Shakespeare's activity and reputation as a writer for London's stages was significant by 1592. He had to have been known, and to have been a little irritating or intimidating, for an active, older professional writer such as Greene to consider him worth attacking. And Chettle says that "diver of worship" can confirm his "facetious [that is, smooth] grace in writing."

This reputation, the evidence suggests, was based mainly on Shakespeare's ambitious project of producing a trilogy of *Henry VI* plays based on the Wars of the Roses, England's civil wars between the dueling York and Lancaster families from the prior century. The Rose Theatre's manager Philip Henslowe records in his diary a new play called "Harey the vi," performed by Strange's Men, on March 3, 1592. Additional records indicate that this play enjoyed constant crowds and brought Henslowe commercial success. In fact, despite being part one, this play was likely a "prequel" to the already successful *First Part of the Contention* and *True Tragedy of Richard Duke of York* (or the Folio's *2 and 3 Henry VI*).

David Bevington nicely summarizes the theme of *1 Henry VI* as "political division at home leads to military defeat abroad," and these two areas of concern nicely reflected the earlier and present hot topics in English drama. The play dramatically opens with the funeral cortege of the militaristic king Henry V, and almost immediately the new young king Henry VI is opposed and undermined by ambitious churchmen and noblemen. This dramatization of civil strife was similarly accomplished in a very early blank-verse play, *Gorboduc* (1570s). Similarly, today's critics now think that Shakespeare not only benefited from current tastes for historical drama, but also, with these *Henry VI* plays, helped to establish the genre. Marlowe and his *Tamburlaine* in particular must also receive credit for giving form to the nationalist energies and anxieties surrounding the Armada years. In *1 Henry VI*, we witness the first division of the houses of Lancaster (Henry VI's side) and York (represented by the conspiring Richard Plantagenet), symbolized by red and white roses. This domestic opposition undermines England's military efforts in France, concentrated valorously in the figure of Talbot. If Henry VI is a problematic title character, as weak and passive as Marlowe's Tamburlaine is aggressive and awe-inspiring, then the war hero Talbot effectively vies with Marlowe's hero for theatrical power and audience appeal. When compared, Talbot is a more proper hero than Tamburlaine—first of all, he is English, but he is also courageous and disciplined. The audience soon resents the dilettantish, diabolical French who are his enemies, and the weak English leadership who comprise Talbot's natural heartiness. In *Pierce Pennilesse*, Thomas Nashe considers

> How would it have joyed brave *Talbot* (the terror of the French) to think . . . he should triumph again on the Stage, and have his bones new embalmed with the tears of ten thousand spectators at least, (at several times) who, in the Tragedian that represents his person, imagine they beheld him fresh bleeding.

As a possible collaborator on *1 Henry VI*, Nashe may be guilty of self-promotion here (few

Elizabethan writers were above that), but he also memorably expresses the popularity of this particular play and the general power of theater to animate characters, or even to reanimate the country's historical heroes, long dead. Nashe manages to give the impression of both a solemn consecration (with the tears and embalming) and a veritable entertainment industry (ten thousand spectators! several times!). He also evokes the peculiar patriotic intensity and nationalist preoccupation of the time in which the *Henry VI* plays felicitously appeared.

The second play, chronologically if not compositionally, *2 Henry VI*, features Henry VI's French bride, Margaret, and her lover, the Duke of Suffolk, as the main Lancastrian aggressors, and they first take out their malice on Humphrey Duke of Gloucester, who futilely tries to mediate royal authority and the commoners' uprising. He is cut down, and in this way parallels Talbot. Meanwhile, the Yorkist Richard Plantagenet instigates the commoners to sack London, and Shakespeare's memorable handling of the Jack Cade rebellion scenes, with its horrific black comedy, soon led to his being invited to compose similar scenes for other plays. Richard means to seize power during this time of political unrest, but in *3 Henry VI*, he, too, meets his fate, tormented and killed by Queen Margaret and her forces. Henry VI also becomes a casualty, as he meditates on the unique cares of any person with great power: "Was ever King so grieved for subjects' woe? / Much is your sorrow; mine ten times so much." Shakespeare would regularly revisit this theme in later plays. Read with the benefit of hindsight of Shakespeare's long, unmatchable literary career, the *Henry VI* plays naturally seem like the work of a beginner. Some explanations of the political contexts are wordy, and the characters are not fully developed. The pacing can feel monotonous, and the speeches are often stiffly formal—full

Portrait of King Henry VI from the early sixteenth century *(Artist unknown)*

of high terms and thickly applied rhetorical figures that feel too beholden to Marlowe. There are also over-the-top moments more suited to *Titus Andronicus*, such as Margaret's entrance with Suffolk's head. Yet these plays were, to some extent, the Elizabethan equivalent of a patriotic action movie, a summer blockbuster. And they delivered.

Shakespeare also delivered on some startlingly high goals. Taken in the context of a young writing career, these plays are remarkably ambitious, and they immediately established Shakespeare as a major writer for the Elizabethan theater. The nervous Robert Greene knew well what he was talking about. In 1592, Shakespeare was twenty-eight years old, and he had just completed an innovative dramatic project popular with theater audiences. The scope of the plays was daring, requiring huge casts and various settings. It is rather impressive that this young writer pulled it off so smoothly, not to mention completed it in the first place. The number of plays involved was also an accomplishment. Two-part history plays already existed, but no one had yet attempted a trilogy. This achievement grandly harked back centuries—many centuries—to the great tragic trilogies of the Athenian dramatists in the fifth century B.C.

And yet Shakespeare was about to do even better. In the middle of *3 Henry VI*, one of Richard Plantagenet's sons, the Duke of Gloucester, springs to dramatic life with a villainous but wittily boasting monologue. Soon Shakespeare would truly conclude his trilogy by making it a tetralogy, or collection of four plays. His *Richard III*, the greatest of all of his early history plays, would feature the revenge of Plantagenet's sons against the Lancastrians, and their final downfall as well. If this conclusion were not satisfying enough, Shakespeare would also manage, almost as an afterthought, to celebrate in mythic form the creation of the House of Tudor, the royal line of the present monarch, Queen Elizabeth, and represent onstage, in the character of Glouces-ter/Richard III, the conflicts and complexities of human character in ways that had never before been written or seen. By 1592, then, Shakespeare had already accomplished big things, but much greater things lay just ahead.

Sources and Further Reading

Arthos, John. *Shakespeare's Early Writings*. Lanham, Maryland: Rowman and Littlefield, 1972.

Bradbrook, M. C. *Shakespeare: The Poet in His World*. New York: Columbia University Press, 1978.

Edwards, Anne-Marie. *Walking with William Shakespeare*. Madison, Wis: Jones Books 2005.

Halliday, F. E. *Shakespeare*. New York: T. Yoseloff, 1961.

O'Connor, Gary. *William Shakespeare: A Popular Life*. New York: Applause Books, 2000.

Riggs, David. *The World of Christopher Marlowe*. New York: Henry Holt, 2005.

Wiggins, Martin. *Shakespeare and the Drama of his Time*. New York: Oxford University Press, 2000.

SHAKESPEARE'S EARLY SUCCESSES

We are now ready to immerse ourselves in the outpouring of Shakespeare's plays and poems, which were to flow forth for nearly two decades. By the early 1590s, Shakespeare had become an established, rising playwright for London's professional theater industry. Soon, he would also be a formal poet seeking the support of a powerful young nobleman as a patron.

For these next twenty years, Shakespeare's life is best known and appreciated through encounters with these plays and poems. This is not to say that biographical details simply dry up; on the contrary, we are fortunate to have various records of Shakespeare's activity and existence, both in London, where he worked, and back in Stratford, where his family still lived. These records tell us where Shakespeare sometimes resided, who admired him as a person and writer, who (Elizabeth's court, for example) paid him for his services, with whom he became involved in literary debates, what property he purchased as his success increased, and even the fellows with whom he spent festive times. (These final kinds of records admittedly are more on the anecdotal and legendary side.) That said, Shakespeare remains known and interesting to us today, not to mention the most famous writer who has ever lived, precisely because of the work he accomplished during these two decades. In other words, we best appreciate Shakespeare the man by discovering and reading and viewing with greater depth and satisfaction those most important records of all—the literary achievements of Shakespeare the writer.

RICHARD III AND SHAKESPEARE'S INNOVATION OF CHARACTER

Most critics feel that Shakespeare's first great dramatic masterpiece is *Richard III*. Its charismatic yet villainous title character is his first enduring stage creation. The play remains popular today: it is regularly staged at theaters across the world (including a critically acclaimed Iraqi version early in the new century), and recent film versions have featured esteemed actors such as Ian McKellen and Al Pacino. As previously discussed, Shakespeare chose to expand his trilogy of *Henry VI* plays, about that king's embattled reign and his eventual fall, by creating a tetralogy—that is, a grouping of four plays. Through this expansion, Shakespeare set himself up for a number of successes. First, he created an occasion to present onstage the brief rise of the Yorkist party to the English throne, at the expense of the vanquished Lancastrians. The civil strife historically grew more severe during this point of the conflict, and so treating this subject matter would make for a grand climax to the whole story.

Second, in a nice moment of opportunism for any English citizen, he also celebrated the origins of the current monarch Elizabeth I's royal Tudor line. At the end of the play, when the valiant, if a little dull, Richmond defeats Richard III at the Battle of Bosworth Field (the historical battle occurred in 1485), he becomes Henry VII, effectively ending the Wars of the Roses, which fueled the earlier plays' bloodshed. He also, by reconciling the warring sides, establishes the Tudor dynasty that was more than a century old when

Richard III during the Battle of Bosworth Field in Act 5, Scene 5 of *Richard III*. This illustration is from 1864. *(James William Edmund Doyle)*

artistry and compose a more powerful play. This may be so, for in fact *Richard III* does tower in some way above the three *Henry VI* plays that preceded it. However, it is also probable, as Holland says, that Shakespeare at least began this play immediately after the trilogy. In this way, he would have been a dutiful follower of the history chronicles that were his main sources, primarily Edward Hall's pro-Tudor *The union of two noble and illustrious families of Lancaster and York* (1548).

The main support for this view of early composition is found in the middle of *3 Henry VI*, where Richard Duke of Gloucester steps forth and delivers a breakout soliloquy. Shakespeare, it is easy to surmise, already had big plans for this character. First, he emphasizes his ill-formed features, and begins to reveal his troubled psychological depths, which have interested so many for so long, including modern Freudian critics:

> Why, love so foreswore me in my mother's
>   womb;
> And for I should not deal in her soft laws,
> She did corrupt frail nature with some
>   bribe,
> To shrink mine arm up like a withered
>   shrub,
> To make an envious mountain of my back,
> Where sits deformity to mock my body;
> To shape my legs of an unequal size,
> To disproportion me in every part,
> Like to a chaos, or an unlicked bear-whelp,
> That carries no impression like the dam.
>   ["dam" = dame, or mom] (3.2.153–62)

We as modern readers must accept that Richard's description of his physical deformities

Shakespeare began writing. Henry VII was Elizabeth I's grandfather. Once again, Shakespeare was sensitive to the patriotic atmosphere of early 1590s England, and more darkly, these plays all played on citizens' general concern for a smooth succession once their aging, long-serving queen expired.

Third, and most important in literary terms, Shakespeare now had the chance to place one of his most interesting characters from the first three *Henry VI* plays onto center stage. Seizing the opportunity, he wrote this character for all he was worth. The hunchbacked, ruthless, and somehow still mesmerizing Richard Duke of Gloucester would spend half of this fourth and final play seizing the crown for himself, thus becoming Richard III, and the other half brutally defending his prize. The scholar Peter Holland suspects that *Richard III* was a later play than has sometimes been thought. Circumstances involving the plague may have delayed the first performance, and thus given Shakespeare time to develop his

would have registered for early audiences as an exterior reflection of his own internal deformities—in other words, his hunchbacked condition is a symptom for his twisted mind and values. He himself acknowledges this later in the play— "Then since the heavens have shaped my body so, / Let hell make crook'd my mind to answer it." He next reveals to his shocked audience, again in that style of delivery known as an aside or soliloquy, exactly what he is capable of doing:

> Why, I can smile, and murder whiles I
>   smile,
> And cry "Content" to that which grieves my
>   heart,
> And wet my cheeks with artificial tears,
> And frame my face to all occasions.
>   (182–85)

The overall effect is somehow both comic and charming, for all of the horrors of which he boasts. Shakespeare must have known, after writing these scenes, that he had indeed struck theatrical gold with this character, and sure enough, Richard soon graduateed to his own play. At the end of *3 Henry VI*, Richard stabs King Henry, serving as both family avenger as well as full-blown predator, set to wreak havoc in days to come: "I have no brother, I am like no brother; / And this word 'love,' which greybeards call divine, / Be resident in men like one another, / And not in me: I am myself alone." One scholar contrasts Henry VI, who even in defeat expresses a "fraternity of shared pain," with Richard's newfound "narrow and perverse individualism" that makes him so dangerous.

For all of Richard's dazzling dissimulations and diabolical blood-shedding in *Richard III*, the core drama of character involves the human cost of Richard's ascent to and defense of the English crown. He must betray and kill both friends and family, and truly he lives out that boast from the prior play: "I am myself alone." This play opens, however, on a note of bravado, with Richard uttering some of the most famous of Shakespeare's words: "Now is the winter of our discontent / Made glorious summer by this son of York." For the York dynasty, this is a time of festivity, as Richard's brother now reigns as Edward IV. However, Richard already feels alienated, and he confides in his audience both his attitude and his outrageous plans:

> And therefore, since I cannot prove a lover
> To entertain these fair well-spoken days,
> I am determined to prove a villain
> And hate the idle pleasures of these days.
> Plots have I laid, inductions dangerous,
> By drunken prophecies, libels, and dreams,
> To set my brother Clarence and the King
> In deadly hate the one against the other.
>   (1.1.28–35)

Here Shakespeare combines the comic elements of the medieval Vice character with a more timely Renaissance villain, the Machiavel (named after Florentine political theorist Machiavelli), full of "plots" and strategies for political advantage. Richard does just as he promises, killing Clarence and making King Edward think he is responsible. Shaken, the king grows ill, and with further theatrical ploys, Richard soon assumes the throne. He takes as his bride Lady Anne, a widow of Henry VI's dead son who, most improbably, is "wooed" by Richard, her husband's killer, in an early scene. Richard's stage presence and powers of persuasion seem almost magical. Once king, Richard grows paranoid and soon betrays followers such as Hastings and, most dastardly of all, orders the killing of the princes—King Edward's sons and his own nephews—in the Tower.

Not even Richard, however, can forever outrun the consequences of his crimes. On the eve of the Battle of Bosworth, the ghosts of his many

Is there a murderer here? No. Yes, I am.
Then fly! What, from myself? . . .

. . .

. . . Alas, I rather hate myself
For hateful deeds committed by myself.
I am a villain.   (5.3.194–204)

These notes of self-inquisition and confession and doomed resignation are revolutionary—Richard is far more complex than the exaggerated villain we have come to expect. As Holland nicely puts it, Shakespeare immortalizes this passage with the "discovery of a dramatic language never heard before in English drama in its depiction of the inner workings of the disordered mind." We are now prepared for Richard's fall, most memorably signaled with his battlefield cry—"A horse, a horse, my kingdom for a horse!" —and the triumph of Richmond, who promises great things as the soon-to-be first Tudor king.

SHAKESPEARE'S FIRST COMEDIES

Shakespeare also devoted himself to comedies, or sometimes to comic elements in other types of plays. For example, *Hamlet* has some hilarious scenes, and Shakespeare's greatest comic creation is Sir John Falstaff, who first appeared in the *Henry IV* history plays. Shakespeare was a comic writer for the entirety of his long career. As a genre, comedies in Renaissance England clearly had commercial appeal (one may even have been especially requested by Elizabeth I), and their writers could draw upon a variety of sources—English folk tales, the adventurous tales of prose romances, classical comedy based on Roman models, the physical humor and character types of Italy's *commedia dell'arte* tradition, and a more sophisticated kind of Italian comedy, full of dupes and mistaken identities, and refined by accomplished authors such as Ariosto and others.

Posthumous portrait of Niccolò Machiavelli from the late sixteenth century. *(Santi di Tito)*

victims (truly, they make up an entire football team) haunt him. Much like the women in the play, who serve as a mournful chorus, these ghosts repeatedly curse their killer: "Despair and die." They affect Richard, and create in him a restless midnight crisis of conscience, by which the young writer Shakespeare achieves a new kind of immediacy and realism in his characterization, as if the audience were not hearing a grand stage orator but rather overhearing a troubled human being, even one buried under Richard's monstrous actions. After these ghostly visitations, he awakes in his tent with a start:

What do I fear? Myself? There's none else
   by.
Richard loves Richard, that is, I am I.

Shakespeare resorted to each of these traditions as he saw fit, and typically he domesticated and harmonized these different comic strains with a unique versatility and efficiency.

The word "comedy" comes from the Greek word *comus*, and it literally meant "revelry" or "merrymaking." Often it was associated with rustics' jigs or village songs. Loosely defined, it signifies first of all a poem or play written in a lower, more accessible style (or sometimes with high and low diction mixed) and featuring a broad array of characters. In this way it differs from tragedy, which usually featured elevated poetry and noble people—kings and heroes and so forth. Most simply, also unlike tragedy, comedies were expected to end happily. In Renaissance comedy, this almost always resulted in the marriage of main characters earlier at odds, or whose love was confuted by opponents or challenging circumstances. In Renaissance drama, the comic plot is romantic, and the main characters begin amid love's confusions and frustrations and end in a resolved, matrimonial state. That said, and as we shall soon see, Shakespeare sometimes boldly pushed back against the expectation of felicitous composure.

A trio of Shakespeare's plays is generally classified as the "early comedies"—*The Two Gentlemen of Verona*, *The Taming of the Shrew*, and *The Comedy of Errors*. We do not know exactly which play was written first, second, and third, and at which time precisely they were composed. Ultimately, this is less important than recognizing in each play the features of a young writer already working at a high level but still very much learning his craft. Critics find in these three plays telling signs of Shakespeare's first efforts in writing comic drama, including less polished poetry, often less economical plotting, comparatively shallower characterization, and the presence in two of the three plays of a specific kind of rough-and-tumble comedy known as farce. Let there

be no mistake: the above signs should not imply negative appraisals of these early plays. To call these plays "early" is a value-neutral statement of chronology, and to call them "weak" when compared with the masterpieces that Shakespeare soon produced—well, that does not seem entirely fair. On the other hand, if we compare these early plays with the works by Shakespeare's contemporaries simultaneously onstage in the early 1590s, then Shakespeare's youthful artistry appears very impressive indeed.

Compared with others, his plotting has always been considered deft. It was so even at this early stage, especially in *The Comedy of Errors*, with its double mistaken identities and restored family. Poetically, Shakespeare was already capable of great lyrical feats when composing verses in English, assisted especially with the ornamenting skills of rhetoric that he had studied as a boy. In *The Two Gentlemen of Verona*, the young lover Proteus reflects upon his letter from Julia and his pending departure for Milan—and separation from his beloved: "O, how this spring of love resembleth / The uncertain glory of an April day, / Which now shows all the beauty of the sun, / And by and by a cloud takes all away." And already, as well, this young writer could arrive upon a truly moving, deeply human scene. Even in *The Taming of the Shrew*, one of his most uproarious plays, Shakespeare reveals a playwright's delicate touch when the newly married couple, Petruchio and Katherine, cast aside their brassy, bossy personalities, and have an exchange about a public display of affection. "Kiss me, Kate," Petruchio says, and at first Kate is surprisingly bashful: "What, in the midst of the street?" Petruchio insists, and eventually they do kiss. The language here has become most tender: "Is not this well? Come, my sweet Kate. / Better once than never, and never too late." There is, even in this early, swashbuckling play, a recognizably humane note that would only grow and sound more profoundly in Shakespeare's later work.

THE TWO GENTLEMEN OF VERONA

Shakespeare's *Two Gentlemen of Verona* derives from prose romances and is his only early romantic comedy, strictly meant. He may have encountered this tale of false friends and love triangles, of hidden identities and cross-dressing, in the Italian writer Boccaccio's medieval story collection, the *Decameron*, or more immediately in the chivalric romance *Diana enamorada*, by the Portuguese author Jorge de Montemayor.

The play opens on a note of youthful restlessness, as Proteus says farewell to his friend Valentine, departing for the court of Milan. (Those who argue that Shakespeare spent his "Lost Years" in Italy must explain why characters sail by ship from Verona to Milan, a land-locked itinerary across central northern Italy.) Proteus is content to stay, for he loves Julia, but his father is persuaded that he, too, would benefit from life at court, where he would "hear sweet discourse, converse with noblemen, / And be in eye of every exercise / Worthy his youth and nobleness of birth." Resigned to his journey, Proteus vows faithfulness to Julia, and the lovers exchange rings. However, upon arriving in Milan, reuniting with Valentine, and learning of his friend's secret love for Sylvia, the duke's daughter, Proteus swiftly admits that he, too, has become enamored with Sylvia, and he devises Valentine's banishment. Valentine's lamenting reaction shows Shakespeare already capable of strong poetry, even if it displays the influence of "aureate" poets such as John Lyly, known for his elaborate repetitions and verbal patterns:

> What light is light if Sylvia be not seen?
> What joy is joy if Sylvia be not by—
> Unless it be to think that she is by

> And feed upon the shadow of perfection?
> (3.1.177–81)

Meanwhile, Julia, perhaps intuiting troubles ahead, disguises herself as "Sebastian" and travels as well to Milan's court, even as the love-struck Proteus tells Sylvia that his former love is dead. Adding insult to injury, Proteus soon hires Julia/Sebastian as a servant, and instructs him to give a ring—the ring Julia gave him—to his new love. Sylvia flees her father's court, but is soon abducted by outlaws, whom Valentine has lately joined. (In comedy, the number of coincidences often strains probability.) Before Valentine presents himself, Proteus appears, and after repeated rejections by Sylvia, he threatens to love her "like a soldier"—that is, to rape her. Valentine steps forward and intervenes, and instantly Proteus begs forgiveness. Even more shockingly, instantly Valentine grants it. Sebastian/Julia faints and shortly reveals her identity. Proteus now recovers his original love for her. The duke appears and finds Valentine now worthy of his daughter's hand. At Valentine's request, the outlaws also receive pardon. Sylvia, meanwhile, says nothing at all.

Thus *The Two Gentlemen of Verona* ends, but does it end well? Many readers have found the play far from perfect. Shakespeare, it seems, had not yet figured out how to stage a conversation involving multiple characters. The characters seem fairly flat, one-dimensional. The conclusion, especially, is troubling. Proteus attempts to rape Sylvia—"I'll force thee yield to my desire"—and Sylvia's cry of "Heavens!" is the last we hear from her. Her silence is inexplicable, as is Valentine's nonchalant reaction. He deems his friend "honest" again all too quickly. That said, the play does have some memorable strengths. Shakespeare's comic tendencies are already evident here—the heroine whose circumstances push her into a gender-bending disguise, and the general shift in setting from a highly civilized one (the court) to a forest or idealized "green world" or retreat or recovery and then, eventually, back again. The critic Northrop Frye sees, in even this early play, signs of Shakespeare's recognition, beyond the obviously comic plot and formulas of his sources, of comedy's "more profound pattern" of loss and death followed by renewal, reconciliation, and restoration. It can be argued that the other early comedies also reflect this general dramatic pattern.

Finally, the two gentlemen's servants, Speed and Lance, represent the most patently comic aspect here. Just like the cross-dressing and forest settings, servants or clowns also recur in many later plays. The most memorable clown scene here features Lance and his dog: "I think Crab my dog be the sourest-natured that lives . . . He is a stone, a very pibble stone, and has no more pity in him than a dog." Later, even more hilariously, Lance reports to the audience that Crab has made a mess

of a banquet at court, snatching Sylvia's meal and urinating. As a comic writer, Shakespeare seemed to know well what Geoffrey Rush's character Henslowe shrewdly says about audience tastes in the Oscar-winning film *Shakespeare in Love*: "Love and a bit with a dog—that's about all they want." Not only was he sensitive to what London audiences found entertaining, but Shakespeare's comic language, a robust English spoken by these clowns, already sounds pitch-perfect.

THE TAMING OF THE SHREW

The next comedy, *The Taming of the Shrew*, opens on a similarly colloquial note, with the language of the tavern and of Shakespeare's native Warwickshire. (Several locations near Stratford are mentioned in these opening speeches.) The play's first two scenes are "induction" scenes. They frame the main characters and actions by presenting them explicitly as a dramatic performance for the benefit of these first characters onstage. We initially meet one Christopher Sly, a drunken tinker just thrown out of an alehouse. A rich lord encounters the passed-out Sly and decides to play a practical joke. The lord commands his servants to place the sleeping man in a luxurious gown and bedroom and to feed him delicacies. Encountering a group of traveling actors, the aristocrat retains them to perform a play for Sly. The tinker will become convinced that he has awakened from a bad dream and is in fact a "mighty lord." A young servant, Bartholomew, appears in drag as Sly's wife, which leads to further gags. (Shakespeare at this point is showing his audience how all women characters appeared on the Renaissance stage, as young male actors dressed in women's clothes.)

This nineteenth-century illustration of Act 3, Scene 1 of *The Two Gentlemen of Verona* shows Speed reading Lance's letter. *(Engraving by J. Gilbert)*

THE PLAYS: AIDS FOR READING

The past few chapters have introduced numerous plays—perhaps an overwhelming number, and in different genres, no less—by William Shakespeare. Audiences in London's Renaissance theater scene had a massive appetite for these plays, and they created a formidable market for aspiring, industrious playwrights. Competing theater companies regularly introduced new works into their frequently rotating repertory schedules. (They sometimes performed five or six times per week, alternating among twenty or so plays at any one time.) For more than twenty years, through the end of the sixteenth and beginning of the seventeenth centuries, William Shakespeare delivered such plays to theater owners and playing companies—often at the rate of two plays per year, and sometimes even more than that. The First Folio of Shakespeare, first published in 1623, collected no fewer than thirty-six plays, and he was responsible, or partially responsible, for at least two additional plays, and perhaps a few more. Shakespeare was a busy writer!

This book mainly treats Shakespeare's plays in chronological order, in the context of the writer's life. The ultimate goal of this study of Shakespeare's life is to send readers, newly interested in this writer, more forcefully to those things that make him famous—his plays and poems. Although they are wonderful plays, they are not always so easy for modern readers to appreciate, and so naturally some people may wish to consult other resources. The list below is a brief survey of aids that will assist new readers of Shakespeare, or seasoned readers who may not be familiar with a particular play. All of these books share a general format, presenting brief, accessible chapters dedicated to the individual plays.

Absolute beginners will find some accessible volumes among those gathered here, including Andrew Dickson's *Rough Guide to Shakespeare*, Norrie Epstein's *The Friendly Shakespeare*, and Robert Thomas Fallon's *A Theatergoers' Guide to Shakespeare*. The chapters dedicated to individual plays are more or less plot summaries; they identify characters and explain clearly how the plays' plots develop, reach their climaxes, and resolve.

Victor L. Cahn's *Shakespeare the Playwright* focuses especially on major characters in Shakespeare's plays; he intends to point out to readers a "through line" by which these characters reveal and express themselves. Harold Bloom's popular and monumental study, *Shakespeare: The Invention of the Human*, is equally dedicated to Shakespeare's unique representation of character, and how deeply influential that achievement has been in cultural and psychological life in general. With his special praise for Hamlet and Falstaff, Bloom carries on a high critical tradition that proudly looks back to Samuel Johnson in the eighteenth century. He also sends readers regularly to Harold C. Goddard's *The Meaning of Shakespeare*, whose cogent chapters in portable editions are a help to many a reader.

In 1946, the poet W. H. Auden gave lectures on each of Shakespeare's plays at the New School in New York City, and they have been gathered in *Lectures on Shakespeare*. These studies do not attempt to be comprehensive, but they reveal how one great poet reads another poet. Unsurprisingly, Auden's treatment of Shakespeare's sonnets is among his most influential writings on the Bard. It is nonsensical, he says, "to waste time trying to identify characters" in the Sonnets. He sees in them instead a record of a supreme artist "interested in seeing just how much he can stand."

Marjorie Garber's *Shakespeare After All*, based on her popular lectures at Harvard University, is a highly readable survey of the plays, sensitive to various critical trends as they applied to Shakespeare's works in recent years. The latest title of this sort is Tony Tanner's *Prefaces to Shakespeare*, and its elegant, learned

(continues)

(continued)

introductions to the plays have received special praise from esteemed critics such as Frank Kermode and Kenneth Gross. Tanner's title looks back to the still dazzling introductions to the plays in the early twentieth century by Harley Granville-Barker. As an actor, Granville-Barker was largely responsible for helping readers, overly interested in the back stories of Shakespeare's characters, remember that these were first and foremost plays—performances to be brought to vital life onstage. John Wilders has also alluded to Granville-Barker's efforts in his *New Prefaces to Shakespeare*, which were commissioned for television productions sponsored by the BBC and PBS networks in Britain and the United States, respectively.

SEE ALSO:

Auden, W. H. *Lectures on Shakespeare*. Princeton, N.J.: Princeton University Press, 2000.

Bloom, Harold. *Shakespeare: The Invention of the Human*. New York: Riverhead Books, 1998.

Cahn, Victor L. *Shakespeare the Playwright*. New York: Greenwood Press, 1991.

Dickson, Andrew. *The Rough Guide to Shakespeare*. New York: Rough Guides, 2005.

Epstein, Norrie. *The Friendly Shakespeare*. New York: Viking, 1993.

Fallon, Robert Thomas. *A Theatergoers' Guide to Shakespeare*. Chicago: I.R. Dee, 2001.

Garber, Marjorie. *Shakespeare After All*. New York: Pantheon Books, 2004.

Goddard, Harold C. *The Meaning of Shakespeare*. Chicago: University of Chicago Press, 1960

Granville-Barker, Harley. *Prefaces to Shakespeare*. Princeton: Princeton University Press, 1947.

Tanner, Tony. *Prefaces to Shakespeare*. Cambridge, Mass.: Belknap Press of Harvard University Press, 2010.

Wilders, John. *New Prefaces to Shakespeare*. New York: Blackwell, 1988

The main theme of the play is already present here—"transmutation," to use Sly's own word—that is, how powerfully our changed circumstances, along with the fictive powers of drama and rhetoric, can fundamentally alter our sense of ourselves, as well as our social identities. Sometimes we are enslaved to these identities, but sometimes love and comedy can liberate us, can make us feel like new people, people with capacities for peacemaking and maturation. Love and comedy can also prepare us, sometimes by emboldening us, for relationships with new people. As with Christopher Sly's situation, issues of what is and what appears to be—of play-acting and duplicity and disguise and true reality—are central to both of the plot threads that Shakespeare now introduces.

The gentleman Lucentio arrives in the university town of Padua, with his servant Tranio attending him. Immediately he encounters a father, Baptista, who announces that his pretty, younger daughter Bianca cannot marry until her older, ill-tempered sister Katherine does. Lucentio steers clear of Kate, "renowned in Padua for her scolding tongue," but falls in love instantly with Bianca. Soon he switches identities with his servant, to win access to the younger sister in the guise of a tutor. Lucentio will compete for Bianca's affections with rivals, the fop Hortensio and the "pantaloon" character of Gremio, an old, foolish suitor from the *commedia dell'arte* tradition. Overall, this storyline borrows many features of classical comedy and its more recent Italian equivalent, including the disguised lover and the competition among lovers. One of Shakespeare's sources was the earlier play *The Supposes*, by the English writer George Gascoigne, who was himself translating a High Renaissance Italian play written by Ariosto. Hortensio's invitation to his friend Petruchio leads to the primary storyline of

The Taming of the Shrew—the actual rough wooing, or taming, of the shrewish daughter Kate.

We cannot approve of Petruchio's "taming" methods, yet the dramatic energy between him and Kate is undeniable. Their story is properly the most popular one here. Petruchio's character is rough and aggressive. Indeed, in an age of very different sensibilities regarding courtship, marriage, and equality between the sexes, some modern critics and directors have judged Petruchio to be an abusive, mercenary monster. Thus Petruchio has been staged as a churlish man-boy exhibiting arrested emotional development, and more darkly as a conquering force, more or less brainwashing Kate as if she were an enemy combatant. Initially,

it is clear that Petruchio is no sighing romantic: "I come to wive it wealthily in Padua; / If wealthily, then happily in Padua," he declares. This attitude may seem abhorrent today, but it should be remembered that in Shakespeare's day, marriages between two prosperous families were often very consciously financial affairs. In other words, Petruchio's monetary concerns seem baser today than they would have seemed to the well-to-do during the English Renaissance. Kate, too, soon reappears in all of her harsh glory, abusing her sister, Bianca, and, offstage, striking a tutor (the disguised Hortensio) upside the head with a lute.

Petruchio, however, seems intrigued by Kate's ferocity: "Now, by the world, it is a lusty wench; /

Petruchio sends the tailor and haberdasher away in Act 4, Scene 3 of *The Taming of the Shrew*. This engraving is from an 1846 edition of the *Illustrated London News*. *(Illustration by Charles Robert Leslie; engraving by William Luson Thomas)*

I love her ten times more than ever I did." For all of his bombast, Petruchio may glimpse and realize what the suitors of the *seemingly* prim and proper Bianca do not—that Kate has personality and intelligence, and is lashing out at her limited freedom and her sister's goody-two-shoes reputation. He may appreciate better than most that a passionate relationship or marriage should retain a certain wild quality to it. They will be, in Petruchio's own prophetic words, like "two raging fires" that meet together. At this point, the wooing and comic fun really begin.

Petruchio's and Kate's relationship does not begin on a particularly promising note. He seems to mock Kate's bad reputation by speaking of her in excessively sweet terms—she is "my super-dainty Kate" and "sweet as springtime flowers." In swift, back-and-forth conversation, the two characters commence with one of the hallmarks of Shakespearean comedy: witty, punning, flirtatious wordplay. Already Petruchio seems to intimate that he knows Kate's secret self, and knows that they two together can oppose everyone else: "Why doth the world report that Kate doth limp?" Petruchio asks. "O slanderous world!" Petruchio does not so much convince Katherine to marry him as he does wear her down. Besides, he must convince only the father, Baptista, and he soon does so. With their wedding scheduled, the father next considers appeals for Bianca's hand.

Meanwhile, Lucentio (disguised as the tutor "Cambio") reveals himself to Bianca as he teaches her Latin from the poetry of Ovid, author of the *Amores* and *Ars amatoria*. Lucentio soon wins his pupil's heart. The middle of the play presents Kate's wedding day, when Petruchio apparently stands her up. Kate's reaction here is emotionally revealing: she does not stomp about in fury, as we might expect, but seems truly saddened and touchingly embarrassed: "Now must the world point at poor Katherine / And say 'Lo, there is mad Petruchio's wife, / If it would please him come and marry her.'" In Kate's case, she must be careful what she wishes for: Petruchio eventually arrives, but dressed in a motley, rag-tag groom's outfit, and riding an old nag of a horse. Kate is scandalized and her father objects, but Petruchio replies bluntly that she is marrying him, and not his clothes. At the reception, a wide-eyed Gremio reports how Petruchio acted up during the wedding ceremony, even bopping the priest. The couple arrives, and Petruchio scandalizes everyone again by announcing they will not be staying. Kate has finally had enough and objects, but she is answered stoutly by Petruchio:

> I will be master of what is mine own.
> She is my goods, my chattels; she is my
>   house,
> My household stuff, my field, my barn,
> My horse, my ox, my ass, my anything.
> And here she stands, touch her whoever
>   dare. (3.2.235–39)

At this point, modern audiences and readers are often scandalized as well: Kate is Petruchio's "chattels" or property, he claims? How dare he! And yet, however dramatically (or even traumatically), there also seems to be a method to Petruchio's madness. He wishes for Kate to value him, him essentially, and not for the many things (clothes, horse, etc.) that accompany and outfit his person. His sudden departing, also, in the face of Kate's father's protests, seems to be a lesson as well: now married, the couple does not have to bow to Kate's prior narrow circumstances as Baptista's daughter and Bianca's less likeable sister. Note that the different tone in the last line quoted above—"touch her whoever dare"—is not so much imperious and possessive as it is protective. The newlyweds then depart for Verona.

We next hear from a servant in Petruchio's house about the couple's rough journey, how Kate fell in the mud and how Petruchio seems more shrewish than she. Indeed, upon their arrival Petruchio is in full, violent form, striking his servants, throwing food, and generally unsettling his new bride. Uncharacteristically, Kate now sounds like the calming presence: avoid "disquiet," she urges her husband, and be "so contented." Soon Petruchio, via soliloquy, reassures the audience that his outbursts are planned. "Thus have I politicly begun my reign," he begins, and eventually promises, "Ay, and amid this hurly I intend / That all is done in reverend care of her." Still, to modern audiences his "politic" or strategic practices are hard to accept. Kate's meals are withheld, she is deprived of sleep, and Petruchio rejects and returns a cap and gown that Kate had hoped to wear to her sister's wedding to Lucentio.

In Act 4, Scene 5, the two storylines merge. Petruchio and Kate experience together one of the play's great moments of spirited debate, of independence of outlook, of quiet concord. Returning to Padua, they encounter Lucentio's true father, bound for the same city. First, Petruchio urges Kate to call the sun, as he does, the moon. She at first refuses. Petruchio threatens to return home, and expresses what sounds like the first moment of true exasperation during this entire "taming" process: "Evermore crossed and crossed, nothing but crossed!" Kate finally relents, but to my ear, she never loses her own spirited sense of self:

> Then God be blessed, it is the blessed sun.
> But sun it is not, when you say it is not,
> And the moon changes even as your mind.
> What you will have it named, even that it is,
> And so it shall be so for Katherine.
> (4.5.21–25)

These are not the words of a crushed, brainwashed spouse, but rather the recognition of someone who is beginning to understand Petruchio's gamesmanship, his willful defiance of the world's realities. This defiance, if shared by his wife, promises to join them together. And just so, Kate not only accepts Petruchio's outlook, but also runs with his gag, addressing Lucentio's father as "Young budding virgin, fair and fresh." This moment usually draws great laughter from audiences.

In Padua, Lucentio and Bianca secretly marry, and significantly, social disorder ensues. Lucentio's father suspects Tranio of "villainy" against his son, and Bianca's duped father, Baptista, promises to make sense of this "knavery." In the final wedding-feast scene, Petruchio, Lucentio, and Hortensio (who has married a rich widow) make a wager on whose wife will prove most obedient. Bianca claims to be too busy, and there are hints that her sweetness and deference may have been a ruse. As for the widow, she says simply that "She will not come." Kate, on the other hand, obeys and proceeds to give one of the play's most extended, polished speeches. She discourses on women's proper duty to their husbands:

> Thy husband is thy lord, thy life, thy keeper,
> Thy head, thy sovereign, one that cares for
>   thee,
> And for thy maintenance; commits his body
> To painful labor, both by sea and land.
>   (5.2.162–65)

Readers who defend the play's ending are quick to point out that Kate's speech seems to include mutual service of husband and wife. After outlining the husband's efforts, Kate says that love and obedience are "Too little payment for so great a debt." The play ends with Petruchio and Kate having triumphantly won the wager, and retired to bed. Moreover, for Shakespeare and his age, Kate's articulation of a hierarchy in a marriage, however loving and mutually serving, would have seemed natural, and as desirable in a marriage as in a commonwealth, where citizens obey their king. Nevertheless, Kate's speech has struck some readers and viewers as humiliating and degrading, and it is unsurprisingly one of the more controversial endings in all of Shakespeare's plays. The late critic Tony Tanner sums it up well: "If you don't like the play, you don't—and you will not be in bad company." Yet Tanner himself appraises this memorable couple more sympathetically, especially compared with Kate's duplicitous sister and her new husband: "And when, at the end, Petruchio says, 'Come, Kate, we'll to bed,' one cannot but feel that, not to put too fine a point upon it, they will have a better time there than Lucentio and Bianca."

The Taming of the Shrew did not appear in print till the publication of the First Folio in 1623; however, a curious text called The Taming of a Shrew (note the different article) was published in 1594, listed as acted "sundry times" by Pembroke's Men. Scholars for a long time thought that this lesser known, much less artful play was an early version, possibly by Shakespeare himself, or a source revised into the play we now know. However, in recent years the tide of opinion has turned. It is now believed that this other Shrew play, published in 1594, was in fact a rough version of Shakespeare's original script, possibly reconstructed from memory by actors. Thus a record of a performance in 1594 in Newington Butts, farther south from the theaters in Bankside, may refer to one or both of these texts.

One major difference between these versions involves the framing scenes with Sly and the rich lord. In The Taming of a Shrew, the Sly equivalent reappears at the end, announcing that he now knows how to tame his wife. It is all very tidy. Shakespeare's play, on the other hand, never returns to the framing episode. This may be due to textual instability; that is, Shakespeare may have originally had a concluding framing scene,

but it was forgotten or cast aside by the time the play was printed. Alternately, this absence could be intentional and causes an artful evaporation, so to speak, of the Kate and Petruchio story as an explicit performance for Sly's entertainment. Arguably, the couple by the conclusion has become more real, and seemingly with greater freedoms, compared with their first entrances. To return to the framing story, and thus diminish the de facto main characters, would be dramatically counterproductive. If this is so, it exemplifies Shakespeare's rather bold reenvisioning of a very familiar tradition. Petruchio's and Kate's scenario itself had many precedents in popular "taming" literature, some of them stunningly violent and misogynistic. As Tanner points out, "Shakespeare wants to find a better way."

THE COMEDY OF ERRORS

Readers often consider the last of Shakespeare's three early comedies, The Comedy of Errors, to be his earliest attempt at comic writing for the stage because this play, among them all, is most obviously derived from its classical sources. Shakespeare very likely encountered those sources while a student in Stratford. It is written largely in rhyming couplets, and its 1,786 lines make it the shortest of Shakespeare's plays. These aspects make The Comedy of Errors unusual. It may be a young writer's modest first effort and careful following of past masters. On the other hand, dissenting readers find in this swiftly paced comedy a new confidence in plotting, compared with the two previous comedies discussed.

This play is set in Ephesus and opens on a surprisingly dark note for a comedy. Solinus, the duke of Ephesus, enforces a harsh law prohibiting merchants from Syracuse in Ephesus. If they are captured, as Egeon has been, they must pay a fine or face death. Egeon explains why he has risked his life. Long ago, a storm ripped apart the family's ship, separating for these past eighteen years husband and wife, as well as their twin boys and their servant's twins. For five years, Egeon has sought the lost boys, "Roaming clean through the bounds of Asia" to arrive in Ephesus. The duke, pitying these "griefs unspeakable," gives him a day to secure money for the fine, and therefore save his life.

As it turns out, Egeon's lost son, known as Antipholus of Ephesus, resides in the city, along with his servant, Dromio of Ephesus. Meanwhile, Egeon's other son, known as Antipholus of Syra-

Dromio of Ephesus and Dromio of Syracuse. This illustration of *The Comedy of Errors* is taken from *Tales from Shakespeare*, published by the McLoughlin Brothers in 1890.

cuse, has just arrived with his servant, Dromio of Syracuse. The scene is now set for comic confusions and misidentifications, involving misgiven orders and money bags. Soon the beaten Dromio reports to Adriana, the Ephesian Antipholus's wife, that Antipholus is "horn mad"—he has refused to come, and even denied being married. Talking to her sister Luciana, Adriana suspects her husband of an affair. The women confront the (wrong) master and servant, and demand they return home. The two visitors marvel: Antipholus does not know if he wakes or dreams, and Dromio declares that Ephesus is "fairy land" (in fact, Shakespeare wishes to invoke here the city's reputation for the supernatural). Back home, the local Antipholus furiously beats upon his own front door. In his anger, he decides to bestow a new chain to a courtesan, rather than Adriana.

Confusion now increases. The Syracusan Dromio is suddenly betrothed to Nell, the kitchen wench. He shares many off-color jokes about this "globe" of a woman. A mix-up with the chain lands Ephesian Antipholus in jail, and his bail is mixed up, too. (Are you following this?) The three women now appear with Dr. Pinch, a memorable schoolmaster and "quack" exorcist. He has Ephesian Antipholus and Dromio bound and taken away, and the Syracusan pair escape into a priory. The opening story now resurfaces, as the duke leads Egeon onstage to be executed. Ephesian Antipholus and Dromio, escaping crazy Dr. Pinch, bring these confusions to crisis and climax. Egeon greets the pair, but his Ephesian son does not recognize him. This moment is a surprisingly painful one for comedy. The others are led forward by the prioress, who turns out to be Egeon's long-lost wife, Aemilia. Confusions are cleared up, and joyous reunions ensue. The play ends with a feast, where everyone will discourse on "all our fortunes." The twins exit the stage hand in hand.

Shakespeare based this story of mistaken identity on a Roman comedy by Plautus, or in fact, two—principally the *Menaechmi*, but also *Amphitruo*. The young English writer was thus working with an explicitly classical style of comedy. The various character confusions are entertaining, and there is a real satisfaction when everything becomes clear. However, the ending can also be surprisingly moving, in part because of Egeon's framing story. The shipwreck and the lost family are motifs belonging to a different kind of comedy, that of romance. Shakespeare's specific source involves the travels of Apollonius of Tyre, a popular Greek tale that he would later revisit. Egeon's lament at being unrecognized by his son, along with his pending execution, deepens the emotion in this final scene tremendously. One modern reviewer applauded a 1997 Royal Shakespeare Company production for being "straightforward, sharply focused, and attentive to the language." It treated the story it had to tell with deep respect, and less boisterously and farcically than usual. This change was most marked in the ending: revelations following Aemilia's arrival "had a feeling of the miraculous about them." That said, these high and low tones need not be mutually exclusive: the resulting sense of reconciliation, and even resurrection, can make that closing feast all the more festive.

The Comedy of Errors was definitely in existence by December 1594. Yet even a record of a play's *first* performance does not resolve all questions. For example, Philip Henslowe notes in his diary that *Titus Andronicus* was first staged in the Rose Theatre on January 24, 1594. However, did this note signify the first performance at the Rose only? Or the first performance by a specific company of actors? We know from a title page that a few different companies performed the play, including Pembroke's, Derby's, and Sussex's Men. There also exists a priceless drawing by Henry Peacham of a scene from *Titus*; this image gives us a fascinating idea about Renaissance costumes (some actors appear as ancient Romans, others in contemporary dress), but it helps us not a jot with questions of dating. Overall, conventional wisdom suggests that Shakespeare completed the writing of *Titus Andronicus* a few years before Henslowe's record of a performance. Generally the same attitude applies for these earliest comedies by Shakespeare.

Publication dates do not help, either. For example, *Richard III* did not appear in print until 1597. The play's popularity explains, rather than belies, the delayed publication. As long as companies could fill theaters with paying audiences for ongoing performances, they (as actual owners of scripts) had no real interest in seeing the play published. If people could purchase the play, they might be less inclined to pay to attend a performance. Scholars generally agree that *Richard III* is an early play, despite its later publication. Dating Shakespeare's plays, then, is challenging on multiple levels.

SHAKESPEARE, MARLOWE, AND THE LONDON THEATERS

It will be helpful, before proceeding any further, to situate these early plays by Shakespeare, along with the initial success they earned him, within a competitive context—with respect to his greatest rival among playwrights. The vagueness mentioned above in dating plays also complicates theories about influence—either of other writers upon Shakespeare, or of his influence upon them. That said, we should acknowledge one last time the long shadow of Christopher Marlowe upon Shakespeare's early poetic language and the plays themselves. The opening lines of *1 Henry VI*, when Bedford laments the death of Henry V, sound like a pastiche of the dense rhetoric and elaborate imagery of Marlowe's own powerful poetry:

Hung be the heavens with black, yield day
   to night!
Comets, importing changes of time and
   states,
Brandish your crystal tresses in the sky,
And with them scourge the bad revolting
   stars
That have consented unto Henry's death.
   (1.1.1–5)

Marlowe may have smirked when he first heard these lines, recognizing his own sound in his competitor from Stratford. (The two writers were of the same age, but Marlowe was clearly an established force in London theater while Shakespeare searched for his first break.)

There is a wonderful scene in that film mentioned earlier, *Shakespeare in Love*, in which a famous actor boasts about playing the roles of Marlowe's great characters—Tamburlaine, Doctor Faustus, the Jew of Malta—and then he turns, a little remorsefully to young Shakespeare, and adds as an afterthought, "And oh yes, Will, your *Henry VI*." Shakespeare, played winningly by Joseph Fiennes, admits that his *Henry VI* "was a house built upon his foundation." In another hilarious scene, Marlowe gives Shakespeare, suffering from writer's block, the title *Romeo and Juliet*—thus preventing the tentative Will from calling his unfinished play *Romeo and Ethel the Pirate's Daughter*! In short, Marlowe's artistry pointed the way, giving Shakespeare a model for his first attempts at playwriting and pushing him toward greater achievements.

It should be quickly added that influence between these writers apparently did not move in only one direction, or at least not for very long. Most scholars believe that Shakespeare's *Henry VI* trilogy in turn influenced Marlowe's last work, the English history play *Edward II* (1592–93). Whereas Marlowe's first dramas were very protagonist-centered, *Edward II*, despite its similar-sounding title, is a better plotted, more modulated play. Dramatic attention to King Edward is shared with other characters, and thus brings to life the queen; Edward's favorite, or minion, Gaveston; and his nemesis, Mortimer. This development reflected the broad scope and large casts of Shakespeare's first history plays; the old dog Marlowe was learning new tricks.

The stage was now set, so to speak, for a theatrical competition for the ages, one between the established, respected writer Marlowe and the provincial newcomer Shakespeare. The fact that each was writing for a particular playing company only heightened the stakes. By the mid-1590s, primacy over London's theater world was starkly divided between two particular companies. On the one hand, Philip Henslowe soon had the towering Edward Alleyn as a son-in-law. As the main actor for the Lord Admiral's Men, Alleyn promptly drew awestruck audiences to Henslowe's Rose Theatre, where he brought Marlowe's great characters to stage-stalking, speech-declaiming life. On the other hand, Shakespeare may have first been associated with the Queen's Men, early competitors with the Admiral's Men, but their influence lessened. Eventually, in 1594 and during a general reshuffling of companies, actors from Strange's Men helped to form a new troupe called the Lord Chamberlain's Men. Shakespeare became one of their leading figures and, as we will soon see, this new company swiftly eclipsed the initial dominance of the Admiral's Men. Another major figure of this group was Richard Burbage, son of the James Burbage who built the Theatre in Shoreditch. This was in fact the home of this second company, creating a wonderful north-of-London/south-of-London commercial battle with the Admiral's Men at the Rose Theatre in Bankside.

Christopher Marlowe, unfortunately, would never live to see this exciting showdown between these two London theater companies, or be able to lend his literary talents to spur himself and his competitor William Shakespeare to even greater poetic and dramatic heights. Marlowe spent much of the 1590s embroiled in several tumultuous incidents, and rumors grew about his atheism and homosexuality. Consequently, Elizabeth's main cabinet, the Privy Council, ordered Marlowe to appear before its members on May 18, 1593. It is likely that Marlowe had long been familiar with the council and with the queen's secret service in particular. Marlowe reported as requested, on May 20, and was ordered to stay nearby and return on a daily basis. Ten days later, he was dead. He was stabbed in the eye in nearby Deptford, allegedly over an argument about a "reckoning," or inn bill. The circumstances surrounding this sudden, mysterious death have fascinated scholars ever since. The murkiness surrounding Marlowe's activity and his sudden demise invite all sorts of theories; there is likely more to the story than the coroner's report blandly tells us.

More importantly for Shakespeare, his main rival was now suddenly dead. Following Marlowe's abrupt end, along with the generally short careers of other writers active during the 1580s, no other playwright ever came remotely close in the years ahead to competing with Shakespeare as London's most popular, most important writer

for the theater. For the next two decades, center stage and the heart of English drama was his.

Sources and Further Reading

Hamilton, A. C. *The Early Shakespeare*. San Marino, Calif.: Huntington Library, 1967.

Holland, Peter. *William Shakespeare* [a book-length version, in Oxford University Press's Very Important People series, of Holland's entry in the *Oxford Dictionary of National Biography*]. New York: Oxford University Press, 2007.

Newman, Karen. "Renaissance Family Politics and Shakespeare's *The Taming of the Shrew*," *English Literary Renaissance* 16 (1986): 86-100.

Pearlman, E. "The Invention of Richard of Gloucester," reprinted in *William Shakespeare: Blooms Modern Critical Views*, New York: Chelsea House, 2003.

Ryan, Kiernan. *Shakespeare's Comedies*. New York: Palgrave Macmillan, 2009.

Tanner, Tony. *Prefaces to Shakespeare*. Cambridge, Mass.: Belknap Press of Harvard University Press, 2010.

Wells, Stanley. *Shakespeare: The Writer and His Work*. New York: Scribners, 1978.

Wells, Stanley, ed. *Shakespeare in the Theatre*. Oxford: Clarendon Press, 1997.

SHAKESPEARE'S GROWING FAME

By the early 1590s, the twenty-something actor and writer Shakespeare had completed a quartet of history plays on a scale never before seen on the English stage. He had also created one of literature's most memorable stage villains and tragic mouthpieces in the person of Richard III. Additionally, he had produced, as if afterthoughts, a handful of early comedies. Unfortunately, just as Shakespeare's playwriting career was taking off in 1593, he and the rest of London faced the most dreaded of professional disruptions, not to mention mortal perils. A particularly severe occurrence of the bubonic plague struck the city. Shakespeare had survived a similar outbreak once before, as an infant in Stratford. This time, throughout the streets of London, thousands of citizens were not so lucky. Entire families perished, swiftly, in panic-causing multitudes. One commemorative verse in the parish register of St. Peter's Cornhill reads:

> In a thousand five hundred ninety three
> The lord preserved my house and me
> When of the pestilence there died
> Full many a thousand else beside.

Under these terribly deadly circumstances, how would Shakespeare continue his writing? How would he make a living with the theaters closed? More urgently, how would he avoid the plague?

PLAGUE AND POETRY

Epidemics of pestilence were not new to Londoners—previous plague years included 1563, 1574, 1577, 1578, and 1581, and they would recur throughout the first decade of the seventeenth century as well: Shakespeare's actor-brother Edmund may have been a plague victim upon his death in 1607. More broadly, the "sickness" had reached England in 1348 and would not subside entirely till after the Great Fire of London, in 1666. Still, in the present case, London had enjoyed a long hiatus from the plague when symptoms and fatalities began to reappear as early as the summer of 1592. The problem worsened in August, after the theaters had already been closed for most of the summer following June riots. By October, the queen issued a proclamation banning persons from visiting the court, and also commanding her attendants not to travel to London. It became customary for authorities to close down the theaters if the weekly death count reached forty people, and the Queen's Privy Council ordered this closure on January 2. It prohibited "all manner of concourse and public meetings of the people," at theaters or elsewhere. Except for brief stretches, such as when Sussex's Men staged *Titus Andronicus* in January 1594, London's public theater industry ceased to exist for nearly a year and half. Public theaters did not reopen till June 1594.

During times of plague, London's city leaders also acted quickly to shut down the theaters. They already strongly disapproved of the public playhouses, condemning the "lewd" content of the plays themselves, and fearing that performances encouraged civic disorder among the unsavory people in attendance. As we have seen, the theaters were built in the "liberties" just beyond the city limits, and so theaters were tainted by the reputation of their rougher neighborhoods, crowded as they were with bear-baiting pits, thieves' rings, and brothels. Theaters, then, helped to corrupt youth and encourage idleness. Plague times increased these anxieties even further. One letter from the Lord Mayor to the queen's councilors expresses concern that "many having sores . . . take occasion hereby to walk abroad and to recreate themselves by hearing a play. Whereby others are infected . . . " This image of plague spreading easily throughout an already dirty, disreputable crowd invited the city's aggressive action against both theaters and actors. It was not yet known in the Renaissance that the plague spread from fleas that would bite rats and then humans. Rats were a staple of city life, as much then as now, and they often found a welcoming habitat in the thatched roofs of London buildings.

Citizens tried to protect themselves from the plague by bloodletting, or with nutmeg or rosemary, which they placed in their ears and noses. Usually it helped little: at its deadliest, the plague caused a thousand deaths a week, and one chronicler estimated that ten thousand died in 1593 alone. Infected houses were boarded up and marked with a cross. Shakespeare seems to recall this time of enforced quarantines in *Romeo and Juliet*, when Friar John is prevented from delivering an all-important letter to Romeo. We hear that officials in Mantua, "Suspecting that we both were in a house / Where the infectious pestilence did reign, / Sealed up the doors, and would not let us forth."

Clearly this was no atmosphere in which actors could make a living, especially when London's preachers and aldermen framed the plague as a sign of divine judgment against the city's wicked practices, including playgoing. One woodcut features a skeleton standing atop caskets, menacing Londoners with an arrow. "Lord, have mercy on London," reads the top of the image, as

Seventeenth-century woodcut depicting the plague in London.

lightning flashes, a sign of God's disfavor. "We die. Keepe out," it reads below. The once thriving theater companies may have received modest support from patrons, but it was not enough. Unable to work and back on their heels, the actors had to set out on tours of the countryside, performing wherever they could and making whatever wages were to be had. However, it seems plausible that Shakespeare chose not to do this.

Shakespeare obviously had recourse to his home and family in Stratford, and he likely spent time there during the nearly two years of inactivity in London's theaters. Who knows? His wife, Anne, may have even been glad about this professional setback; William's having no stage to act on or write for meant that her husband was home more often. It is reasonable to think so, although we have no evidence. A different kind of evidence exists, however, indicating that Shakespeare was likely moving and working in another social milieu. The evidence consists of two books of narrative poetry, *Venus and Adonis* and *The Rape of Lucrece*, which were published in 1593 and 1594, respectively. They were Shakespeare's first printed works. This new social setting was the rarified circle around a powerful, wealthy twenty-year-old nobleman, Henry Wriothesley, the third

Earl of Southampton. This exclusive, fashionable circle was far removed from either the quiet hearth scene of Stratford or the urban ravages of London's streets.

Shakespeare's literary productions during these plague years indicate that he was actively pursuing a new writing identity—not the popular entertainer scribbling plays for a pastime that many found questionable, but rather an elegant courtly poet, dedicating learned poetry to a patron capable of socially advancing his favored writers. He intended to compose a more rhetorically eloquent verse, with Greek and Roman mythological characters and narratives drawn from Ovid's *Metamorphoses* and other classical sources. Whereas Ovid's story of Venus and Adonis takes seventy-five lines, Shakespeare's poem expands to 1,200 lines, amassing along the way sensual imagery and artful paraphrases and restatements. Shakespeare, the provincial writer without a university education, was hoping to gain a more sophisticated readership: university men, future lawyers at London's Inns of Court, and, of course, a certain young nobleman to whom his two longer poems were dedicated.

HENRY WRIOTHESLEY AND SHAKESPEARE'S CLASSICAL POEMS

Who was this young nobleman Southampton? He was the fellow to whom Shakespeare addressed the only letters of his we have in our possession, thanks to their having been printed. Henry Wriothesley's father and older brother died when he was a boy, and he was educated under Queen Elizabeth's most powerful councilor, William Cecil, Lord Burghley. His guardian wished the young nobleman to marry his own granddaughter (thereby strengthening his own family), but Wriothesley resisted, much to Cecil's anger. The young man became a generous patron to many writers and scholars. We have already encoun-

tered some of them: the Italian tutor John Florio, Gervase Markham, and Shakespeare's fellow London writer Thomas Nashe, who dedicated his prose narrative The Unfortunate Traveller to the earl in 1591. A later edition appeared without the florid dedicatory letter, suggesting that Nashe did not receive the reward from Wriothesley that he had anticipated. Shakespeare's poetic efforts apparently met with greater success.

His first poem, *Venus and Adonis*, was published in April 1593, just a few months after the theaters had been closed indefinitely. It appeared as a small but handsome volume (the size of a modern paperback), and its mistake-free printing suggests a carefully prepared manuscript copy. Shakespeare may have been a concerned poet who had the leisure to visit the print shop every day and oversee his book's production. If he did so, he probably had occasion to hear about gossip back in Stratford. The printer, Richard Field, was a fellow townsman, and the young, heretofore unpublished poet may have caught a local's break in connecting with one of the best printers then working in London. Field had apprenticed with the master printer Thomas Vautrollier, and upon his death he took over his boss's printing shop in the Blackfriars area. Was Shakespeare living somewhere nearby or elsewhere? Perhaps the poet had taken up residence in Southampton House in London, or alternately, to protect himself better from the plague raging in the city, maybe he had retired with Wriothesley and other artists, writers, and musicians to the family's country home near Tichfield, in Hampshire. One contemporary called it a "right stately house" with a "goodly gate." (Known as Palace or Place House, the property is today in ruins.) Some scholars have argued that Shakespeare may have arranged theater performances in this home; one room has even been identified as the "playhouse room."

This hypothesis is certainly tenable, and if Shakespeare the dramatist was also writing a new play there, one additional comedy that comes to mind is *Love's Labour's Lost.* The dialogue there is more sophisticated than in other early comedies, more metaphorically dense and full of the courtly language that shows the writer John Lyly's influence. The setting and plot of this play, about the romantic mishaps of a retinue of courtly men in retreat from the real world, does indeed reflect well the plague-fleeing situation of Southampton and his followers. It is very possible that Shakespeare was working on this and perhaps other

plays, some of which would be ready for staging when the theaters reopened. It is also easy to imagine him, as we shall see, writing sonnets to or about Southampton, or merely as challenging lyrical exercises, at a furious pace. However, his most likely projects during this time, based on their publication shortly afterward, were those two narrative poems, *Venus and Adonis* and *The Rape of Lucrece.*

Highly decorative and full of sensual titillation, *Venus and Adonis* narrates an erotic encoun-

Venus and Adonis, ca. 1560 *(Titian)*

ter in a fecund forest setting. In Shakespeare's version of this myth, Venus becomes the ardent suitor, and Adonis the lovely youth reluctant about the goddess's advances. "I'll be a park, and thou shalt be my deer," Venus says suggestively, "Feed where thou wilt, on mountain or in dale":

> Graze on my lips, and if those hills be dry,
> Stray lower, where the pleasant fountains lie.

Talk of Venus's "Sweet bottom-grass" and "Round rising hillocks" and the elaborate description of Adonis handling a steed all seem coordinated to please a young nobleman. (Never mind that the haughty youth is eventually gored and killed by a "foul" boar.) The poem's language, like Venus's body teasingly presented, is luscious. It splendidly fulfilled the fashionable, worldly poetic subgenre of the epyllion, involving more or less an Ovidian love narrative. Thomas Lodge's *Scilla's Metamorphosis* (1589) was an early English example, and Christopher Marlowe completed his masterpiece of erotic verse, *Hero and Leander*, around the same time as Shakespeare was writing. It was not published till 1598, but Shakespeare may have read it in manuscript form. A "love book" described in *The Two Gentlemen of Verona* may refer to Marlowe's poem.

However aware he was of these similar poems, Shakespeare certainly had high hopes for his poetic gift to Wriothesley. A Latin epigraph from Ovid's *Amores* contrasts "what is cheap" and "common" with his own Apollonian, Muse-given poetry. The accompanying letter from the author, despite its conventionally self-deprecating tone, should be read with that epigraph in mind. Shakespeare was striving to present his patron or potential patron with something clearly literary (and thus unlike mere plays), something highly artful, and unapologetically artificial, too:

> Right Honourable, I know not how I shall offend in dedicating my unpolished lines to your Lordship, nor how the world will censure me for choosing so strong a prop to support so weak a burden, only if your Honour seem but pleased, I account my self highly praised, and vow to take advantage of all idle hours, till I have honoured you with some graver labour. But if the first heir of my invention prove deformed, I shall be sorry it had so noble a god-father: and never after ear so barren a land, for fear it yield me still so bad a harvest, I leave it to your Honourable survey, and your Honor to your heart's content, which I wish may always answer your own wish, and the world's hopeful expectation.
>
> Your Honor's in all duty,
> William Shakespeare

Stephen Greenblatt describes the tone here as "formal" and "emotionally cautious." Perhaps the dedication's talk of "all idle hours" refers to the writer's necessary flight from London because of the plague, as well as the time for writing that Southampton's support made possible. Or maybe he is appealing for support that he has not yet received; we can almost hear the offer of a transaction here—you provide me with "idle hours," and I will provide you with "some graver labour." He did just this in the following year, with the completion and publication of the far more sober poem about an ancient Roman's chastity and violation, *The Rape of Lucrece*. First of all, though, the author is anxious that this first poem please its intended, ideal reader, Wriothesley. The very existence of a second poem, and the warmer tone of its dedicatory letter, suggests that Shakespeare himself was heartened by the nobleman's reaction.

There is ample evidence that Shakespeare's *Venus and Adonis* pleased numerous other readers as well. The multiple printings the book enjoyed—nine times within a decade and sixteen by 1636—most obviously proves its popularity. This early poem would turn out to be Shakespeare's best-selling book during his lifetime. Anecdotal evidence also exists. A Cambridge University play from a few years later, *The Return from Parnassus*, features a character who dismisses Chaucer and Spenser in favor of "sweet Mr. Shakespeare, and to honour him I will lay his *Venus and Adonis* under my pillow." The same character elsewhere promises to keep Shakespeare's picture in his study, as if our famous writer were a teen heartthrob. "We shall have nothing but pure Shakespeare," went the cry on campus. Far more surprising is the record of a lapsed friar reading and enjoying this narrative poem with its erotic, pagan content!

It is also just possible that we should read *Venus and Adonis* within a sensitive social context. It may have been a timely lesson for Wriothesley, a text meant as a warning, if gently and subtly so, about the young earl's stubbornness regarding his guardian Cecil's wishes for him to marry. The powerful Cecil was threatening enormous fines against the young man, and one of his secretaries composed for his ward a Neo-Latin poem, *Narcissus*, that seems to dramatize Wriothesley's isolated, self-contented state of mind with the title character. Narcissus famously falls in love with his own image in a pool of water. Of course Adonis would be the doppelgänger in Shakespeare's poem, and Venus indeed accuses the reticent young man of being, like Narcissus, too proud of his own beauty. Perhaps Adonis's scornful smile matches that of the poem's primary reader, and sometimes his refusals of Venus sound downright surly:

> "I know not love," quoth he, "nor will not
>   know it,
> Unless it be a boar, and then I chase it;
> 'Tis much to borrow, and I will not owe it;
> My love to love is love but to disgrace it;
> For I have heard it is a life in death,
> That laughs and weeps, and all but with a
>   breath.

This defiant comment also expresses, if we listen closely, a genuine fear of love and all that it involves—a relinquishing of independence, a vulnerability, an awareness that love, like all earthly things, is transient ("all but with a breath"). On the other hand, perhaps the poem has it both ways—seeming to lecture Wriothesley on his matrimonial resistance, and thus reassuring various worrisome people surrounding the young man, but all the while aware of the recipient's true desires. Because the poem is largely from the point of view of the lusting Venus, many passages describe Adonis's highly desired male body, giving the poem a homoerotic charge overall.

Shakespeare's "graver labour" appeared in May 1594. Richard Field also printed *The Rape of Lucrece*, and its high quality suggests authorial oversight similar to that of the first poem. Shakespeare's second and final letter available to us is included in the volume, yet again public and formal:

> To the Right Honourable Henry Wriothesley, Earl of Southampton, and Baron of Tichfield.
>
> THE love I dedicate to your lordship is without end; whereof this pamphlet, without beginning, is but a superfluous moiety. The warrant I have of your honourable disposition, not the worth of my untutored lines, makes it assured of acceptance. What I have done is yours; what I have to do is yours; being part in all I have, devoted yours. Were my worth greater, my duty would show greater; meantime, as it is, it is bound to your lordship, to whom I wish long life, still lengthened with all happiness.
>
> Your lordship's in all duty,
> WILLIAM SHAKESPEARE.

If any letter today sounded like this address to Southampton, it would be a formal thank-you note, or perhaps a letter to an employer. That said, the tone here in this second letter sounds a little warmer. It is easy to imagine that Shakespeare's relationship with Wriothesley had grown closer. This seems to be the case professionally, at least, following the reception of the first poem the year before, and we may find signs of a writer's growing loyalty to and appreciation for his patron in this letter: "What I have done is yours; what I have to do is yours[.]" Or is there something more personal in such a declaration? As many have thought, the poet's and nobleman's relationship may have been developing more than professionally as well, as will be discussed.

The Rape of Lucrece is a more ambitious poem, although some readers find that it lacks the freshness and gorgeous strokes of its predecessor. It is nearly 1,900 lines long, composed in the elegant seven-line stanza known as rhyme royal. Shakespeare again returned to Ovid for his source in Roman legend, and consulted ancient historians such as Livy as well. The story involves a Roman nobleman, Collatinus, who boasts of the beauty and virtue of his wife, Lucrece, and foolishly persuades others to visit her and see for themselves. Sextus Tarquinius, the son of King Tarquin, sees her and becomes consumed with lust. His advances initially repulsed by the chaste wife, Tarquin ravishes her. Eventually the shamed Lucrece reveals her rape to her husband and father. Naming the perpetrator, she demands revenge, stabs herself, and dies. The poem ends with Brutus vowing to drive the Tarquins into "everlasting banishment," giving Shakespeare's poem an anti-tyranny subtext that would have been viewed, within England's own Tudor monarchy, as a bold theme.

The tragedy of Lucrece, though dramatic, is still rather thin for a somber 2,000-line poem.

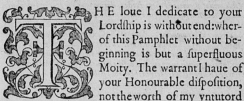

Shakespeare's dedication of *The Rape of Lucrece* to Henry Wriothesley in 1594.

Thus Shakespeare takes advantage of several occasions for extended descriptions or more highly passionate narrations (as of Lucrece's suicide). Her formal complaint following her rape attacks the personified conditions that have made it possible—Night, Opportunity, Time. Awaiting Collatinus's return, Lucrece focuses on a wall hanging depicting the Fall of Troy. This attention gives Shakespeare an opportunity for ekphrasis, or extended description of a visual object:

> For much imaginary work was there,
> Conceit deceitful, so compact, so kind,
> That for Achilles' image stood his spear,
> Grip'd in an armed hand, himself behind
> Was left unseen, save to the eye of mind:
> A hand, a foot, a face, a leg, a head
> Stood for the whole to be imagined.

(continues on page 84)

SHAKESPEARE'S BOOKS

The above title does not mean "those books that belonged to Shakespeare," although, in some cases, echoes in certain plays make it clear that Shakespeare owned or at least had access to books by authors such as Ovid, Plutarch, and Montaigne. Sometimes he clearly wrote with these source books beside him—right there for nearly verbatim copying, as we find in some passages. But "Shakespeare's Books" here means those books—from the early 1590s to our own time—that featured Shakespeare's writing, both with and without his name attached, or in some cases connected Shakespeare's name with writing that was in fact not his.

We would love to have work by Shakespeare that reflected his habits of composition—his first drafts of plays or poems, or, more complicatedly, copies of his writing that we could safely call "authorial," meaning that we could know it was his writing as intended, and not altered (and often shortened) for the stage, or edited later by collaborators or revisers. These manuscript materials were often called a writer's "foul papers" in the Renaissance. When a manuscript of a play was marked by a theater company's scrivener and prepared for rehearsal and performance, it was then called a "promptbook" or "playbook." One rare manuscript of this sort that exists today is a promptbook called "The Book of Sir Thomas More." It is most famous because of the 147 lines (by "Hand D") that many scholars believe to be by Shakespeare. If this is so, then these are his only handwritten lines available to us. In any case, this play is also useful because it clearly shows the highly detailed collaborative process that often led to the creation of Renaissance plays; evidence reveals that several writers were involved in the writing of scenes for "Sir Thomas More."

Usually plays would be published only after their popularity on the stage had waned. Then the theater company (rather than the author, who in this era retained no rights to his work) would register the manuscript with London's stationers—a general term for printer, publisher, or bookseller. Soon these volumes would appear in print, ready to be sold among the booksellers who gathered in Paternoster Row in London, in the shadow of St. Paul's Cathedral. They were called "quarto" editions because the printed paper was folded into fourths. They were not unlike today's trade paperbacks or mass market paperbacks—popular, reasonably priced, portable, and, unfortunately, often ephemeral as well. Some editions were literally read out of existence. When one book by Shakespeare's dead contemporary Christopher Marlowe appeared, the publisher wrote that "Marlowe's ghost" was now haunting the booksellers' area, a sign of how personally identified books were with their authors, especially in posterity.

As best as scholars can tell, books of poetry, not to mention collections of sermons, almanacs, and other kinds of books, sold far more briskly than printed versions of plays. It is not surprising, then, that Shakespeare's first publications were his two narrative poems—*Venus and Adonis* and *The Rape of Lucrece*—that appeared in 1593 and 1594, respectively. For a few years, these were the only volumes that featured Shakespeare's name, and the only ones that ever featured formal dedications by the author. Shakespeare's first play to become a book was *Titus Andronicus*, published in 1594. A couple of Shakespeare's *Henry VI* plays appeared in print in 1594–95 (though with different titles), followed by *Richard II*, *Romeo and Juliet*, *Love's Labour's Lost*, *Richard III*, and *Henry IV* during the next few years.

By 1598, Shakespeare's name began to appear on the covers of these quarto editions—"Newly corrected and augmented by W. Shakespere." In 1600, four plays featured his name. To put it in familiar terms, Shakespeare was becoming a famous writer. However, others were realizing that a work by Shakespeare's name on it would sell, regardless of its quality. A poetry anthology called *The Passionate Pilgrim* claimed to be by Shakespeare, although only five of the poems it contained were his—two of his sonnets, and three passages from a play. Similarly, several plays in the early seventeenth century were published under Shakespeare's name, but are probably not by him. Still, his authorship of a couple of these titles is still debated. A volume of particular interest Is Shake-Speares Sonnets (1609), the first printed collection of his sonnets likely published without his approval. Was he embarrassed or angered by their being made available, these intense poems of desire and love? We do not know. He never said, at least not in print.

By the time the great collection of Shakespeare's plays, the First Folio, appeared in 1623, twenty of Shakespeare's thirty-six plays had already appeared in smaller quarto editions. A folio volume, by contrast, was folded only once, and thus was a larger, more expensive, more formal book. The Folio's editors were clearly proud of this edition of their fellow actor Shakespeare's works. (They also hoped, let us not forget, to sell copies and to make back a considerable investment.) Their opening letter in the Folio promises "all his plays," and furthermore, it boasts that

where (before) you were abused with diverse stolen and surreptitious copies, maimed and deformed by frauds and stealths of injurious imposters that exposed them: even those are now offered to your view cured, and perfect of their limbs; and all the rest, absolute in their numbers, as he conceived them.

The editors probably have in mind many of these earlier quarto editions, which may have been memorial reconstructions (that is, composed from memory by opportunistic actors—pirated, basically). Some of them do seem far inferior and often shorter compared with the Folio volume's version, which (the editors seem

Title page of the First Folio, published in 1623. *(Copper engraving of Shakespeare by Martin Droeshout)*

to claim) derived from Shakespeare's original manuscripts. Some scholars today still favor the quarto versions because they feel these texts better reflect original performance conditions—that is, what the first audiences would have seen acted on the Renaissance stage. And remember, despite all of the prior quarto editions, there were still *sixteen* plays that appeared in print for the first time in the Folio. The editors' work was valuable indeed.

This editorial care for Shakespeare's writings has continued through the centuries. The

(continues)

(continued)

eighteenth century saw a procession of editors who helped to restore Shakespeare's original lines and better appreciate their meanings. The Cambridge Shakespeare in the mid-nineteenth century achieved a new level of scholarly sophistication, and was an influential series for many decades. Today, several popular and reliable editions of the complete works are available, edited by David Bevington, Stanley Wells and Gary Taylor, Stephen Greenblatt, G. Blakemore Evans, Jonathan Bate and Eric Rasmussen, and others. For individual plays, the most thorough editions appear in the Arden, Cambridge, and Oxford editions, while volumes in the Pelican, Folger, and Modern Library series often provide inexpensive classroom texts.

SEE ALSO:

Brooks, Douglas A. *From Playhouse to Printing House: Drama and Authorship in Early Modern England.* New York: Cambridge University Press, 2000.

Erne, Lukas. *Shakespeare as Literary Dramatist.* New York: Cambridge University Press, 2003.

Jowett, John. *Shakespeare and Text.* New York: Oxford University Press, 2007.

Murphy, Andrew. *Shakespeare in Print: A History and Chronology of Shakespeare Publishing.* New York: Cambridge University Press, 2003.

Stern, Tiffany. *Making Shakespeare.* New York: Routledge, 2004.

Taylor, Gary and Stanley Wells. *William Shakespeare: A Textual Companion.* New York : Oxford University Press, 1987.

(continued from page 81)

Lucrece considers her own fate in the figures of Hecuba and Helen, and sees in the Greek betrayer Sinon her Roman assailant, Tarquin. Altough the villain, Tarquin is memorably rendered as well, as someone at war with himself, someone who must go against conscience to commit his crime. In this way, he resembles later characters such as Angelo in *Measure for Measure* or Macbeth, who imagines a personified Murder moving "With Tarquin's ravishing strides." However, as scholar and editor F. T. Prince puts it, if *Lucrece* resembles Shakespearean tragedy elsewhere, it is closer to the early Roman tragedy *Titus Andronicus* than to later triumphs such as *Macbeth* or *King Lear*. Still, *The Rape of Lucrece* proved popular with readers, too. If not as frequently as *Venus and Adonis*, Shakespeare's second narrative poem was nevertheless reprinted seven more times before 1640, a respectable publishing success.

SHAKESPEARE'S "SUGARED" SONNETS

Through the centuries, Shakespeare's *Sonnets* have become far more famous than his two narrative poems, and more likely than not, he also composed many of these fourteen-line lyrical poems during the plague years and with the help of Wriothesley's support. The nobleman may also be, at the risk of oversimplifying the dramatizing potentials of lyric poetry, a subject or addressee in many of the sonnets. The sequence of these poems, as we have it, contains 154 sonnets. However, since Shakespeare apparently did not oversee publication, we have no way of knowing if they are in the order he intended, or if he ever gave a thought to forming a lengthy "sonnet sequence" out of these many individual poems. As is, there seems to be some thoughtfulness about the ordering of the sonnets: some go together in pairs or smaller groups, and larger groups still tend to focus on shared themes or circumstances. This may sound like an astounding number, 154 sonnets total, but we should be careful about presuming many years of composition by quantity alone. When Philip Sidney's highly influential sonnet sequence *Astrophil and Stella* appeared in 1591 (though composed nearly a decade earlier), it kicked off a sonnet craze throughout the next decade that led to several copy-cat sequences with many individual sonnets therein. Readers found in Sidney's sonnets various "screen" scenarios in verse that lyrically dramatized real events at court, as well as characters that could both be, and not be, real persons, namely Sidney himself and his alleged lover, Penelope Rich. Similarly, the majority of Shakespeare's sonnets are addressed to a young man, fair youth, or "lovely boy" (or more than one). Elsewhere a rival poet appears, and a short sequence at the end focuses on a dark lady. Shakespeare, for practical and evasive—or fictive and artful—reasons, identified the figures in his sequence without specific names or as clever, punning personas.

Perhaps Shakespeare joined Wriothesley's circle as a sonnet writer already. In fact, the range of tones and possible real-world clues in individual sonnets suggest repeated efforts with this popular literary form at different stages of his life and career. For example, sonnet 145's possible pun on Anne Hathaway in the line "'I hate' from hate away she threw" has led some scholars to date the sonnet as early as 1580 or 1581, making it a courting poem of a young Stratford man. Likewise, sonnet 128—"How oft, when thou, my music, music play'st"—is a perfectly pleasant poem and perfectly conventional. A literary commentator likely had this and poems like it in mind when, in 1598, he claimed the "sweete wittie soule of Ovid lives in mellifluous and hony-tongued Shakespeare, witness his *Venus and Adonis*, his *Lucrece*, his sugared *Sonnets* among his private friends." The phrase "sugared sonnets," on the other hand, fails to convey some of the amazing heights and depths of love and companionship, so amazingly voiced throughout these sonnets. Nor does the description encompass the challenging relationships suggested in different poems, or the revulsion, betrayal, and self-loathing dramatized there. The *Sonnets* are full of, in the scholar Stephen Orgel's words, "emotional turmoil and non-vanilla sex," yet they supremely exhibit, when treated as the artful poems that they are, Shakespeare's own "transforming power of the mind."

The comment above, about Shakespeare's sonnets "among his private friends," indicates that they—or more likely, some of them—were circulating in manuscript within Shakespeare's immediate circle of friends and readers. Copies in diaries and commonplace books from the period suggest that this distribution widened soon enough. Curiously, the *Sonnets* did not appear in print until 1609, and then did so in a volume most likely unauthorized by Shakespeare. Why had it taken so long? Had the popularity of sonnet sequences passed by the time Shakespeare wished to publish them? Alternately, maybe he did not wish to see them printed because some of the contents and circumstances were more personal and still considered sensitive. If we apply the storylines of the *Sonnets* to Shakespeare's own life, this hesitation to broadcast these poems certainly becomes understandable. We will examine more details surrounding this mysterious 1609 publication when we consider Shakespeare's later career.

There is a long, sometimes outrageous history of reading Shakespeare's sonnets in similarly autobiographical fashion. Consider titles such as Arthur Acheson's *Shakespeare's Sonnet Story* or Charles Armitage Brown's *Shakespeare's Autobiographical Poems*. Readers' curiosity about Shakespeare the man and writer, and their hope of finding clues about him concealed in these poems, is doubtless one reason why the *Sonnets* remain popular today. They have been used to substantiate a number of things about Shakespeare: that he suffered from a physical disability (37: "So I, made lame by fortune's dearest spite"), that he was ashamed of his theatrical career (110: "Alas, 'tis true, I have gone here and there / And made myself a motley to the view"), that he was old and pondering death (73: "That time of year thou mayst in me behold"), that he felt pangs of conscience about one or more adulterous relationships (152: "In loving thee thou knowst I am foresworn"). One major narrative in the later sonnets (from 127 to 152 in particular) connects Shakespeare's persona, if not the poet himself, with an affair with a "dark lady," which may mean dark in complexion or something more figurative (morally nebulous, harmful to the speaker, etc.).

Readers should proceed carefully when trying to apply lines of complex poetry to Shakespeare's biographical record. For example, we know Shakespeare was an actor, so sonnet 23's opening seems patently autobiographical: "As an unperfect actor on the stage . . ." However, in the world of the poem, the speaker is merely saying he is *similar to* an actor forgetting lines: "So I, for fear of trust, forget to say / The perfect ceremony of love's rite." Likewise, many critics agree that Shakespeare is dramatizing here a patron-poet relationship, in which case the speaker's social status in the sonnets would certainly be a vexed matter. That does not necessarily mean that Shakespeare himself was ashamed of his theater career. Much evidence suggests otherwise. The topic becomes less about personal revelation and more about dramatic opportunities.

The relationship between male speaker and admired young man also requires care from modern readers, since friendship between men in the Renaissance was highly valued, and often expressed in effusive, affectionate terms that would embarrass many male friends today. This fact does not necessarily imply that this primary relationship in the sequence is platonic, since the overall dramatic expression in the sonnets makes this a strained conclusion. Nevertheless, many early readers, uncomfortable with the homoerotic implications of the *Sonnets*, were happy to subscribe to this "high friendship" or "esteemed patron" reading. (One editor in 1640 went so far as to change the "he" and "him" in various poems to "she" and "her.")

In this same sleuthing spirit, ongoing interest in identifying the major characters of Shakespeare's *Sonnets*—the Fair Youth, the Rival Poet, the Dark Lady—seems all but inexhaustible. How true are the details in Shakespeare's many sonnets, and to whom did they happen? Who is the poet addressing through the fictive "screen" of his lyrical persona? To take one example, does the poet reveal himself in sonnets 135 and 136, where we encounter the punning character named "Will," or is this just one more level of fictive masking? These two sonnets remain unusual in giving a name so explicitly. In this way, Shakespeare's sonnets differ significantly from others' sequences, where we encounter allegorical lovers such as Astrophil and a range of beloveds such as Stella, Idea, Diana, Rosalind, and Delia. The lack of poetical names in Shakespeare's poems arguably creates a greater sense of veracity, as if lyrical masks have been stripped away, and his sonnets' dramas were the Renaissance version of "reality TV." Yet this may be one more fiction-making trick of a supreme poet, or a playwright prancing coyly before us. More certainly, the feelings recorded in the sonnets—about love, lust, jealousy, betrayal, disappointment, forgiveness, ecstasy, aging, death, memory, and literary immortality—have always struck readers, including the earliest ones who copied out Shakespeare's lines, as deeply genuine.

Historical candidates, therefore, have always been sought. Alleged dark ladies have included the wife of Shakespeare's printer Richard Field, the poet Emilia Lanyer, who was also a mistress of a later patron of Shakespeare's, and many others. Rival poets have centered on Christopher Marlowe and George Chapman especially (the latter's verse style accords well with sonnet 86's "proud full sail" comment). The main debate about the fair youth's identity will be picked up later; it involves the publication of the *Sonnets* in 1609 and arguments about when the sonnets were composed. For now it is sufficient to identify Henry Wriothesley as a longstanding choice, which presupposes that Shakespeare wrote many of the sonnets to him or about him during the plague years of 1592–94. It also is compatible with the patron relationship dealt with more publicly in Shakespeare's dedicatory letters to the two narrative poems. Maybe these sonnets' events reflect a professional relationship between the writer of twenty-nine and the young man of twenty; maybe that relationship soon grew into something more intimate. The sonnets themselves give us no definitive answers.

A homosexual relationship between the nobleman and (gasp!) a stage player hardly would have been the desired outcome for Wriothesley's family, especially if you find convincing one theory about the genesis of the first seventeen sonnets, called the "procreation" sonnets. This theory posits that Wriothesley's mother may have employed Shakespeare to write those poems, which do in fact have a made-to-order quality compared with later, more emotionally intense sonnets. This group of poems diversely urges the young man to "breed"—that is, to marry (and remember how Wriothesley was resisting his guardian's wish for him to marry)—and to recreate himself in a male heir, who will keep the young man's beauty alive. Soon, however, the poems arrive at a different solution—the sonnets themselves will immortalize

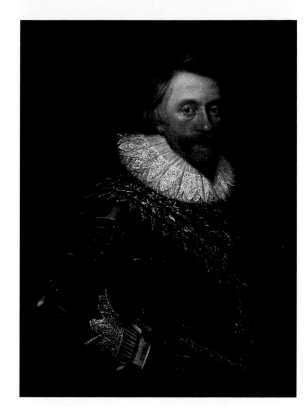

A seventeenth-century portrait of Henry Wriothesley, third Earl of Southampton and Shakespeare's patron. Shakespeare dedicated his poems *Venus and Adonis* and *The Rape of Lucrece* to Wriothesley. *(Daniel Mytens)*

the young man's beauty: "Yet do thy worst, old Time: despite thy wrong, / My love shall in my verse ever live young" (sonnet 19). Many of the following poems rehearse this theme of immortality through great poetry, which the Roman writer Horace famously declared in his *Odes*. Shakespeare echoes that confidence in sonnet 55: "Not marble nor the gilded monuments / Of princes shall outlive this powerful rhyme[.]" Our continued reading of these sonnets today makes this argument more convincing, and likewise persuasive are some sonnets' famous pronouncements of love: "Shall I compare thee to a summer's day?" (18), "Let me not to the marriage of true minds" (116), and so forth. No, these later poems and the closeness they imply would not have pleased Wriothesley's mother at all, and she would have been as scandalized by the class difference of the men (nobleman vs. actor) as by their difference in ages or the same-sex nature of their relationship.

Again, we must proceed cautiously. Here details of biography quickly pass over into theory, and if we look for secret codes and hidden names in the sonnets, as some have done, we go even farther afield into conspiracy theory. The esteemed biographer Samuel Schoenbaum is right to warn us against "biographical license" when reading the sonnets, for "the ambiguous language of poetry resists the fragile certitude of interpreters." Yet we might usefully conclude this focus on the *Sonnets* with an anecdote, found in early biographies, that Wriothesley gave Shakespeare one thousand pounds "to enable him to go through with a Purchase which he heard he had a mind to." Some have doubted this legendary gift: the amount is almost absurdly high, and the nobleman was in fact facing financial difficulties by the mid-1590s. One also wishes for more information about that "Purchase." However, there were a few things, all requiring significant financial outlay, that Shakespeare may have had in mind, as we shall soon see.

THE THEATERS REOPEN: THE LORD CHAMBERLAIN'S MEN

Following the plague years, the public theaters finally reopened in June 1594. Several details about these first resumed performances point to a weakened industry. First, the Lord Admiral's and the newly established Lord Chamberlain's Men had to team up to present a joint season. They performed on alternating days. Second, this season was extremely short—a mere ten days. Third, they performed at Newington Butts, in a theater farther from London than either the Rose in Bankside or the Theatre in Shoreditch. Were these first shows, in effect, public rehearsals, a chance for these tentative companies to mount productions before a more formal return? Were they not yet allowed to stage shows in London?

One thing is clear: the theater companies had suffered great financial setbacks during the long period of inactivity caused by the plague. This reemergence of the theater industry proved to be a time of regrouping, of reorganization, and, soon enough, a time of new power dynamics among the companies. Once dominant, the Queen's Men were already waning in influence in the early 1590s. Their number of performances at court (an ongoing sign of comparative esteem) declined, and Lord Strange's Men began to appear there more frequently. No matter how successful the Queen's Men had been in London previously, when the plague struck and the city's theaters closed, the company had no choice but to perform throughout the provinces. Pembroke's Men were forced to do this also, and it did not go well. The theater manager Philip Henslowe reported in September 1593 that this last company had been home for five or six weeks "for they cannot save their charges [i.e., expenses] with travel as I hear, and were fain [i.e.., desperate] to pawn their apparel for their charge." What we witness here is a dissolution of a once prominent acting company. Nevertheless, Strange's Men had no other option but to try their fortunes on tour.

Fortunately there exists a warrant for travel, granted by the Privy Council in May 1593, that lists the actors. Edward Alleyn appears there. He was already famous as the main tragedian in Christopher Marlowe's plays. He had transferred to Strange's Men, but would return to the Admiral's Men when that company regrouped, eventually performing once again at the Rose Theatre. The warrant does not list Shakespeare's name, but it does include various actors with whom he would soon work: William Kemp, Thomas Pope, John Heminge, Augustine Phillips. We remember them today because they were original members, and fellow actors with Shakespeare, in this new company known as the Lord Chamberlain's Men. The name derived from their powerful patron, Henry Carey, first Baron Hunsdon and Lord Chamberlain. In October 1594, he requested of London's Lord Mayor that his "nowe company of players" be permitted to perform throughout the winter at the Cross Keys Inn, in Gracechurch Street. The company was fortunate to recruit Richard Burbage, who eventually would overtake Edward Alleyn as the greatest actor of the age (largely thanks to roles Shakespeare was to write for him). Burbage's family connection with the Theatre, which his father built, must have made that a natural location for the new company's future performances.

The Lord Chamberlain's Men made another, even more fortunate, acquisition when William Shakespeare joined the company. He may have been a part of the band of Strange's Men who joined initially (a "reunion of friends," according to one historian), or he may have been recruited slightly later. He would have appealed to Chamberlain's actors as an experienced actor himself, but was likely most attractive to them as an active, reliable playwright. He had already scored a number of stage successes before the plague struck. Soon he would be the company's "poet in ordinary," or house writer, providing the group with a regular supply of new plays, on average two per year, and sometimes, unfathomably, even more. The first recorded performance of *The Comedy of Errors*, on December 28, 1594, at Gray's Inn, one of London's law schools, may give us a glimpse of Shakespeare's new professional association. Were "the players" mentioned in the school diary the Lord Chamberlain's Men? If so, it is telling that they chose to perform one

of Shakespeare's (likely) existing plays. The performance punctuated a night of holiday dancing and general revelry. The diarist adds that the event was "ever afterwards called, *The Night of Errors*." This no doubt pleased the playwright. Imagine if you and your friends spent a memorable night together, part of which was spent seeing a film, after which you referred to that night out as "The Night of [Name of Film]." Any writer would be gratified by the work in question catching, and defining, playgoers' or moviegoers' memories.

The Lord Chamberlain's Men twice staged more important, and more verifiable, shows during this same holiday season, before Queen Elizabeth at the royal palace in Greenwich. These holiday performances are highly valuable because a record of payment exists, made three months later:

> March 15 [1595] To William Kempe, William Shakespeare, and Richard Burbage, servants to the Lord Chamberlain . . . for two several comedies or interludes showed by them before her Majesty in Christmas time last past . . .

This priceless record is the first to connect Shakespeare with his new playing company. It is the only official documentation of his name related to a specific dramatic performance. We may reasonably conjecture that Shakespeare was already a leading member of the Lord Chamberlain's Men, since he is listed with Kempe (the company's main comic actor) and Burbage (its main tragedian) as a joint payee. What's more, Shakespeare was also a shareholder in the company, that is, a partial owner, along with the other five actors mentioned above. This fact may argue for Shakespeare being an original member, or for his importance to the company in being allowed to make this investment.

The initial cost must have been great (this may have been the "Purchase" previously heard of with respect to Wriothesley's gift to the poet), but once paid, the prospect of profit sharing with other shareholders would have been a happy one. As he would repeatedly do, he made a shrewd business move. Shakespeare, by investing in the Lord Chamberlain's Men, found himself in an extremely rare and enviable position for a professional writer during the Renaissance. When he signed on, he could not have known the stability he would enjoy. Nearly twenty years later, Shakespeare would retire from this same company. Much sooner, almost immediately, he dazzled his fellow members with a series of outstanding plays.

NEW PLAYS AND A NEW POETIC LANGUAGE

In his wonderfully imagined essay "Shakespeare at Thirty," the poet and critic John Berryman attempts to take his readers to April 22, 1594, William Shakespeare's thirtieth birthday. "It would be an error to imagine him very young," Berryman helpfully reminds us. "He has been married almost twelve years, has (at least) three children, and Elizabethans age fast." So far Shakespeare has chiefly made his living as an actor, and lately he has found some traction as a poet seeking patronage from Henry Wriothesley. On this birthday, he is two weeks away from registering his *Rape of Lucrece* for publication. Most important, he is an ambitious playwright. Awaiting the reopening of London's public theaters, he is about to have what some would call an *annus mirabilis*—a miraculous year. The scholar Jonathan Bate recognizes in these new plays the fresh fruits of a sabbatical, even one enforced by plague. Shakespeare returned to the theater, Bate argues, "with a new-minted verbal art." In short order, the comedies *Love's Labour's Lost* and *A Midsummer Night's Dream* appeared, both of

which seem to have no immediate source. This may be a sign that Shakespeare was attempting to spread his wings artistically, although he—and Renaissance writers generally—had no qualms about imitating sources, whether ancient or recent. He would borrow existing storylines for the rest of his career.

A Midsummer Night's Dream represents Shakespeare's first great masterpiece of plotting. With almost eerie effortlessness, he weaves together four narratives: the Athenian hero Theseus and his fair Hippolyta, whose "nuptial hour / Draws on apace," as heard in the play's very first lines; the confused and confusing young lovers, Hermia, Helena, Lysander, and Demetrius; the powerful Oberon and Titania, rulers of fairy land; and the loveable "rude mechanicals," including Peter Quince and Nick Bottom, craftsmen and amateur thespians whose vigorous language makes them sound like comical, colorful laborers from Shakespeare's London, rather than anyone from ancient Athens.

Hermia's father, Egeus, wants his daughter to marry Demetrius, and appeals to Theseus to enforce his wish. Hermia, however, is in love with Lysander. Soon the young lovers defy the father and governor by fleeing Athens for the forest. Helena loves Demetrius, but he is too taken with Hermia to appreciate her. Both of them follow the first pair of lovers into the forest. Love, as is usually the case, is topsy-turvy in this play. To complicate matters further, a quarrel between the fairy king and queen erupts. Oberon sends his assistant, Puck or Robin Goodfellow, to apply to Titania a magical potion, which will make her enamored with the first person she sees. Oberon also orders Puck to apply some to Demetrius's eyes, since he has seen the truculent Athenian flee from the lovelorn Helena. Unfortunately, Puck uses the potion on Lysander, who awakes and instantly falls for Helena. Correcting himself,

Puck applies it to Demetrius as well. Suddenly, both young men are wooing Helena, who can only imagine she is being mocked. When poor Hermia awakes, she discovers herself abandoned. The two men are chasing after Helena.

"The course of true love never did run smooth," says Lysander, and he unwittingly prophesies the play's hijinks. Even so, Shakespeare deftly resolves these many comic tangles, and the play ends with a series of marriages. This conclusion is common enough in comedies, but the especially festive, ceremonial quality to this play's ending, or endings (one public, one private), have caught some critics' attention. They argue that the play was first performed at a manor house to celebrate a private wedding (thus Puck's concluding blessing of the "best bride-bed"). Similarly occasional may be Oberon's talk of a "fair vestal thronèd by the west," often taken as words in praise of Queen Elizabeth.

The play's comic high point is incontrovertibly the mechanicals' production of the Ovidian story of Pyramus and Thisbe. Their antics are ridiculous, and we are invited to laugh along with the more dignified lovers. Yet there remains something magical in the amateur troupe's enthusiasm and camaraderie. When Bottom tells his fellow actors, "our play is preferred," we may just hear how the Lord Chamberlain's Men reacted when they received invitations to perform at court. Finally, we also find here those qualities most beloved in Shakespearean comedy. These include visions of transformation, as when Bottom's head is "translated" into a donkey's head, and yet Titania still adores him, thanks to the magic potion. Another staple of Shakespeare's comedies is meditation on love, art, and imagination:

The lunatic, the lover and the poet
Are of imagination all compact:
One sees more devils than vast hell can
    hold,

That is, the madman: the lover, all as
    frantic,
Sees Helen's beauty in a brow of Egypt:
The poet's eye, in fine frenzy rolling,
Doth glance from heaven to earth, from
    earth to heaven;
And as imagination bodies forth
The forms of things unknown, the poet's
    pen
Turns them to shapes and gives to airy
    nothing
A local habitation and a name.

The poetry throughout is glorious, and nowhere more so in the lines above, when Theseus broods on the lovers' adventures outside Athens. These woods represent an early example of Shakespeare's celebrating the green world—a

Titania lavishes affection on Bottom in Act 4, Scene 1 of *A Midsummer Night's Dream*. This painting is from 1793–94. *(Johann Heinrich Füssli)*

place of retreat from regular society, with its laws, institutions, and careful distinctions. Characters may arrive in this "space set apart" in a state of disorder, or encounter disorder there, but this space also invites self-discovery, social harmony, new wisdom.

Love's Labour's Lost features a retreat of a different sort. There King Ferdinand of Navarre vows to turn his court into a "little academe, / Still and contemplative in living art." Women are banned from his "silent court" for three years, but when the Princess of France, her attendant Rosaline, and other ladies arrive, Navarre and his courtiers—Berowne, Longaville, and Dumaine—promptly fall in love with them. Disguises and sonnet intrigues ensue in this mannered comedy, which like Midsummer meditates variously on love and desire. Also like Midsummer, Love's Labour's Lost features inset performances, from the lords disguised as Muscovites to the Pageant of the Nine Worthies. The latter play ends on a vastly different, more mournful note, however. The Princess learns that her father has died, necessitating the ladies' immediate departure. Marriages are on the horizon, we are promised, but there is neither resolution nor consolation now: "Our wooing doth not end like an old play; / Jack hath not Jill[.]"

John Berryman, our opening critical voice above, sees more wit than heart in this elaborate, intellectualized play, although he claims a third play, Romeo and Juliet, was the "first dramatic labour ever to fully engage Shakespeare's heart." This tale of woe about "a pair of star-crossed lovers" was well known, and the play relies on Arthur Brooke's lengthy poem, "The Tragical History of Romeus and Juliet" (1567, reprinted 1587). Yet another play was produced during this magical period of 1594–95, Richard II, and like Romeo and Juliet, it had clear sources as well, this time in the chronicles of English history by the likes of Edward Hall and Raphael Holinshed. Each of these plays deserves some brief comments and appreciations as well.

Berryman and others have suspected that Romeo and Juliet was the first play Shakespeare completed for the Lord Chamberlain's Men. This may explain the bravura sensed throughout its lines, as well as its experimental spirit in terms of genre (it is tragic in its ending, but steadily comic in its romance, talk of courtship and marriage, and puns and gags). It is tempting to imagine the author himself speaking the Chorus's opening lines: "Two households, both alike in dignity, / In fair Verona, where we lay our scene"— this last phrase makes explicit the playwright's work of making this tragic tale from Italy believable, somehow, on a Renaissance London stage. This focus continues when he describes what is to follow—"The fearful passage of their death-marked love"—as, in essence, "the two hours' traffic of our stage."

From the outset, the play is full of heated emotions. The conflict here involves the warring Montague and Capulet families, and Romeo's and Juliet's doomed attempt at love despite this familial strife. Aggression and hostility permeate the play, until dulled by the leaden reaction to the youths' deaths. The energy of adolescent love both lightens the mood and makes it feel emotionally turbulent. In an early speech, Romeo's friend Benvolio reports how "A troubled mind drave me to walk abroad / Where, underneath a grove of sycamore" he saw Romeo. Both young men, it seems, suffer from love melancholy: "Towards him I made, but he was ware of me / And stole into the covert of the wood." On the other hand, as Stanley Wells has lately argued in Shakespeare, Sex, and Love, this is "also one of the bawdiest of Shakespeare's plays, riddled with sexual puns, double meanings, and bawdy innuendo." This verbal transgression finds its character equivalents in some of the male supporting roles, especially Mercutio, Romeo's randy friend, and Tybalt, Juliet's Capulet cousin. Even the Nurse, who memorably recalls Juliet's early days, is rendered with new dramatic power.

The writing in *Romeo and Juliet* achieves a number of virtuostic displays (such as Mercutio's extended speech on Queen Mab), and it ornaments its best scenes with lyrical beauty. That opening choric speech is in sonnet form, and Shakespeare places a sonnet within the play as well. He also did this in *Love's Labour's Lost*, but there the sonnets are recited as such, straightforwardly. In *Romeo and Juliet*, he is altogether more artful and subtle when Romeo first meets Juliet at the Capulets' masked ball. There the quatrains, or four-line stanza units, determine the pace of the dialogue, giving it a flirtatious, back-and-forth quality. Both say a single line at the end to form, fittingly, a concluding couplet to the sonnet, which they further punctuate with their first kiss.

Romeo notes Juliet's beauty even in death in Act 5, Scene 3 of *Romeo and Juliet*. This painting is from 1809. *(Johann Heinrich Füssli)*

Of course, some of the play's most famous lines, in one of the greatest love scenes in literature, occur at Juliet's balcony. "But soft! What light through yonder window breaks?" asks Romeo upon seeing Juliet above, likely in the theater's gallery space. "It is the East, and Juliet is the sun!" Soon he overhears her pondering their feuding families and fated meeting: "O Romeo, Romeo! wherefore [i.e., why] are thou Romeo? . . . What's in a name? That which we call a rose / By any other name would smell as sweet." *Romeo and Juliet* remains one of Shakespeare's most frequently read and staged plays. You may know firsthand one explanation for this durability: its status as a standard play for reading in English classrooms and staging in high school, college, and community theaters. Some treat the play begrudgingly, as a traumatic school experience. One humorous Internet list of student exam responses reflects this. When asked "How does Romeo's character develop throughout the play?" one reader, apparently frustrated with Romeo's highly rhetorical language, replied, "It doesn't, it's just self, self, self, all the way through." For many, however, it is a formative work for reading or acting, encountered during that transition from childhood to young adulthood. This early tragedy is, in short, a classic. Yet like many classics that have taken root in culture, it is also capable of continuous change in style and emphasis. Therefore it can refract our contemporary values and anxieties back upon us. For example, influential films by Franco Zeffirelli and Baz Luhrmann have visually interpreted Shakespeare's text for their own generations. And various pop songs or films such as *Letters to Juliet* constantly keep the iconic lovers in our imaginations. More seriously, the educator Sue Gregory points out that seismic world events, and children's exposure to them, also shape how literary works are received in the classroom. She focuses on the opening of Luhrmann's popular movie, in which a discarded cigarette ignites a pool of gasoline. It creates a visual introduction to "the fiery Tybalt," but for Gregory, it cannot but be associated with the ubiquitous television imagery of the attacks on the World Trade Center on 9/11. In this way, Shakespeare remains vital, insofar as he remains both culturally and educationally inviting and troubling.

Richard II is the final play that seems to burst out of Shakespeare's imagination in 1595, with a new level of poetic expression. Despite being a history play, *Richard II* is generally held up as one of Shakespeare's most "literary" works—its title character acts and thinks more like a poet than a king, which is precisely his problem. It is also composed entirely in verse. Often the play is grouped within a sub-genre of English history plays known as the "weak-king" plays. *Thomas of Woodstock* and, more importantly, *Edward II*, Christopher Marlowe's last great play, are other examples, and against them the dramatic and poetic maturity of *Richard II* compares well. It is also important as a history play because it inaugurated Shakespeare's second, even greater tetralogy of history plays, which occupied him for the last half of the 1590s. The following plays were to be *Henry IV*, parts 1 and 2, and *Henry V*; the whole series is popularly known as the *Henriad*. Taken together, the plays represent Shakespeare's greatest accomplishment in the genre of the history play.

Shakespeare's *Richard II*, like the earlier history play *Richard III*, also follows a tragic arc, and is sometimes associated with this genre as well: the storyline here concludes with the eventual murder of King Richard II. More deeply, his tragedy results from being the wrong kind of person for his given, sovereign role. We quickly encounter in Richard an incompetent, decadent ruler too easily led by greedy favorites at court, called "caterpillars of the commonwealth." Shakespeare pow-

erfully juxtaposes this lack of rule and harmful influence with scenes and speeches framing England patriotically. They show a country worthy of a greater leader, and include a superbly rendered garden scene, and John of Gaunt's famous speech, still heard on U.K. tourist commercials, in praise of "This royal throne of kings, this scepter'd isle

Portrait of Richard II, ca. 1390 *(Artist unknown)*

/ . . . / This blessed plot, this earth, this realm, this England." Such a leader tantalizingly appears in the figure of Henry Bolingbroke, who defies King Richard and returns from exile, ostensibly to reclaim lands and titles wrongfully seized from him. Richard is impolitic and underestimates Bolingbroke's threat to his seemingly secure royal power. "Not all the water in the rough rude sea / Can wash the balm off from an anointed king." Henry is more aware that force sometimes wins out over legitimate rule. When he defeats Richard in battle, Henry seems unprepared for the necessary consequences of his success—Richard's deposition and death, and Henry's own assumption to the throne.

Shakespeare boldly dramatizes Richard's deposition, a highly sensitive event, especially in the waning years of the aging Elizabeth's own reign. (This scene would not be included in publications of *Richard II* till 1608.) That said, the personal rather than the political is the most poignant matter. However unworthy Richard has proven to be as king, he retains a royal aspect. It only grows in nobility and dignity as he endures his removal and suffering and death late in the play. Majestic descriptions of Richard give way to those of the martyr, and Richard himself compares his outcast state to that of Jesus: "So Judas did to Christ. But he, in twelve, / Found truth in all but one; I, in twelve thousand, none." Richard, peering into a mirror, soon shatters it into a "hundred shivers," a symbol not only of his deposition, but of his personal dissolution as well. The play becomes a solemn testimony about the surprising trials of kingship.

THE EMERGENCE OF SHAKESPEARE THE AUTHOR

The earliest tribute to Shakespeare in which he is expressly named appeared in 1594: "Yet Tarquin plucked his glistering grape, / And Shake-speare paints poor Lucrece's rape," a clear reference to Shakespeare the poet, and his *Rape of Lucrece* in particular. It was also a critical year for Shakespeare's reputation as a playwright. His first plays began to appear in printed form, in quarto format. His name was not attached to any of these books, however. *Titus Andronicus* was first published in this way, followed by *The First Part on the Contention betwixt the two famous houses of York and Lancaster* (a version of *2 Henry VI*) and, more tenuously, a play called *The Taming of a Shrew* (notice the article difference), that corrupt version of Shakespeare's original play, or one inspired by the original and loosely resembling it. The absence of an author's name on these quarto publications was no slight to Shakespeare directly. The age generally undervalued authors, especially playwrights: plays belonged to the theater companies, and writers received no compensation, or royalties, upon publication of their plays later. In almost all cases, publishers didn't bother to include the author's name on a play's title page. To illustrate, consider this witty exchange between a producer and theater manager in the film *Shakespeare in Love*: "Who's that?" the first asks, pointing to a young Will Shakespeare. "Nobody, he's the writer," responds the manager.

In 1595, there appeared *The True Tragedy of Richard, Duke of York* (a version of *3 Henry VI*). Two years later, a trio of Shakespeare's works appeared in print: *Romeo and Juliet*, *Richard II*, and *Richard III*. All of these plays soon enjoyed further reprintings. The next year, 1598, was a watershed: plays began to bear Shakespeare's name. *Love's Labour's Lost* is by "W. Shakespere" [sic], followed in 1599 by a reprinting of *1 Henry IV* (first published anonymously the year before), "Newly corrected by W. Shakespeare." Now, this identification didn't change everything—other plays continued to appear anonymously—but clearly Shakespeare's fame was increasing by the late 1590s. His name was now something to reckon with commercially. The absence of Shakespeare's name from his plays (or of dedications, or commendations from others) has supported the popular myth that he never cared about the publication of mere plays. However, recent books such as Lukas Erne's important *Shakespeare as Literary Dramatist* and the collection *Shakespeare's Book* have challenged that tradition. Erne's persuasive argument suggests that Shakespeare worked all along as a poet-playwright for the page, as much as for the stage, even when his plays appeared anonymously.

Shakespeare's fame reached a new level in 1598, thanks to a comment in Francis Meres's *Palladis Tamia* ("Wit's Treasury"). Meres himself is now famous for giving the first detailed evidence of Shakespeare's fame, or at least his very high standing among London literary types:

> As *Plautus* and *Seneca* are accounted the best for Comedy and Tragedy among the Latins: so *Shakespeare* among the English is the most excellent in both kinds for the stage; for Comedy, witness his *Gentlemen of Verona*, his *Errors*, his *Love Labors Lost*, his *Love Labours Wonne*, his *Midsummer Night Dream*, & his *Merchant of Venice* : for Tragedy his *Richard the 2. Richard the 3. Henry the 4., King John, Titus Andronicus* and his *Romeo* and *Juliet*.

Meres's catalog appears in a section entitled "Comparative discourse of our English poets, with the Greek, Latin, and Italian poets." Just before, he compares Shakespeare as a poet to Ovid, and here, breathtakingly, he compares him to both the comedy writer Plautus and the tragedy writer Seneca. He simply says that Shakespeare is England's most talented, accomplished playwright "in both kinds for the stage." Additionally, the list he provides of Shakespeare's known plays to date is priceless for scholars and theater historians today. That said, his list was not even complete, and the corpus of plays it sought to compile was already growing. Shakespeare was becoming famous, and all the while he remained highly industrious. New heights were still ahead.

Sources and Further Reading

Akrigg, G. P. V. *Shakespeare and the Earl of Southampton.* Cambridge, Mass.: Harvard University Press, 1968.

Berryman, John. "Shakespeare at Thirty," *Berryman's Shakespeare.* New York: Farrar, Straus and Giroux, 1999.

Callaghan, Dympna. *Shakespeare's Sonnets.* Malden, Mass : Blackwell Pub., 2007.

Cook, Judith. *Shakespeare's Players.* London: Harrap, 1983.

Erne, Lukas. *Shakespeare as Literary Dramatist.* New York : Cambridge University Press, 2003.

Hyland, Peter. *An Introduction to Shakespeare's Poems.* New York: Palgrave Macmillan, 2003.

Murphy, Andrew. *A Concise Companion to Shakespeare and the Text.* Malden, Mass : Blackwell Pub., 2007.

Wells, Stanley. *Shakespeare, Sex, and Love.* New York: Oxford University Press, 2010.

Wilson, F. P. *The Plague in Shakespeare's London.* Oxford, U.K.: Oxford University Press, 1999.

SHAKESPEARE BACK IN STRATFORD

The line between fact and conjecture is often thin. And with Shakespeare, frequently it is awfully thin. We know this much, and this knowledge, however basic and bare in detail, is reassuring: Shakespeare lived in Stratford, and had a family in Stratford, and increasingly he worked in London. We don't know how much time he spent in one place and how much in the other. We don't know how long he stayed once he arrived in either place. We do know about how long his travels would have taken from Stratford to London. We do know which routes he likely would have traveled. Oxford lies along one very common route to London, and the university city has long claimed Shakespeare for itself, at least as a passerby if not as a student. There exists one story, which has become by now a suggestive commonplace in biographies, that Shakespeare had an affair with one Mistress Davenant at the Cross Inn in Oxford. This incident, and the reputation it presupposes, is in fact consistent with other stories, anecdotes, or alleged traces in Shakespeare's plays and poems. Taken together, they present a picture of a middle-aged writer hardly squeamish in matters of the flesh, and possibly prone to extramarital romps. However, it must be remembered that this is merely a story, which is to say no documents or other evidence exist that would prove or even solidly support that story.

For that matter, nor do any records exist placing Shakespeare's wife, Anne, or any of his children with him during his London residence, although certainly this arrangement is not impossible. Nonetheless, the popular image has him writing alone, acting with his company, and hanging out with his friends while in the city—a sort of second bachelorhood, if not childhood. John Aubrey, in his late-seventeenth-century collection of *Brief Lives*, reports that Shakespeare "was wont to go to his native country once a year."

In fact, he may have been present in Stratford far more often, and for greater lengths of time than usually imagined, especially when it was off-season for London's theaters. It will be important for us to remember—as we soon survey diverse traces of Shakespeare in London and summarize the increasing number of plays he wrote for London's stages—that his family life in Stratford did not vanish during his residence and working days in the city. Quite the contrary. Stratford may have remained foremost in his mind, and the people there those he most valued. At the very least, and more verifiably, a few developments from this same period make it clear that Shakespeare's long-term interests, with respect to properties and investments, were far more focused on his hometown and his family there. Sometimes family demands, or losses, called him home as well.

A TRAGEDY IN STRATFORD

The Stratford Burial Register includes the following listing for August 11, 1596: "Hamnet filius William Shakspeare" (Hamnet, son of William Shakespeare). It is a concentrating, clarifying moment in Shakespeare's life—one of those shattering family events that defines a person's life, and continues to assail grieving parents. Shakespeare's lost son was eleven years old. Some historians would argue that the word "tragedy" used above belies how an English Renaissance family must have reacted when mortality struck, an all-too-frequent occurrence. Should we call Hamnet's death a "tragedy," exactly, when (by some accounts) one third of children did not live any longer than Shakespeare's son? The writer himself had lost sisters during his boyhood, and when the plague struck Stratford, a neighboring home soon lost all four of its children to the epidemic. Unquestionably, death was a more common fact of life (so to speak) in Shakespeare's day compared with our own, and families would have confronted losses of their kin and friends and neighbors in more straightforward ways, if no less painfully.

We must not minimize the impact of such a death, nor can most of us presume to know what a parent goes through following the loss of a child. On the other hand, it seems easy, or at least fairly safe and justifiable, to imagine that the death of Shakespeare's only son must have struck him as a devastating blow. His immediate family—his wife, Anne; his daughters, Susanna and Judith (Hamnet's twin sister); his parents, John and Mary—must have been especially affected since, unlike the boy's father, they had seen Hamnet grow up day by day, all living together in the Shakespeares' Henley Street home.

As we consider this loss, we would hope that Shakespeare had been present for his son's burial at Stratford's Holy Trinity Church. It may or may not have been so. If Hamnet had suffered a gradually worsening illness, then Shakespeare may have gotten word of his son's decline well before his death. This news would have taken three to four days to reach the father, who then would need three to four days to travel the nearly one hundred miles to Stratford. The father may have also been farther afield from London, performing on the road with the Lord Chamberlain's Men during a summer that was turbulent for London theaters. By then, if Hamnet's death were sudden, the boy may have been dead, and buried even, before his father arrived. Those present on August 11 must have heard the words of the Anglican burial service:

> . . . we therefore commit his body to the ground, earth to earth, ashes to ashes, dust to dust; in sure and certain hope of the Resurrection to eternal life.

The family's neighbors, Hamnet and Judith Sadler, for whom the twins were named, would almost certainly have been present, too. The baker and his wife would have shared the family's state of mourning.

Shakespeare's rival Ben Jonson was also a father, and also suffered the loss of children of a young age, but with one major difference: Jonson as a poet commemorated the deaths of both a son and a daughter in memorable elegies. "Farewell, thou child of my right hand, and joy, / My sin was too much hope of thee, loved boy," he writes movingly in the short poem "On the Death of His Son." No such poem exists by Shakespeare, although some readers have traditionally found less personal, more refracted feelings of a parent's grief in the plays' diverse dramatic contexts. For example, critics have often remarked upon the seeming paradox that Shakespeare responded to his son's death with a series of comic masterpieces in the years following—characters such as Falstaff, Benedick and Beatrice, and Rosalind, along with plays such as *As You Like It* and *Twelfth Night*. But isn't this a simplistic way to measure the complicated feelings within any person, much less in one of literature's great creators? It also risks evaluating genres too simplistically. For example, both of the late comedies mentioned above begin under the threat of death or are haunted by deep loss. In *Twelfth Night*, we first meet Olivia in seven years' mourning for her dead brother, and Viola spends most of the play believing her brother Sebastian has perished in a

Hamlet and Horatio speak with the gravediggers in Act 5, Scene 1 of Hamlet. This painting is from 1839.
(*Eugène Delacroix*)

shipwreck that separated them. Of course, *Hamlet* (note the similarity of names) is a play that is also haunted—most obviously by the ghost of a dead father, but also by the memory of a dead son. Even later in his career, Shakespeare in *The Winter's Tale* has one character describe a "young prince" as "all my exercise, my mirth, my matter," and soon King Leontes's son Mamillius becomes ill and dies. Different readers, directors, or actors will find varying degrees of biography in such scenes.

KING JOHN

One of the most memorable examples of this grief-stricken writing and representation appears in *King John*. It may seem an unlikely source, considering that the play is one of Shakespeare's stray English history plays, a popular dramatic genre throughout the 1590s. If he completed the play after Hamnet's death in 1596, then the character of Constance, who laments the imprisonment and death of her son, Arthur, would make a startling mouthpiece for the author's own reality as a mournful parent. Some critics, however, date this not entirely successful play earlier, anywhere from 1594–95 back to the very beginning of Shakespeare's playwriting career. In any case, Constance's words can still make one shudder, as when she addresses Cardinal Pandulf: "And, father cardinal, I have heard you say / That we shall see and know our friends in heaven: / If that be true, I shall see my boy again." Unfortunately, she can only imagine her "pretty Arthur" as utterly changed by death, and so "hollow as a ghost" that she will not recognize him in the "court of heaven." Furthermore, neither the cardinal nor King Philip is particularly sympathetic, a stance that draws from Constance an even more passionate expression:

> Grief fills the room up of my absent child,
> Lies in his bed, walks up and down with
>   me,

> Puts on his pretty looks, repeats his words,
> Remembers me of all his gracious parts,
> Stuffs out his vacant garments with his
>   form;
> Then, have I reason to be fond of grief?
> Fare you well: had you such a loss as I,
> I could give better comfort than you do.

Arthur's mother is not the only character to register the absence of the legitimate prince, whose death has been ordered by the suspicious King John. "How easy thou dost take all England up," cries Falcounbridge upon seeing Hubert carry Arthur's corpse. Falcounbridge is, along with Aaron the Moor in *Titus Andronicus*, one of Shakespeare's greatest early dramatic achievements. Whenever he speaks, we are aware of a fully characterized figure onstage. He is also called Philip the Bastard. Early in the play, he discovers that his father is actually Richard the Lionheart, much to the adulterous embarrassment of his mother, Lady Falcounbridge. As the bigger political landscape of the play comes into focus, Falcounbridge will fight courageously and be unwavering in his loyalty to England.

The play opens with the French adversaries, King Philip II and his son, Lewis the Dauphin, threatening and eventually invading England. The pope and the Roman Catholic Church, present in the legate Cardinal Pandulph, further challenge English independence. Eventually King John will surrender his crown to the papacy, only to be crowned again by its authority. Shortly afterward, John retreats to a monastery, where a monk poisons him. These anti-papal and anti-clerical details made John's reign a ripe one for strongly anti-Catholic histories and dramas. At least two plays prior to Shakespeare's, including *The Troublesome Reign of King John* (1591), presented John as just such a proto-Protestant hero. The Protestant chronicler John Foxe included John's fate in his highly influential *Acts and*

Monuments, popularly called the "Book of Martyrs" and full of examples of papal tyranny and wickedness. This same focus was restored in a later, eighteenth-century adaptation of Shakespeare's play. Most interesting here is Shakespeare's strikingly exceptional point of view. Far from an English patriot and religious hero, his King John has come to the throne illegitimately, murders his nephew, loses territory to the French, and bends to papal intimidation. Shakespeare may or may not have been Catholic in his personal sympathies, but he certainly wished to go against the prevailing Protestant appropriation of King John and his story. That said, Shakespeare the writer for the popular stage was no dummy; he knew well how to capture and reflect the spirit, or "pressure," of his times, and his audiences' beliefs and passions. Therefore, his character Falcounbridge repeatedly steals the show and seizes the audience's applause, from his rant on "commodity" and duplicity at court, to his exhorting defense of his—and his audience's—native land: "This England never did, nor never shall, / Lie at the proud foot of a conqueror . . . / . . . Naught shall make us rue / If England to itself do rest but true." Curiously, Shakespeare chose not to include one detail for which historians today most remember King John: his signing in 1215 of the Magna Carta, a concession to his disaffected noblemen.

CONTINUED UNCERTAINTIES IN LONDON

Following his son's burial, Shakespeare likely was still reeling from news of another death just a few weeks earlier. On July 22, 1596, Henry Carey died. He was the queen's cousin, the Lord Chamberlain, and for the past two years had served as the powerful patron of Shakespeare's company of actors. His influential court position passed to one William Brooke, Lord Cobham, and this fact must have deeply worried Shakespeare and

his coworkers. Brooke was not inclined to these actors, or theatrical shows generally. In fact, around this same time he led a charge to ban performances of plays at inns, in effect eliminating the Lord Chamberlain's Men's run of winter performances at the Cross Keys Inn. Shakespeare himself may have felt more personal resentment toward Brooke. He was an adversary of the Earl of Southampton, who as we have seen was likely a patron of Shakespeare's poetry, and possibly quite close to the author himself. A theater controversy was about to break out, and it suggests that Shakespeare soon found himself in a full-blown feud with the powerful Brooke.

Shakespeare's company was taken over by Carey's son George, Lord Hunsdon, meaning that Shakespeare briefly wrote and acted for Lord Hunsdon's Men. The feeling among the men may have resembled that of a professional sports team today, when its front-office organization is shaken up by an ownership change. The publication of four of Shakespeare's plays during the next few years may be one sign of an ongoing struggle for the company, faced with long-term uncertainty or a precarious financial situation. Although the printing, sale, and circulation of these playbooks—*Richard II*, *Richard III*, *Love's Labour's Lost*, and *1 Henry IV* (quite a recent play to be appearing in print already)—helped to extend Shakespeare's reputation among London readers, the texts were technically the property of the troupe. Companies usually resisted publication because they feared it would compromise future performances by reducing the size of paying audiences.

It seems, then, that Shakespeare's company was in need of funds, and sought proceeds from the sale of these plays. That said, it is also possible that Shakespeare or the company wished to make available in book form authoritative editions of the plays; already a few pirated books had appeared, in one early biographer's words, "surreptitiously and lamely printed." The company received no profits from such editions, which typically featured incomplete or otherwise corrupted texts. For example, a 1597 printing of *Romeo and Juliet* was superseded by a better 1599 version, touted on its title page as "Newly corrected, augmented, and amended." The 1598 edition of *Love's Labour's Lost* is similarly announced as "Newly corrected and augmented," although no earlier copy has surfaced.

SHAKESPEARE'S POSSIBLE WORK "BEHIND" THE KNOWN WORKS

The extent of Shakespeare's involvement—correction, revision, or addition—of his plays as they were appearing in print raises the question of other writerly activities that may have kept him busy. For example, a tragedy entitled *Locrine* was published in 1595, and, according to its title page, was "Newly set foorth, overseene and corrected, by *W. S.*" Do we take these to be the initials of William Shakespeare? The play today is generally held to be the work of another, lesser writer. Likewise, his entire name would appear on the title page of *The London Prodigal* in 1605, and three years later, on a play entitled *A Yorkshire Tragedy*, now attributed to Thomas Middleton. All of these plays, along with a few others, were included in subsequent editions of the Folio, the "official" collected volume of Shakespeare's plays, and then eventually excluded as textual critics became more doubtful of their authenticity. Today, these suggestive initials may signal a couple of things: *Locrine* may have been the first of many publications that would attempt to make up for mediocre writing by attaching to itself the increasingly popular and prominent name of William Shakespeare. Alternately, it is just possible that his initials indicate a kind of signature of work completed—that is, he may have been responsible for completing or otherwise overseeing this anonymous play into print.

The most famous example of Shakespeare's early collaborative activity occurs in a complicated manuscript known as "The Book of Sir Thomas More." Never printed, this fascinating collection of scenes illustrates better than any other document the sometimes messy business of composing and completing a play for the English Renaissance stage. The play was first written by Anthony Munday, a writer of several different kinds of books (travel exposé, journalism, prophecy, ballads, historical chronicle, plays, romances in translation), and perhaps by Henry Chettle as well, either in 1593–94 or 1600–04—scholars have not been able to agree on the composition dates. The original copy was submitted to the Master of the Revels, Edmund Tilney (the queen's censor, in effect), and he demanded various changes. "This must be new written," he demands in one place. Munday's first version was then extensively revised: passages were deleted, and scenes removed or rearranged. Moreover, a number of new passages or scenes was added to the manuscript, and these additions display at least five different handwriting examples. In other words, a host of new writers was brought in to complete the play in a satisfactory way. These included Thomas Heywood; Thomas Dekker, who likely provided scenes heavy with apprentices' dialogue; and, it has been believed since 1871, William Shakespeare. That belief is as strong as ever today: *Sir Thomas More* has just appeared as a new title in the prestigious, scholastically authoritative Arden Shakespeare series.

Most scholars today believe, or wish to believe, that the sixth scene of "The Book of Sir Thomas More," commonly called the "Ill May Day" scene, features three folio pages written by, and full of corrections by, Shakespeare. Known as "Hand D," this handwriting, if it is Shakespeare's, is the only example we have of the writer at work—and, in this case, extensively so. The scholar John Jones describes the section as a first draft of a "focal episode" in the play. In this particular scene, Thomas More must speak eloquently to dissuade May Day rioters from attacking London's immigrants, or "strangers":

Grant them removed, and grant that this
    your noise
Hath chid down all the majesty of England.
Imagine that you see the wretched
    strangers,
Their babies at their backs, with their poor
    luggage,
Plodding to th' ports and coasts for
    transportation,
And that you sit as kings in your desires,
Authority quite silenced by your brawl,
And you in ruff of your opinions clothed:
What had you got? I'll tell you: you had
    taught
How insolence and strong hand should
    prevail,
How order should be quelled. And by this
    pattern
Not one of you should live an aged man;
For other ruffians, as their fancies wrought,
With selfsame hand, self reasons, and self
    right,
Would shark on you, and men, like raven-
    ous fishes,
Would feed on one another.

This scene of uprising (or "insurrection," as the censor objected), taking place in London, would have been a highly sensitive one; it surely would have drawn the authorities' scrutiny. Shakespeare, as the theory goes, might have been called in as a "rebellion-scene" specialist in order to ensure that this episode in Thomas More's story

was handled carefully, and perhaps to make sure that the title character was properly articulate—and in favor of order—at this crucial moment. In this respect, Shakespeare (if Hand D was indeed his) did not disappoint. Indeed, Shakespeare did have a knack for such scenes, from his rendering of Jack Cade's rebellion in *2 Henry VI* to his later treatment in *Coriolanus* of Menenius Agrippa calming the Roman crowd. More's powerful lines against disorder and "innovation" would have appeased the authorities, or so it seems, yet the play remained unpublished till the twentieth century. Whether or not it was ever performed remains a mystery.

The Reign of King Edward III represents another play increasingly attributed to Shakespeare—or rather, certain scenes may be by him. The play first appeared in print in 1596, described as "sundry times played about the city of London." It must have greatly appealed to its first audiences, focusing as it does on a popular king and his legendary son, the Black Prince, a martial hero whom we see achieve victory at the famous battles of Crécy and Poitiers in France. The story of *Edward III* is largely taken from Holinshed's *Chronicles*, a source that Shakespeare often adapted, and Froissart's *Chronicles of France*. Edward's military aggression led to the Hundred Years' War in the fourteenth century, and this monarch fared much differently from his ill-fated father, Edward II, whose tragic reign Marlowe had successfully dramatized a few years earlier. Was Shakespeare interested in one-upping his greatest rival with a play about a more theatrically promising monarch? The best poetry in this play, which is exclusively written in verse, features the king's attempted seduction of the beautiful Countess of Salisbury in the second act. The final line of Shakespeare's sonnet 94 even appears there. Again, he may have been hired in an ad hoc way to spice up or diversify one more

This portrait of King Edward III was done long after his death, probably in Shakespeare's time, around the late 1500s. *(Artist unknown)*

dent plagiarism, showed two hundred matches of phrases of three or more words between *Edward III* and Shakespeare's other plays and poems. It moreover suggested that Shakespeare may have collaborated with his fellow Elizabethan dramatist Thomas Kyd. No doubt this debate will continue.

Additionally, we must also consider that sort of literary activity that, by its very nature, is never retained or has escaped recording. The scholar John Berryman, being a poet himself, could more easily imagine Shakespeare beginning this or that project but then setting it aside, a false start destined to be left unfinished. Homer nods, as the saying goes, and no creative writer, not even Shakespeare, performs perfectly, or even satisfactorily, every single time.

We also have mystery works, which may have been completed but now are lost to us, such as the play tantalizingly listed by Francis Meres in 1598: *Love's Labour's Won*. Was this simply another title for *The Taming of the Shrew*, as has been suggested, or did Shakespeare instead follow up the abrupt, incompletely comedic ending of *Love's Labour's Lost* with a happier, more traditional sequel?

In poetic realms, too, Shakespeare seems to have stayed busy, or at least others stayed busy for him. In 1599, William Jaggard published *The Passionate Pilgrim*, a poetry anthology attributed in its entirety to "W. Shakespeare." In truth, only five poems appear to be his: two genuine sonnets, 138 ("When my love swears that she is made of truth") and 146 ("Two loves I have, of comfort and despair"), in print for the first time here, along with three sonnets extracted from their dramatic contexts in *Love's Labour's Lost* ("Did not the heavenly rhetoric of thine eye"; "If love make me forsworn, how shall I swear to love"; "On a day (alack the day!)"). Even if Jaggard hadn't claimed that Shakespeare was the author of all selections

history play, to make it stand out from a crowded field of similar works.

Edward Capell was the first editor, in the eighteenth century, to add the play to Shakespeare's canon, doing so on the basis of its being good enough that no other contemporary could have written it. There has been little agreement on Shakespeare's authorship since then, although in recent years his case has grown. The Royal Shakespeare Company first produced the play in 2002, and an edition is now available in the esteemed New Cambridge Shakespeare series. (It also appears in the authoritative Riverside and Oxford Shakespeare volumes of Shakespeare's complete works.) As recently at 2009, the scholar Brian Vickers reported to *The Times* of London that a computer program, designed to detect stuin *The Passionate Pilgrim*, Shakespeare might still have resented not being asked permission, especially about the last three of his own poems. What had been contextually apt poems in *Love's Labour's Lost*, finely and comically modulated to the characters reciting them, in this context seem like the poet Shakespeare's best efforts. Shakespeare had to get used to such treatment: the following year another collection, *Belvedere, or, The Garden of the Muses*, culled more than two hundred passages from his plays and poems.

THE MERCHANT OF VENICE AND MUCH ADO ABOUT NOTHING

Whatever else occupied Shakespeare's time, during these years he was continuing to dedicate himself to the writing of new plays. Until the opening of the new Globe Theatre demanded bold new works, he focused exclusively on two genres that fit the time: Italianate comedy, as seen in *The Merchant of Venice* and *Much Ado About Nothing*, and English history, which Shakespeare raised to an even higher level in that series of plays known as the *Henriad* (to be treated in the next chapter). These last three history plays would connect both with *Richard II*, to form a second tetralogy, and with his first tetralogy of history plays completed earlier in the decade. Thus Shakespeare began his exciting new phase of writing and performing at the Globe with the kind of momentum most writers could only dream of experiencing.

Shakespeare completed *The Merchant of Venice* in 1596–97, perhaps during a longer stint at home in Stratford, or perhaps during any free time he could seize from his busy theater days in London. In any case, this comedy has proven to be one of his most popular, and controversial, plays. For one thing, it is by no means always played as a comedy. Some have heard, through the conflicted character of Antonio, a melancholy note that sounds throughout the play—"in sooth, I know not why I am so sad," he says at the beginning. Antonio's deep affection for Bassanio, and his willingness to support his friend's desires, lead him to imminent danger: this Christian merchant of Venice will overextend himself—by bonding his very flesh to Shylock, a Jewish moneylender—to make possible Bassanio's grand trip to Belmont to woo Portia. The play then becomes a tale of two places: the mercantile world of Venice, where law is stern and unyielding, versus the more free, feminine, and dreamlike world of Portia's Belmont. This latter setting will happily seal the nuptial resolutions there, as Portia and her servant Nerissa return from their saving work, disguised as men: "That light we see is burning in my hall. / So shines a good deed in a naughty world."

Portia has traveled to Venice to save her new love Bassanio's friend, Antonio, who is on trial. He must be spared from the clutches of the law and from the cruel determination of Shylock to have, as the bond allows, a pound of Antonio's flesh if he must be financially forfeit. Her main appeal, delivered while disguised as a male lawyer, becomes one of Shakespeare's most famous speeches:

> The quality of mercy is not strain'd;
> It droppeth as the gentle rain from heaven
> Upon the place beneath. It is twice blest—
> It blesseth him that gives, and him that
>   takes.
> 'Tis mightiest in the mightiest. It becomes
> The throned monarch better than his
>   crown.

Taken out of context, it sounds like a speech of extreme gentleness and meekness, but in the play, Portia is just about to turn her argument and bring the full force of Venetian justice upon Shylock; ironically, she is better able to hold to the letter of the law than he, and her sparing of Antonio and ruining of, and forced conversion of, Shylock create a range of mixed reactions in modern audiences. No matter one's response, in Portia Shakespeare had achieved a new level of representation in this strong, articulate, incredibly pragmatic heroine.

More centrally, and with regard to Shylock's fate, this comic play's genre tensions have increased in the wake of cataclysmic modern events, primarily the Holocaust, or the Nazis' deportment, detainment, and mass killing of Europe's Jewish population during World War II. So heavily does history weigh on *The Merchant of Venice* that often in productions today, Shylock becomes the protagonist, or at least a character capable of earning our deep sympathy, while the Venetians frequently appear crass and hypocritical at best, or cruel Christian persecutors at worst.

It is safe to say that Shakespeare never intended for Shylock to become the hero of this play. For example, often Shylock is as dismissive of the Venetian Christians as they are of him: "I will buy with you, sell with you, talk with you, walk with you, but I will not eat with you, drink with you, nor pray with you." Furthermore, he sometimes comes off unsympathetically as the father of Jessica, who soon elopes with Lorenzo. We hear of his reaction to her flight only in caricature, as reported by two Venetians, Salerio and Solanio: "My daughter, O my ducats, O my daughter!" they report him saying, letting the audience connect his own equivocation of his child and the riches she has taken. Shortly Shakespeare raises the dramatic stakes by presenting Shylock in his own, vindictive words: "I would my daughter were dead at my foot."

Most problematically, Shylock seems genuinely to expect a pound of flesh to be carved from Antonio's body, thus honoring the bond and fulfilling his murderous wishes. Mainly, Shylock must have seemed to Shakespeare's early audiences an *exotic* figure, since Jews had been expelled from England since 1290. Now, this lack of familiarity could lead to ugly caricatures. Shakespeare most definitely would have known a play by his great predecessor Christopher Marlowe, *The Jew of Malta*, whose title character is so excessive and flamboyant in his villainous acts that at times he seems like a mix of the medieval Vice figure and Shakespeare's own Richard III. An existing inventory list tells us that Marlowe's Jewish character wore onstage a red wig and a prosthetic nose.

Compared with Marlowe's play, which T. S. Eliot described as a "savage farce," *The Merchant of Venice* and Shylock in particular suddenly do seem to possess striking capacities for generating sympathy and compassion. It is hard to imagine Marlowe's Jew, pointedly called Barabas, saying these lines of Shylock's:

> I am a Jew. Hath not a Jew eyes? Hath not a Jew hands, organs, dimensions, senses, affections, passions? fed with the same food, hurt with the same weapons, subject to the same diseases, healed by the same means, warmed and cooled by the same winter and summer as a Christian is? If you prick us, do we not bleed? If you tickle us, do we not laugh? If you poison us, do we not die? And if you wrong us, shall we not revenge? If we are like you in the rest, we will resemble you in that.

Shylock's questions are deeply dignified, and keenly persuade us of humanity's universally shared experiences. Conversely, his final explanation about revenge—we seek revenge because in that we follow you, who claim to be above it—is fiercely confrontational, and in truth, the Venetians often seem too frivolous or biased to be capable of an adequate reply to that challenge.

Shylock hands Jessica his key in Act 2, Scene 5 of *The Merchant of Venice*. This painting is from 1887. *(Maurycy Gottlieb)*

and delicate desires," and so Claudio's feelings for Hero can grow. Yet he really only woos Hero once he realizes she is Leonato's sole heir. Is the young military hero capable of being a true lover? Or is he a fair-weather opportunist? Soon enough, the substance of Claudio's love, and the faithfulness therein, will be sorely tested—repeatedly so.

Leonato also has a niece, now orphaned, named Beatrice, and early in the play, she coolly asks after one Benedick, with whom she pretends to be unimpressed. Hailing from Padua, Benedick arrives and almost immediately begins his verbal battles with Beatrice; the "merry war" between the two of them soon became the most famous part of the play, although in one sense they are the secondary, initially non-romantic couple. In this respect, *Much Ado About Nothing* resembles in many ways Shakespeare's earlier play, *The Taming of the Shrew*, where the less promising, harsher relationship between Petruchio and Katherine soon blossoms, quickly overshadowing Lucentio's traditional but less interesting (and far less honest) courtship of Bianca.

The title of the present play suggests the ongoing theme of misapprehension, an error common in love, and one especially prevalent in the various plots here. For example, the vanquished Don John is allowed to join the festivities as well, though he quickly admits that he remains a "plain-dealing villain." He attempts to convince Claudio that Don Pedro intends to win Hero's heart, but this ploy doesn't work, and soon Claudio and Hero are betrothed. His next plan, however, is devastatingly effective. On the night before their wedding, Claudio is tricked into thinking he sees Hero acting unfaithfully, and promptly proceeds to condemn her and abandon her at the altar. Hero faints, and upon awaking, even her father rejects her claims of innocence. The play seems to nosedive as a comedy when it is announced that Hero has died of sadness.

And thus our sympathies among the characters will continue to oscillate.

Shakespeare likely completed another comedy, *Much Ado About Nothing*, by or around 1598. Instead of Venice, this play is set in Messina, in Sicily. There Don Pedro, a prince newly victorious over his illegitimate half-brother, Don John, has come to enjoy the hospitality of the local governor, Leonato. Claudio, who has distinguished himself in the wars, soon falls in love with Leonato's chaste daughter, Hero. The post-battle, courtly atmosphere invites all sorts of "soft

The play's darker aspect is also heard in Beatrice's fury on Hero's behalf. She wishes she could be a man to avenge her cousin. Barring this, she bluntly solicits Benedick's help: "Kill Claudio." Benedick suspects that Don John is up to no good, but nevertheless agrees to challenge Claudio. In the fifth act, the mournful Leonato laments the difficulties we all face in sympathizing with others' suffering:

> . . . Therefore give me no counsel.
> My griefs cry louder than advertisement. . . .
> I pray thee peace. I will be flesh and blood;
> For there was never yet philosopher
> That could endure the toothache patiently,
> However they have writ the style of gods
> And made a push at chance and sufferance.

Fortunately, all confusion is soon cleared up, Hero is revealed to be alive, and she and Claudio are reconciled. Most improbably, Don John's destructive plan is intercepted and reported for what it is by the comically misspeaking constable Dogberry and his assistant, Verges. Shakespeare clearly wrote this character for Will Kemp, the Lord Chamberlain's Men's best comic actor, famous for his clown-like behavior. (There is evidence for this identification in Shakespeare's First Folio, where the name "Kemp" appears instead of "Const," an abbreviation for "constable.") Kemp soon left the Chamberlain's Men, for reasons unknown, and in 1600 became the talk of London when he successfully jigged his way to Norwich over the course of nine days.

Throughout the ups and downs of Claudio's and Hero's relationship, Shakespeare works out the theme of misapprehension in a lighter, more fruitful way in the characters of Beatrice and Benedick. Certainly both lovers seem less than ready for, or even receptive to, love at the play's beginning. "That a woman conceiv'd me, I thank her," says Benedick, later adding that "Because

I will not do them the wrong to mistrust any, I will do myself the right to trust none." Likewise, a famous song, sung by Balthasar, captures Beatrice's feelings well: "Sigh no more, ladies, sigh no more, / Men were deceivers ever . . ." If they seem wary of love, it is because both demand a great deal from their ideal lovers. In their cases, it will take dissimulation to bring them together, constructively carried out this time. And so the couple's friends convince both partners that each is secretly in love with the other one. In other words, they must be tricked into believing what is, in actuality, true all along. Even so, the pair is hesitant to reveal any true feelings, until the same friends make public Beatrice's and Benedick's secret love sonnets. Finally, love and kisses triumph over verbal jabs and a sense of, or wish for, self-sufficiency, which is love's enemy.

HAPPIER DEVELOPMENTS IN STRATFORD

Shakespeare's social stature, as a citizen and family man in Stratford, grew significantly during the time. Two months after Hamnet's death, the entire Shakespeare family received good news, in October 1596, some twenty-five years in the making. Back in the early 1570s, Shakespeare's father, John, had applied for a coat of arms. As a bailiff or mayor of Stratford, his wish to achieve this gentleman's status was not unreasonable. However, it was discovered only in the 1980s that John Shakespeare was caught up shortly thereafter in questionable dealings, including usury, or money-lending, and the unauthorized buying and selling of large quantities of wool. John risked massive fines with this undertaking, but perhaps his need for income felt desperate enough to warrant the risk. In 1576, it will be recalled, John abruptly stopped attending town council meetings, although his fellow townsmen kept him on the rolls for a decade afterward. Throughout the

1580s, he was reduced to selling family properties and found himself increasingly caught up in legal proceedings.

A "Mr. John Shackspeare" was included in a March 1592 list of absentees from church, which has led some scholars to suspect that he was a secret Catholic, or recusant, who refused to attend Anglican services on the grounds of religious principle. However, another list from six months later makes it clear that John was avoiding church for fear of encountering creditors there: "It is said that these last nine come not to church for fear of process for debt," says this second document. John's original application for a coat of arms, made at the height of his professional career two decades ago, must have seemed far from his mind during this long stretch of professional embarrassment and fiscal insolvency that followed.

His son William, however, was doing well financially by the mid-1590s, less for his writing than for his acting, and for co-owning of a theater above all. It was very likely he who renewed his father's long-forgotten application to the Herald's College in London. The herald's draft speaks of John as "of good wealth," so presumably his fortunes had been restored by his playwriting son or by some other means. The herald rather exaggeratedly describes the Shakespeare family's distinguished line, and assigns them a shield of gold and silver, atop which a falcon shakes a spear, which also looks like a writer's quill. (Both the shaken spear and the quill are probably visual puns.) The design's motto was *Non sancz droict* ("Not without right"). If this motto sounds slightly defensive, Shakespeare had good reason to be. At least four other players from the Lord Chamberlain's Men would similarly obtain gentleman's status, but some naysayers found it to be a distasteful show of upward mobility at best, or even worse, an outright transgression of social rank.

Ben Jonson mocked Shakespeare's pretensions by having his character Puntarvolo, in the play *Every Man Out of His Humour*, suggest to a rustic clown that his gentlemanly motto should be "Not without mustard." Jonson was also critical of his peer in the preface to *Every Man In His Humour*; one begins to understand why an early biographer wrote of Shakespeare and Jonson that "they were profess'd Friends; tho' I don't know whether the other ever made him an equal return of Gentleness and Sincerity." The herald's draft itself, perhaps unintentionally, makes a joke of the family motto with one stroke of punctuation; by first writing "Non, sanz droict," the phrase risks becoming a double rejection of the family's claim of status—"No, without right." And with Shakespeare's sole male heir now dead, however much the family name was deemed "with right," it was now without a future.

John Shakespeare submitted another application in 1599, to connect the arms of his in-laws, the Ardens, with his own. Nothing seems to have come of this effort. A more serious objection arose three years later, when the York herald accused his counterpart, who had granted the Shakespeare arms, of elevating unworthy applicants. He supported this accusation with a list of twenty-three examples, including a reproduction of the Shakespeare family crest under which appears "Shakespeare the Player." This reference to William's career in the theater is doubtless meant negatively, as if to say, "How could a playwright or *actor* ever be worthy of social elevation or gentlemanly status?"

A more material, less debatable example of Shakespeare's growing status occurred the year after the coat of arms was granted. In May 1597, he purchased from a lawyer an impressive house in the heart of Stratford. Known as New Place, this "pretty house of brick and timber" was said to be the second-largest home in town. It stood across from the Gild Chapel and Shakespeare's old school, and came with extensive grounds, including two barns, two gardens, and two orchards. Shakespeare's family had very likely remained in his parents' Henley Street home before moving into New Place, possibly in the "back," a section that projected into the garden and could stand as a little independent residence.

Today, the entire property is now only a few foundation walls and a lovingly cultivated Great Garden. Landmarks include a mulberry tree said to derive from one planted by Shakespeare and an "oaken tunnel" in the Knot Garden. A later owner of the home, increasingly exasperated by the regular visitors there, tore it down in 1759. The adjacent Nash House has been preserved, named after Thomas Nash, the husband of Shakespeare's granddaughter Elizabeth. Its early-modern atmosphere gives visitors at least an approximate sense of how Shakespeare's neighboring house may have appeared within while he was alive.

Fortunately, an eighteenth-century sketch of the home exists, giving some sign of its opulence: it had three stories, five gables, ten fireplaces, prominent beams, and a street-side façade of some sixty feet. Although it was standard for young families to live with parents, the Shakespeares' excitement at moving into their own home must have been heightened by the recent reduction of the Henley Street home's living space, following the threat of fire to one of its sides. Serious fires had struck the town in 1594 and 1595, destroying at least one hundred and twenty homes. Some fires were blamed on poorly built hovels that housed the poor or town transients, heightening class tensions in Stratford. Citizens also suffered from epidemics and food shortages. It also seems likely that Shakespeare's sister Joan and her new husband, the hatter William Hart, took up the space in the family home vacated by William's family.

Shakespeare's increased prosperity must have stuck out from this general landscape of setback and deprivation. Yet as is often the case, it was from these reduced circumstances that new signs of wealth arose. For example, many of Stratford's fine timber-framed buildings date from the years immediately after the fires, including the ornate Harvard House on High Street. Built by the bailiff Thomas Rogers, the house is named for Rogers's famous grandson John Harvard, founder of America's first university. Shakespeare's formal residence at New Place is verified by a corn and malt survey of February 1598, in which he is listed with hoarders of malt. This was a potentially serious offense, particularly during a time of bad harvests and grain shortage. Was Shakespeare preparing to sell this malt at a higher price as it became more scarce? Whatever his motivation, the appearance of his name on this list uncomfortably implicates him further as an increasingly powerful "have" among a growing number of town "have-nots." Only two Stratford residents had stockpiled more malt than our author.

His domestic and economic activity in Stratford continued for the next several years. In 1598, the town paid Shakespeare ten pence for a ton of stone, which was used for bridge repair. Shakespeare may have had material left over from building projects at New Place, or possibly the stone derived from the remains of a barn pulled down. In September 1602, he bought a cottage in Chapel Lane, likely an extension of his new property. Four months earlier, he purchased at great cost more than a hundred acres in the farming country of Old Stratford, north of town, and he paid an even larger amount (£440!) for a share of Stratford's tithes (basically an investment in tillable lands and their annual returns of corn, grain, hay, and so on).

The 1598 correspondence of two Stratford men, Abraham Sturley and Richard Quiney (both

Great Garden of New Place, Stratford-upon-Avon, England *(Photograph by Michelle Walz Eriksson)*

of whom had suffered losses during the fires), further suggests Shakespeare's considerable standing in his hometown. Sturley wrote to Quiney in London that "our countriman Mr. Shaksper" was willing to disburse money for some land outside of Stratford. They think of Shakespeare as a possible investor, then, and perhaps someone eager to build his real estate portfolio and reputation generally. This purchase, Sturley adds, "would advance him in deed." Quiney is the author of an even more interesting letter, the only one we have addressing Shakespeare himself. "Loving countryman, I am bold of you as a friend, craving your help with £30," Quiney's note begins. "You shall friend me much in helping me out of the debts I owe in London." He writes from the "Bell in Carter Lane," an inn near St. Paul's Cathedral.

Quiney had accrued this debt while residing in London for the sake of town business. Stratford was petitioning for reduced taxes in the wake of the town's fires. (His mission proved successful.)

Apparently Quiney never actually posted this letter, for it was found in his papers in the town archives. Did he decide against sending it? Or did he run into the playwright in London and make his appeal in person? We will never know, but a biographical tradition, more wishful than factual, soon developed that Shakespeare immediately showed Quiney great generosity. (In truth, the sum requested was substantial.) This inference relies upon a final letter, from Sturley to Quiney again, in which Sturley refers to a letter from Quiney written on the same day as Quiney's letter to Shakespeare. Biographers were quick to hear in

Sturley's reference that "Mr. Wm. Shak. Would procure us money" that Quiney had, somehow, already secured funds from Shakespeare on the very same day, as if with great swiftness of generosity. In fact, Sturley takes Quiney's solicitation of Shakespeare as that only—he will be keen to hear if anything comes of this arrangement: "which I will like of as I shall hear when, and where, and how." Whatever sort of "paymaster" (as Quiney calls him) Shakespeare was or was not in this case, clearly the writer had become one to be reckoned with economically in Stratford.

Sources and Further Reading

Bearman, Robert. *Shakespeare in the Stratford Records*. Stroud, England: Alan Sutton, 2006.

Halliday, F. E. *Shakespeare*. New York: T. Yoseloff, 1961.

Jones, John. *Shakespeare at Work*. New York : Oxford University Press, 1995.

Schoenbaum, Samuel. *William Shakespeare: A Documentary Life*. Oxford, U.K.: Clarendon, 1977.

SHAKESPEARE'S TRIUMPHS AT THE GLOBE

Shakespeare's company, the Lord Chamberlain's Men, began constructing the Globe playhouse in February 1599. An inventory from May of that year described the theater in Latin as a "new edifice," one "in the occupation of William Shakespeare and others." The most resplendent, enduring glories of the English Renaissance stage would soon be performed there. Mainly, though, it must have been a time of great relief for Shakespeare and his coworkers. The company had regularly faced an uncertain existence during the past five years, staging shows at a number of venues that included the Theatre, north of London, which had been built by the father of its best actor, Richard Burbage; the Curtain nearby, a lesser and (it seems) multi-purpose location; and possibly even the new theater known as the Swan, across the River Thames in Bankside. Now, the Chamberlain's Men were more firmly relocating to that suburb of Bankside, or Southwark.

As the players raised the new octagonal structure, beam by beam, their work surely did not go unnoticed for long. Just around the corner stood the company's main competition, Philip Henslowe's Rose Theatre, where the Admiral's Men regularly performed. Shakespeare's group would increasingly overshadow this competition in the years ahead. By 1600, Henslowe conceded commercial defeat: he abandoned the Rose, leased a new lot in Finsbury, another neighborhood north of London's city walls, and soon built the Fortune there. This new playhouse distinguished itself by being square in design. (Fortunately for theater historians, Henslowe's exact specifica-

tions exist.) As for the Globe, Bernard Beckerman in *Shakespeare at the Globe, 1599–1609*, speaks of the "splendid decade" that was about to occur in this new playhouse. The Lord Chamberlain's Men had enjoyed a series of theatrical successes, and now they would benefit from an unparalleled degree of stability and productivity. This new situation would be a welcome change from prior years, when the company was just barely surviving crises of leadership and residence, as well as rejection from one London neighborhood and near abolishment of the entire theater industry by both city and court authorities.

THE LORD CHAMBERLAIN'S MEN IN THE LATE 1590S

After their triumph at court during the holiday season of 1594–95, the Lord Chamberlain's Men soon took up residence in the Theatre. A long, prosperous partnership might have been predicted, but unfortunately the Burbage family's lease, for the Shoreditch land housing the wooden theater itself, was set to expire in April 1597. Their landlord, Giles Allen, was difficult to work with, and his Puritan sympathies made him suspicious of his dealings with actors, whom he probably considered disreputable. James Burbage, the Theatre's owner, may have sensed that negotiations with Allen for a new lease on the current land would prove difficult, if not impossible. He began searching for a new performance site, and in February 1596 paid a very considerable sum for the old dining hall once occupied by the monks at Blackfriars, in the heart of London.

Choirs and children's acting companies successfully performed in such spaces, as did the Lord Chamberlain's Men themselves whenever they presented shows at court. This new, indoor space would allow the increasingly popular company to perform for a longer season. Also, a potential residence in what was a more exclusive neighborhood might attract more well-to-do audiences and help to set the Chamberlain's Men apart from public-theater competition. Unfortunately, the aristocratic inhabitants of Blackfriars actively resisted this invasion of their neighbor-

hood by "common" players, and they successfully appealed to the Privy Council to prohibit performances in this new space. The Burbages had a fancy new theater, but could not use it. Exacerbating matters, the father, James Burbage, died in February 1597. The problems of the Theatre's lease and the stalled Blackfriars investment now fell to his sons Richard and Cuthbert.

Facing two impasses, the Chamberlain's Men needed to find alternate locations for their shows. One option was the new Swan Theatre, built by the wealthy goldsmith Francis Langley in the Bank-

HOW TO MOVE A THEATER

The story of the birth of the Globe Theatre, where Shakespeare's greatest plays were first staged from 1599 till his retirement in 1613, sounds like something taken from a summer action movie, with the stealth and suspense of *Mission: Impossible* or the group bravado of *The A-Team*, Renaissance London style.

It was unusually cold on December 28, 1598. The snow was falling and the River Thames was nearly frozen over. A dozen or so men gathered in Shoreditch, a neighborhood just north of London and home to some of the city's most popular public theaters—including the first one built, called the Theatre, and the nearby Curtain, in the vicinity of Finsbury Field, where Shakespeare's company the Lord Chamberlain's Men had recently been performing. Early that morning, the group arrived at the Theatre, which had been empty for two years, following a dispute between the Chamberlain's Men and their landlord, Giles Allen.

Risking trespassing charges and a property dispute, the group intended to dismantle the large wooden structure of the theater. They were armed with saws and axes. They knew Allen would intensely object, but they were determined to remove the wood and materials of the theater itself from the landlord's property. The theater, they believed, was rightfully theirs. Two

brothers at the front of the group, Richard and Cuthbert Burbage, had good reason to think so: their father, James Burbage, had first built the Theatre in 1576. But the father was now dead, the company was stalled in its efforts to perform in an indoor theater in central London, and attempts to extend the lease for the current Theatre location with the landlord, Allen, had gone nowhere. Allen's brother was a former Lord Mayor of London, and he had powerful connections. Even so, the Lord Chamberlain's Men were taking matters into their own hands.

The landlord had been threatening to tear down the theater himself and retain the valuable materials, but he was away in Essex for the Christmas holiday. The theater troupe had to act now. Shortly after the dismantling began, a crowd assembled and a standoff soon developed—some of the onlookers were supporters of the absent landlord, while others favored the rights of the Lord Chamberlain's Men. Legal action was threatened, but the actors kept working. Peter Street, a master craftsman overseeing the project, supervised as the pegged posts and groundsills were separated. Later in the day, the team loaded the oak posts onto wagons, which horses led southward through the city. The group passed through Bishopsgate, quite near the parish church where records show Shakespeare

side neighborhood of Paris Garden. The company likely performed there for a short while, but the revived Pembroke's Men soon took over residence in February 1597. That troupe's comeback did not last long, however. It was responsible in July for a scandalous play, *The Isle of Dogs*, that caused an uproar among city leaders and the queen's Privy Council alike. The authors, Thomas Nashe and Ben Jonson, were promptly arrested, and there was even some threat of the "final suppressing" of plays—that is, tearing down the theaters for good. The councilors condemned the "lewd" play with its "seditious" matter, and citing a "confluence of bad people," it shut down performances throughout the city. The Chamberlain's Men again had to resort to touring the provinces, and it likely did so till returning to London later that fall.

The company soon commenced performances in the rougher Curtain Theatre, also in Shoreditch, after the summer scandal had died down. Both the Chamberlain's and Admiral's Men also performed at court that winter, despite ongoing uncertainty as to the fate of their profession in London. The Curtain was no permanent worshipped, and onward to Street's warehouse near the river. The men would store the materials there throughout the winter, and then ferry them across the river for the building of the Globe, once the foundation was laid. The theater company would face legal challenges from a furious Allen, but eventually the Lord Chamberlain's Men prevailed, and the new Globe Theatre was standing and ready for performances by late summer of 1599.

In 1599, Shakespeare was thirty-five, the traditional, biblical midpoint of a human life. (Although, truth be told, Elizabethan life spans were far shorter, averaging in the late thirties or early forties.) He was already a successful London writer: plays were now appearing with his name upon them, and a popular collection of lyric poems appeared in this year, entitled *The Passionate Pilgrim by W. Shakespeare*. Only five poems in that volume were in fact by Shakespeare, but we see how an opportunistic printer was eager to associate any book of his with this proven writer's name. Yet based on the work that would follow, this change of scenery from Shoreditch, in north London, to Southwark, south of the Thames, must have quickened him all the more, given him a refreshed sense of his career as a writer and member of a theater company. So regarding the year 1599, according to the critic James Shapiro: "as critics have long recognized, it was a decisive one, perhaps the decisive one, in Shakespeare's development as a writer."

Thus it is easy to imagine Shakespeare as inspired by the relocation of Lord Chamberlain's Men's theater and the rise of the Globe on Bankside. Practically speaking, Shakespeare may have appreciated a new wave of audiences that the company's new neighborhood would invite, or he may have felt incredible pressure as the company playwright to produce plays that would begin the Globe's first season on a high note. He did not disappoint, completing for this opening year *Henry V*, *Julius Caesar*, *As You Like It*, and a draft, at least, of *Hamlet*. Arguably his accomplishments mark the first year of the Globe Theatre as one of the most remarkable ones for any writer ever, in all literary history.

SEE ALSO:

Gurr, Andrew. *The Shakespeare Company, 1594-1642*. New York: Cambridge University Press, 2004.

Shapiro, James. *A Year in the Life of William Shakespeare 1599*. New York : HarperCollins Publishers, 2005.

Sohmer, Steve. *Shakespeare's Mystery Play: The Opening of the Globe Theater, 1599*. Manchester: Manchester University Press, 1999.

Thomson, Peter. *Shakespeare's Theatre*. New York: Routledge, 1992.

solution, however, and in the meantime, the relationship with the hostile owner of the Theatre's land was worsening. Expecting eventually to arrive at an agreement, the Burbages had let the prior lease expire in April 1597, which gave Allen increased leverage. While the lease was in effect, it was clear that the theater itself belonged to the Burbage brothers, but now, sans lease, Allen was additionally claiming possession of the structure standing upon his land. And his terms for renewing the lease were extravagant. The Lord Chamberlain's Men had to take matters into their own hands, decisively and dramatically, and they did just that. At the end of December 1598, when they knew Allen was out of town, they assembled at the Theatre, dismantled it over and against the protests of Allen's allies, and hauled the timber along Bishopsgate Street and toward a waiting warehouse. Allen returned to a vacant lot, his leverage evaporated. Shrugging off legal action from Allen, the company signed the aforementioned agreement for its new location in February 1599, and the building of that new playhouse, the Globe, was soon underway.

This time, the lease was not only with the Burbages, but also with five of the actors themselves, including Shakespeare. This happy resolution invites us to stand back and marvel for a moment. "For the first time in England, and perhaps anywhere in the world," writes the theater historian Peter Thomson, "a theater was to be designed by actors, run by actors and built on land leased and paid for by actors." It was a high moment, and Shakespeare's forthcoming plays would suit these historically important circumstances well.

TRACES OF SHAKESPEARE IN LONDON

Records in London's Exchequer office show that Shakespeare was keeping a residence in the city's Bishopsgate ward during the mid-1590s. It was an attractive, prosperous area, full of inns and with a new conduit that delivered fresh water. Shakespeare had chosen a location within convenient walking distance of the Theatre in Shoreditch just to the north; he wished to be close to work, and this trend, it seems, would continue as his company worked in successive locations. His name turned up on a November 1597 list of residents in St. Helen's parish who had failed to pay taxes. Shakespeare still owed £5, which had been due in February. He next appeared on a 1598 list, and one marginal note suggests he did not pay this levy, either. Other evidence suggests he hadn't paid because he no longer had goods in that ward, and a second marginal note indicates that he was now living across the river, in the district known as the Clink, in Southwark. This tax bill remains unpaid in a 1600 document as well.

When did Shakespeare change neighborhoods, and does it help to explain his apparent tax dodging? Maybe he had already left Bishopsgate by February 1596, when he is first listed as delinquent. His great biographer Edmund Malone claimed in 1796 to have evidence (now lost) that he had relocated by 1596. He may have moved there because the Lord Chamberlain's Men were then playing at the Swan, not far from his new neighborhood. Another legal document connects Shakespeare with Francis Langley, the Swan's owner. In it, one William Wayte in fall 1596 requests a surety of the peace against "William Shakspere," Langley, and, intriguingly, two women. The phrasing is dramatic—Wayte fears he is in danger of death or bodily harm—yet Shakespeare may have also simply found himself in an ongoing dispute involving a professional contact. Alternately, he might have moved to Southwark as late as 1599, and if then, likely because the Chamberlain's Men were completing final preparations for the opening of the Globe on the same side of the river.

Whichever his neighborhood at any given time, Shakespeare soon became as much a London writer as an ongoing Stratford resident. His works, taken together, reveal a local's knowledge of the many streets, monuments, and landmarks of the great city. He alludes to Watling Street, a direct route between Stratford and London, and mentions the Tilt Yard, Star Chamber, and White Hall in Westminster, to the west of the city proper, along the bend of the River Thames. There also appears the "cathedral church of Westminster" and the Jerusalem chamber in the abbey. Neighborhoods described in the plays include Charing Cross, Smithfield, St. Paul's, Blackfriars, and Eastcheap, and on the other, eastern side of London, we repeatedly hear of "Julius Caesar's ill-erected Tower" (that is, the Tower of London), Tower Hill, and London Bridge.

A 1596 sketch of the interior of the Swan Theatre, made by a traveler from Holland. *(Drawing by Johannes de Witt)*

Crosby Place is where Richard Duke of Gloucester conspires in *Richard III*, and was a building no doubt familiar to Shakespeare when he lived in Bishopsgate. Just to the north, near London's first theaters, Holywell Priory may be alluded to in *The Comedy of Errors. Love's Labour's Lost* makes a metaphor of Tyburn, a gallows west of the city and on the road to Paddington. (The spot today is a traffic island, just beside Hyde Park and Marble Arch.) *Twelfth Night* features some more central London locations, including the Inns of Court ("Temple hall") and "the bells of St. Bennet," a church at Paul's Wharf, on the London side of the Thames. Some place names reflect Shakespeare's time in Southwark, including the inn known as the Elephant, St. George's Fields, and Marshalsea Prison. Likewise, the late play *Henry VIII* reflects the author's later residences in its inclusions of Blackfriars.

By the late 1590s, Shakespeare's reputation as a London writer was growing. Epigrams and poems by Richard Barnfield, John Marston, Robert Tofte, and John Weever mention him or his writings. Shakespeare may also be the man behind the "gentler shepherd" Aetion in the poet Edmund Spenser's *Colin Clout's Come Home Again* (1595), or even "Our pleasant Willy" with "that same gentle spirit" in an earlier poem by the same author. Equally complimentary is William Covell's speaking of "sweet Shakespeare," also in 1595, although he may be describing less the man than his poetic style, which is elsewhere called "mellifluous," and its author "honey-tongued."

One tradition suggests that Shakespeare, as a prominent member of the Chamberlain's Men, helped Ben Jonson get his first break with the company. Actors were about to reject a play submitted by Jonson when Shakespeare "luckily cast his Eye upon it," as his early biographer Nicholas Rowe narrates it, "and found something so well in it as to engage him first to read it through, and afterwards to recommend Mr. Johnson and his Writings to the Publick. After this they were profess'd friends." We may wish to read this with a grain of salt, for certainly Shakespeare comes off here in saintly fashion, as a benign literary godfather, as well as an exquisite tastemaker: in 1598, the Chamberlain's Men were advancing a new style of play with Jonson's popular *Every Man In His Humor*. Later a printed version of the play listed Shakespeare atop a list of its "principal comedians," or comic actors. Another early biography asserts that the two writers were city observers together; they "did gather Humors of men daily wherever they came"—gathering material for future stage creations, no doubt.

It is hard not to accept wholesale (for so pleasant are they) the cherished myths of Shakespeare's good company with his fellow actors and writers, and their rollicking nights of gossip, jokes, and drinking at the Mermaid Tavern and other London haunts and hangouts. One story, recorded in Thomas Fuller's *Worthies of England* (1662), presents Shakespeare and Jonson engaged in lively verbal battles:

> Many were the wit-combats betwixt him and Ben Jonson, which two I behold like a Spanish great Gallion and an English Man of War; Master Jonson (like the former) was built far higher in Learning; Solid but Slow in his performances. Shakespeare, with the English man-of-War, lesser in bulk, but lighter in sailing, could turn with all tides, tack about and take advantage of all winds, by the quickness of his Wit and Invention.

Fuller's description is remarkable in the way it compares the two men's tactics to the Spanish Armada's fate off England's coast in 1588: the quick, dangerous English fleet, though "lesser in bulk," devastated the less maneuverable, "built far higher" Spanish ships. Just so, Shakespeare appears as the better rival, thanks to his native gifts, namely, his quick wit and versatility as the course of conversation turned. We also see here, in Shakespeare's equation with England's miraculous victory, a very early vision of the Stratford man as England's National Poet. This focus on his shrewdness recurs as well, as when a fellow author speaks of him as "Shakespeare, that nimble Mercury thy brain, / Lulls many hundred Argus-eyes asleep."

Another anecdote involves Shakespeare and his main actor, Richard Burbage, who already had brought to life Richard III and Romeo:

> One evening when Richard III was to be performed, Shakespeare observed a young woman delivering a message to Burbage in so cautious a manner as excited his curiosity to listen to. It imported, that her master was gone out of town that morning, and her mistress would be glad of his company after Play; and to know what signal he would appoint for admittance. Burbage replied, three taps at the door, and it is I, Richard the Third. She immediately withdrew, and Shakespeare followed 'till he observed her to go into a house in the city; and enquiring in the neighborhood, he was informed that a young lady, lived there, the favorite of an old rich merchant. Near the appointed time of meeting, Shakespeare thought proper to anticipate Mr. Burbage, and was introduced by the concerted signal. The lady was very much surprised at Shakespeare's presuming to act Mr. Burbage's part; but as he (who had wrote Romeo and Juliet) we may be certain did not want wit or eloquence to apologize for the intrusion, she was soon pacified, and they were mutually happy till Burbage

A 1588 painting of English ships and the Spanish Armada *(Artist unknown)*

came to the door, and repeated the same signal; but Shakespeare popping his head out of the window, bid him be gone; for that William the Conqueror had reigned before Richard III.

This story supports utterly our vision of Shakespeare and his merry company—actors who are popular, possibly oversexed, and more prone to amusement than offense. Shakespeare's curiosity marks him as a bright writer, but also one of the world; he is as intrigued by amorous rendezvous as great poetry. He also comes off in this story—as in some examples above—as shrewd and quick to act. He is highly skilled in wooing women, and, in besting the vigorous actor Burbage, vigorous himself. His boldly proclaiming his bed conquest to his friend's face introduces a note of bombast, as does the final, punning comparison of these actor-lovers with the famous English monarchs whose names they bear. This story is recorded in a law student's diary in March 1602, a surprisingly early date considering the tale's legendary qualities. However made up or embellished this story, it should give us pause, lest we too quickly imagine that the "gentle, honest" Shakespeare of his friends' commendations was a super-sensitive, retiring writer. He seems, in fact, to have been a sociable man and good friend; some of Chamberlain's actors eventually left him bequests in their wills.

His relationship with Burbage deserves special appreciation. Some have suggested, in part from the above story, a dark competition existed between the two men, yet this underestimates their mutually advantageous professional relationship. Because of Burbage, Shakespeare felt confident to create some of his most demanding roles, characters capable of in-depth expressions across thousands of lines. On the other hand, Burbage's fame largely depended on the raw material of those powerful, memorable parts that Shakespeare wrote for him. They were also, let us not forget, actors who performed together. The poet John Davies, when writing of those "guerdoned [rewarded] not, to their deserts," lists in the margins the "Stage players" and a pair of initials: "W.S." and "R.B."

THE *HENRIAD* AND CONTROVERSY

Often Shakespeare seems to have enjoyed lucky timing, or else he had a terrific sense of how to time things well. For example, one of the plays that opened the first season at the Globe in 1599, *Henry V*, was not only a stirringly patriotic play about a popular English soldier-king, but was also a triumphant culmination. It concluded on a high note Shakespeare's second tetralogy of English history plays. This second series began with *Richard II* in 1595. Savvily the epilogue of *Henry V* circles back and, by mentioning the forthcoming reign of Henry VI, links chronologically with the very first play of the first tetralogy. In other words, the second four plays written actually take place historically prior to the events covered in the first four plays. Thus the final lines of *Henry V* ambitiously conceive of a grand cycle of English history across the entire eight plays, and across nearly a decade of Shakespeare's writing life.

Henry V also concluded, on a smaller scale but just as impressively, a sequence of the three final plays known as the *Henriad*. In short, these three plays tell the story of Henry Bolingbrook's accession as Henry IV and, more importantly, the story of his son, Prince Hal, who is destined to become the victorious, glorious Henry V. Shakespeare returned to the narrative arc of an earlier play, *The Famous Victories of Henry V*, and his *Henriad* is mainly Hal's/Henry's story. These history plays, arguably the best Shakespeare ever wrote in the genre, tell how Hal eventually becomes King Henry V, including the trials he faces and overcomes, and the necessary rejections he must make.

A preview of Hal appears in *Richard II*, when the concerned Bolingbrook asks about "my unthrifty son":

> Inquire at London, 'mongst the taverns
>   there,
> For there, they say, he daily doth frequent,
> With unrestrained loose companions, . . .

He hears that his son is associated with commoners and stews, or brothels, and is disappointed yet hopeful:

> As dissolute as desperate; yet through both
> I see some sparks of better hope, which
>   elder years
> May happily bring forth.

Here, then, is the action of the *Henriad* in brief: Hal must grow up to give his country hope in his "elder years." However, early in *1 Henry IV* we find Hal in just such a tavern lamented by his father, who is now Henry IV. The play opens with the king, whose own questionable usurpation of

Portrait of King Henry IV made long after his death, probably in Shakespeare's time, around 1600. (Artist unknown)

the English throne will continue to haunt him in both the first and second parts of *Henry IV*. His reign will never be peaceful, but always on the brink of rebellion: "So shaken as we are, so wan with care," he admits, having to put off a desired journey to the Holy Land to contend with England's battles with Scotland, the capturing of the nobleman Mortimer, and with the fiery young Hotspur's refusal to yield his prisoners to the crown. Hotspur's meeting with his father (Northumberland) and uncle (Worcester) sets the stage for a rebel faction, which henceforth acts in counterpoint against Henry IV and his beleaguered court. The two sides' showdown will mark this play's climax.

Moreover, Shakespeare triangulates the settings, by in effect splicing son from father, or

Prince Hal and his tavern world in Eastcheap from Henry IV at the court. The son is also contrasted early on with Hotspur, whose prowess overshadows the dissolute Hal. He behaves like the son Henry IV wishes he had, and, painfully, Hal knows this. A part of Hal's own maturation will involve confronting Hotspur, and proving himself the better hero, the true prince. He will do so, but Shakespeare extends his artistry here by giving Hotspur a fully defined character, as well as some of the play's most memorable lines:

> By heaven, methinks it were an easy leap,
> To pluck bright honour from the pale-faced moon,
> Or dive into the bottom of the deep,
> Where fathom-line could never touch the ground,
> And pluck up drowned honour by the locks;
> . . .

Hotspur's departure—at times comic, at times poignant—from his wife, Kate, is also formidable, and is arguably Shakespeare's most memorable domestic scene to this point. All of these competing worlds satisfyingly collide and resolve in the second half of *1 Henry IV*, at the Battle of Shrewsbury presented there.

First, Hal must make his journey there, both literally and figuratively. He fascinates us because from the outset he is terribly aware of the distance between the escapist tavern and the glories of the battlefield. We soon meet his companions: Sir John Falstaff, Poins, Bardoph, Peto. They are incredibly attractive, funny company—and Falstaff may just be the masterstroke of the *Henriad*—but there is never any mistaking Hal's consciousness of his true habitat and standing. He is deeply aware of the burdens of his now royal family, and expresses these tensions in a dazzling first soliloquy:

I know you all, and will awhile
     uphold
The unyoked humour of your
     idleness:
Yet herein will I imitate the sun . . .
My reformation, glittering o'er my
     fault,
Shall show more goodly and attract
     more eyes
Than that which hath no foil to set
     it off.
I'll so offend, to make offence a skill;
Redeeming time when men think
     least I will.

Hal's greatest obstacle to this redemption is also the play's most beloved presence—Falstaff, the fat old knight with an equally gigantic wit. He is Hal's fellow tavern reveler, and also relates to Hal as a more easygoing, affectionate father figure. (The pair quarrels all the time, but the fights are lighthearted, and hilarious.) Falstaff,

Hotspur dies in Act 5, Scene 4 of *Henry IV*, Part 1. This painting is from 1864. *(James William Edmund Doyle)*

too, must participate in the battle against the rebels, but he remains a radically undercutting figure; he questions the whole enterprise of martial valor ("What is honor? A word.") and is not above playing possum on the battlefield ("The better part of valor is discretion."). The first part of *Henry IV* ends with king and prince victorious, and Falstaff cagily alive. Yet there are more rebels to face.

The civil strife continues in *2 Henry IV*, although tonally this play feels very different from its predecessor. Its urban world is darker compared with the tavern fun of part one, and is populated with more violent figures such as Pistol or the sheriff's men, Fang and Snare. The play opens with news of Hotspur's death, and soon the Chief Justice berates Falstaff for his bad influence on Hal. Meanwhile, the king is dying.

"Uneasy lies the head that wears a crown," he says gloomily. The scenes and their language repeatedly conjure a world of greed, self-interest, weariness, and faithlessness—overall, a vision of a sick commonwealth. Similarly, Hal's brother John's double-crossing of the rebel forces is effective as a ruthless act of realpolitik, but dramatically it lacks the thrilling valor of Hotspur and Hal battling. Falstaff's trickery and comic language dominate the play, but this fact also makes the second part feel narrower. And if Falstaff is the mainly appealing part, then inevitably the play's power must dim at the end, when the newly crowned Henry V decisively rejects his erstwhile friend, mentor, and father figure:

I know thee not, old man: fall to thy
     prayers;

How ill white hairs become a fool and
jester!
I have long dream'd of such a kind of man,
So surfeit-swell'd, so old and so profane;
But, being awaked, I do despise my dream.

Having enjoyed the special, uniquely lively relationship between these two, the new king at the moment of his rejection is painful to watch. King Henry's severity continues at length: "know the grave doth gape / For thee thrice wider than for other men. / . . . / Presume not that I am the thing I was." Once a warm, feisty companion, the king, newly appreciative of his sovereign obligations, can only view him now as "the tutor and the feeder of my riots." Those days, we come to understand, are long gone, and he banishes Falstaff from the royal presence. This banishment punctuates an earlier, painful confrontation between father and son, when Hal awkwardly dons the crown of his sleeping father. Awaking, Henry IV believes his son has wished him dead; "I stay too long by thee," he says, "I weary thee." The son's remorse and father's forgiveness follow, but the strained, gloomy atmosphere still hangs over the play.

Falstaff stands center stage for much of the play, praising sack, his drink of choice, and arguing energetically with Mistress Quickly and Doll Tearsheet at the Boar's Head Tavern. However, some critics have seen Falstaff as an increasingly sinister character in the center of this play's rougher world. At the midpoint, he travels to Gloucestershire, where he unscrupulously recruits lean, poor men who will soon become "powder" in battle. He also encounters there an old classmate, Justice Shallow, whose nostalgic talk is sometimes silly (Falstaff rightly sends him up). Yet Shallow nevertheless adds a spirit of wistfulness to the play's world. Falstaff plans to embezzle from his host, and then receives word of Hal's accession to the throne. He is overjoyed, believing overreachingly that "the laws of England

are at my commandment." Hal, now Henry V, determines otherwise. First he praises Falstaff's nemesis, the Chief Justice, for sternly doing his duty to the realm, and after Falstaff is rejected, it is this character who will convey the forlorn friend to a naval prison. Where should our sympathies lie? Has the new king done the necessary thing, however difficult? Or instead does he do it too easily, thus betraying his old dear friend? His definitive distancing from Falstaff has repulsed some readers, who believe what Hal has grown into is deplorable—a heartless, calculating, mercenary ruler, intent only on political advantage and consolidation of royal power. Incidentally, *2 Henry IV* has never been as popular as its counterpart play, although in modern times the two plays are increasingly performed together, or conflated into one long dramatic narrative.

The popularity of Falstaff soon embroiled Shakespeare in controversy with that powerful nobleman William Brooke. The character's original name of Oldcastle was the more precise reason that Brooke took offense. Brooke, like the historical Oldcastle, was Lord Cobham, and he counted Oldcastle as an ancestor from the early fifteenth century, and a proto-Protestant soldier and sufferer to boot. John Foxe had honored Oldcastle in his popular "Book of Martyrs." It naturally irked Brooke and probably others that now Catholic writers were dismissing Oldcastle as a "ruffian knight," "jovial roister," and "coward," and awkwardly pointing to "comedians on their stages" to support their deflating contentions. Shakespeare may have meant Falstaff's original name as a hostile gesture toward the Brooke family, who were no lovers of the theater, but he may have also simply found the name "Oldcastle" in his source play. An opportunistic group of rival playwrights soon wrote a competing play, *Sir John Oldcastle*, for the Admiral's Men, featuring, a little self-righteously it must be said, "no pampered glutton" but a "valiant martyr and a virtuous peer."

The pushback must have been great because Shakespeare soon changed the fat knight's name to Falstaff, although echoes are still mischievously present, as when Hal addresses him as "my old lad of the castle." The playwright sounds a little scorched and penitent in his epilogue to *2 Henry IV*: "Falstaff shall die of a sweat, unless already 'a [i.e., he] be kill'd with your hard opinions; for Oldcastle died a martyr and this is not the man." Scholars have put forward other examples, from this very play, of Shakespeare's paying back enemies by immortalizing them as less than savory characters. For example, Justice Shallow may be a figure of William Gardiner, a justice of the peace and stepfather of William Wayte, Shakespeare's legal opponent discussed earlier. Or, looking back much further, Shallow has also been conceived as Sir Thomas Lucy, the Stratford man who legendarily caught the young Shakespeare poaching deer. It was even suggested, by the great editor Edmund Malone in 1780, that Falstaff was based on not the historical Oldcastle, but a fellow Stratford citizen who had refused to sell Shakespeare lands adjacent to his own property. All of these specific identifications of Falstaff will strike many readers as too limiting of his character, for one of Falstaff's great dramatic qualities is his sense of being a universal representative, and so he is. "Banish plump Jack," Falstaff tells Hal, "and banish all the world."

FALSTAFF AND *THE MERRY WIVES OF WINDSOR*

Generally, the character of Falstaff remains the most enduring creation in the *Henriad*. Even those who believe Hal necessarily rejected him nevertheless concede that Shakespeare, in Falstaff, fashioned one of the great comic characters in all of theater history. He is regularly uproari-ous, and ultimately heartbreaking, as we shall see when his death is reported in *Henry V*. "I've never been so afraid of doing a role," recalls the accomplished actor Kevin Kline about his playing Falstaff in a 2004 production. "He doesn't have one bad line," he realized. But Kline was also sensitive to Falstaff's darker, destructive side: "He is not a fuzzy, cuddly guy." The critic Harold Bloom asserts that Falstaff symbolizes the pinnacle of the Shakespearean imagination. He and Hamlet, for Bloom, "are the fullest representations of human possibility." Today as much as ever, Falstaff "retains a vitalism that renders him alive beyond belief," Bloom writes.

Such estimation and outright affection developed early. "Falstaff is allow'd by every body to be a Master-piece," declares an early-eighteenth-century biographer, and if an early legend is accurate, Queen Elizabeth herself called for a sequel featuring Falstaff, "to show him in Love." The result of this alleged commission was the outlying comedy *The Merry Wives of Windsor*. The first reference to this command performance appeared in 1702, when John Dennis mentions a little defensively—he is introducing his own adaptation of Shakespeare's comedy—that the original was completed in only fourteen days, and that it had still pleased "one of greatest Queens that ever was in the World."

The Merry Wives of Windsor may have pleased Elizabeth, but it typically has not pleased critics, many of whom find the humor beneath Shakespeare's other romantic comedies and the character of Falstaff much reduced. In the play, he attempts to seduce mistresses Ford and Page, and to make them "exchequers" of their husbands' money. But the women are smarter than he. They devise a number of humiliations for the knight, and eventually their husbands get in on the pranks. "Have I liv'd to be carried in a basket like a barrow of butcher's offal?" Falstaff

Mistress Ford and Mistress Page hide Falstaff in a basket in Act 3, Scene 3 of *The Merry Wives of Windsor*. This painting is from 1792. *(Johann Heinrich Füssli)*

cries during one of his indignities. Elsewhere his circumstances force him to dress as a woman. Meanwhile, three suitors woo Page's daughter, Anne. The comical Slender and Doctor Caius end up eloping mistakenly with disguised boys, while Anne runs off with and marries her beloved Fenton. As these descriptions suggest, the comedy here is of a lower variety, mainly involving bawdy *fabliaux* stories, farcically physical humor, character types, and ironic knowledge of disguises on the audience's part. There is no transformation, which so delights us in other comedies, nor is

there a lyrical grace to the language. (Shakespeare wrote the play almost entirely in prose.)

That said, some of Falstaff's prose passages are as vigorous as those in *Henry IV*, and *The Merry Wives of Windsor* features some well-known phrases: "Why, then the world's my oyster," Pistol says, and "as good luck would have it" and "the short and the long of it" also appear. Local English settings, including Windsor Park, Frogmore, Datchet Mead, and the Garter Inn, distinguish the play. *The Merry Wives of Windsor* is also notable for celebrating the shrewd virtues of its middle-class characters. The knight Falstaff attempts his tricks on them, but he does not succeed. Finally, a comic scene of grammatical instruction between parson Hugh Evans and his pupil "William" may be the author's own fond recollections of his Stratford school days. Less warmly, Shakespeare may have relished one final dig at his now deceased nemesis William Brooke, Lord Cobham, when the husband Ford assumes the alias "Brook." Like the name "Oldcastle," this one soon had to be changed—to "Broom."

Other clues suggest a celebratory occasion for this play, likely the festivities in April 1597 related to George Carey's induction into the prestigious Order of the Garter. Carey's father had founded the Lord Chamberlain's Men, and the company briefly became Lord Hunsdon's Men when patronage transferred to the son. It would be natural for Shakespeare and his coworkers to honor their patron in this way, with the comic reprise of one of their most popular characters, and with various allusions to Carey's own ceremonial honor. Around this same time, the queen appointed Carey to his father's old position of Lord Chamberlain. The company was most likely doubly pleased: it could once again use its former name, Lord Chamberlain's Men, and its enemy the Brooke family no longer controlled this powerful position. Carey may have even commissioned *The Merry Wives*, the better to show off his premier company. Presumably he enjoyed the play as much as Queen Elizabeth did, again presumably.

The play may be only so-so, but the royal relationship surrounding *The Merry Wives of Windsor* is almost too good to be true, in part because we love to imagine two great celebrities of any age cavorting together. "Queen Elizabeth . . . without doubt gave him many gracious Marks of her Favour," says the same early biographer. A later nineteenth-century story imagines the queen even crossing the stage one night, expecting Shakespeare to cease his impersonation of a king in order to greet her. However, he resisted to "throw off his character," leading Elizabeth to drop her glove before him. Without missing a beat, he retrieved and delivered it, "aptly" giving a speech and staying in character as he exited the stage. It is a charming tale, but Richard Dutton and many other scholars believe that Elizabeth never once stepped foot in a public theater—when she wished to see a play, the actors came to her, and performed at court. In this respect John James Chalon's painting of Shakespeare, as he thoughtfully reads at the court to an appreciative Elizabeth from a thin folio volume, may be less strained historically, although it, too, retains a pleasantly fanciful quality.

THE GLOBE'S GRAND OPENING: *HENRY V*

The Globe, the exciting new theater of the Lord Chamberlain's Men, probably began staging the company's shows in the spring of 1599, or possibly on June 12, based on an astrologer's optimal prognostications. The theater took shape amid the garden plots and marshy grounds of Bankside, just south of Maiden Lane. *Henry V* may have been the opening play at the Globe, or in any case was one of Shakespeare's first works performed there. Looking backward, the play represented the grand finale of a sweeping sequence of history plays, while in the present setting of the Globe it was one of two new plays with tales of historical interest—one about England's medieval victory at Agincourt, and the other, *Julius Caesar*, about Caesar's assassination in classical Rome.

Audiences of *Henry V* would have sensed immediately that something was different, something newly ambitious and self-conscious, when the Chorus entered and delivered the play's justly famous prologue:

O for a Muse of fire, that would ascend
The brightest heaven of invention,
A kingdom for a stage, princes to act
And monarchs to behold the swelling scene!
. . .
　　　can this cockpit hold
The vasty fields of France? or may we cram
Within this wooden O the very casques
That did affright the air at Agincourt?
O, pardon! since a crooked figure may
Attest in little place a million;
And let us, ciphers to this great accompt,
On your imaginary forces work.

It is as if Shakespeare wanted to "try out" the fine new space and push his dramatic ambitions ever onward, to the very point where stage representation must break down. At first the voice sounds a little abashed, with talk of "this unworthy scaffold," "this cockpit," and "the girdle of these walls." It certainly shows a new attention to the theater's material dimensions, in which "two mighty monarchies"—that is, England and France—must be confined. It may seem foolish to foreground one's weaknesses, that is, the limitations of staging a grand historical show. However, the Chorus's overall goal is to urge the audience to grow, too, and to use their imaginations to fill in the glorious story of English military victory, about to be told in "this wooden O." For example, onlookers must add an imagined one million to the single soldier onstage. The Chorus will make similar speeches before each act, punctuating shifts in the story with elevated lyrical force ("Now all the youth of England are on fire"), while also serving helpfully to fill in details of setting and narrative ("And thence to France shall we convey you safe"). On the eve of the battle of Agincourt, before act four, the Chorus explains how its disguised king, a "little touch of Harry in the night," visits the tattered,

modestly sized English army, with "lank-lean cheeks and war-torn coats."

This patriotic, martial hero is Henry V, made famous through the centuries and dear to English hearts. Their isle, "the world's best garden," is roundly celebrated here. He sounds his fiery defiance of France, whose leaders mistakenly believe the new king remains Hal, the wayward youth he once was. The Dauphin, who initially serves as a foil to Henry, much like Hotspur did in *1 Henry IV*, flippantly gives the English king the taunting gift of tennis balls, meant as a symbol for the adolescent frivolousness he wrongly associates with Henry. "This mock," the king replies, "Has turned his balls to gun-stones, and his soul / Shall stand sore charged for the wasteful vengeance / That shall fly with them; for many a thousand widows / Shall this his mock mock out of their dear husbands, / Mock mothers from their sons, mock castles down." Henry achieves his greatest moment with his rousing speech on St. Crispin's Day, when he is outnumbered five to one by French troops at Agincourt. He wishes for no more men, for then he would have to share the coming honor. Inviting anyone "who hath no stomach" to depart, he forges an exalted fellowship amid the fighters present:

We few, we happy few, we band of brothers;
For he to-day that sheds his blood with me
Shall be my brother; be he ne'er so vile,
This day shall gentle his condition . . .

Henry here verbalizes, as king speaking to his soldiers, a radical experiential equality, and his men are sufficiently inspired. Shortly they achieve a miraculous victory, suffering only a few casualties while ten thousand French soldiers and noblemen lay slain.

Shakespeare's play has loomed large in the English imagination ever since. Winston Churchill, the country's great leader during World War II, had clearly imbibed Henry's rhetoric, which he echoed when he spoke as a new prime minister facing Nazi invasion in 1940: "Let us therefore brace ourselves to our duties, and so bear ourselves that if the British empire and its Commonwealth last for a thousand years, men will still say, 'This was their finest hour.'" Later, in 1989, the young English actor Kenneth Branagh played a more introspective hero in a powerful independent-film version of Shakespeare's play. The movie was nominated for an Oscar, and ushered in two decades of heavy Hollywood engagement with Shakespeare.

Henry V rises above mere propaganda or jingoism, however, because Shakespeare takes care to show, and to have his hero fully aware of, the costs and compromises of war. Victory, the play uneasily suggests, requires cruelty, and so at the siege of Harflour, in the middle of the play, we hear threats that "poor maidens" will be raped and "naked infants spitted upon pikes." These lines are not as famous as other, more noble lines in this speech—"Once more unto the breach, dear friends, once more," or "God for Harry, England, and Saint George!"— but these horrible images of the brutal collateral damage of warfare are just as present. Likewise, when Henry does not have enough men to secure his French prisoners, as is proper, he orders their execution, and he is also ruthless with some of his old Eastcheap tavern cohorts: Bardolph is executed for robbing a church, and a commander bludgeons the disrespectful Pistol, who also reports to us the death of Nell Quickly, his wife.

The most powerful death reported, of course, is that of Falstaff. When the tavern crew hears of his illness, Nell says bluntly about his recent rejection by Hal, "The king has killed his heart." Her later report of Falstaff's cold body is justly famous, and for lovers of those opening tavern scenes in *1 Henry IV*, hard to bear.

At its best, the play neither glorifies nor stigmatizes, but presents the responsibilities and

Portrait of King Henry V made long after his death, probably around Shakespeare's time. *(Artist unknown)*

consequences of war in all of its complexity. For example, as pleasing as is Henry's speech after receiving the tennis balls, it is undercut by his actions just beforehand—consulting with his Archbishop about how best to justify his dubious claims to the French throne. The most powerful scene of this sort occurs on the eve of battle, when Henry disguises himself as a Welsh soldier, Harry Le Roy. He is sobered by his men's varied responses about duty and the state of their—and his—souls. Arguably, Henry is at his strongest dramatically when he is most revealingly vulnerable before us, meditating on the cold comfort of "thou idol ceremony," or begging God not to think of his father's "fault." As it turns out, Henry V is still burdened by his father's usurpation of the English crown from Richard II, and fears divine judgment will ruin him on the battlefield. In these unguarded human moments, Henry is here, more than anywhere else, the true "star of England."

Once victorious, Henry's last action, too, is morally complex and ranging. He woos the French Princess Katherine in an effort to establish a long-lasting peace between "England and fair France," and he refuses to be deterred by either "nice customs" or their cultural distance—for example, the fact that she can speak only French. The play ends like most comedies, then: with a marriage. Yet the scene can be played diversely: as a romantic match bringing welcomed levity at the end of a war play, or as one more stage of Henry V's aggressive, politic rule.

Elizabethan politics also entered Shakespeare's play at one critical point, in a passage that was more contemporary and partisan than is found elsewhere in the usually poker-faced writer's works (at least when it came to political opinions or current events). The Chorus voices this moment, in the speech describing Henry V's triumphant return to London as a "conqu'ring Caesar"—

> As, by a lower but loving likelihood,
> Were now the general of our gracious
>   empress,
> As in good time he may, from Ireland
>   coming,
> Bringing rebellion broached on his sword,
> How many would the peaceful city quit,
> To welcome him! much more, and much
>   more cause,
> Did they this Harry.

The "general" in Shakespeare's comparison refers to a powerful nobleman, Robert Devereux, the Earl of Essex, for a long time the queen's much younger favorite. Elizabeth becomes the "gracious empress" in the passage, awaiting her courtier-warrior's triumphant return from Ireland, where he had been dispatched to crush an Irish rebellion.

Unfortunately, Essex's trip was becoming a military and political disaster in the spring of 1597. He agreed on a humiliating truce with the Irish and returned abruptly to the court, all without the queen's permission. She was furious, detained him in the Tower, and stripped him of his dignities. Suddenly Shakespeare's explicit praise of Essex, whom he may have supported because of the nobleman's alliance with Henry

Portrait of Robert Devereux, second Earl of Essex, ca. 1597. Devereux attempted a failed rebellion against Queen Elizabeth I. *(Marcus Gheeraerts II)*

THE GLOBE THEATRE TODAY

The original Globe Theatre burnt to the ground in 1613, and its successor was pulled down for good in 1644. Since 1997, however, the theater, now officially known as "Shakespeare's Globe Theatre," stands in Bankside once again, instantly recognizable in its iconic fidelity to the earlier playhouses.

This reconstructed Globe was the dream of Sam Wanamaker, an American actor and director, who in 1970 established the Shakespeare Globe Trust. In an interview, Wanamaker recalls as one of his early inspirations a visit to a replica Elizabethan theater, as part of a mock English village, at the Chicago World's Fair. He later envisioned a new structure in London that could "absorb the spirit of the original theatre" and be "an enrichment."

His dream of a new Globe in Southwark, as it turned out, would take nearly three decades to realize. Advised by the theater historian John Orrell, Wanamaker eventually oversaw the initial construction work, but sadly, he did not live to see the new theater in its finished state, in all of its reborn glory. He died in 1993.

The new Globe's grand opening occurred in 1997, although the first "preview" performance, of *The Two Gentlemen of Verona*, took place in August of the previous year. Mark Rylance starred in that production and went on to serve as the theater's artistic director till 2006, when Dominic Dromgoole succeeded him. As an actor, Rylance also starred in several highly regarded Shakespearean shows at the Globe. Performances are usually held from May to October and in the afternoon, much like in Shakespeare's own day.

The builders of the new theater sought to make it as historically accurate as possible, and the shows are performed with a spirit of faithfulness. Thus the Globe has the first thatched roof permitted in London since the Great Fire of 1666, and the trademark thrust stage, along with the three tiers of seating surrounding it, have also been carefully recreated. Neither spotlights nor microphones are used, and musicians play live songs on instruments from the Renaissance period. Sometimes the company follows the male-actor-as-female-character practices of their early modern predecessors. The sounds of seagulls, too, are the same today as a few centuries ago.

There are a few key differences, however. The seating capacity in the new Globe is only about half of the number of Renaissance Londoners who packed into the original Globe. Sprinklers in the roof, a concrete floor, and a modern lobby, restaurant, gift shop, and visitors' center also differ from the Renaissance version of the Globe. The location of the new theater is different as well, being about eight hundred feet to the north of the original site, and now closer to the bank of the Thames. The first location can still be glimpsed on nearby Park Street. The semicircular outline, seen through a fence, marks the foundation discovered in 1989, under a parking garage. A plaque commemorating the first Globe now hangs on the wall of a beer-bottling factory.

In many ways, to best understand Shakespeare the man, one must experience the place where his plays were first performed. Wanamaker revered the location of the Globe and the neighborhood around it as "the birthplace of the work." All Shakespeare biographers, and readers of such biographies, should take note and plan a visit.

SEE ALSO:

Day, Barry. *This Wooden O: Shakespeare's Globe Reborn*. New York: Limelight Editions, 1998.

Gurr, Andrew and John Orrell, *Rebuilding Shakespeare's Globe*. New York: Routledge, 1989.

Kiernan, Pauline. *Staging Shakespeare at the New Globe*. New York: St. Martin's Press, 1999.

Mulryne, J. R. and Margaret Shewring, *Shakespeare's Globe Rebuilt*. New York: Cambridge University Press, 1997.

Shakespeare's Globe. New York: Films for the Humanities and Sciences, 2006.

Wriothesley, the Earl of Southampton, must have felt deeply embarrassing. Nor was this the only fallout Shakespeare and his company would suffer by Essex, whose situation soon worsened.

The nobleman's impulsiveness led to his debacle in Ireland, and just so, his great pride made the queen's treatment of him insufferable. He grew increasingly agitated and unpredictable, and soon began conspiring to overthrow the aged Elizabeth. Some followers approached actors in the Lord Chamberlain's Men, "to have the play of the deposing and killing of King Richard the Second to be played the Saturday next." Essex's men offered a handsome extra payment to convince the company, which had been resisting on the grounds that the play was "so old and so long out of use that they should have small or no company [audience] at it." Shakespeare's troupe performed it, as it turned out, on the eve of Essex's attempted uprising in London, in February 1601. He set out from his London mansion and passed through Ludgate, intent on raising up citizens around him and overthrowing the unsuspecting queen.

The wish for the staging of *Richard II* now begins to make perfect sense. As will be recalled, that history play features a controversial deposition scene, where the ascendant Bolingbrook usurps Richard II. Essex was hoping that the performance would fire up his countryman to do likewise, with he himself playing the role of Bolingbrook in real life. Essex's followers supported him, but the rest of London did not, leaving the rebelling nobleman and his retinue to march down eerily quiet city streets. He returned to his home to await his prompt arrest, and was beheaded as a traitor a month later. (Southampton was convicted, too, but his life was spared. His sentence was reduced to life in the Tower.)

The quotations above are found in a government examination of one of Shakespeare's fellow actors, Augustine Phillips, following the attempted coup. Phillips must have persuaded the queen's examiners that the Lord Chamberlain's Men had been duped by the conspirators and knew nothing of Essex's intentions. Still, it was probably a nerve-racking close call, to have been questioned about and nearly implicated in an act of high treason. The company must have also found it uncomfortable to perform before the queen on the eve of Essex's execution. Yet work at the court could hardly be disparaged, and fortunately for the company, records indicate that the Chamberlain's Men did not suffer a reduction of court appearances in the wake of the Essex entanglement. As for the shrewd Elizabeth, her servant William Lambarde recorded an incident when the queen commented upon the frequent performances "in open streets and houses" of the play. "I am Richard II," she said. "Know ye not that?"

THE GLOBE'S FIRST RECORDED SHOW: *JULIUS CAESAR*

Thomas Platter, a Swiss traveler visiting London in the fall of 1599, recorded the following diary entry for September 21:

> . . . after dinner, at about two o'clock, I went with my party across the water; in the straw-thatched house we saw the tragedy of the first Emperor Julius Caesar, very pleasantly performed, with approximately fifteen characters; at the end of the play they danced together admirably and exceedingly gracefully, according to their custom, two in each group dressed in men's and two in women's apparel.

It is generally agreed that Platter describes here a performance of Shakespeare's *Julius Caesar* by the Lord Chamberlain's Men. His praise of their skills is unsurprising; foreign travelers to London frequently remarked on the quality of its theaters and actors. We might wish for more comments on the play itself, but a few of Platter's remarks helpfully remind us of certain practices. First, he focuses inordinately on the jig that concluded every performance, whether comedy or tragedy. It may take one aback, to imagine a company finishing a tragic play such as *King Lear* and then commencing a dance. Yet this was the convention, and it has been revived by the troupe at today's Globe Theatre in London. He also points out the convention of male actors playing female roles—were the "two in women's apparel" here the actors playing Calphurnia and Portia? It is very likely so.

Shakespeare chose his subject wisely in preparing *Julius Caesar* as an early "kick-off" show at the new Globe. Caesar was one of the most famous figures from ancient history. Renaissance generals appropriated his military skills, while monarchs sought to have their own glory reflected in the durable, uncontestable example of Caesar's imperial power. For example, England was about to welcome a new Stuart monarch, James I, who would fashion himself as a new Caesar Augustus, an even more powerful successor of Julius Caesar. The connection, for these kings or dukes, was strikingly literal. Both the Tudor and Stuart dynasties traced their genealogy from Brute, a legendary English ruler who was held to be the great-grandson of Aeneas, the mythic founder of Rome. Thus Caesar's power had transferred from classical Rome, through the Holy Roman Empire, and to whichever Renaissance monarch needed to justify and valorize his or her authority. The scholar Lisa Hopkins has recently argued that the issue of authority was central to any Renaissance treatment of ancient Rome, and she goes so far as to say that concerns about power could not be fully considered separate from the specters of Rome's emperors. Indeed, questions of authority lie at the heart of Shakespeare's *Julius Caesar*. We hear how Caesar "doth bestride the narrow world / Like a Colossus, and we petty men / Walk under his huge legs." Do we marvel at his power and sway here, or react against it? Is such concentrated authority in the national interest, or does it threaten to undermine that interest? Shakespeare, it should also be said, is daring in asking these political questions when he did, in the wake of Essex's uprising and very late in Elizabeth's reign. Issues of succession, royal legitimacy, and civil strife were on the tongues of all Englishmen. Famine, pestilence, a renewed threat of Spanish invasion, and the moans of maimed veterans blighted the realm.

Julius Caesar has proven to be Shakespeare's most popular out of a handful of Roman plays, and the Renaissance age loved Roman culture in general. Lisa Hopkins has also shown how Shakespeare and other English Renaissance writers used Rome and its history and symbolism to engage with and reflect indirectly, and thus more safely, their own early modern British identity. Rome as a source and analogue for this engagement must have seemed sensible, if not inevitable. Schoolboys, working by a humanist curriculum that valued Roman literature and its eloquently composed Latin language (compared with more medieval ecclesiastical Latin), found their heroes and villains in the very figures Shakespeare brought to life in his new play—Julius Caesar above all, but also the republican conspirators Brutus and Cassius, and Mark Antony, who along with Octavian (the future Caesar Augustus) ushers in at the end of the play a new regime, and one beset with exactly the same problems surrounding just rule.

Renaissance students' or writers' habit of following, in their own compositions, the ancient, revered works of others was known as *imitatio*, or imitation, and it had none of the pejorative connotations inferred when the word is used in artistic contexts today. Charles and Michelle Martindale have studied how Shakespeare carried out this very practice when composing his various Roman plays and, more importantly, how he occasionally adapted his sources for his own dramatic purposes. For *Julius Caesar*, Shakespeare followed very closely the prose account of the events surrounding Caesar's assassination in Plutarch's *Lives of the Noble Grecians and Romans*, written in Greek very early in the first century A.D. Shakespeare, as Ben Jonson claims, had "little Latin and less Greek," and in any case Plutarch's Greek text was not as widely available in the Elizabethan era. Echoes in Shakespeare's play make it clear that he in fact consulted Thomas North's English translation of Plutarch, published in 1579 and itself rendered from a French version of a Latin translation of the original. (Richard Field, the publisher of Shakespeare's narrative poems and a fellow Stratfordian, was responsible for this English edition, leading some to believe that Shakespeare may have obtained his copy of Plutarch from Field.) The Martindales show that Shakespeare typically followed his sources incredibly carefully, often using the same language as North's translation and merely shaping it into iambic pentameter, or blank-verse, lines of poetry. His divergences, though, are where his dramatic instincts really display themselves. He would alter his source text for the sake of adding wit, or deepening a character's motives, or changing given facts into possible realities, ones still to be confirmed or lost forever, and thus considerably enriching the overall theatrical experience.

Early in *Julius Caesar* a soothsayer warns the triumphant title character to "Beware the ides of March," or the month's midway point, March 15. Caesar proceeds to the Capitol, while other Romans, Cassius first among them, react uneasily to the crowd's adoration of Caesar: "this man / Is now become a god," Cassius says. On the other hand, Caesar, seeing Cassius and Brutus converse, suspects Cassius's "lean and hungry look." Cassius determines to persuade the high-minded Brutus toward conspiracy against Caesar by delivering fabricated letters of incitement—"Speak, strike, redress," says one that we soon see Brutus reading in his orchard. Soon Cassius and other conspirators arrive there, and convince Brutus of the rightness of their killing of Caesar, without "personal cause" and all for the sake of the Roman republic. Cassius suggests they kill Mark Antony, too, but Brutus resists, saying they will be "sacrificers" but not "butchers." Already Brutus is attempting to frame the murder of Caesar as not only a political act, but also a sacral and religious one. He is true to his better character in resisting the proposed murder of Antony, but it is also a decision that will have, for Brutus, fatal consequences.

In Caesar's house, the title character is awakened by the prophesying nightmare of his wife, Calphurnia. Later she urges him not to visit the Capitol that day, being the ides of March, but he responds with a mix of courage and fatalism: death will come when it will come, he says, and "Cowards die many times before their deaths." Caesar almost listens to his wife, but then Decius arrives and, playing on "mighty Caesar's" vanity, convinces him to depart. This scene is most striking for its depiction of a personal, vulnerable Caesar—here we see the emperor, but he is in his nightgown, and troubled by Calphurnia's entreaty. We see or hear other examples of Caesar's weaknesses throughout the play, which complicate our sense of the great man and our sympathies for him. We are told he refused the crown three times at the Capitol, and "swooned" in a seizure, foaming at the mouth. He has previously been feverish, crying out "as a sick girl," and Cassius seems disgusted at being a better swimmer than Caesar, and having saved him from the Tiber river. Now Cassius must "bend his body" at Caesar's very whim. Caesar's presence seems almost tiny, on this night of storms, omens, and portents. (For the Elizabethans, ancient Rome was a highly supernatural, pagan city.)

The fateful day comes at the play's midpoint. Defending his constancy, Caesar is soon stabbed by Casca and many others. Upon seeing Brutus among his killers, the fallen leader utters one of the most famous questions in English literature—and it isn't even in English: "Et tu, Brute?" (And you, Brutus?) "Then fall, Caesar," he says with his dying breath. Mark Antony soon arrives, and feeling cornered and outnumbered, he feigns support, shaking each killer's hand and arranging to speak at Caesar's funeral. Alone onstage, he vows to avenge his fallen comrade. The rest of the third act features two dueling orations, Brutus's defensive one and Antony's speech that arouses the passions and fury of the citizens. The different spirit of the speeches can be heard in the very first line of each—"Romans, countrymen, lovers" vs. "Friends, Romans, countrymen." Notice how the latter, Antony's opening, lifts upward and outward, one-two-three syllables, building in power from its opening address: "I come to bury Caesar, not to praise him." Yet Antony praises Caesar

Four senators surround Julius Caesar (Amleto Novelli) in this image from the 1914 film version of *Julius Caesar*.

indeed. Claiming it is not the right time to say how Caesar loved the citizens, he unpacks illustrations of Caesar's love. Antony here is a masterful, if manipulative, rhetorician. And just so, his ringing refrain, "And Brutus is an honorable man," quickly turns from endorsement to hollowed out, sarcastic accusation. Caesar's murder was "the most unkindest cut of all." The angry crowd marches off, and quickly kill Cinna the Poet, mistakenly thought to be a conspirator of the same name. Cassius and Brutus have already fled the city, and, as Antony says, mischief is afoot.

The final two acts dramatize the disintegration of Cassius's and Brutus's relationship and the defeat of their army. Brutus is already grieving at news of the death of his wife, Portia, and now a new triumvirate, consisting of Antony, the young Octavian, and Lepidus, are marching toward the conspirators. The ghost of Caesar visits the troubled Brutus, and predicts their meeting at Philippi. Cassius soon kills himself. Brutus, happening upon his dead ally, follows him. No servant will kill Brutus, so he runs himself upon his sword. When the victorious Antony finds Brutus's body, he praises his dead countryman, and seems to honor his pure motives: "This was the noblest Roman of them all," he says, adding that only he acted without personal envy. At this point, however, it is difficult to presume that Antony is even capable of speaking with sincerity, so powerful was his rhetoric before the body of Caesar. As this brief summary suggests, Shakespeare carefully distributes lines, as well as his attention and sympathy, across these characters, who are variously in conflict with one another. It is telling, for instance, that the title character has died by the third act. These multiple perspectives are natural, and possibly necessary: Robert Miola, in his influential study *Shakespeare's Rome*, argues that the idea of Rome was so pervasive in Renaissance culture that it had multiple meanings and values. Thus the imperial Caesar can be seen as an ideal Roman, but so can Brutus, the freedom-loving citizen who determines to kill Caesar and preserve Rome's ancient republican virtues. More darkly, the more self-interested conspirator Cassius equally represents another Roman aspect—a unique pride and insatiable grasping for power. These different illustrations of "Romanitas" take center stage at different points in *Julius Caesar*. Although the play is named after Caesar, in truth it is Mark Antony who delivers its most famous speech, and Brutus is arguably its true protagonist. In his conflicted brooding, struggles with conscience (he is "with himself at war"), and stoic acceptance of his fate, he clearly looks ahead, starting with Hamlet, to some of the great tragic characters of the coming years. In one respect, *Julius Caesar* most resembles the history plays, and with its multiple points of view, it is akin to *Richard II* in particular.

Yet most fundamentally, the play returned Shakespeare to the dramatic genre of tragedy, after he had spent the past few years on histories and comedies. *Titus Andronicus* had been a primitive version of a Roman tragedy, and *Romeo and Juliet*, though technically a tragedy, borrowed much tonally and stylistically from the lyrical and comic works of the mid-1590s. *Julius Caesar*, therefore, represents a new achievement for Shakespeare in the genre of tragedy. The strong, even austere language fits the Roman setting, and both the action-driven plot and the elevated themes of the play benefit from the author's stripping away of excessive, highly rhetorical language and poetic figures. Although their qualities of language differ, *Hamlet*, a play that Shakespeare was already working on, has much in common with *Julius Caesar*. Both are highly political plays, and Hamlet likewise contemplates man's mortality and the transience of reputation: "Imperious

Caesar, dead and turn'd to clay," he remarks in the graveyard scene. A different sort of Caesarian presence may be found in Polonius's seemingly throwaway line about having played Julius Caesar in a past university production. One hypothesis casts this actor as the same who may have played the title role of *Caesar* the year before, in effect creating a clever, possibly winking meta-theatrical reference for those again assembled at the Globe.

In discussing *Hamlet*, we have reached a new, marvelous stage in Shakespeare's career as writer and maker of theater. For now, it is enough to appreciate these first two opening triumphs at the Globe, in the crucial year of 1599. James Shapiro has recently focused on this single year of Shakespeare's life, declaring it a "decisive" one for him both creatively and professionally. It was a "fraught and exciting" year generally, even by the Renaissance's eventful standards, but for Shakespeare specifically, then in his thirty-fifth year, it may have been a miraculously productive year—the year of *Henry V*, *Julius Caesar*, and the late comedy *As You Like It*, along with the bulk of the work on *Hamlet*. This, then, was the year that "Shakespeare became Shakespeare," Shapiro argues, or, more precisely, the year that "Shakespeare went from being an exceptionally talented writer to one of the greatest who ever lived." He made this leap even while performing with the Lord Chamberlain's Men almost year-round, spending mornings in rehearsal, acting in afternoon shows, and attending to theater business on many an evening. Shakespeare, therefore, was by now spending most of his days, and most of each day, in the Globe Theatre and its surrounding precincts.

One lover of Shakespeare and culture generally, when imagining what it must have been like to see these plays for the first time, how it must have felt to be utterly unaware of how they ended,

has called this little area one of the most favored places in all of history. It is a bold statement, but fairly made.

Sources and Further Reading

Beckerman, Bernard. *Shakespeare at the Globe, 1599-1609.* New York: Macmillan, 1962.

Dutton, Richard. *William Shakespeare: A Literary Life.* New York: St. Martin's Press, 1989.

Hackett, Helen. *Shakespeare and Elizabeth: The Meeting of Two Myths.* Princeton: Princeton University Press, 2009.

Hopkins, Lisa. *The Cultural Uses of the Caesars on the English Renaissance Stage.* Burlington, Vermont: Ashgate, 2008.

Jones, John. *Shakespeare at Work.* New York: Oxford University Press, 1995.

Maher, Mary Z. *Actors Talk About Shakespeare.* New York: Limelight Editions, 2009.

Martindale, Charles and Michelle. *Shakespeare and the Uses of Antiquity.* New York: Routledge, 1990.

Miola, Robert. *Shakespeare's Rome.* New York: Cambridge University Press, 1983.

Shapiro, James. *A Year in the Life of William Shakespeare: 1599.* New York: HarperCollins Publishers, 2005.

Thomson, Peter. *Shakespeare's Theatre.* New York: Routledge, 1992.

SHAKESPEARE THE LITERARY LION

The Lord Chamberlain's Men, thanks largely to the active quill of its company writer William Shakespeare, successfully inaugurated its new theater, the Globe, during the second half of 1599. The already established troupe must have been the talk of London's many playgoers for much of this year. The players would stage successful shows for years to come. Londoners in the know gravitated toward the Chamberlain's Men's bold new plays, and the exciting new "wooden O" where they performed. As the home of Shakespeare's plays, the Globe quickly became a timbered imagination chamber. The stage was set, so to speak, for Shakespeare's greatest achievements.

A more stable theatrical atmosphere in the city and increasing financial rewards for the company were all to his benefit. The main actors were also co-owners of their theater, and royal patronage would soon be at hand. In the meantime, the company enjoyed regular invitations to perform at court before the queen. They staged plays there twice during the holiday season in 1598–99, twice again in 1599–1600 and 1600–01, and three times in 1601–02. These conditions encouraged a deeper, more fruitful season of artistic engagement and exploration for Shakespeare.

Most biographies point out his general falling off of productivity during the early years, and entire first decade really, of the seventeenth century. This fact is not so much false as rather ungenerous in the way it assesses Shakespeare's remarkable achievements. True, Shakespeare's almost inconceivable writing pace during the mid- to late 1590s, during which time he pro-

lifically completed multiple comedies, history plays, and two very different tragedies, did begin to slow down. But surely this comment cannot, must not, be treated as criticism. How could it have been otherwise? And should we really focus on the "slowing down" during the early 1600s, when the works Shakespeare did complete were of the highest order, by turns more challenging or more inspiring, but always increasing in their powers? The new plays included *Hamlet*, *Othello*, *King Lear*, *Macbeth*. In short, they were some of the greatest tragedies ever written or performed. They also included Shakespeare's last great high comedy, or pure comedy, *Twelfth Night*, though it, too, was seasoned, or mellowed, by the presence of loss and time passing. Included here as well was a trio of plays so tonally mixed and evasive in genre that a whole new designation has been created for them—the problem comedy. This intense period of accomplishment begins with one final play from the prior phase. That play is *As You Like It*, which, along with *Twelfth Night*, stands as one of the great examples, by Shakespeare or anyone, of comic drama.

AS YOU LIKE IT

As You Like It may have opened the new season of the Globe in 1599, although traditionally it is thought to be slightly later than "opening" plays such as *Henry V* and *Julius Caesar*. It appeared in the Stationers' Register, a record of publishing intentions kept with the printers' guild, on August 4, 1600. This title is marked "stayed," which suggests the play was still popular onstage then. You see, the Chamberlain's Men were less interested in printing the play than keeping others from doing so while they were still performing it. Being a festive comedy, it would have suited well the enthusiastic, "grand opening" atmosphere of the Globe. From beginning to end, the play displays a conscious engagement with its relatively new audiences in Bankside. The very title enacts a kind of commercial promise: come one, come all, the title seems to proclaim, satisfaction guaranteed. And then there is the Epilogue, in which the character of Rosalind, played at that time by an adolescent male actor, addresses the theatergoers: "It is not the fashion to see the lady the epilogue," says Rosalind, yet "good plays prove the better by help of good epilogues." The actor may be speaking on behalf of the playwright, in a rare moment when a goal is forcefully expressed: "My way is to conjure you," says Rosalind, who then promptly pulls down the fiction of her female sex: "If I were a woman, I would kiss as many of you as had beards that pleased me."

It is enjoyable to imagine the crowd's reaction to the young actor's peek-a-boo moment here: did they react with surprise at the bold action of an actor pointing out the make-believe inherent in all female characters on the English Renaissance stage? Or did they break into fits of laughter, as the young man coyly played Rosalind, then set her imagined personality aside as the play world's magic dissolved back into the world of real-life London? In this way, the two main settings in *As You Like It*, the green world that is the Forest of Arden and what Rosalind calls "this working-day world" of the court, find their parallels in the renewing, conjuring world of the theater on one hand, and our normal lives on the other. Arden is an Anglicized Forest of Ardennes, and various names here suggest a French locale, yet any student of Shakespeare's life will quickly recognize the personal significance of the place for him. His mother's family

name was Arden, and a forest of that name stood near Stratford.

As these two opposed settings suggest, *As You Like It* is also Shakespeare's most explicitly pastoral play, one of the most popular literary genres during the Renaissance, and abounding with shepherds, rustics, and country lasses. Looking all the way back to the Greek poet Theocritus's *Idylls* and the Roman poet Virgil's *Eclogues*, the genre features shepherds in dialogue, extolling the virtues of a simple country life and talking leisurely about enduring topics—love, time, nature, and so on. (Indeed, these are the very themes of Shakespeare's play.) However, these shepherds are also highly articulate about art and art-making, and typically they hold forth in a surprisingly polished, ornate style. In short, these are not true shepherds, but poets, courtiers, and even kings masquerading as simple folk in an elaborate game of fiction-making. Pastoral as a literary genre risked becoming ludicrous once it became popular and widely practiced by accomplished poets and sophisticated fellows at court. To his credit, then, Shakespeare in his play not only celebrates the pastoral ideal but also scrutinizes its paradoxical (for a supposed country setting) artificialities as well. The play's language, a mix of prose and poetry energetically shared across social classes, reflects this balance, too. Here the language struts with its highly polished lyricism, and there it settles "into so quiet and so sweet a style," for which the lord and singer Amiens praises the exiled Duke Senior.

The play opens on discordant notes of exile, usurpation, and family negligence. Oliver, who "stays me here at home unkept," hates his younger brother Orlando. When Orlando prevails in an exciting wrestling match, his life is soon at risk and he must flee to the Forest of Arden. At court, Duke Frederick has usurped leadership from his brother, Duke Senior, whom we soon find overseeing a thoughtful, peaceful anti-court in

Rosalind and Celia watch Orlando defeat Charles in Act 1, Scene 2 of *As You Like It*. This painting is from 1750. *(Francis Hayman)*

the same forest. "Sweet are the uses of adversity," he says of his exile, for here in the woods he has left behind the world's "painted pomp" and finds "sermons in stones, and good in every thing." Soon Orlando happens upon the Duke, and is taken aback by the Duke's welcoming hospitality; he has not experienced such kindness in the real world. The play's central character is Rosalind, the exiled Duke's daughter, who remains uneasily at court until Duke Frederick banishes and threatens to kill her. Rosalind and Celia, Frederick's daughter, vow to escape to the forest as well. To protect themselves, they dress as young men and assume the aliases of Ganymede and Aliena.

Already Orlando is in love with Rosalind—he spends his time in Arden carving love poems into trees—but when they next meet, he does not recognize her, and she will be unable to reveal herself. Their conversations in the following scenes are some of the most charming dialogues that Shakespeare ever composed. Rosalind, as Ganymede, explicitly demands that Orlando practice his wooing by treating her, Rosalind, as "Rosalind." The gender and identity shuffles here are mindbendingly delightful. More profoundly, Rosalind's disguise enables her to speak freely to her beloved Orlando. She achieves a level of freedom and directness unheard of for early modern women. In effect, she is able to teach Orlando how a young man becomes a grown lover, and they go so far as to have a mock wedding. Some of the more powerful moments between them feature her gentle rebukes of Orlando's excessively amorous expressions. For many men, such words are all talk and no substance. "Men have died from time to time, and worms have eaten them, but not for love," she tells him, responding to Orlando's showy romantic desperation. Their growing love takes its place amid two other couples in the forest, representing romantic extremes. Silvius and Phebe are shepherd and shepherdess, taken directly from the highly stylized pastoral romances popular during Shakespeare's day. On the more earthy side, the clown Touchstone takes up with the country girl Audrey.

As You Like It ends with spectacle and reconciliation. Hymen, mythological god of marriage, makes a startling entrance to celebrate the play's multiple marriages. In one of Shakespeare's main sources, Thomas Lodge's *Rosalynde, or Euphues' Golden Legacy* (1590, and frequently reprinted), the usurping duke eventually meets his just death, but in *As You Like It*, both Frederick and the wicked brother Oliver experience conversions and repent past deeds. They in turn receive forgiveness, this being a comic world.

A final appreciation of a few of the play's characters introduces precious biographical details. First, Jacques is the resident melancholy grump in the Forest of Arden. As we shall see, he may have been one of a few parodying representations of Ben Jonson that would appear in the next couple of years. "I can suck melancholy out of a song as a weasel sucks eggs," Jacques sneers, and in his joyless self-containment, he acts in counterpoint to the deeper, more affirming spirit of the lovers Rosalind and Orlando. That said, Shakespeare clearly did not mean to belittle Jacques completely, since he gives him one of the greatest speeches he ever wrote, "The Seven Ages of Man":

> All the world's a stage,
> And all the men and women merely players:
> They have their exits and their entrances;
> And one man in his time plays many parts,
> His acts being seven ages.
> . . .
>   Last scene of all,
> That ends this strange eventful history,
> Is second childishness and mere oblivion,

> Sans teeth, sans eyes, sans taste, sans
>   everything.

The metaphor may reflect the new theater setting: "all the world" equates with the Globe, and the comparison of world and stage echoes a Latin motto displayed at the theater's entrance. Some readers have found the successive characters in this famous speech to match well with those in the play. The old servant Adam, for example, would be the last age mentioned. Incidentally, relatively early treatments of Shakespeare and his plays connected him as an actor with the role of Adam.

Touchstone sounds like a different comic figure compared with those in Shakespeare's other plays, and in fact he wrote the role for a comic actor, Robert Armin, new to the Lord Chamberlain's Men. This difference marked one huge transition in the company's life: the departure, sometime after signing the lease for the Globe in February 1599, of Will Kemp, the Chamberlain's Men's most popular comedian. Kemp had gained fame by playing characters such as the bumbling constable Dogberry, discussed in the last chapter, and Shakespeare may be dramatizing his departure when the wittier, sharper Touchstone deflates the more clown-like William (as in "Will"), late in *As You Like It*. Maybe Kemp left because he felt the Globe's financial prospects were uncertain, or maybe the company initiated his departure, wishing its new comedy to be something beyond the popular jigs for which Kemp was beloved. More importantly, Armin's presence led Shakespeare to create for him more intelligent, more somber clown figures, including Feste in *Twelfth Night* and the Fool in *King Lear*.

Less directly, Shakespeare paid homage to his great early model and rival, Christopher Marlowe, when Phebe addresses the "Dead shepherd" and asks, "who ever loved that loved not at first sight?" She echoes a line from Marlowe's erotic poem *Hero and Leander* (characters also mentioned in Shakespeare's play). The address, "dead shepherd," likewise connects the deceased poet to his highly popular lyric poem "The Passionate Shepherd to His Love." Marlowe had been dead for six years, so why was Shakespeare honoring him now? Perhaps because *Hero and Leander* had just appeared in print, and had also been ordered confiscated by a controversial Bishop's Ban. Marlowe's name was in the air again, and Shakespeare paid him this tribute. The historical actor behind these characters is unfortunately unknown to us.

Shakespeare had created powerful female characters previously, Juliet and Portia among them, but he must have recruited or discovered one or more incredibly talented young male actors who were worthy of new, stronger female roles, beginning with Rosalind, continuing with Viola, and onward to Lady Macbeth. Working from his source, *Rosalynde*, Shakespeare chose to reduce Orlando's role, which is action-packed in Lodge's version, and amplify Rosalind's part considerably. She does many things in this wonderful play, but most of all she makes a game of love, with a spirit of play that brightens encroaching shadows in *As You Like It*. Unsurprisingly, generations of strong actresses have coveted the chance to play Rosalind, including Peggy Ashcroft, Katharine Hepburn, Vanessa Redgrave, and, more recently, Gwyneth Paltrow. The play seems to have succeeded early, too: the popular composer Thomas Morley had already set one of its songs to music ("'Twas a lover and his lass") by 1600.

SHAKESPEARE AS POET OF "DEEP ENGLAND"

The pastoral mode of *As You Like It* helpfully reminds us of how comfortable Shakespeare was with dramatizing—and how frequently his language reflects—the country or village settings of his upbringing and adult family life. We too easily think of Shakespeare as champing at the bit to escape his dead-end town of Stratford, and accomplishing all of his literary work as a thoroughly urban poet. Yet this simplifies the matter biographically, and it also risks overlooking the ever-present nature poetry throughout his plays and poems. In short, this poetry drinks deep of what the contemporary Caribbean poet Derek Walcott calls the "ale-colored skies of Warwickshire." It is there in Shakespeare's verses long before the present play. The early work is full of floral imagery—violets, cowslip, columbine, bluebells and harebells, daffodils, primroses in the hedgerows—drawn from familiar landscapes in and around Stratford, which John Leland in his *Itinerary* (c. 1540) described as "upon plain ground . . . fruitful of corn and grass." The biographer Peter Levi emphasizes the large quantities of elm trees in Stratford: "it must have looked and sounded like a woodland settlement."

A Midsummer Night's Dream features roughly forty-two kinds of flowers, trees, and shrubs ("I know a bank where the wild thyme blows, / Where oxslips and the nodding violet grows"), and Jessica Kerr has pointed out that Shakespeare often uses familiar names of flowers, as in these lines from *Love's Labour's Lost*:

> When daisies pied and violets blue,
> And lady-smocks all silver white,
> And cuckoo-buds of yellow hue
> Do paint the meadows with delight.

Cuckoo-buds are better known as buttercups today, and elsewhere Shakespeare shows his Warwickshire origins by calling pansies "love-in-idleness." Other touches of country life variously occur. He frequently knows the medicinal uses of plants, and when the goddess happens upon the gored beloved in *Venus and Adonis*, Shakespeare describes her recoiling "as the snail, whose tender horns being hit, / Shrinks backward in his shelly cave with pain, / And there, all smoth'red up, in shade doth sit, / Long after fearing to creep forth again." In *Midsummer*, a play full of Midlands fairies and artisans, we hear of Puck that he "frights the maidens of the villagery" and skims the milk. As Levi elsewhere says, "Everyone was familiar with freezing cold, with physical hard work, and at least with the sight of all the operations of agriculture: milking, shearing, ploughing, harvest, and so on." Shakespeare's early posthumous reputation continued to associate him with rural life, or "deep England": many commemorative poems connect him with the "lucid Avon," and we hear of him as "Warwickshire Will" or "Sweet Willy O."

Shakespeare's countryside experience affected all levels of his writing and thinking. For example, his texts feature several curious regional spellings, such as "scilence" instead of "silence." As for thinking, we may look to Touchstone's and Corin's talk in *As You Like It* of a "natural philosopher," meaning one who studies the natural world, but also, as David Bevington puts it, one who is "innately gifted and wisely self-taught." This emphasis continues to operate in various spheres of Shakespearean activity today. Scholars have been quick to apply the emergence of environmental criticism toward "Green Shakespeare" or "EcoShakespeare," as in Gabriel Egan's recent study where he considers the presence of "food and biological nature" in *As You Like It*. Alternately, the *Guardian* reviewer of Jez Butterworth's *Jerusalem*, a recent play and smash hit in London, described its "vision of Englishness" (it is set in rural Wiltshire) as "infused with the spirit of Shakespeare." Performers more directly uphold Shakespeare's natural appreciations with summertime "Shakespeare in the Park" productions and repertory seasons, staged everywhere from Central Park in New York City to community theaters across the country. Numerous

Shakespeare gardens, spaces dedicated expressly to showcasing the flora mentioned in the plays, also exist across the United States, for instance at Central Park, the Brooklyn Botanical Garden, Golden Gate Park, and Northwestern University. Even at the height of Shakespeare's professional busyness in London, we better understand his life if we remember his ongoing presence and investment in Stratford and his native orientation.

TWELFTH NIGHT

Shakespeare's name increasingly appeared on title pages of printed books, a host of which appeared in 1600: *2 Henry IV, Henry V, The Merchant of Venice, A Midsummer Night's Dream*, and *Much Ado About Nothing*. The last of the high comedies, *Twelfth Night* was likely performed early the following year, on January 6, 1601, at Whitehall Palace. The occasion was the annual Christmas revels at court, and the play's very title alludes to this holiday emphasis: Twelfth Night is the last of the twelve days of Christmas, otherwise known as Epiphany, on January 6. Queen Elizabeth may have requested this new play to honor her guest, the young Italian duke Virginio Orsino. A lovesick duke, also named Orsino, delivers the opening lines of *Twelfth Night*: "If music be the food of love, play on; / Give me excess of it, that, surfeiting, / The appetite may sicken, and so die." More assuredly, a performance of the play took place at the Middle Temple, one of the law schools at London's Inns of Court, about one year later. On February 2, 1602, John Manningham wrote in his diary that

> At our feast we had a play called *Twelfth Night, or What You Will*, much like *The Comedy of Errors* or *Menaechmi* in Plautus . . . a good practice in it to make the steward believe his lady widow was in love with him by counterfeiting a letter as from his lady . . . and then when he came to practise, making believe they took him to be mad.

We encountered this same diarist earlier, as the fellow who recorded the curious story about Shakespeare's and Richard Burbage's alleged bed conquests. Here Manningham sounds more intellectual, noting similarities between *Twelfth Night* and other plays.

Although these occasions were festive and the play's comic themes involve love and pranks, *Twelfth Night* actually begins on notes of grief: Orsino pines for Olivia, who mourns for her dead brother, and soon Viola arrives on the coast of Illyria, the play's faraway setting. She has just suffered, though survived, shipwreck. However, she is disconsolate over the loss of her twin brother, Sebastian, at sea. Disguised as the male "Cesario," Viola enters Orsino's service, and she soon falls in love with him. Her obstacles are two: she appears as a young man, and she must relay or "unfold" Orsino's love to Olivia, clad all in black. Olivia has vowed to mourn her brother for seven years, but soon she falls for the charming "Cesario." This motif of lost twins is a staple in Roman comedy, although here Shakespeare makes the twins of different sexes, thus necessitating a cross-dressing storyline so that one is mistaken for the other. He also found the story of a disguised woman serving the ruler she loves in a contemporary work by Barnabe Rich, *Farewell to Military Profession*.

Viola (Viola Allen) after the shipwreck in Act 1, Scene 2 of *Twelfth Night*, in this photograph published by the Byron Company in 1903.

The primary topic of *Twelfth Night* is love or, more specifically, desire, in all of its kinds and expressions, from food and drink to the most idealized unions of lovers. The play's subtitle, *What You Will*, nonchalantly hints at this varied exploration of desire. Viola delivers some of the most lyrically beautiful evocations of love—including grief at having lost it, and the passionate commitments of those in love. As "Cesario," she enraptures Olivia by explaining what she would do if she were Orsino facing such rejection:

Make me a willow cabin at your gate,
And call upon my soul within the house;
Write loyal cantons of contemned love
And sing them loud even in the dead of
    night;
Halloo your name to the reverberate
    hills
And make the babbling gossip of the air
Cry out "Olivia!" O, You should not rest
Between the elements of air and earth,
But you should pity me!

Later, Viola, indirectly talking of her own unspoken love for Orsino, tells him of her father's daughter who "never told her love, / But let concealment, like a worm i' th' bud, / Feed on her damask cheek . . . She sat like Patience on a monument / Smiling at grief." The plot's confusion grows when Viola's brother, Sebastian, accompanied by his friend and rescuer Antonio, also arrives in Illyria. Antonio saves the frightened Viola from a dual, thinking it is his friend Sebastian, while the real Sebastian thumps the naïve upstart Sir Andrew Aguecheek, and then promptly falls in love with Olivia. Eventually the twins encounter each other and movingly reunite. Seeing a production at London's Old Vic, the author Virginia Woolf described the siblings "looking at each other in a silent ecstasy of recognition." At play's end, Olivia and Sebastian are already married, and Orsino, discovering his page is the lovely Viola, also proposes marriage.

As in the other late, great comedy *As You Like It*, Shakespeare diversely enriches this play world with a colorful cast of characters. At the two extremes, there is Olivia's cousin Sir Toby Belch, who, as his name suggests, has a little of the drunken, gluttonous Falstaff in him. He is regularly at odds with one Malvolio (his name means "ill will"), Olivia's sour, humorless steward. For Shakespeare's early audiences, Malvolio in his stern proscriptions evoked the city's Puritans; battles between Sir Toby and Malvolio reflected class tensions as well, between the aristocracy and middle class. Of course, their personalities also differ greatly: "Dost thou think, because thou art virtuous, there shalt be no more cakes and ale?" asks Toby. In other words, Malvolio's severity should not be categorically applied to one and all. The festive characters resist, and then punish, Malvolio for his delusions of power and presumptions of Olivia's favor. This tricking, or "gulling," of Malvolio introduces a dimension of satire into *Twelfth Night*, a harsher spirit of comedy that was by then a trend on London's stages.

In Shakespeare's hands, the treatment of Malvolio, which involves a forged love letter that he all too quickly believes is from Olivia, begins in a madcap way, culminating in Malvolio's appearing, by request of the letter, in cross-gartered yellow stockings and wearing a ridiculous smile. We would do well today to imagine a contemporary fashion that would most humiliate a super-serious servant—maybe wearing a Speedo bathing suit, or a rapper's baggy jeans. Audiences tend to enjoy Malvolio's comeuppance, and they savor the pranksters' taunt that the "whirligig of time brings in his revenges." The joke worsens from here, however. Malvolio, thought mad, is apprehended and confined in a dark room. Soon the play's Fool, Feste (another shrewd role for the actor Robert Armin), dresses up as the curate "Sir Topas" to evaluate the "notoriously abused" Malvolio. At this point, the play's hierarchies have become topsy-turvy, creating an inverted social world suitable for the Feast of Fools, a carnival-like pagan holiday still celebrated on Twelfth Night during the Renaissance. Most painfully, Malvolio finally stands before Olivia, only to learn that he has been tricked: she does not love him. Thus this subplot, too, enacts the same topics of love and desire, but in this case they turn out poorly for the foolishly aspiring lover. Nor will he forgive, or adapt himself to comedy's expectations of resolution: "I'll be revenged on the whole pack of you!" he cries. Shakespeare prevents us from writing off Malvolio's dark fate, and threat, too quickly.

Although a minor character involved in a buffoonish subplot, Malvolio was immediately seen as a prominent part of *Twelfth Night*. The star actor Richard Burbage played the role, and we saw earlier how the diarist Manningham focused most on the "practice" against Malvolio in his summary of the play. By 1623, it was performed at court as *Malvolio*, and a 1640 poem proclaims, "The Cockpit galleries, boxes, are all full / To hear Malvolio, that cross-gartered gull." The critic Kenneth Burke defends Malvolio and other minor characters as also reflecting the height of Shakespeare's artistry. "To a degree their appeal is in their sheer value as inventions," he explains. "They are a nimble running of scales; they display the poet's farthest reaches of virtuosity . . . —the feeling that brilliance is being given out with profusion and overwhelming spontaneity." Finally, the darker resolution of the Malvolio storyline is tonally consistent with other melancholic moments in *Twelfth Night*, intimations of age and death often crystallized in songs: "Youth's a stuff will not endure," sings Feste, or "Come away, come away, death, / And in sad cypress let me be laid." The refrain of the final song continues this dirge-like note—"For the rain it raineth every day"—although there is also a countering glimpse, of triumph and an acting company's growing confidence: "But that's all one, our play is done, / And we'll strive to please you every day."

SHAKESPEARE'S NEW HEIGHTS: *HAMLET*

Between 1599 and 1602, between the eyewitness report about *Julius Caesar* and the diary entry about *Twelfth Night*, Shakespeare wrote (or rewrote) a new tragedy, entitled *Hamlet*, his first unparalleled masterpiece. This play, about an introspective young Danish prince whose father's ghost urges him toward revenge against his uncle, who has usurped the throne and hastily married the queen, is one of the greatest accomplishments in world literature. *Hamlet* is possibly the most powerful tragedy in the English language (that is, unless we prefer another Shakespearean tragedy). It has never gone out of fashion, but has held "the mirror up to nature" for every age that has read and performed it. The Shakespeare biographer Park Honan nicely catalogues those qualities that made *Hamlet* so innovative: its complex, intelligent hero; fresh, subtle word-play; new treatment of the revenge motif; refined, elegant soliloquies; philosophical richness.

Shakespeare's Hamlet displays his deepest emotions and thought processes repeatedly throughout the tragedy bearing his name, as in his first soliloquy. There, Hamlet, clad in black, mopes at the Danish court at Elsinore. He awkwardly refuses the oily persuasions of his uncle/ stepfather/king, Claudius, and the general festivity surrounding his and Queen Gertrude's wedding:

O, that this too too solid flesh would melt
Thaw and resolve itself into a dew!
Or that the Everlasting had not fix'd

His canon 'gainst self-slaughter! O God!
    God!
How weary, stale, flat and unprofitable,
Seem to me all the uses of this world!
Fie on't! ah fie!

Hamlet employs images of corruption throughout the play—unweeded gardens, cankers, ulcers, hypocrites' garments. The chief abuser is his uncle, the new king. The Ghost has not yet told Hamlet that Claudius has committed both regicide and fratricide against the prince's father, but already Claudius's seizure of the throne and quick marriage to his mother appall him. Hamlet compares his deceased father, "so excellent a king," to Claudius as Hyperion (or a Titan) to a satyr. The actor Richard Burbage first gave life to Hamlet's theatrical thinking, doing so upon the Globe's thrust stage. And such thinking, as Northrop Frye argues, always advances the action of *Hamlet*. In Hamlet's soliloquies, for example, he consistently achieves a fresh realization about his condition or circumstances (if not an outright course of action). Audiences have rarely been so privileged to overhear this interior speech.

By 1602, the Lord Chamberlain's Men had already opened their *Hamlet*, although no record exists of any performance during Shakespeare's lifetime. That said, the publication of a pirated, "bad" first quarto in 1603, announced as "diverse

Two pages from the first quarto, also known as the "bad quarto," of *Hamlet*, published in 1603.

times" acted by the company "in the City of London," makes this timing very likely. This first edition could not be allowed to stand as Shakespeare's text, for some of the most famous speeches are almost unrecognizable in their garbled state (the result of actors trying to reconstruct the entire script, and thereby make a few pence from an unscrupulous printer). Thus a second edition appeared in 1604, expanded and vastly superior, suggesting that Shakespeare had supplied his own manuscript for corrective publication. This textual mystery regarding *Hamlet* would deepen in 1623, when the First Folio presented a version lacking some of the quarto lines but featuring additional passages never before printed.

Shakespeare seems to have overwritten *Hamlet*; that is, its great length has almost always made the play unactable in its complete form, which would run to five hours onstage. The famous actor John Gielgud recommended that *Hamlet* be performed in repertory, alternating with other plays, because no actor could sustain the demands of playing Hamlet every night. As James Shapiro puts it, if Shakespeare were in love with anything at this time, "it was with words." He had pushed himself to a new creative level, and now had a play "that was better than anything he had ever written." The English poet Ted Hughes describes Shakespeare's even greater fluency as a "pincer movement" of Latinate and Anglo-Saxon words, and many critics have noticed a rhetorical pattern of doubling throughout *Hamlet*. The result, says Hughes, is a "weirdly expressive underswell, like a jostling of spirits." Faced with such verbal amplitude, therefore, directors have always made necessary cuts for their productions, and these differing early texts may reflect altered stage versions as well.

In any case, the swift appearance of these quarto editions suggests popularity, as does a further note on the first quarto's title page, about its being acted "also in the two Universities of Cambridge and Oxford, and elsewhere." These university locations are significant, since around this time the public theaters were facing rival companies with indoor settings and more satirical, sophisticated shows. In this respect, Shakespeare may have been asserting, with *Hamlet*, the Chamberlain's Men's broad appeal, capable of both popular "blockbuster"-type shows and philosophical, linguistically dazzling creations. *Hamlet*, like no other play before it, was both. It pursued with great eloquence some of the most challenging topics in Renaissance thought. For example, Shakespeare echoes the Italian humanist Pico della Mirandola and other thinkers when Hamlet exclaims, "What a piece of work is a man!" His speech, moving from man's impressive form and faculties to his being, ultimately, "this quintessence of dust," comments upon Pico's observation that man is peculiar in nature, in between angels and animals. Yet also, with its curious revenger-prince, *Hamlet* caught the imagination of popular culture as well.

The university tutor and man of letters Gabriel Harvey wrote in the margin of a book that "The younger sort takes much delight in Shakespeare's Venus & Adonis: but his Lucrece, & his tragedie of Hamlet, Prince of Denmarke, have it in them, to please the wiser sort." Anthony Scoloker, in 1604, speaks of "Friendly Shakespeare's" mixed-genre tragedies, and how "it should please all, like Prince *Hamlet*." More oddly, in a 1605 pamphlet, *Ratseis Ghost*, named after a recently dead outlaw, the title character ventures "all the money in my purse" against Burbage, "to play Hamlet with him for a wager." The play was even performed far from London, on an English ship off the coast of Sierra Leone, as early as 1607.

The presence of Hamlet's father's ghost was an especially popular element for early audiences. This brings us to the "Ur-Hamlet," an early version of Shakespeare's story that does not exist in present form but which scholars believe must have been known by 1589. Certain scholars, including Peter Alexander and Harold Bloom, conclude that this early version, too, was by Shakespeare, and was perhaps his earliest dramatic work. Alternately, Thomas Kyd may have written it; he already could take credit for English theater's most popular play of this kind, *The Spanish Tragedy*. Yet another writer in 1596 described one who "looks as pale as the Visard of the ghost which cried so miserably at the Theater like an oyster wife, 'Hamlet, revenge.'" This detail indicates that the Ghost was featured in the earlier play. These Renaissance versions, likely influenced by supernatural elements in Seneca's popular tragedies, differed from their medieval source by Saxo Grammaticus. (Shakespeare knew it in Belleforest's popular collection.)

In the source story, the evil brother (named Feng, not Claudius) kills the king in public. Thus the king's son, here called Amleth, has no need of the Ghost to inform him of the crime. However, the source story makes him very young and powerless, and so the prince must fake madness for years until he can properly get revenge on Feng. In Shakespeare's *Hamlet*, the Ghost dramatically appears in the opening scene, and then soon reappears to tell his son the horrible truth: "The serpent that did sting thy father's life / Now wears his crown." At this point, in revenge plays, the revenger trusts the ghost without hesitation and undertakes his revenge. In *Hamlet*, Shakespeare blows up the genre and its demands for swift action. By doing so, he creates a far more philosophically interesting play, and a more intellectually vexed revenger. First, Hamlet may simply be too sensitive to carry out this traditional violence. The Ghost demands action of his son, but Hamlet, a student at Wittenberg and prone to deep thoughts, does not sound convincing when he vows to "sweep to my revenge" with "wings as swift / as meditation or the thoughts of love." Meditation? Thoughts of love? That is not terribly intimidating.

The Romantic writer Goethe described Hamlet as a "beautiful, ineffectual dreamer," who has a "lovely, pure, noble, and most moral nature, without the strength or nerve which forms a hero." For centuries critics and directors have treated Hamlet as a poet for whom revenge killing is too coarse or downright absurd. Lately scholars have sought to return Hamlet to his early roots in action-oriented revenge tragedy—a protagonist who jumps in an open grave, is a skilled swordsman, and does, finally, kill the wicked king. Released from the interior chamber of his soliloquies, scholars such as Margreta de Grazia and Alan Stewart have foregrounded Hamlet's material situations in the play, from his relationship to spaces, including graves and kingdoms, to the many letters he sends to those around him. Hamlet, in short, is not an idea, a mental state, or psychological condition. In the world of *Hamlet*, he is a living person, and one of the most alive characters ever encountered on page or stage.

FAMILY QUESTIONS: FOR HAMLET, FOR SHAKESPEARE

Hamlet reacts to the Ghost as a skeptic, or at least with fear and procrastination masquerading as skepticism. This quality is more dramatically fruitful for Shakespeare and his play than a simple inability to act. Instantly, upon seeing the Ghost, Hamlet frames it ambiguously: "Be thou a spirit of health or a goblin damned," from heaven or hell, "Thy intents wicked or charitable," he inquires. He does not know if he can trust the Ghost's story. Overall the play asks, what is true? How can I know what is true? And how can I make myself act, in any way, if I remain uncertain about the authenticity of my information or motivation? The Ghost, to a strikingly modern character such as Hamlet, is a "questionable shape" indeed. It has been frequently pointed out that the play's very first words are exceedingly fitting—"Who's there?" asks one sentry approaching another—in being a question, and in seeking to identify. Repeatedly Hamlet will worry, and thus pause in his revenge, that he has encountered a "damn'd Ghost," even a devil, armed with the ability to appear as his father, who "Abuses me to damn me." This same uncertainty marks the play's most famous speech:

> To be, or not to be: that is the question:
> Whether 'tis nobler in the mind to suffer
> The slings and arrows of outrageous
>   fortune,
> Or to take arms against a sea of troubles,
> And by opposing end them? To die: to sleep;
> No more; and by a sleep to say we end
> The heart-ache and the thousand natural
>   shocks
> That flesh is heir to, 'tis a consummation
> Devoutly to be wish'd.

Readers through the centuries have never exactly agreed on what these illustrious words mean: what *is* the question? Is it about life after death (the "undiscover'd country")? Or about suicide? Or revenge and its consequences? The line most consistent with Hamlet's attitude toward the Ghost appears toward the end of the soliloquy: "Thus conscience does make cowards of us all"—that is, his very awareness of what he is so radically unaware of (whether it be the Ghost's nature or the guessed-at afterlife) kills his "native hue of resolution" and makes him inactive.

If not inactive, it at least makes him indirect, and inscrutable. Hamlet's subsequent plan to act mad, or "put an antic disposition on," after meeting the Ghost creates even greater uncertainty for readers. Hamlet is the hero and title character, yet for much of the play we do not know if he is actually mad, or feigning madness for the sake of substantiating the Ghost's claims and dodging Claudius's suspicions. Or, as one critic has memorably explained, perhaps his act of madness is masking his genuinely mad state. That sort of ironic confounding of what is and what appears to be ("I know not seems," Hamlet says) is squarely in the spirit of this play, whose uncertainty of knowing makes it a firm harbinger of the coming seventeenth century, with its new discoveries, "new philosophy" (which puts all in doubt, as one poet famously wrote), and new explorations of human character and destiny.

The uncertainty or theatricality that Shakespeare insists upon reaches out to other parts of *Hamlet*. Midway through the play, Hamlet welcomes a group of traveling players to Elsinore, and it may be Shakespeare's way of cleverly celebrating some of his fellow actors, who had performed in Denmark in the 1580s. It also becomes an occasion to hold forth on his theories of acting and the day's theater gossip, as we will see. More relevantly to plot and theme, Hamlet employs the players to present *The Mouse Trap*, an indicting play-within-a-play by which he hopes to confirm Claudius's guilt. *Hamlet* is a play that explores the power of plays, as well as the troubling ability of actors to show more emotion and seeming resolution than those with real-life reasons to do so ("What's Hecuba to him, or he to Hecuba?" Hamlet meditates). It goes likewise with Ophelia, whose relationship with Hamlet is palpable if now past, but about which we can determine very little, between her understandable indirections before her snooping father and Hamlet's dismissive playacting, regrettably harsh madness, or some combination thereof. We are also invited to ponder how much Queen Gertrude knows. Does she not see her marriage with Hamlet's uncle as too quick, not to mention incestuous? Might she have even conspired with Claudius in Hamlet's father's death?

Painting of Ophelia from 1894 *(John William Waterhouse)*

sion (1948) played up this angle of maternal-filial angst.

At its core, *Hamlet* is a play about a royal family broken, and even more sweepingly, about three families broken. Hamlet's own challenges of young adulthood in a complicated family are mirrored in Ophelia's oppressive circumstances. Her father, Polonius, is a bumbling version of Claudius, with his own sinister edges. Her brother Laertes, a student as well, also mirrors Hamlet. When Hamlet accidentally kills Polonius, Laertes swiftly returns to Denmark and almost single-handedly causes revolution; he is the true avenging son, quick to do what Hamlet cannot. And on the outer edges of the play, but stepping center stage at the end, is Fortinbras, who marches his army against Denmark to seek revenge on behalf of his father, who fell to Hamlet's father. Both of these more active sons put further pressure upon Hamlet's own complicated mission. On the other hand, when Hamlet returns to England, having avoided Claudius's murderous designs for him, he has grown out of his earlier paralysis: "There is special providence in the fall of a sparrow," he tells his friend Horatio. Hamlet, then, does seem to achieve resolution, although never with the kind of laser-like aggression of Laertes or Fortinbras. There remains an eerie feeling that the fatal events of the play's conclusion happen *to* Hamlet, rather than because of him. John Cox is certainly right that Hamlet's perceptible change "functions to heighten his tragedy by deepening our recognition and understanding of him and our admiration for him."

Almost certainly details from Shakespeare's personal life shaped, to varying degrees finally unverifiable, certain aspects of *Hamlet*'s fictive world. Less than authoritatively, one early reporter claimed that Shakespeare wrote the Ghost's parts in *Hamlet* "in a charnel house in the midst of the Night." Less fancifully, a number of biographers

One of the play's most climactic moments involves Hamlet's confronting of his mother in her bedroom, upon her very bed. Sigmund Freud developed the influential theory in the early twentieth century that Hamlet is a textbook sufferer of the Oedipus Complex: "How does he explain his irresolution . . . ? How better than through the torment he suffers from the obscure memory that he himself had contemplated the same deed against his father out of passion for his mother?" Laurence Olivier's famous film verhave noted both a change of mindset and the effects of home life within the play. For example, some see signs of a "daring transformation" in Shakespeare's life, leading to a cascade of new words in his writing. What charged him in this way, or rather was he shocked or made anxious by something? If we look broadly, we might point to the Essex rebellion discussed previously, although Shakespeare was almost certainly underway on *Hamlet*, if not finished, by early 1601. (It wasn't entered in the Stationers' Register till July 1602.) Performing regularly at court, he might have also felt some disturbance at the sight of his declining queen, Elizabeth. Who would succeed her, and would it be a peaceful transition? Elizabeth had ruled for nearly a half century, and would be dead within two years. As a countryman and subject, Shakespeare may have been racked with the mortal broodings that mark Hamlet's mindset.

Shakespeare during this time experienced more personal, local losses as well. "Family love is at the play's center," writes Honan, who says in *Hamlet* Shakespeare draws upon "the complicating pressures of Elizabethan domestic life." Recall that his son, Hamnet, had died fewer than five years ago. It must have been a strange experience—a series of tiny pullings upon the heart— to repeatedly write his son's name, or something very close to it, as he worked on his manuscript. (In records from the time, the names "Hamnet" and "Hamlet" are interchangeable.) He may have also remembered a much earlier incident in Stratford when composing the news of Ophelia's death by drowning. A woman died in this way just outside of Stratford in 1579; she was named Katherine Hamlett.

Other deaths soon struck the family as well. In the spring of 1601, the Hathaway family's shepherd, Thomas Whittington, died. His will mentions forty shillings "due debt unto me, being paid to mine executor by the same William Shaxpere."

Perhaps the shepherd had lent Shakespeare money, but the total may also represent wages not yet paid or funds kept safely with the family—an early modern savings account, in other words. Later that year, an entry appeared in the Stratford Burial Register: "1601 Septemb. 8 Mr. Johannes Shakspeare." Shakespeare's father, then, was still living when *Hamlet* was completed and first performed, but perhaps he was already ailing. An artifact associated with John's death, a "small paper-book," was discovered in 1757 in the Henley Street home, having been hidden between tiling and the roof. Although the original is now missing, and its authenticity is therefore very much uncertain, copies of thus strikingly Catholic confession survive. Consisting of fourteen short articles or paragraphs, it is known as John Shakespeare's "Spiritual Last Will and Testament." In it John solicits his family's

Painting of Edwin Booth as Hamlet from 1873 *(Library of Congress)*

"holy prayers" to quicken his "long while in Purgatory," which brings to mind the Ghost's comment to Hamlet that he is "Doomed for a certain term to walk the night / And for the day confined to fast in fires / Till the foul crimes done in my days of nature / Be burnt and purged away."

It is hard to resist making some sort of connection between the decline or loss of John Shakespeare and the absence of Hamlet's father and the Ghost's appearances. We also hear a passionate articulation of a son's grief in Laertes's reaction to Polonius's death. Or perhaps Shakespeare transferred, for the sake of dramatic distance, his mourning for his son onto a not-yet-faced grief for his father. He may have also imaginatively stepped into his father's shoes, since

AN OVERLOOKED SHAKESPEARE POEM

Is a writer more of a literary lion when a distinctive voice marks—and seems to broadcast from—any passage he or she has written, or alternately, when that writer shows such range of voice that two pieces may have been written at the same time, and yet sound absolutely different? At least in 1601, Shakespeare displayed his greatness by the latter means. During that year, it is well known that he was likely writing or possibly revising Hamlet, one of his greatest tragedies and a veritable fountain of newly coined English words. This play is also punctuated throughout with powerful, rhetorically charged soliloquies in blank verse, and it shows exquisite sensitivity to how different characters speak and think differently. He was also writing Troilus and Cressida, probably, or even one of the other problem comedies.

However, Shakespeare also saw another poem published during this year, just the third time he had seen his poetry into print. (This does not include the unauthorized inclusion of five sonnets by Shakespeare in The Passionate Pilgrim in 1599.) The sixty-seven-line poem, among the most mysterious of his writings, is entitled "The Phoenix and the Turtle" (though apparently not titled by him originally). It is lyrically beautiful without being particularly comprehensible. Or rather, one intuits a distant, veiled meaning behind the poem's allegorical narrative about the phoenix, a mythical bird known for arising again from its own ashes, and a turtle dove. Yet efforts to elucidate that meaning from the storyline and the given words leave a reader with tentatively held ideas at best.

Robert Chester printed this curious, underappreciated poem by Shakespeare in a collection called Love's Martyr: Or, Rosaline's Complaint. Allegorically shadowing the Truth of Love, in the constant Fate of the Phoenix and Turtle. The book was dedicated to Sir Robert Salisbury, and the various poets featured here, including Ben Jonson, John Marston, and George Chapman, use the "phoenix and turtle" motif to elegantly celebrate Salisbury's family, or perhaps a specific wedding in the family. Others have seen it as a veiled lament for the Earl of Essex's fall from favor and his execution. No other connection between Shakespeare and the nobleman has been discovered.

Drawing on the "Parliament of Birds" convention popular in medieval poetry, Shakespeare meditates on the death of ideal love between the phoenix and turtle. The poem is, in one sense, a ceremonial mourning song for the pair. It has also been called a philosophical hymn. Here, "Every fowl" is ordered to "Keep the obsequy so strict," or observe the funeral proceedings. The birds are presented as "Love and Constancy":

So they loved as love in twain
Had the essence but in one,
Two distincts, division none:
Number there in love was slain.
. . .

tradition connects him most as an actor with the role of the Ghost. In James Joyce's *Ulysses*, Stephen Daedalus theorizes that John Shakespeare's death made William more sensitive to his own fragile, wounded fatherhood. "Remember me," the Ghost commands Hamlet. "Ay, thou poor ghost, while memory holds a seat / In this distracted globe," the son responds, referring to his head as globe but also cleverly pointing out the show's location—the Globe Theatre. If Shakespeare played this role, he in a certain sense trades places with his dead son. He, the father, now speaks from the grave, to an intelligent son whose blood still pulses. Perhaps the great character of Hamlet is a dramatist's extended eulogy, and the play itself a series of prayers for the dead, which were no

Property was thus appalled,
That the self was not the same;
Single nature's double name
Neither two nor one was called.

Readers will notice here the evasive quality to the statements here. They exist within a tradition of philosophical paradox—how can there be both two and one?—and such cerebral poetry was about to become very popular. Later critics would speak of this kind of poetry as of the "metaphysical" school, made most famous by John Donne, a poet slightly younger than Shakespeare.

A "threnos," or formal lament for the dead, concludes the poem. The five stanzas of this final section shrink to tercets, or three lines per stanza, from quatrains previously, giving the poem an intensifying effect, even as the tonal solemnity continues. "Death is now the Phoenix' nest," declares the poem, boldly rewriting the expected mythic narrative of the phoenix rising from its ashes. The runic, riddling quality of the verse remains—"Truth may seem, but cannot be, / Beauty brag, but 'tis not she"—but the poem ends with a simple, pitying command, "For these dead birds sigh prayer." Germaine Greer has called Shakespeare's "The Phoenix and the Turtle" the "most perfect statement of the Platonic ideal in English poetry."

On the other hand, we should not too quickly create a cryogenic chamber of abstractions and idealism around this poem. It tells us something biographically: Shakespeare neither had given up entirely his activity as a lyric poet nor was uninterested in his writing appearing in print. Instead he was, in the phrase of Patrick Cheney, a "literary poet-playwright," and interested in what Lukas Erne has previously framed as literary authorship—an interest that reached to the publication of the plays as well.

Speaking of the plays, let us remember, too, that Shakespeare must have remained very busy at the Globe in the year that this pensive, reposeful poem was published. The American poet Marvin Bell nicely captures in his poem "Shakespeare's Wages" our professional mover and shaker, working with others and with an eye on the profits: "Him again, the bard of bards, bard of the boards, he of the company and crew. / He wears a bag of coins, his purse, his recompense, his toll, his confidence. / It's a pigskin bag for one, without a thought of silk, altogether common." Like the main paradox in his poem, Shakespeare's single poetic voice could flourish in two contrasting literary worlds.

SEE ALSO:

Bell, Marvin. "Shakespeare's Wages," *Poets Respond to Shakespeare*. Iowa City: University of Iowa Press, 2005.

Cheney, Patrick. "'An index and obscure prologue': Books and theatre in Shakespeare's literary authorship," *Shakespeare's Book: Essays in Reading, Writing, and Reception*. Manchester: Manchester University Press, 2008.

Greer, Germaine. *Shakespeare*. New York: Oxford University Press, 1986.

Honan, Park. *Shakespeare: A Life*. New York: Oxford University Press, 1998.

longer permitted in Protestant England. Marvin W. Hunt, in his recent study of *Hamlet*, movingly speaks of the play as a "benediction for a dead boy."

THE WAR OF THE THEATERS

In 1600, the Burbages made a business decision that soon led to fierce competition between the Lord Chamberlain's Men at the Globe and what were generally known as the "private theaters"— that is, companies of child actors that performed indoors, favoring sophisticated plays enjoyed by usually more privileged audiences. Such companies may sound strange today, but they had a long history in Renaissance England, in part because (as in England today) many young men participated in choirs connected with cathedrals, college chapels, or grammar schools. After the Theatre opened in London in 1576, these groups increasingly expanded into dramatic performances. The two most distinguished companies were the Children of the Chapel Royal, associated with the court, and the Boys of St. Paul's Cathedral, connected with the prestigious school there. The Chapel Royal company performed in the early years of Elizabeth's reign, and even resided in a theater in Blackfriars throughout the 1580s. The ornate writer John Lyly composed his best plays when the Boys of St. Paul's were in their heyday, from 1587 to 1590. Fortunately for Shakespeare's adult company and the public theaters generally, these troupes lay dormant throughout the 1590s. But that was about to change.

The Burbages had been sitting on hall space at Blackfriars monastery. Their father, Richard, had purchased it in 1596, hoping to establish Chamberlain's Men's shows there immediately, but the neighborhood resisted. For the next few frustrating years, the space was unusable as a theater, thus this major investment was a bust. In 1600, the family leased the space to the Master of the Chapel Royal, who promptly restored that company and began producing shows. Perhaps sensing a craving for something new among London's theatergoers, the Boys of St. Paul's had already resumed activity in 1599.

The theater landscape was suddenly more crowded, and much more competitive. Moreover, thanks to the influence of the boys' companies and their more exclusive audiences, plays themselves trended toward a different kind of comedy, known as comic satire. The humor was typically more pointed in tone and language, and aimed at real persons' expense. In other words, these playwrights did not flinch from attacking rivals. Blistering parodies soon appeared on their stages. This mix of new competition and more aggressive new comedy led to a series of back-and-forth salvos among the playwrights of the Globe and those writing for the private theaters. The battle later became known as the War of the Theatres, and for those involved, it was the "Poetomachia" (Poets' War).

London's literary landscape had already become harsher and more vindictive by the summer of 1599, leading the city's bishop to order "That no Satires or Epigrams be printed thereafter." This prohibition probably spurred one satirist, John Marston, toward playwriting. (His poetry had already been ordered burnt.) His first play, *Histriomastix*, was a tale about law in a corrupt society, in which the character Chrisoganus bore a clear resemblance to Ben Jonson, Shakespeare's friend and fellow playwright. Marston may have meant it as a compliment, but the prickly Jonson took it otherwise: late in 1599, the Chamberlain's Men performed Jonson's new comedy, *Every Man Out of His Humour*. It mocked Marston and his bombastic writing style with its character Clove, who frequently quotes clumps of Marston's verses. Jonson also berated another writer for the children's companies, Thomas Middleton. The war was on.

It was a bold answer from the Chamberlain's Men; Jonson's play would doubtless incite further attacks, but perhaps controversy, they felt, would increase audiences at their new theater. Jonson continued his offensive in another play, *Cynthia's Revels*, performed this time by the Chapel children, as was *Poetaster* in the autumn of 1601. There, Jonson's virtuous Roman doppelgänger, the true poet Horace, gives two posers representing Marston and Dekker a pill that makes them vomit their silly, infated words. He also took swipes at Shakespeare's plays, their friendship notwithstanding. Finally, in *Satiromastix* Marston and Dekker struck back, crowning Jonson's fictional counterpart Horace with nettles. Jonson by now had attracted government suspicion, and so he restrained his vitriol, bringing the literary battle to a close.

Shakespeare was not a primary participant in these battles, but inevitably he was caught up in this major standoff. A poem from this time suggests that Shakespeare's disposition made him unfit for the scabrous attacks of the Poets' War, and the theaters' turn to satire generally. It presents him as honest and gentle: "Thou has no railing, but a reigning wit," and praises him as "our English Terence." However, one contemporary Cambridge play chose to celebrate a more rough-and-tumble author: "Why here's our fellow Shakespeare puts them all downe," it crowed. While praising Jonson's outrageous vomiting scene in *Poetaster*, it also claimed firmly that Shakespeare "hath given him a purge that made him beray his credit." This comment may apply to Shakespeare's next play, *Troilus and Cressida*, whose surly characters Ajax and Thersites represent Jonson and Marston. Marston's play *The Malcontent* makes fun of *Hamlet*, and his *What You Will* seems to respond to *Twelfth Night* by appropriating its subtitle and presenting its own Malvolio, whom Shakespeare may have based on

Marston. The Chamberlains' Men even stole *The Malcontent* and performed it themselves, to get back at the Chapel Royal children for adopting one of their repertory plays.

Less confrontationally, Shakespeare also decided to comment on the state of the theaters in passages in *Hamlet* that feature the traveling actors. Today, these passages are thought to be later additions to an earlier completed manuscript, whereby Shakespeare made his play speak to "current events." In the first quarto, Hamlet's classmate Guildenstern explains why the players must travel: "novelty carries it away" and the principal public audience "are turned to private plays, / And to the humour of children." In the Folio version of *Hamlet*, the other classmate Rosencrantz speaks of an "aerie of children, little eyases"—that is, a nest of little hawks—that now "berattle the common stages." No play was viable, we shortly hear, unless "the poet and the player went to cuffs." Guildenstern then summarizes, "O, there has been much throwing about of brains." The children's companies have won the day, even against "Hercules and his load too." This last line was a sensitive one, since a painted sign outside of the Globe featured Hercules holding the world atop his shoulders. In another scene between Hamlet and the players, Shakespeare takes the opportunity to disapprove of exaggerated overacting associated with the larger, outdoor stages. "Speak the speech, I pray you, as I pronounced it to you, trippingly on the tongue," Hamlet advises the actors, as if serving as a mouthpiece for the writer himself. He is greatly offended, he says, when he hears a "robustious, periwig-pated fellow tear a passion to a tatters."

These added passages sound a note of uneasiness: Shakespeare as a mid-career writer, established with a particular company and theater, expresses concerns about a trendy new style of playwriting, along with the popular children's companies in their indoor theaters. He is aware of his own public theater's limitations, and fears his own plays will grow outdated and stale. As he usually did, he soon responded to these changing tastes with an answer, incorporating style change of his own.

THREE "PROBLEM" PLAYS

During the next three years, from 1601 to 1604, Shakespeare completed a trio of plays—*Troilus and Cressida*, *All's Well That Ends Well*, and *Measure for Measure*—that have for a long time confounded critics. They are comedies, technically speaking, yet they differ widely from his previous comic writing. The tone is often more challenging, compromising, and caustic. Shakespeare in these plays seems more willing to create an imposing work, one less concerned with pleasing audiences. In an extreme example, the character Thersites concludes *Troilus and Cressida* by speaking of his syphilis and promising to "bequeath you my diseases." This is hardly a gentle requesting of applause, as in other plays' epilogues. Harold Bloom has spoken of the darker, wearisome, festering world of these comedies as illustrations of "the rancid." Characters are often predatory, fantasies dark, and physical bodies repulse and betray rather than delight and unite. What's more, these plays' endings and many scenes therein are, well, fundamentally not comic. Either the whole storyline's worth has been radically called into question, or this or that character remains so unappealing that the narrative resolutions fail to be satisfying overall.

These plays do serve as fitting corollaries or complementary works to the tragedies Shakespeare was composing during this period. He had finished *Hamlet*, was in the middle of *Othello*, and may already have had *King Lear* and *Macbeth* in mind. It is reasonable to suppose that Shakespeare, having written a tragedy of *Hamlet*'s caliber, simply could no longer write the kind of high romantic comedies of the previous years. Or perhaps this change of tone was more personal: the scholar Edward Dowden in the late nineteenth century ordered Shakespeare's life and writings into four phases. He described this period as "out of the depths"—a time when the playwright was wrestling with evil and suffering. "Shakespeare had been reached and touched by the shadow of some of the deep mysteries of human existence," says Dowden. If this is so, then Shakespeare may have been speaking through his character Achilles, who says, "My mind is troubled, like a fountain stirr'd; / And I myself see not the bottom of it."

While it is perfectly possible that Shakespeare's soul may have encountered Dowden's "terrible forces of the world," we should not overlook literary tastes and market demands as valid explanations for the change in tenor in the three above plays. James P. Bednarz, in *Shakespeare and the Poets' War*, argues that Ben Jonson had sought to escape Shakespeare's shadow by veering toward a harder kind of comedy, "comical satire." His success in three early plays demanded that Shakespeare respond. He did more than this; he refashioned his own proven style. According to Bednarz, we can see Shakespeare appropriating Jonson's influence in a "counter-trilogy" of *As You Like It*, *Twelfth Night*, and *Troilus and Cressida*. Using this last play as a "hinge work," we next witness Shakespeare deepening and/or undercutting this comic engagement with *Troilus*, *All's Well*, and *Measure for Measure*. The very tension suggested here, between these plays themselves and their flouting of comedy's expectations, led F. S. Boas in 1896 to coin the phrase "problem plays." Lately scholars have backed away from the phrase, pointing out that many of Shakespeare's plays do not fit perfectly into the prescriptive boxes of this or that genre. Still, to employ another phrase sometimes used, these three plays do seem more alike than different in being grouped together as "dark comedies."

Troilus and Cressida dramatizes the great founding legend of the classical world, the Greeks' siege of Troy to recapture Helen. As read in Homer's enduringly popular epic poems, the Trojan War was a high occasion of valor, heroism, and the dignified sadness of war. Shakespeare produced his version of this famous narrative in the shadow of a similarly named play by the Admiral's Men, as well as the 1598 publication of George Chapman's bold English version of the first seven books of Homer's *Iliad*. Shakespeare's title characters refer to young Trojan lovers, who are separated when Cressida's father defects to the Greek camp. This more courtly, romantic focus reflects later treatments by Chaucer and other medieval sources. Strikingly and summarily, Shakespeare deflates the very validity of one of history's greatest conflicts. Not even those in the midst of battle either believe in the cause or come off particularly well. Thersites, debauched and abusive even by clowns' standards, declares that "all the argument is a cuckold and a / whore; a good quarrel to draw emulous factions / and bleed to death upon." The resulting play is a cynical, pessimistic exploration of war and love, represented respectively by their deformed spokesmen, Thersites and the pimp-like Pandarus. He brings together the lovers, but Cressida soon cheats on Troilus with Diomedes, a betrayal that reflects the initiating adultery of Helen with the Trojan Paris. In this world, nothing is faithful or worthy of belief and the efforts on its behalf.

The early history of *Troilus and Cressida* remains mysterious. It was entered in the Stationers' Register in 1603, likely to prevent publication by others, and it was published in 1609. The first title page announced it as written by Shakespeare and performed at the Globe. Yet that page was soon retracted, and a second quarto appeared with a preface: "Eternal reader, you have here a new play, never staled with the stage, never clapper-clawed with the palms of the vulgar, and yet passing full of the palm comical . . . " The author seems to say here that this play has never been performed ("staled with the sage"), although the dismissal of the "vulgar" suggests that the *public* stages are meant. An indoor performance would explain some of the differences between this play and Shakespeare's prior works—the harsher tone and more heavily Latinate language, for example. The play was neglected till the early twentieth century, when George Bernard Shaw, buoyed by the more naturalistic theater of Ibsen, became its champion. These days, it has become a play that increasingly speaks to our own complicated, disappointed times. This play is also the most complicated in terms of genre: the 1609 quarto's preface speaks of it as a comedy, while that edition's title page announces "The Famous History of Troilus and Cressida." Moreover, in the First Folio, it appears with the tragedies.

Charles Williams admitted in the middle of the last century that *Troilus and Cressida* "has the signs of a great play, yet it hardly succeeds in being one; indeed it hardly succeeds in being a play at all." This sense of looming failure is right there in the play's prologue: "hither am I come / A prologue arm'd, but not in confidence / Of author's pen or actor's voice[.]" Some of the most powerfully written scenes are prose denunciations of major characters, as when Thersites attacks Ajax or mocks Achilles and his companion Patroclus. Shakespeare reserves Ulysses to give voice to some of those great signs about which Williams spoke above. "Time hath, my lord, a wallet at his back / Wherein he puts alms for oblivion," he warns Achilles, urging his fellow Greek not to rely on his past glories in battle, which are already being forgotten. Likewise, Ulysses's discourse on hierarchy and order has been diversely influential:

"Take but degree away, untune that string, / And hark what discord follows." John Adams evoked this passage when pondering the best political path for the young democracy that was the United States. This example involving an early American president is convenient, for to fully appreciate the sting of Shakespeare's bitter play, we must imagine our own cherished history being ruthlessly exposed—imagine the Founding Fathers not as courageous patriots and statesmen, but as greedy landowners, slave drivers, and adulterers.

For *All's Well That Ends Well*, Shakespeare drew upon a tale in the medieval author Boccaccio's *Decameron*. The action occurs at the courts of Roussillon and Paris, and a battle camp in Florence. The play's heroine, Helena, is unfortunately not desired by the man she loves, Bertram, and so she spends the entire play heroically overcoming his resistances: his immaturity and surliness generally, his arrogance about his higher social ranking, and his own ongoing reservations about marriage, which seem little diminished at the play's conclusion. Helen's story of obstacles defeated is the thing of fairy tales, but there is no fairy-tale ending here. The play opens with sadness, as both Bertram's and Helena's fathers have recently died. Helena's real grief, though, is for the imminent departure of Bertram, who must relocate to Paris. There the king will be his guardian. Helena fully realizes the social gulf between her and Bertram—"'Twere all one that I should love a bright particular star / And think to wed it, he is so above me"—yet she persists. She, too, travels to Paris, where she soon cures the ailing king. She is allowed to choose any husband, but Bertram, once chosen, promptly flees to the wars in Italy.

In a letter to his mother, Bertram swears off marriage until Helena successfully removes an ancestral ring from his finger, and then bears his child. He thinks this means forever, but the enterprising Helena, with the help of a "bed trick" that

occurs here and in the next play, manages to meet even these extreme conditions. Back in France, Bertram finds himself in a confusing bind with the king, but the pregnant Helena soon appears to resolve all problems. Bertram's follower Parolles, out for himself and eventually a betrayer of his countrymen, adds to the gloomy quality of *All's Well*. As a lord says, "The web of our life is of a mingled yarn, good / and ill together." With so much ill abounding, maybe there is a glimpse of good in Bertram's late promise to love Helena "dearly, ever, ever dearly."

In Italy, Bertram speaks of "my sick desires" for the maid Diana, and the final problem play, *Measure for Measure*, devotes a great deal of attention to desire, both at the individual level and widespread across a culture. We first encounter Duke Vincentio, ruler of Vienna, and learn that he not only has tolerated vices in his state for the past fourteen years, but also wishes to relinquish his governing role and "formally in person bear me / Like a true friar." Thus will he see better "what our seemers be" in Vienna, if citizens are in fact what they appear to be. Yet it is also suggested that he is running from his own vices: "He had some feeling of the sport, he knew the service, and that instructed him to mercy," says the worldly Lucio, explaining Vincentio's leniency. In other words, "The Duke had crotchets in him," or strange whims that he has kept private. Perhaps he wishes to retire from public life to indulge himself further.

The duke designates his "strict deputy," the "precise" Angelo, to succeed him, and soon his government enacts harsh, reactive measures: the city's brothels are being demolished, and Claudio, imprisoned for fornication, is to be executed. His sister, Isabella, about to enter a convent, first visits Angelo to seek mercy for her condemned brother. Two intense scenes of debate occur, the first in which Angelo becomes enamored with Isabella.

Shakespeare achieves great moral expressiveness in showing us Angelo's conflicted state of mind. He will resort to villainy, but he is the more admirable character in realizing fully his great hypocrisy and abuse of power:

> Can it be
> That modesty may more betray our sense
> Than woman's lightness? Having waste
> ground enough,
> Shall we desire to raze the sanctuary
> And pitch our evils there? O, fie, fie, fie!
> What dost thou, or what art thou, Angelo?
> Dost thou desire her foully for those things
> That make her good? O, let her brother live!

In their second meeting, he agrees to spare Isabella's brother—if she will submit her body to him. She chastely refuses, and is angry when Claudio urges her compliance. He understands her anger, but his following explanation of his fear of death echoes some of Hamlet's famous lines:

> Ay, but to die, and go we know not where;
> To lie in cold obstruction and to rot;
> This sensible warm motion to become
> A kneaded clod; and the delighted spirit
> To bathe in fiery floods, or to reside
> In thrilling region of thick-ribbed ice;
> To be imprison'd in the viewless winds,
> And blown with restless violence round
> about
> The pendent world; or to be worse than
> worst
> Of those that lawless and incertain thought
> Imagine howling: 'tis too horrible!

Isabella does not sympathize: "Die, perish," she says severely as she departs.

Fortunately the Duke, disguised as Friar Ludowick, now intervenes, and undertakes the kind of manipulation of events that makes him resemble a playwright. He convinces Isabella to accept Angelo's offer, as long as Mariana, whom Angelo has previously scorned, replaces Isabella. Despite Angelo's ignorance of the "bed trick" played on him, he nevertheless orders Angelo's death anyway. There follows what one critic has called a "head trick": the Duke ensures that Claudio's life is spared, but not before Isabella and Angelo think the execution has taken place. The head of an expired pirate is sent instead. Upon the Duke's official return, Isabella demands justice. Soon the Duke is revealed to be the friar, leading to Angelo's confession and wish for death. He is ordered to marry Mariana, and then told he will suffer Claudio's presumed fate. Isabella—and this moment is a breathtaking one—pleas for his life. The play concludes in a series of marriages, including, surprisingly, the Duke's asking for Isabella's hand. The fact that she says nothing afterward may signal a pointed silence, if not outright rejection, that Shakespeare has built into his ambiguous play.

Measure for Measure is today treated increasingly as a successful work, despite its status as a "problem play." Its ideas—about human nature, moral values, self-control, political liberty, dissimulation, death, and forgiveness—are ambitious for any stage production. The play, nowhere more so than at its ending, demands audiences to assess the relative virtues and vices of its deeply flawed characters. "We are all frail," Angelo tells Isabella—as he is planning to have his way with her. These clear moments of human brokenness may be one reason why this is Shakespeare's most theological play. Its very title comes from a biblical phrase: Jesus, in his Sermon on the Mount, says, "For with what judgment ye judge, ye shall be judged: and with what measure ye mete [i.e., give out], it shall be measured to you again."

The play also addresses political leadership with thoroughness. This theme seems especially bold when we realize that Shakespeare was now writing for a new monarch. *Measure for Measure* was performed before James I during the Christmas revels in 1604, less than two years after the new king assumed the throne. "Tired with all these, for restful death I cry," Shakespeare writes in sonnet 66, which may date from this time. At the least, it shares with the problem plays an extreme tiredness and even disgust with life. It was an ironic feeling for Shakespeare to dramatize in these plays, for, as we shall see, he was now working and writing right at the center of England's political universe.

Sources and Further Reading

Bednarz, James B. *Shakespeare and the Poets' War*. New York: Columbia University Press, 2001.

Burke, Kenneth. *Kenneth Burke on Shakespeare*. West Lafayette, Ind.: Parlor Press, 2007.

Cox, John. *Seeming Knowledge: Shakespeare and Skeptical Faith*. Waco, Tex.: Baylor University Press, 2007.

Dowden, Edward. *Shakespeare: His Mind and Art*. New York: Harper, 1899.

de Grazia, Margreta. *Hamlet Without 'Hamlet'*. New York: Cambridge University Press, 2007.

Honan, Park. *Shakespeare: A Life*. New York: Oxford University Press, 1998.

Hunt, Marvin W. *Looking for Hamlet*. New York: Palgrave Macmillan, 2007.

Kerr, Jessica. *Shakespeare's Flowers*. New York: Thomas Y. Crowell Co., 1969.

Levi, Peter. *The Life and Time of William Shakespeare*. London: Macmillan, 1988.

Stewart, Alan. *Shakespeare's Letters*. New York: Oxford University Press, 2008.

JACOBEAN SHAKESPEARE

Shakespeare and the rest of the Lord Chamberlain's Men performed for Queen Elizabeth on February 2, 1603. It would prove to be the company's last appearance before her. The queen had moved up the River Thames to Richmond Palace, and she died there on March 24. On the same day, her council proclaimed James VI of Scotland as her royal successor—he was now King James I of England. The Jacobean era had begun. Elizabeth had ruled since 1558, and so her death and James's accession signaled a seismic change in England's national life. And the differences were pronounced. Elizabeth's long continuation of the Tudor dynasty gave way to the house of Stuart. She had assumed the throne as a young, vulnerable monarch, and remained unmarried and childless, whereas James began his reign as a monarch already, accompanied by his queen, Anne of Denmark, and three children, Henry, Elizabeth, and Charles. The new age would be less heroic but more worldly.

Elizabeth's and James's personalities were very different as well: she had always been shrewd and prudent, whereas James was sophisticated, extravagant, and sometimes even scandalous. The court immediately reflected his influence. He imprisoned Sir Walter Ralegh, his predecessor's favorite and an anti-Spanish seadog, and rewarded those who were more modern and cosmopolitan. He released Henry Wriothesley, the Earl of Southampton and Shakespeare's patron, from prison (he was being held there following Essex's rebellion); he knighted the young intellectual Francis Bacon, a great legal mind and man of court; and Robert Cecil, the son of Elizabeth's

great secretary Lord Burghley, he made the Earl of Salisbury. Cecil quickly became James's main political counselor.

James dramatically expanded the court, dispensing knighthoods and other titles generously (not to mention profligately), and he brought to it a new spirit of opulence and revelry. This changed atmosphere was about to benefit Shakespeare's theater company tremendously. Furthermore, the

Portrait of King James I of England and VI of Scotland, ca. 1606. James became the patron of Shakespeare's company after his ascension to the monarchy. *(John de Critz the Elder)*

new king's Scottish background, his high view of a monarch's absolute sovereignty, and his broader focus on a united Britain helped to determine the subjects of and give form to some of Shakespeare's later plays.

THE CREATION OF THE KING'S MEN

James made his way southward from Scotland to England throughout April 1603, and he arrived in London by May 7. A mere ten days into his rule there, he issued a resounding sign of support for Shakespeare and the rest of his company. His royal warrant of May 17 reveals how strongly aware the new king already was of the Lord Chamberlain's Men, and their superior standing among London's theater companies:

> Know ye that we, of our special grace, certain knowledge, and mere motion, have licensed and authorized, and by these presents do license and authorize, these our servants, Lawrence Fletcher, William Shakespeare, Richard Burbage, Augustine Phillips, John Heminges, Henry Condell, William Sly, Robert Armin, Richard Cowley, and the rest of their associates, freely to use and exercise the art and faculty of playing comedies, tragedies, histories, interludes, morals, pastorals, stage-plays, and such other, like as they have already studied or hereafter shall use or study, as well for the recreation of our loving subjects as for our solace and pleasure when we shall think good to see them, during our pleasure. And the said comedies, tragedies, histories, interludes, morals, pastorals, stage-plays, and such like to show and exercise publicly to their best commodity, when the infection of the plague shall decrease, as well within their now usual house called the Globe, within our county of Surrey, as also within any town halls or mote halls or other convenient places within the liberties and freedom of any other city, university town, or borough whatsoever within our said realms and dominions, willing and commanding you and every of you, as you tender our pleasure, not only to permit and suffer them herein without any of your lets, hindrances, or molestations during our said pleasure, but also to be aiding and assisting to them, if any wrong be them offered, and to allow them such former courtesies as hath been given to men of their place and quality. And also what further favor you shall show to these our servants for our sake we shall take kindly at your hands.

James directed this request regarding "The Players' Privilege" to his Keeper of the Privy Seal, who two days later formally issued the royal patent. So sweeping was this show of favor, the company would no longer be known by the same name. Now they could proudly call themselves the King's Men, or as they are elsewhere spoken of, His Majesty's Players. James himself, instead of the Lord Chamberlain, became the official patron of the company.

This vital relationship was reflected not only in the king's permitting and authorizing the troupe to perform, but also in the warrant's solicitations for support and courtesy, or at least acceptance, from anyone whom the new company might encounter in the course of its theatrical work. The company could now work more confidently and with more security under the king's validation and protection. Soon other existing theater companies were brought under royal patronage as well. Thus Shakespeare's company's main rivals, the Admiral's Men, became known as Prince Henry's Men, while another company known as Worcester's Men became Queen Anne's

Men. Even the Children of the Chapel Royal, the group performing at Blackfriars and taking away business from the public theaters, were rebranded the Children of the Queen's Revels. However, the patronage of the king himself was clearly the most coveted and most lucrative.

King James in the above warrant clearly shows himself as knowledgeable about theater. In fact, the first actor mentioned, Lawrence Fletcher, had acted as a "comedian" at the king's court in Scotland, and James may have insisted that he be a part of any company that bore his name. Fletcher seems to have been welcomed by the existing actors (he is left something in one of their wills, for example), but he is not mentioned among the "Principal Players" in the First Folio of Shakespeare's plays. Presumably he did not remain with the King's Men for the long term. The company received additional new blood in John Lowin, who also joined in 1603. He began as hired man, but soon became a shareholder or "adventurer" in the company, which he stayed with for nearly forty years. On the portly side, he has been traditionally connected with the roles of Falstaff and Henry VIII. In the warrant, King James also appears aware of London's theater scene specifically. Twice he articulates the main genres of plays (comedy, tragedy, history) as well as types of plays previously dominant and still staged (interlude, moral) and even styles of plays and poems that reflected current taste (pastoral). He also speaks of the former Chamberlain's Men's workplace, the "their now usual house called the Globe."

A new patron, who was the sovereign ruler of their nation; new actors; soon-to-be regular opportunities to perform at court, before the royal family and England's most powerful courtiers and noblemen; and the generous payments and gifts that often followed these performances: clearly it was an exciting time for the King's Men.

However, Jannette Dillon and others have argued that there is a more ominous aspect to this new, royal association. Perhaps King James shared political leaders' nervousness about the theaters satirizing current events and inciting disorder. He may have wanted the most influential company close at hand, easily supervised and influenced. Being rewarded and maintained by James, the King's Men would therefore be inclined to show support for royal prerogative.

Regardless of their kept circumstances, the company quickly showed itself capable of provoking James's wrath. Ben Jonson was called before the Privy Council and accused of treason and popery (that is, being Roman Catholic) after his play *Sejanus* created a scandal. The timing was awkward: it was performed at court during the first Christmas season of James's reign. In the following year, a play about a 1600 conspiracy against James when he was Scotland's king also drew his displeasure. "I hear that some great counselors are much displeased with it," reported a gossipy letter writer, "and so is thought [it] shall be forbidden." Shakespeare may have written this lost play, and he also may have collaborated with Jonson on *Sejanus*, based on the latter's comment in its 1605 preface about a more pleasing "genius." No proof or trace of this work exists. Censorship was always a very real prospect for Shakespeare and his fellow playwrights, even for the company (and perhaps especially so for them) that enjoyed the privilege of being the King's Men.

More positively, the king's existing interest in the theater and in Shakespeare's company led directly to a significant increase in the number of plays performed at court. Six or seven performances on average were annually staged for Queen Elizabeth; James I requested nearly twenty shows per year, and the King's Men were responsible for the great majority of them. Their activity at court grew from roughly three shows

SHAKESPEARE THE KING'S MAN

When the Scottish king James I assumed the English throne in 1603, a new political and cultural age was at hand. He was the first of a Stuart line of kings, after more than a century of rule by Tudor monarchs. The last of these Tudor rulers, Elizabeth I, wore the crown as England's queen for nearly fifty years. The styles of Elizabeth and James were vastly different. Her court was associated with mindful management if not outright frugality, and often she stood in a kind of English isolation and defiance against various European and Catholic powers bent on overthrowing or greatly weakening her. On the other hand, James's court was, from the outset, a place of extravagance and decadence. He was a lover of cultured festivity and freely dispensed his royal prerogatives, such as noble titles and valuable properties, among his increasing number of courtiers. There was also an initial promise of a détente or softening of conflict in terms of religious divisions, and likewise James sought to establish a much more cosmopolitan, broadly governing leadership style and court atmosphere. Thus he was celebrated as ruler of a United Britain—that is, not just England, but Scotland and Ireland as well—and at different times at court, Spanish political influence and French tastes and fashions were prevalent.

Shakespeare and the Lord Chamberlain's Men experienced a drastic professional change when James I arrived. Shortly they were renamed the King's Men, a royal association that served as testament to their general reputation as the most accomplished, successful acting company in England at the time. Royal support had its material benefits as well: during one procession through London, the company, being official servants of the king, wore opulent red liveries, or retainers' outfits. More importantly, this royal patronage also meant that one of the King's Men's most frequent and appreciative audience members was James I himself. During the first decade of the seventeenth century, Shakespeare's company was present at court on numerous occasions, especially during holiday festivities, and they performed a variety of plays there. From November to February 1604–05, for example, the company performed eleven plays before the court. Needless to say, these many performances were handsomely compensated by the crown, giving the King's Men not only stature but significant profits as well.

However exciting and financially advantageous it was to be enjoying royal support, this privileged position could sometimes make visiting actors squeamish. Most obviously, sometimes the king did not appreciate, or even disapproved of, certain performances, as with the company's poorly received production of Ben Jonson's *Sejanus* during the first winter at court. The play dramatizes Roman wickedness, intrigue, and injustice at the court of Tiberius— perhaps its subject was too sensitive for a new king, and it certainly didn't make a good first impression for the theater company.

Residence at the Jacobean court also exposed the actors to decadence or excesses for which James soon became notorious. The Jacobean court atmosphere seemed to have made an impression on Shakespeare later in his career. While average Englishmen struggled with a number of problems during the decade from 1603 to 1613—including food shortages, a year during Elizabeth's reign to thirteen for James, more than those by all other companies combined. And naturally, the majority of the King's Men's shows consisted of plays by Shakespeare, both new productions and old favorites.

James's wife, Queen Anne, was also an avid fan of the theater, further increasing demand at court for plays. One record exists in which a servant of Anne's is desperately seeking out a new play from London's actors. Richard Burbage replied that

plagues, fears of Catholic plots, and so forth—James I ruled as a spendthrift, racking up huge expenditures for which he awkwardly had to ask Parliament's help. Many found the moral compass of his court questionable as well, and worried that James was too lax of a ruler and full of too much levity and debauchery for a Christian man of any sort.

The brooding of the typical, increasingly disappointed English citizen finds its way into the plays Shakespeare wrote during this decade. The Roman drama *Coriolanus* explores the various duties of the body politic, and how different parts of a polity should properly relate to and work with one another. *King Lear* expresses concern for "unaccommodated man," and however tragically noble Lear becomes, we never forget that he is a king who has been neglectful—"I have ta'en too little care of this," Lear says. We find similarly resigned or abdicated rulers in later plays such as *The Winter's Tale* and *The Tempest*. The suspect ruling figure is even there in *Measure for Measure* (1604), which Peter Thomson calls a *caveat rex*, or "king's warning," for the new Stuart monarch. The court's and city's tendency toward sexual profligacy also comes under examination in this play. The Duke, disguised as a friar, lambastes the bawd Pompey Bum:

> . . . Do thou but think
> What 'tis to cram a maw or clothe a
>   back
> From such a filthy vice; say to thyself,
> From their abominable and beastly
>   touches
> I drink, I eat, array myself, and live.
> Canst thou believe thy living is a life,

> So stinkingly depending? Go mend,
>   go mend.

The character Marina in *Pericles* encounters a similarly repulsive world of sexual exploitation and predation. Finally, that comparatively minor, misanthropic play *Timon of Athens* offers comment (sometimes veiled and sometimes barely so) on the greed and prodigality at court. "Lived loathed and long, / Most smiling, smooth, detested parasites," Timon rails against his false friends, who have denied him in his own time of need. In a more proverbial vein, this play, too, seems to offer James I a warning about his host of sycophants and hangers on, always fickle. As Apematus says, "Men shut their doors against a setting sun."

As the sun of Shakespeare's career was also setting, these were the moral and ethical concerns found in his plays performed at court, making his writing for the Jacobean stage seem all the more bold and courageous.

SEE ALSO:

Astington, John. *English Court Theatre, 1558-1642.* Cambridge, U.K.: Cambridge University Press, 1999.

Kernan, Alvin B. *Shakespeare, The King's Playwright: Theater in the Stuart Court, 1603-1613.* New Have : Yale University Press, 1995.

Marino, James J. *Owning William Shakespeare: The King's Men and Their Intellectual Property.* New Haven: Yale University Press, 1995.

McGuire, Philip C. *Shakespeare: The Jacobean Plays.* New York: St. Martin's Press, 1994.

Milward, Peter. *Jacobean Shakespeare.* Naples, Fla.: Sapientia Press of Ave Maria University, 2007.

the queen has seen every play in the King's Men's repertory (no small number!), but fortunately the company has just revived *Love's Labour's Lost*, "which for wit and mirth he says will please her exceedingly."

Between 1603 and Shakespeare's death in 1616, the King's Men performed at court nearly two hundred times. They were compensated handsomely for these more exclusive occasions, and naturally their reputation was greatly enhanced. However, the prosperity that was to follow for more than a decade could not be anticipated in 1603. In fact, for several terrible months in 1603–04, life itself could hardly be counted on. At the time when the above warrant was issued, in May 1603, it seems that Shakespeare and his new company were not even able to perform: notice that James in the above warrant allows his King's Men "to show and exercise publicly" (that is, to perform in London) only when "the infection of the plague shall decrease." The situation was about to grow far worse before becoming better.

THE PLAGUE STRIKES AGAIN

Even as King James was establishing his royal residence in and around London, another presence was again growing in the city—the plague. The resulting outbreak in 1603–04 would prove to be the most deadly occurrence of the plague in Shakespeare's lifetime. Aside from the personal peril involved, this outbreak of plague worsened an already professionally harmful season of inactivity for London's theater companies. In the spring of 1603, Shakespeare's company ceased performing, first because of the church season of Lent and then because of Queen Elizabeth's declining health. Her counselors grew anxious about possible uprisings following her death. They did not want the "dangerous matter" of plays that might encourage "rogues" and "discontented persons" to rebel. After the queen's death, the theaters closed for a time of mourning, and remained so before the new king's arrival in London, perhaps as a sign of decorum. The first signs of plague extended this inactivity. When James speaks of the "pestilence" in his May warrant, the theaters were already closed, even though that week's record shows only eighteen plague deaths.

The mortality rate soon spiked: 72 by the end of June, 917 one month later. James's coronation occurred on July 25. The ceremony was deemed necessary for the proper transfer of sacral rule to the new king, but the traditional progress by the monarch through London was postponed. Only a select few possessing tickets were allowed to witness the coronation, and guards stood at London's gates, prepared to bar citizens from visiting the ceremony at Westminster Abbey. By the last week in August, the plague claimed more than three thousand victims. For the theaters, its peak commercial season of summer was totally lost. The companies' only option was to vacate London and tour the countryside. The plague was so widespread, however, that even this plan had to be curtailed. Oxford to the north and Dover to the south were also infected, but records referring to the "King's players" suggest that Shakespeare and his troupe did manage to perform in Bath, Coventry, and Shrewsbury. It was the best thing the company could do in response to an outright financial emergency. They were hopeful that London's theaters would reopen in the fall, but the crisis persisted: fifty to a hundred people were still dying weekly at the end of the year, and conditions did not improve till the following spring. Overall, thirty thousand people succumbed to the plague.

King James had also fled London for safer locales. He took his court to Winchester in the fall, and then moved on to Salisbury, and to the Earl of Pembroke's elegant residence of Wilton House in particular. From October to December, England's government was effectively located there. Shakespeare's company seems to have fled the city, too, possibly to the actor Augustine Phillips's new home in the respectable suburb of Mortlake, upriver and west of London. The King's Men finally gave their first performance before their patron at Wilton House on December 2, and an expense record describes them as "coming from Mortlake." The play may have been *As You Like It*. James next moved to Hampton

Court, a royal residence just outside London, and the Christmas Revels were held there, despite the plague. The King's Men performed seven shows, including *A Midsummer Night's Dream*. The king must have been impressed with his first glimpses of the royal company, and with the creations of its main writer in particular. In the same year, the chronicler William Camden included Shakespeare among ten of "the most pregnant wits of these our times."

Tradition has it that the writer earned the friendship of the king, who "was pleas'd with his own Hand to write an amicable Letter to Mr. Shakespeare." Alas, this letter was never printed and is unavailable today. James also may have been responsible for a payment to the King's Men on February 4, 1604, for their "maintenance and relief," presumably because they remained unable to perform publicly in London and were enduring hard times. The theaters finally reopened in April 1604. However, the proclamation also made it clear that if plague deaths rose above thirty persons per week, the companies would "cease and forbear" immediately. Although never as severely as in 1603–04, London would intermittently face extended playhouse closings due to plague for the next six years.

PUBLIC EVENTS IN LONDON

James I made his ceremonial progress through London on March 15, 1604, a month before the theaters reopened. Elaborate triumphal arches were constructed at various points along the route, each praising the new king by a different theme. One featured a miniature of the city itself, welcoming its new sovereign and celebrating fresh political hopes; others featured a Garden of Plenty or the New World, a symbol perhaps of James's international interests. The King's Men did not perform during the progress, although playwrights such as Ben Jonson and Thomas Dekker contributed short dramas to the "Magnificent Entertainment" of the new monarch.

Yet as James's servants, technically speaking, Shakespeare's company may have walked behind the king as a part of his royal retinue, or even stood along the streets to observe the procession and pay homage. We know that they were dressed appropriately for such a festive occasion. The office of the Master of the Wardrobe has a record of a grant of four yards of "Red Cloth bought of sundry persons," to nine of the company's actors, in their capacity as Grooms of the Royal Chamber. This cloth was used to outfit the men in scarlet liveries, or courtly uniforms, befitting royal employees. Shakespeare, this time, is listed at the top of the list.

The year was proving a busy one for the new king. In January, he had called the Hampton Court Conference in response for Puritans' requests for church reforms. The most lasting outcome of this conference was the commissioning of the Authorized Version of the Bible. Not completed till 1611, and forever known as the King James Version, it was a new, less confessionally partisan English version that all subjects could read in good faith. In the meantime, the king resisted Puritan calls for rigorous enforcement of ecclesiastical and theological matters. He was more moderate and inclusive in outlook, and his internationalist ethos inclined him toward an acceptance even of Roman Catholics. (However, James's latitude and leniency would change dramatically a year later, following a nearly successful plot against him, his family, and all of England's leadership.) Thus James alienated his Puritan constituency for the first time, and this tension reemerged in March when the first Jacobean Parliament met. Immediately the two sides began to wrangle over who had which powers, and the basis for the independence of each side.

For eighteen days in August 1604, the King's Men served the Spanish Ambassador at Somerset

House, the queen's palace, during sensitive peace negotiations between England and Spain. They may have done what they did best—perform plays for everyone's entertainment after tense days of official business—or they may have assisted the ambassador in more mundane ways. There is a record of payment for twelve men. It does not name Shakespeare specifically, but he was almost certainly present at such an important occasion on the king's behalf. It would have been an excellent chance for him to observe an array of great men. The royal family hosted a ball at the end of the Spaniards' stay. Prince Henry danced a galliard, the queen and various courtiers danced a *brando*, and then several revelers danced a *correnta*. Perhaps some of these politically powerful, highly sophisticated participants became models for the proud Roman characters (or, in *Antony and Cleopatra*, partying ones) that Shakespeare was about to create.

PRIVATE RESIDENCE IN LONDON: THE CASE OF *BELOTT V. MOUNTJOY*

We have the rare benefit of knowing where Shakespeare was living during 1604. He was a lodger on the corner of Silver Street and Muggle (or Monkswell) Street, and "lay in the house" of one Christopher Mountjoy, who lived and worked there with his wife and daughter. The home was in Cripplegate ward, a middle-class area in northwest London, and Silver Street was so called because of several prosperous silversmiths there, living in "diverse fair houses." A few companies such as the Barbers (similar to labor unions today) had impressive halls in the area. The Mountjoys themselves were also professionally successful, working as "tire-makers" (as in, attire)—they crafted wigs and exquisite headpieces made of gold, silver, and jewels, usually produced for noble ladies or, in this family's

case, for Queen Anne herself. Charles Nicholl, in a book devoted entirely to Shakespeare's life on Silver Street, suggests that the playwright himself may have introduced the Mountjoys to their royal client.

Shakespeare possibly became a tenant of the family's through his acquaintance with the Fields, who lived nearby. Recall that the husband was both from Stratford and the printer of Shakespeare's narrative poems, and his wife attended the French church with the Mountjoys, who were a Protestant or Huguenot family. This means they had fled France because of religious persecution. For all of their success and church respectability, however, these landlords of Shakespeare's were also, as it turns out, involved in bedroom hijinks and courtship intrigues. These activities, in which Shakespeare was soon caught up, sound like a slapstick film in today's cinemas, full of shifts and liaisons like the plot of a "city comedy." (This type of drama was becoming popular in London's theaters just as Shakespeare was living on Silver Street.) For example, we know from a doctor's notebook that Mrs. Mountjoy feared that she was pregnant by her lover, a cloth trader who lived nearby. Fortunately for her, there was no pregnancy, and her marriage stayed intact. Another love match involved Shakespeare, directly and centrally: he was asked by Mrs. Mountjoy to negotiate a marriage between one Stephen Belott, a fellow Frenchman and apprentice to the family, and the Mountjoys' daughter, Mary.

We know of this wooing strategy today, and Shakespeare's role in it, because of the discovery—by an eccentric American couple in London's Public Records Office in 1910—of what is sometimes called the Wigmakers' Lawsuit. It consists of a series of legal documents taken from a 1612 case before the Court of Requests, which was a little like our small-claims court today. Unfortunately, eight years after the apprentice Belott courted and married the Mountjoys' daughter, the son-in-law was now suing the father regarding broken promises of a dowry and legacy, or inheritance. The apprentice would have expected both gifts, if they were indeed formally promised, to provide significant substantial support for him and his new wife. He now asked the court to order Christopher Mountjoy to make good on this withheld financial contribution. These records contain a deposition, or written testimony, from "William Shakespeare of Stratford-upon-Avon in the Countye of Warwicke, gentleman of the age 48 or thereabouts," about his remembrance of details surrounding the young couple's courtship and marriage. Shakespeare was one of three witnesses called on the first day of hearings, on Monday, May 11, 1612. It is one of the few days when we know precisely where Shakespeare was and how he spent at least part of his day. What would he and the other witnesses remember? Could they help to resolve this legal standoff and in-law animosity?

Five questions or "interrogatories" are put to Shakespeare, who honestly does not have much to say. His memory often fails him, or so he says. He claims to have known both litigants "for the space of tenne yeres of thereaboutes," which, if taken precisely, may mean Shakespeare was living with the Mountjoys as early as 1602. Some biographers have posited that the especially severe outbreaks of plague in Southwark and near the Globe, where we last know Shakespeare to have lived, may have led him to seek out a safer neighborhood by 1603. He describes the plaintiff, the son-in-law Belott, as a "very good and industrious servant" who did "well and honestly behave himselfe," and yet he never heard Mountjoy claim that "he had got any great profit and commodity" from his apprentice. He next remarks on the apparently affectionate relationship between the parties, and confirms the parents' wishes that Belott marry

their daughter. We learn, too, that Mrs. Mountjoy "did solllicitt and entreat" Shakespeare "to move and persuade" the apprentice. Suddenly Shakespeare appears like his character Pandarus, a go-between to encourage a budding romance, and Belott resembles no one so much as Bertram (a Frenchman, too, incidentally), the reluctant lover of the tenacious Helena.

Another witness declares that the couple "made sure by Mr Shakespeare," which raises the stakes of his involvement significantly. The phrase implies that he actually presided over the couple's formal betrothal, known as a "troth-plighting" or "handfasting." This act of "giving each other's hand to hand" was a binding ceremony, the civic, or laity's, version of a priest presiding over the solemnization of holy matrimony, which took place in a nearby parish church on November 19, 1604. Shakespeare seems to have taken Mrs. Mountjoy's request seriously. He next asserts that the father offered the apprentice a dowry, or "porcion," comprising money and "household stuff," but he no longer remembers the sum discussed. Perhaps the father and son-in-law quickly failed to get along. Soon the apprentice moved out of the Mountjoys' home and established a rival shop. The couple returned to Silver Street upon Mrs. Mountjoy's death in 1606, but the quarrels grew worse, and they left again. Sadly, by the time of Shakespeare's deposition, Mountjoy's character and fortunes had crashed. The French church court condemned both men as "debauched," yet still ordered the father to pay the son-in-law something. He refused, hence the court case involving Shakespeare.

He was scheduled to testify again in June, but did not. Overall, the record, and the incident it records, is a curious one. Shakespeare was forty years old at the time, and although the Mountjoy home may not have been a "hotbed of sexual intrigue," as Ron Rosenbaum claims, it became an awkward, probably irritating, and potentially embarrassing situation. On the other hand, biographers have not been sheepish in inferring even more scandal from the case, and some interpretations of the story present Shakespeare as the adulterous lover of Mrs. Mountjoy, or, as Charles Nicholl suspects, of Mary, the daughter. Furthermore, another witness in the case, one George Wilkins, gives an altogether less pleasant, more tawdry taint to the case. He claimed to be a "victualler" in his deposition, but truly he was a brothel-keeper, pimp, thief, and known abuser of women. His connection with the Mountjoys further darkens our estimation of that seemingly upright, professional household. Likewise, we would like to think that this foul fellow witness must have doubly troubled Shakespeare. Perhaps he did. Yet, in fact, Wilkins was also a writer, a provider of plays for the King's Men—and yes, even a later collaborator with Shakespeare, on *Pericles* in 1607–08. As always, Shakespeare becomes more mysterious, rather than more understandable, the more we learn about him.

Reviewing Shakespeare's deposition, Rosenbaum hears something *Shakespearean* in the answers—a "patterned ambiguity," he calls it, "creating double meanings, revising himself, rewriting himself." Both he and Nicholl value the glimpse the case gives us of Shakespeare the everyday man in workaday London. However limitedly and incompletely, we see the "texture of the life" here, and the "physical and cultural circumstances" of Shakespeare's days, more readily verifiable in this case because of the legal occasion that arises later. Both critics also marvel that in these documents, and only in them, we hear, even if faintly, what Nicholl defines as "the only occasion when his actual spoken words are recorded." True, they are rendered generic by the question-and-answer framework of the deposition, but Nicholl also hears a "note of perfunctoriness,

or perhaps impatience." For him, Shakespeare's statements are "adequate and no more." His signature adorns the bottom of his sworn statements, and although space is not an issue, he gives his name in abbreviated fashion—"Willm Shaks." He may have wanted simply to be done with it all.

The company performed *Measure for Measure* at the end of 1604, on December 26. It was a court performance in the Banqueting House at Whitehall Palace, and its themes of leadership and justice seem presented as a cautionary lesson for the new ruler. The play becomes rather bold when seen in this context. What is more, many critics argue that the main characters, the absconding duke Vincentio and his "precise" lieutenant Angelo, reflect England's new king and severe Parliamentarians. More domestically, there is also an interesting parallel to be made between Shakespeare's involvement in the tetchy Belott-Mountjoy betrothal and the appearance of resistant lovers and bed tricks in both *Measure for Measure* and *All's Well That Ends Well*.

OTHELLO

From his rented room in the Mountjoys' place, Shakespeare could have easily walked from Silver Street to St. Aldermanbury's parish, where his colleagues Heminges and Condell lived with their large families, or, if desiring to keep to himself, to Paternoster Row, a few blocks to the south. This area, in the shadow of St. Paul's Cathedral, was home to London's numerous printers and booksellers. Charles R. Forker in "How Did Shakespeare Come By His Books?" asks if he were wealthy enough to have a large library, and considers possible lending sources: Ben Jonson, his noble patron Southampton or maybe the Herbert brothers, the theater company itself. Forker does believe that Shakespeare was affluent enough "to accumulate a useful working library as his interests and specific needs arose." Shakespeare's most convenient source for books would have been the bookstalls of Paternoster Row. Perhaps while living with the Mountjoys, and on his way to the riverside and a wherry to carry him across the Thames to the Globe, he encountered among the shops a copy of *Hecatommithi* (1565), a collection of a hundred sensational tales by the Italian writer Giraldi Cinthio. One story, of a "very valiant" and "handsome" African soldier who lives in Venice and is ruined by jealousy, supplied the action for Shakespeare's second great tragedy, *Othello*. He seems to have read the story in the original Italian, or possibly in a French translation.

Discovered in 1842, a revels book exists that lists various plays performed for the king during the 1604–05 holiday season at court. Several of the entries identify Shakespeare under the column "The poets which made the plays," where he is called "Shaxberd." It has been suggested that the spelling is so strange because one of James's Scottish followers, newly arrived to London, recorded the entry. Between November 1 and mid-February, the King's Men performed at court eleven times, and seven of the plays were Shakespeare's. The offerings ranged from early comedy (*The Comedy of Errors*, *Love's Labour's Lost*) to late (*Measure for Measure*). They staged *Henry V* and two satirical comedies by Jonson, and *The Merchant of Venice* was requested twice in three nights—perhaps James liked it immensely and wished for others to see it. The first play on this list, though, is *Othello*, performed on November 1, 1604. This timing is probably no coincidence. The tragedy's newness would have generated interest, and this swiftly moving play, with its exotic hero Othello, chaste heroine Desdemona, and betraying villain Iago, seems designed to be a crowd-pleaser. The author K. L. Cook has praised this play as masterful in its narrative strategy and dramatic design; it is "the most perfectly constructed" of all Shakespeare's works, he says. From its richly rendered poetic speeches to its shocking ending, *Othello* stands as a perfect play to open a critical revels season during which Shakespeare's sovereign's and patron's approval was sought.

The full title of Shakespeare's play is *The Tragedy of Othello the Moor of Venice*. What was a Moor, exactly? The word has a geographical root, deriving from the area of ancient Mauretania in North Africa, where Algeria and Morocco are today. Moorish presence expanded to Europe in the eighth century, when an Islamic empire was established through much of Spain. Renaissance Englishmen often used the words "Moor," "Muslim," and "blackamoor" interchangeably, and applied them vaguely to any black or Arab person. There were very few Africans in England at this time, and so the Moor became thought of in the popular imagination as an exotic, pagan, and brutish figure. Elizabeth I's Moorish ambassador, dramatically depicted in an existing portrait with his turban and large sword, drew much attention. This may be why Shakespeare had already created stage Moors in previous plays, including the almost laughably evil Aaron in *Titus Andronicus* and the pompous, bombastically speaking Prince of Morocco, one of Portia's suitors in *The Merchant of Venice*. As you may recall, she sends him away with a joke about his "complexion," a moment usually offensive to modern audiences. The European Renaissance mindset, and there is no reason to exclude Shakespeare from it, generally believed in racial differentiation and saw connections between race and capability and moral bearing. Prejudiced views, unacceptable today, were far more widespread. And it is just this attitude that makes Shakespeare's very conscious choices and emphases in *Othello* so striking.

The play begins with the manipulation of this early modern European disdain for and anxiety about people of dark complexion, and it frames this anxiety or even disgust in explicitly sexual and, to some degree, economic, terms. We first meet Iago and his dupe Roderigo. Iago, a standard-bearer for Othello, is about to betray his master: he calls from the shadows of the street to Brabantio, a prosperous Venetian father, and informs him in coarse terms that his daughter Desdemona has eloped and is intimate with the "old black ram" Othello. The father soon confronts Othello, calling him "thou foul thief," suspecting he has used exotic spells to enchant Desdemona. Both men appeal to the Venetian senate, and Desdemona soon arrives to vali-

date the new marriage. In a compelling speech, Othello describes how he wooed Desdemona with stories of his travels and hardships. "She loved me for the dangers I had passed, / And I loved her that she did pity them." The couple acquits themselves, but the father's warning to Othello will haunt the rest of the play and the hero's peace of mind: "Look to her, Moor, if thou hast eyes to see, / She has deceived her father, and may thee." Meanwhile the Venetians hear about a Turkish attack of Cyprus, and soon they dispatch Othello in defense. Turkish military aggression against

This painting from 1880 is entitled *Othello Relating His Adventures to Desdemona* *(Karl Becker)*

Christendom, as well as England's increased discovery and mercantile activity, inspired a host of plays featuring the Turks, and yet here a paradox arises, as one suspected foreigner defends Venice against a traditionally foreign threat. The play's racial dynamics and connotations become further complicated.

Othello promises to become one big sea battle, but a storm providentially ruins the Turkish fleet, meaning that the play's attention can turn to love and festivity at its midpoint. A domestic tragedy soon emerges. Ironically, Othello's safety and sanity become imperiled soon after the Turkish menace disappears, and he and his wife and servants land triumphantly on Cyprus. "When I love thee not, Chaos is come again," vows Othello to Desdemona, and this destruction of love and eruption of Othello's personal chaos is precisely what occurs. From the outset, Iago is the frighteningly calculated, cold-blooded instrument of this turbulent change. Ironically, Iago, a white Venetian, represents the play's diabolical figure, despite language about the "blacker devil" or devils putting on the "blackest sins" and other racially demonizing speeches. In *Othello* as in life, Shakespeare seems to say, looks—and cultural outlooks—can be deceiving.

Iago mesmerizingly speaks in scheming soliloquies, often telling the audience directly what he intends to do: he will frame Cassio, whom he envies for having been named Othello's lieutenant. On Cyprus, Iago gets Cassio drunk and then instigates a fight between him and Roderigo. Cassio is soon humiliated and demoted. Next Iago encourages Cassio to seek an advocate in Desdemona, and her speaking on Cassio's behalf soon creates jealousy and anger in Othello. Iago ruthlessly flames this distrust, transforming Othello's "free and open nature" into a state of mental, marital torment. Why does Iago wish to destroy Othello? He gives different reasons at different

times: to get revenge for being overlooked professionally; because he believes (or says so, at least) that Othello has seduced Iago's own wife, Emilia; and even because he, too, like Roderigo, loves Desdemona and wants her for himself. Amid this crowd of reasons, the more terrifying conclusion is that Iago has no good reason, except that he devilishly savors destruction. For the poet W. H. Auden and many others, Iago steals the play: free of all traditional ethics or morals, he is like a chameleon, a cancer cell, a deadly joker in the pack. He often seems utterly unknowable, like an isolated space alien of evil. (For this reason, Shakespeare eliminated Iago's child, who appears in his source.) He repulses us, but we cannot look away, and before we know it, we as a knowing audience are in league with his lethal goals.

In the guise of being a concerned servant, Iago single-handedly convinces Othello of infidelity between Desdemona and Cassio. The temptation scene (3.3) features the play's most chilling interaction. Iago warns Othello about the "green-eyed monster" jealousy, though the overall effect is to fill his lord with a jealous rage. He torments Othello with images of Desdemona's sexual voracity, so much so that the hero falls into a trance. Soon Othello's language becomes coarse and misogynistic like Iago's, and his intentions grow murderous. He enlists Iago to murder Cassio, and says of his sweet wife, "I will chop her into messes!" Instead, at Iago's suggestion, he strangles Desdemona in their marriage bed. "Put out the light," he says in their chamber, treating his bride as a votive candle, an ironic symbol of her actual sainthood. With her last gasps, as the rest of the characters arrive upon the scene, she blames herself rather than Othello for her death.

It must have been surprising for early audiences to find Othello the Moor as a title character of a serious tragedy, and not only for racial reasons. He is a mere soldier employed to protect

Venice, not a prince (tragic heroes were supposed to be noble, royal figures), and his main obstacle in the play involves his love of and trust in his new wife, Desdemona. This topic, too, is unusual for a tragedy. Indeed, it centers most of all on the usually comic figure of the suspicious husband, and its action turns on the loss and unscrupulous use of, and misunderstanding about, a love token Othello has given to Desdemona. Shakespeare devotes to this critical object his typical poet's eye for specificity—so that what is merely a vague "Moorish device" in the original tale becomes a handkerchief "spotted with strawberries." Still, critics have regularly found Othello's fall too simplistic, and too dependent on this comic device. The early critic Thomas Rymer, a fierce critic of *Othello*, thought in 1693 that it should be called "The Tragedy of the Handkerchief." "What can be more absurd?" he asks with exasperation. Considering everything, it is even more surprising that we feel such sympathy for Othello. We must condemn the murderous jealousy that marks his tragic fall, but we also understand it, as well as his fragility socially and emotionally. As he says about himself, he is "one that loved not wisely, but too well."

In *Othello* Shakespeare achieves a new complexity of character, a dramatic virtue that characterizes all of the great tragedies of his mature years. As is often the case, he allows actors and directors a range of interpretation. Othello can seem noble and towering, or fierce and terrifying in his later obsessions. He at times seems pathetic, as "ignorant as dirt," as Emilia says. "Is Othello Stupid?" asks Fintan O'Toole; the blunt question is a chapter title in his study of the tragedies. Others find Othello's vulnerability all too convincing. Declan Donnellan, in his production a few years ago, made Othello childlike, utterly defenseless against Iago's masterful manipulations. "Speak of me as I am," Othello says in conclusion, and fans of the play have been trying to do that for centu-

Emilia and Desdemona speak while Desdemona prepares for bed in Act 4, Scene 3 of *Othello*. This painting is from 1849. *(Théodore Chassériau)*

ries now, and will continue to do so. Audiences, it seems, were positive from the outset. The play may have influenced Ben Jonson's fashionable *Masque of Blackness* at court, where just as Richard Burbage had painted his face to play Othello, now Queen Anne and her waiting woman dressed as "blackamoors." Later performances of *Othello* were recorded in 1610–12, and ongoing popularity onstage may explain why a quarto did not appear till 1622. This text differs in key ways from, and is 160 lines shorter than, the Folio version of the following year.

Othello remains one of Shakespeare's most popular works on stage or screen today, and most of the great Shakespearean actors have attempted the role: Paul Scofield, Anthony Hopkins, Patrick Stewart, Ben Kingsley. Controversy has arisen when these white actors play the role, which has also attracted some great black actors: Ira Aldridge in the nineteenth century, and the great Paul Robeson, whose convictions about racial equality and interracial relationships made his popular run in *Othello* in 1930s and 1940s America an important social, as well as theatrical, event. Othello's precise appearance seems intentionally clouded by Shakespeare. Iago and Roderigo are guilty of racist stereotypes in calling Othello "lascivious," or in mocking his "thick lips," and throughout the play Othello is associated with blackness. However, phrases such as "Barbarian" or "Barbary horse" or "turbanned Turk" (Othello's own description) suggests North African origins and lighter skin. Some critics have seen this ultimately imprecise identity as both a symptom of Othello's weakness and a factor in the play's ongoing relevance. *Othello* increasingly seems like the play among the great tragedies best suited for the present. In a post-9/11 world, for example, the Islamic aspects of Othello's Moorish identity have become much more discussed as broader debates between the Muslim world and western nations develop. Similarly, the play's disturbing complications of heritage and identity resonate more than ever in our own global and racial, or post-racial, age.

KING LEAR

If Shakespeare were back in Stratford in April 1605, he very likely attended the wedding of Katherine Rogers, the daughter of his neighbors, to Robert Harvard. The new couple soon returned to the groom's hometown of Southwark, and took up residence near the Globe. A son was born to them two years later, and his name would forever be known in America—John Harvard, eventual founder of Harvard University. One month after the wedding, Shakespeare received less happy news: his longtime fellow theater-man Augustine Phillips had died. This loss was a blow to all of the King's Men, for Phillips had been an experienced actor, musician, and even an acrobat. His will also suggests he was a well-liked team player: he left gifts for both his fellow shareholders and more temporary, hired actors, and he also bequeathed "a thirty shillings piece in gold" specifically to Shakespeare and another actor, Henry Condell. One critic has imagined that Shakespeare must have written a verse tribute for his lost colleague, perhaps for a memorial performance for Phillips, but no evidence exists regarding this supposition.

In April 1605, Shakespeare was likely back in Stratford as well, for he was then making one of the great business deals of his life, at least of those on record. He was investing nearly five hundred pounds in the tithes of the fields and farm lands around his home and north of Stratford (discussed earlier). Curiously, during this very time when Shakespeare's financial prosperity was most on display, and when he was seeking to invest his growing wealth in ways to ensure continued returns, he was almost certainly working on *King Lear*, a tragedy that unflinchingly explores questions at the core of human experience, identity, and destiny. What accommodation does man require? Why is nature so uncaring of these needs? How much must we respect human dignity? Can we overcome or create our own fortune? And how strong are the social bonds we most rely on—bonds of kinship, friendship, and formal service? Shakespeare struggled with these questions with unparalleled artistry in this, his third great tragedy.

The play begins with a self-assured monarch handing over his royal "business" to his three daughters. Yet he wishes for each to prove her worthiness. The first two, Goneril and Regan, praise their father effusively, and he in turn rewards them and their husbands (the dukes of Albany and Cornwall, respectively) with a third of his kingdom. Cordelia, however, refuses to flatter. "Nothing begets nothing," Lear warns her, but she will not budge. The line also reflects the erasing of kinship between father and daughter that is now at hand. He angrily, impulsively banishes her. One of her suitors, Burgundy, no longer desires her, but the king of France still wishes to marry the "Fairest Cordelia," whether with dowry or not. One of Lear's advisors, the Earl of Gloucester, tries to warn the king against rash action, but he is banished as well. We also learn, in the very opening scene, that Gloucester has a natural son, Edgar, and a bastard son, Edmund. The latter possesses much of the scheming, cold charisma of Iago, and he informs the audience by soliloquy that he will frame and usurp the privileges of his legitimate brother, mainly because he has the power to do so. Edmund is rational, natural man, a maker of his own fortunes: "Why 'bastard'? Wherefore 'base,' / When my dimensions are as well compact, / My mind as generous and my shape as true / As honest madam's issue?" Soon Edgar must flee his father's misplaced wrath. Meanwhile, Goneril grows tired of Lear and his retainers, who are living with her. She commands that he reduce his "insolent retinue." Lear is again furious, railing against her ingratitude. More profoundly, his madness, or at least the play's existential crisis, begins: "Are you our daughter?" he asks. "Does any here know me?" He storms off to Regan's palace.

Slowly a truer, more loyal retinue develops around the ousted, disrespected king. The exiled Edgar soon dresses up as "Poor Tom," and simulates insanity. A Fool accompanies the king, and shifts between jesting to cheer and console Lear and pointed comments meant to bring his master to self-realization. He will soon become aware of his faults and poor judgments. The Earl of Kent, too, disguised as "Caius," remains in Lear's service, but he is soon put in the stocks as punishment for defending the king. Lear is further angered to see his servant treated so, and then is rejected and criticized by Regan. He curses his second daughter mightily. A storm rises, a symbol of the play world's social discord and Lear's coming madness. The daughters lock out their father, leaving him to the elements of such a "wild night," and word comes that France is preparing for war against England.

Lear's suffering in and defiance of the storm occupies the play's midpoint. "Blow, winds, and crack your cheeks! Rage, blow!" he cries, bellowing much like the tempest around him. He feels himself losing his mind, and the Fool begins to sing to him. They seek out shelter and find "Poor Tom" (Edgar) there. Even in this dire context, though, Lear is beginning to learn: he thinks of "poor naked wretches" and becomes a "poor, bare, forked animal" himself by stripping away his clothes. He becomes a terribly modest, utterly abased version of Edmund's "natural man"—stripped down to his flesh, unaccommodated in nature. Soon Gloucester happens upon the group and leads them forward. The dramatic space for the characters feels increasingly like something purgatorial: infirm in the present, they nevertheless work away their more profound infirmities through present suffering. Soon the evil sisters and their husbands betray Gloucester, pressing out the "vile jelly" of his eyes. Symbolically, as soon as he is physically blinded, he receives illumination, discovering that his son Edgar is innocent and Edmund the true villain.

The fourth act contains some of the most amazing moments in all of Shakespeare. Edgar is reunited with his blind father but remains disguised. He takes Gloucester to a heath, which he mistakenly thinks is the edge of a Dover cliff. He makes a suicidal leap, but of course falls forward harmlessly. Edgar, now as himself, reapproaches his father, speaking of the miraculous. Lear and his party soon encounter the father and son, and the king, adorned with wildflowers, gives a floral coronet to Gloucester. Meanwhile, the antagonists are fraying. A servant loyal to Gloucester has killed Cornwall, and Albany, so repulsed by Gloucester's blinding, has a moral awakening. The wicked sisters begin to fight over Edmund. Lear finally reunites with Cordelia. "I am old and foolish," he says, begging forgiveness, which is granted. However, eventually the English army captures them. Goneril poisons Regan and then stabs herself. Edmund is apprehended, but warns that he has ordered the murder of Lear and Cordelia both. Lear shockingly enters carrying Cordelia's corpse. We soon learn of Edmund's death, and Lear's crown is restored, but that matters little to him now. He, who had first banished Cordelia in rage and then refused to see her face for shame, now looks intensely for any sign of life:

> And my poor fool is hanged: no, no, no life?
> Why should a dog, a horse, a rat, have life,
> And thou no breath at all? Thou'lt come no
>   more,
> Never, never, never, never, never.

Lear enters the camp with Cordelia's body in Act 5, Scene 3 of *King Lear*. This painting is from 1786–88 (*James Barry*)

Just as the ancient Greeks dictated for tragic heroes, Lear has suffered into knowledge, and he, too, now expires. Many of the characters grow in this way, as Millicent Bell points out. The opening scene features Gloucester coarsely talking about fathering Edmund out of wedlock, and even Cordelia is at first "drearily literal," in Bell's view. But Edmund, too, changes by the play's end. The dead are carried away with Edgar's final words: "The oldest hathe borne most; we that are young / Shall never see so much nor live so long."

Shakespeare achieved his most powerful, unsentimental tragedy in *King Lear*. Hardly any actions in his plays feel as lamentable as those of these families, Lear's and Gloucester's. Each family breaks down in the course of the play. Some questions must remain unanswered: Why this intolerable suffering? Is the cause human agency, or fate, or the gods' caprice? The play's ending, and Cordelia's death particularly, was thought so severe and devastating that a different version, altered into a happy ending by Nahum Tate, was performed from 1681 to 1838. The great Shakespeare scholar Samuel Johnson could not bear to read Shakespeare's original ending, and he preferred Tate's revision because it is an injustice that the "virtuous miscarry" at the end: "since all reasonable beings naturally love justice, I cannot easily be persuaded that the observation of justice makes the play worse." Yet Johnson seems to deny one convincing point: "Tragedy, for Shakespeare," writes the present-day Shakespearean David Scott Kastan, "is the genre of uncompensated suffering." The emotional truth of characters' struggles with suffering is at the center of his tragic plays, and *Lear* especially. R. A. Foakes, in his interesting book *Hamlet Versus Lear*, argues that in the 1950s and 1960s, the former play ceased to be commonly held as Shakespeare's "greatest," as it had been for centuries. Instead, *King Lear*, "Shakespeare's bleakest and most despairing vision," spoke with new authority to "cataclys-mic world events" such as world wars, the atomic bomb, political turmoil, and assassinations.

King Lear may or may not have been performed in 1605; the first recorded performance is slightly later, on December 26, 1606, before the court. As with *Measure for Measure*, the interrogation of the duties and cares of kingship in *King Lear* would have been a bold choice to perform for a royal audience. The negligent, suffering, ruminating Lear looms large as a powerful caveat for James I. On the other hand, some have seen its dramatization of a kingdom divided and the subsequent disorder as implicitly supporting King James, who at this time was debating Parliament about a united Britain. There was also a known case in 1603 of a younger daughter, named Cordell, preventing her older sister from having their father declared insane. Shakespeare found the story of Lear, a legendary pre-Christian English king, in one of his favorite resources, the historical collection known as Holinshed's *Chronicles*. Its cautionary tale about prematurely relinquishing royal power made it popular in Renaissance England. An earlier theater company, the Queen's Men, had a *King Leir* in its repertoire during the early 1590s. This play was printed in 1605, and its appearance may have stimulated Shakespeare's own treatment of this tragic king.

Shakespeare's version appeared in print relatively quickly, in 1608, although it is significantly different from the text that appeared in the First Folio fifteen years later. A few modern editors go so far as to treat the two versions as necessarily distinct texts, and publish them together in one volume. With the 1608 quarto, for the first time Shakespeare's name appears at the very top of the book, with the title and performance context underneath: "M. William Shake-speare: His True Chronicle History of the Life and Death of King Lear and his Three Daughters." With respect to authorship, publication, and reputation, Shakespeare found in this particular book a sure sign that he had "made it big."

TIMON OF ATHENS

There is a specific strain in *King Lear* that attacks the glittering spectacle of the prosperous world, a strain that becomes the primary theme in another play written around this same time, or perhaps slightly later, *Timon of Athens*. Lear offers a diagnosis of his own previous outlook, marked by callous luxury: "Take physic, pomp, / Expose thyself to feel what wretches feel[.]" *Timon*, too, broods on the hollow excess of banquets and gold compared with true human needs and contentment. Shakespeare found the character of Timon in Plutarch's *Lives*, one of his favorite sources, and at first glance, his is not the most promising of stories for drama. The first half of the play features him in luxury's lap, his assured attitude contrasting with that of the cynical philosopher Apemantus. In the second half, Timon learns he has become broke. Able to offer only himself and his friendship, he quickly realizes how many of his "mouth-friends" were flatterers, "those wolves" who abandon him once the banquets are past. The second part more or less comprises one long, variously interrupted speech by the now misanthropic title character against his fickle friends. Timon becomes as cynical as Apemantus, yet he fulminates far more emotionally against the world's evils. *Timon of Athens* is necessarily a severe, pessimistic play. Shakespeare adds a more tender element toward the end, however, in the figure of Timon's steward Flavius. Timon's death is unavoidable, but the faithful, friendly Flavius partially draws his master from his hate-filled isolation, his cocoon of gall.

The problematic printed version of *Timon*, from the First Folio of 1623, likely derives from an unreliable, incomplete manuscript, and so it is of special interest to scholars searching for clues about Shakespeare's writing habits in the middle of composition. The blueprint for the whole play is present, but presumably Shakespeare later intended to develop scenes and characters (minor characters especially) that are just barely sketched out here. Characters' names are inconsistent, the text shifts from poetry to prose and back, and from polished passages to those clearly awaiting revision. Shakespeare may have written like the modern Irish poet W. B. Yeats, by rendering a thought or expression in prose and then versifying it into poetry later.

The play's collaborative character further complicates the state of the text. Today, scholars generally agree that *Timon* marks a resumption of co-writing for Shakespeare, in this case with the younger but already successful playwright Thomas Middleton. He was the author of *The Revenger's Tragedy*, a successful play for the King's Men, and he may have also helped with the witches' scenes in *Macbeth* and made revisions to *Measure for Measure* before it was printed in the First Folio. In turn, other plays of his were originally attributed to Shakespeare, namely *A Yorkshire Tragedy* and *The Puritan*. This association was no doubt a commercial strategy in part, but it is also possible that Shakespeare collaborated with Middleton on his plays as well. A new literary partnership was at hand, and others would soon follow for the older Shakespeare, as we will see in the next chapter. Perhaps he began to feel that his plays needed the younger blood of other writers, ones willing to push limits and be more sensitive to ever-evolving literary tastes. Even a highly successful playwright may soon find that, like Timon, the happy feasts of earlier theatrical successes could pass by all too quickly.

THE GUNPOWDER PLOT AND MACBETH

Macbeth, written in 1606, is Shakespeare's shortest tragedy, but it is long in its dramatic and poetic powers, confirmed by centuries of acclaim from readers and audiences. As with *King Lear*, Shakespeare found his material for *Macbeth* in Holinshed's *Chronicles*, and again, he takes many liberties with history, appearing more interested in moral dilemmas, ideas, and an impression throughout of great forces at work, both supernatural and cosmic. *Macbeth* is one of Shakespeare's greatest examinations of ambition, marital conspiracy, and the effects of crimes and cover-ups on the human psyche. It also represents the play in which Shakespeare seems most intent on writing for and flattering his king and patron, James I. Most obviously, he chose from his chronicle source the reign of a king from Scotland, which reflected James's background and the site of his recent rule. Thus *Macbeth*, Shakespeare's fourth great tragedy, repeatedly includes topics of interest to the king (witches and ghosts, the sovereignty of rulers, his own royal lineage). Shakespeare also takes care to reflect the current events that were on the minds and in the mouths of Londoners generally.

The primary event had to be the Gunpowder Plot, a Catholic conspiracy that most Englishmen thought was diabolical and that seismically changed the country's religious attitudes. Today, we could call the conspirators' plan an attempted terrorist attack. On November 5, 1605, Guy (or Guido) Fawkes, a Catholic soldier from northern England, amassed firewood and fuses and

This 1606 etching, entitled *The Execution of Guy Fawkes*, shows the members of the Gunpowder Plot being hanged, drawn, and quartered. *(Claes Jansz Visscher)*

twenty barrels of gunpowder underneath England's Parliament building, the Palace of Westminster. With one "thunderclap," Fawkes and what we might call his Jacobean sleeper cell hoped to blow up the king, royal family, Parliamentarians, bishops, knights—in short, all of the nation's ruling classes. The plotters hoped ultimately for a national crisis, a leadership vacuum, and the eventual restoration of Catholicism in the shaken, reeling country. Fortunately the plot was discovered, and national disaster averted. When interrogated, Fawkes revealed not only religious radicalism but also strong sentiments against the king and his countrymen, saying that "his intent was to have blown them back to Scotland."

Shakespeare also refers in *Macbeth* to a controversial trial in spring 1606 of Henry Garnett, a Jesuit father who had supported the conspirators. The Garnett trial focused in part on the debated practice of equivocation, or giving indirect answers in good conscience to avoid harm, and *Macbeth* raises this topic explicitly, in the memorable words of his Porter: "Knock, knock," he says. "Faith, here's an equivocator that could swear in both scales against either scale, who committed treason enough . . ." The first audiences must have known exactly what, or whom, the Porter meant here. Clearly Shakespeare kept abreast of his age's current events, and he seems to have followed texts relating to religious controversies especially carefully. For example, he also faintly echoes this divided confessional landscape when he includes in *King Lear* various quotations from a polemical tract written in a charged style, *A Declaration of Egregious Popish Impostures* (1603). Written by Samuel Harsnett, chaplain to London's bishop, the book attacks purported exorcisms performed by Jesuits in 1586–87. Some of the priests attacked were from Shakespeare's region, and one was the brother of his old Stratford schoolmaster, so he may have had special

local interest in Harsnett's screed. It seems he took special pleasure in some of the devils' names listed, for they end up in Edgar's mouth, when he speaks in the guise of "Poor Tom" a little comically and crazily: "Hobbididence prince of dumbness . . . Fibbertigibbet of mocking and mowing." Perhaps Shakespeare includes these phrases to mock the book, yet he may have also, as a great poet and dramatist, simply relished in the strange names and phrases that Harsnett's account puts into print and into the light of day.

It is worth noting that a handful of poems written from Catholic perspectives seem to show an impatience with Shakespeare. A writer of his talents, their arguments go, should be more earnestly involved in religious matters, and willing to include telling religious topics and expressions in his writings. Bringing up "lewd Venus" and Adonis, for example, John Davies may mildly chastise our author: "Fine wit is shown therein: but finer 'twere / If not attired in such bawdy gear." Another poem by "I.C." rejects Troilus and Cressida, Richard III, and Tarquin—all Shakespearean characters—in favor of "greater conquests, warres, and loves," namely the life and conversion of Mary Magdalene. The poem points to Shakespeare's "wrong-headed authorship," as Alison Shell argues, and holds up the saint as a "reproachful alternative" to the writer's classical, secular, religiously opaque creations.

As for *Macbeth*, it also seems less concerned with overtly religious matters, but shows immediate interest in issues of fate, agency, and free will. Returning victorious from battle, Macbeth, "valor's minion," and Banquo encounter three witches, the Weïrd Sisters. They tell Macbeth that he will soon be Thane of Cawdor and King of Scotland, and inform Banquo that his heirs will be kings. Macbeth quickly receives the first title, King Duncan having transferred it to him from a just-defeated traitor. Were the witches prophets, then, and what of their promise of Macbeth's becoming king? Shakespeare found these "wither'd" and "wild" women in his source (Holinshed) and imbued them with a sinister supernaturalism. He may have had in mind hag fortune-tellers at nearby London Bridge, and very likely he also knew King James's own work on the supernatural, *Daemonology* (1597), in which he describes witches' powers:

> They can be-witch and take the life of men or women, by roasting of the pictures . . . They can make folks to become frantic or manic . . . And likewise they can make some to be possessed with spirits, and so to become very demoniacs.

Today, directors and critics treat the characters in diverse ways. One recent production by the Royal Shakespeare Company turned the witches into grieving mothers whose children the soldier Macbeth had slaughtered. Their interactions with him are thus fueled by parental revenge, shifting the play's moral dynamics.

The witches' designation as "weird" may simply be a clever reference to Johan Weyer, an influential author on witchcraft whom James refers to as "Wierus." More surely, it is less related to our sense of the word today, but instead derives from an Old English word for "fate." Thus they become the fated or fateful sisters—or do they? Is their announcement about Macbeth's honors and subsequent news of the first being fulfilled mere coincidence? If so, must Macbeth bear sole responsibility for his murderous obsession with the crown that follows? A similar philosophical tension is felt at the beginning of the second act, when a dagger appears before Macbeth. "Come, let me clutch thee!" he exclaims, while pondering whether it is a "fatal vision, sensible / To feeling as to sight," or rather merely a "dagger of the mind, a false creation[.]" It influences him, like

every other thing and person he confronts in these opening scenes, but does it compel him? Thus begins the play's deep interrogation of the character, psyche, conscience, and soul of its title character. Without question, though, the Scottish landscape that Macbeth inhabits is murky (literally, morally, and otherwise): "Fair is foul, and foul is fair," the witches chant.

King Duncan intends to honor Macbeth by visiting him at his castle in Inverness. Macbeth breathlessly writes of everything to Lady Macbeth, whom we first meet as she reads his letter and contemplates their upcoming actions. She fears her husband's nature is "too full o' th' milk of human kindness" to carry out the deeds necessary to become king. Next, she sounds every bit as diabolical as the witches, boldly calling on spirits to "unsex" her and fill her with "direst cruelty." Most critics have interpreted Lady Macbeth's words as a wish to set aside her own female nature, and to proceed with a male ambition and ruthlessness that Macbeth himself may apparently lack. Alternately, Rebecca W. Bushnell has argued that Lady Macbeth ultimately desires feminine power; her asking that her mother's milk be turned to gall is to "convert her female sexuality into a form of cruelty." Soon the king arrives, and Macbeth and Lady Macbeth debate their course of action, with the wife challenging her husband's manhood. He has reservations and fears failing, and her simple reply—"We fail"—is an actor's delight, inviting multiple intonations. One recent Lady Macbeth, Sian Thomas, said the lines not as a question, or something hard to imagine, but rather as a carefree "So be it!" She sees the character's motivation here as her "one clear chance" to escape being the "timid, domestic creature she was afraid she might be." They devise a plan that involves getting the king's chamberlains drunk and then framing them for the murder. The clock strikes midnight, and soon Macbeth returns. He has "done the deed." He is so shaken that Lady Macbeth must return the dagger to the crime scene and help to rationalize his action.

The Porter makes his speech as a knocking at the door is heard, which turns out to be Macduff arriving. He discovers the king's corpse, and shock reverberates among those in the castle. Macbeth claims he has murdered the chamberlains in anger at their crime. Duncan's sons, Malcolm and Donalbain, sense foul play and flee the scene, which invites suspicion that they have killed their father. Amid confusion, Macbeth is crowned king. The new royal couple is to hold a feast, but Banquo and his son Fleance are absent. Macbeth remembers the witches' prophecy about Banquo's royal heirs, and so fears he has committed his wicked deed for a "fruitless crown." He has Banquo murdered, but Fleance escapes. Banquo's ghost invades the feast, causing it to end abruptly. Lady Macbeth scolds her husband (she thinks he hallucinates) for being "unmanned." Meanwhile, Macduff and Duncan's son Malcolm have taken refuge in England, and are preparing for war against Macbeth. The new, embattled king returns to the witches, who again supply him with enigmatic prophecies. A final vision displays Banquo and his royal line. This infuriates Macbeth, and when he hears of Macduff's escape, he orders his family destroyed, "in one fell swoop," as the devastated Macduff says upon learning of his loss. He marches against the "fiend of Scotland." We see Lady Macbeth one last time, sleepwalking and crying, "Out, damned spot, out I say!" She speaks as if she still has blood on her hands, and her state is a dramatically original way for Shakespeare to illustrate her guilty subconscious. In a final battle scene, Macduff defeats the tyrant Macbeth and carries his head onstage. All depart for Malcolm's coronation.

To achieve the play's dramatic power, Shakespeare made several key changes to the story found in the chronicle. First of all, he compressed events of Macbeth's rule from seventeen years to one year. The play's King Duncan is no feeble young man, but an old, venerable ruler; his murder seems all the more shocking and transgressive. The character of Banquo is similarly altered: he conspires with Macbeth in the prose source, but in the play he remains noble and innocent. This shift places the responsibility for the crime squarely on Macbeth, but there is another, more politic reason for the change. Banquo also assumed special importance because James traced his royal line back through Banquo. For example, in the fall of 1605, three Oxford students, dressed as prophetic sibyls (paralleling the witches?), greeted the king as Banquo's descendant.

Shakespeare dazzlingly visualizes this royal connection in his own play. For one, when Macbeth revisits the witches in the fourth act, they sound different. Their speeches are lighter and more deferential. It has been proposed that when the First Witch speaks of "this great king" welcoming their charms and dance, she may refer to King James himself, present in the room. In other words, it is a moment recorded in the Folio text of a royal performance, possibly one staged at Hampton Court. The final vision given to Macbeth features a "show of eight kings." He comments on what he observes: "And yet an eighth appears who bears a glass [mirror] / which shows many more." It may be that an actor positioned the mirror to reflect James in his chair of state, making his image present onstage as one of the triumphant "many more" belonging to Banquo's future line. Of course, this effect would be impossible at the Globe, such as when the physician Simon Forman saw it in April 1611. The moment represents nicely the "double life" of any King's Men play—one version for the general public and one for the court, with person-specific references and effects.

In this 1827 print, Macbeth sees the witches' "show of kings" in Act 4 of *Macbeth*.

King James himself may have requested from Shakespeare a play about Scottish history to go with the author's many treatments of English monarchs, and it is probable that the King's Men performed *Macbeth* in August 1606, when James hosted his brother-in-law, Christian IV of Denmark. Not yet thirty years old and a heavy drinker, the visiting king was prone to festivity during his stay in England, the first state visit of this sort in any Englishman's lifetime. *Macbeth* would have been lively entertainment for these two monarchs, to say the least.

That said, Shakespeare was not willing to please at the expense of his drama. For example, Banquo is cleared of wrongdoing, but he remains a conflicted character: he consents to Macbeth's accession, despite questionable circumstances, and he may, like Macbeth, be too excessively focused on the witches' prophecy to him. "But hush, no more," he tells himself, as if pushing away temptation. Naturally it is Macbeth who is the most conflicted character, and Barbara Everett has argued that the play's most remarkable aspect is his being simultaneously a brutish tyrant and yet highly sympathetic. "I have supped full with horrors," he says, remaining always lucid of his crimes, maintaining a moral awareness surprising for a soldier whom we first hear has split apart an enemy from jaw to naval. He is also capable of the most powerful, soul-haunted poetry:

Tomorrow, and tomorrow, and tomorrow
Creeps in this petty pace from day to day
To the last syllable of recorded time,

And all our yesterdays have lighted fools
The way to dusty death.

These verses bespeak Macbeth's sense of futility, his terrible resignation regarding his fate and, we are led to believe, about living generally, about all of our lives. In *Women of Will*, a recent work created by the actor Tina Packer, her fellow performer Nigel Gore plays Macbeth and recites these lines as he holds the dead Lady Macbeth, played by Packer, in his arms.

Subsequent productions of *Macbeth* always face great challenges, from preventing the fourth and fifth acts from lagging to overcoming a tradition of technical gaffes and performer pitfalls associated with this supernatural play. To this day, actors (still a superstitious lot) cautiously refer to this play not by its name, which is said to invite bad luck, but as simply "The Scottish Play." Nevertheless, this tragedy continues to beckon with opportunities for theatrical and poetic excellence. Park Honan declares that, with *Macbeth*, Shakespeare had reached the "quintessence of his career."

STRATFORD AGAIN, AFTER THE PLOT

The Gunpowder Plot, that national event that hovers behind the conspiracy, demonism, and regicide of *Macbeth*, had interesting connections to Shakespeare's Stratford as well. His family knew some of the plotters, who hailed from Warwickshire gentry families and were fellow landowners. For example, the wealthy young Catholic Ambrose Rookwood had become Shakespeare's new neighbor at Clopton House. The day after the plot was foiled, constables raided this residence. (Was Shakespeare home at New Place, and aware of the raid?) Rookwood had fled, but was apprehended two days later and soon executed. Other conspirators were also captured in the Midlands, and suspects were numerous enough in Stratford that authorities made an extended visit there early the following year to investigate the plot and those involved in it. Similar trials and executions must have given the plot a strangely proximate quality for the playwright.

The reactionary anti-Catholicism that followed the Gunpowder Plot was nationwide, but became personal for Shakespeare in May 1606, when his twenty-two-year-old daughter Susanna appeared in an "act book" of the parish's ecclesiastical court. The churchwarden had cited her and twenty other defendants, including Shakespeare's neighbors the Sadlers, for failing to take Easter communion a few weeks earlier. Her signature appears in the record, so we know that she could sign her name; for her sister Judith, we remain unsure. This list represents a government crackdown on "church papists"—Catholic citizens who attended the Anglican services to avoid fines, but still refused to take what they considered to be a "heretical" communion. Following the plot, authorities were growing less tolerant. Susanna's case was eventually dismissed, suggesting she had agreed to receive communion in the interim.

A happier record a year later exemplifies the religious complexities of the age, and for any family. On June 5, 1607, the town marriage register marks the wedding of "John Hall, gentleman, and Susanna Shaxspere." A Cambridge-trained doctor's son, Hall had been working in Stratford as a physician for nearly a decade—and he had strongly Protestant, even Puritan, sympathies. If Susanna did have Catholic religious leanings, they did not prevent her from falling in love with and marrying Hall, and presumably accepting, at least, his own Protestant convictions. This matter aside, the father in Shakespeare must have been proud of his daughter's choice of spouse: various records exist praising Hall's skills in medicine and commitment to his patients. So single-minded was he in his profession that he resisted town appointments and later rejected a knighthood. Shakespeare seems to have provided the couple with a generous dowry—more than one hundred acres of land in Old Stratford. More good news followed in 1608, as noted in the baptism register: "Februar. 21 Elizabeth, daughter to John Hall, gen." The family must have rejoiced in the arrival of this grandchild, Shakespeare's first.

It is sometimes hard to comprehend that Shakespeare remained a "normal" actor, theater owner, servant to the king, and family man even while he was writing his greatest tragedies. How do you keep appointments and relate to people when you are devising Iago in your head ("I am nothing if not critical"), or giving voice to Lear's deprivations, or imagining the "black and deep desires" of Macbeth? In the case of his new granddaughter, however, the connection between his work and life becomes touching. Both *King Lear* and *Macbeth* involve disasters of inheritance and lamentations or anxieties about heirs (think of Lear's losing Cordelia, or Macbeth's obsessing over Banquo's progeny). Shakespeare's increasing investments and the safe birth of Elizabeth meant that his own experiences with these topics appeared much more prosperous, and were causes for happiness and hope. Furthermore, the appearance of new life in the Shakespeare household, in the toddling person of their granddaughter, forecasts other exciting beginnings about to occur professionally for our writer later in 1608—a new, prestigious indoor theater for the fresh staging of plays, and a wholly new kind of play, those magical "romances" that would occupy Shakespeare for the last phase of his career.

Sources and Further Reading

Barroll, Leeds. *Politics, Plague, and Shakespeare's Theater: The Stuart Years*. Ithaca: Cornell University Press, 1991.

Bell, Millicent. *Shakespeare's Tragic Skepticism*. New Haven: Yale University Press, 2002.

Bushnell, Rebecca W. "Thriftless Ambition: The Tyrants of Shakespeare and Jonson," reprinted in *Macbeth: Bloom's Major Literary Characters*, ed. Harold Bloom. New York: Chelsea House, 1994.

Dillon, Janette. "Theatre and controversy, 1603-1642," *The Cambridge History of British Theatre, Volume 1: Origins to 1660*. Cambridge, U.K.: Cambridge University Press, 2004.

Everett, Barbara. *Young Hamlet: Essays on Shakespeare's Tragedies*. New York: Oxford University Press, 1989.

Foakes, R. A. *Hamlet Versus Lear*. New York: Cambridge University Press, 1993.

Goldberg, Jonathan. *James I and the Politics of Literature*. Baltimore: Johns Hopkins University Press, 1983.

Kastan, David Scott. "'A rarity most beloved': Shakespeare and the Idea of Tragedy," *A Companion to Shakespeare's Works, Volume 1: The Tragedies*, ed. Richard Dutton and Jean Howard. Malden, Mass.: Blackwell, 2003.

Nicholl, Charles. *The Lodger Shakespeare: His Life on Silver Street*. New York: Viking, 2008.

O'Toole, Fintan. *Shakespeare Is Hard, But So Is Life*. New York: Granta, 2002

Rosenbaum, Ron. *The Shakespeare Wars: Clashing Scholars, Public Fiascoes, Palace Coups*. New York: Random House, 2006.

Sharpe, James. *Remember, Remember the Fifth of November: Guy Fawkes and the Gunpowder Plot*. London: Profile Books, 2005.

Thomson, Peter. *Shakespeare's Professional Career*. New York: Cambridge University Press, 1992.

Wilson, F. P. *The Plague in Shakespeare's London*. Oxford, U.K.: Oxford University Press, 1999.

LATE SHAKESPEARE:
A NEW THEATER, NEW PLAYS, NEW BOOKS

The appearance of Shakespeare's name atop the quarto edition of *King Lear*, which the publisher advertised as "played before the King's Majesty at Whitehall," is evidence of the high success that he had enjoyed for years and that he was now enjoying more than ever. Shakespeare was prosperous as a professional playwright, a co-owner of the most popular outdoor theater in London, and, back in Stratford, a propertied and increasingly powerful village gentleman. Many playwrights, if their plays were printed at all, were not known and esteemed enough to have their name featured on the title page. None received top billing—that is, before Shakespeare. If that were not enough, he benefited from the patronage (along with his fellow company men) of King James I himself.

It was 1608. Shakespeare was forty-four years old. Given the much lower life expectancy in early-seventeenth-century England, it was a more advanced age and stage of life than would typically be thought today. Fresh off the achievements of his four great tragedies (*Hamlet, Othello, King Lear,* and *Macbeth*), he was likely taking stock of what might yet lie ahead, thinking carefully about what plays to write next, or more generally, what type of play to turn to, following his thorough, triumphant engagement with tragedy. It does not overstate the matter to suggest that Shakespeare, at this point in his life and career, may have been thinking more frequently about how to make a good end, to perform well what his London contemporary and fellow poet John Donne called his own "play's last scene."

If there was one thing that Shakespeare was not, he was not naïve about the pending realities of his increasing age, his future, and all of our futures. He had just explored, at new literary and theatrical heights and depths, his tragic heroes' dramas of time, fate, and death. Perhaps he intuited that the new direction he would soon take for his next plays might be his last significant phase of productivity as a playwright. Although scholars debate exactly when it happened, and whether

Portrait of John Donne, a famous Jacobean poet. Donne published the majority of his work after Shakespeare's death. *(Isaac Oliver)*

or not it happened gradually or abruptly, Shakespeare's imminent retirement from London's theater life and permanent return to Stratford must have been on his mind. What could he do to ensure these last years of writing and theater ownership were well spent?

How felicitous, then, that around this very time, Shakespeare's theater company, the King's Men, found itself entertaining and promptly seizing upon a wonderful new professional opportunity: the chance to acquire a prestigious indoor playing space, known as Blackfriars, in the center of a well-to-do neighborhood, itself in the center of London. The King's Men were already the dominant theater company in the city, but the acquisition of Blackfriars Theatre would further reinforce this dominance in multiple ways. The company could perform more shows, particularly throughout the colder months when the outdoor theaters had to endure a hiatus. The players would earn a considerably larger income, since tickets in these more exclusive indoor theaters were more expensive, and producing shows there would increase the repertory and extend the theater season through the winter. Naturally, this exclusivity in terms of location and audience would translate directly into an increased cultural prestige for the King's Men, and for theater in London generally.

For Shakespeare in particular, acquiring Blackfriars held out the promise of heightening his own success—he would have a more sophisticated clientele for which to create new plays, and the performance space and generally greater intimacy of an indoor theater invited from the playwright new kinds of dramaturgy, scenic construction, and theatrical thinking. On the other hand, there were attendant pressures: this new, more learned audience, consisting of courtiers, lawyers, and other professional figures, would also be more demanding of Shakespeare. They would desire his plays to smartly reflect the day's popular trends in theatergoing, while not being too popular. Shakespeare, in other words, would have to cater more to high-brow pretensions. Moreover, Shakespeare had written steadily for the public, outdoor playhouses, especially the Globe, for many years, and had encountered repeated success there. What if he simply couldn't conceive of or execute a new kind of play? What if he suddenly seemed behind the times, an old-timer and theater simpleton who could write only for the easily pleased masses? What if, in front of this new, much more elite clientele, Shakespeare flopped? Before proceeding, though, we should take care not to oversimplify: it was not remotely the case that Shakespeare was unused to such audiences. Indeed, during Elizabeth's and especially James's reign, he regularly performed at court for the most powerful, intimidating client of all—the monarch. Alvin Kernan, therefore, reasonably claims that whenever Shakespeare portrays a theater or performance in his plays, he does not—with the exception of the Chorus in *Henry V*—portray a public theater, but rather a performance occuring at a court or nobleman's house.

Nevertheless, the prospect of acquiring the Blackfriars Theatre was a sensitive time for Shakespeare and the King's Men. They were wagering a great investment in this new theater enterprise, both of funds and of reputation. What's more, other instabilities far beyond the theater world prevailed, as we shall see. How would it all turn out? Just as it is today for a suddenly-everywhere new celebrity, a star college athlete who has just turned pro, or the most buzzed-about, swiftly growing Internet start-up company, this season for Shakespeare's company, a pivotal one in a long, glorious history, was almost certainly very exciting and highly stressful all at the same time.

BLACKFRIARS: ITS HISTORY AND ACQUISITION

The King's Men's August 1608 assumption of the lease of Blackfriars Playhouse was, at least for a few of the more longstanding company members, a sweet, long-awaited victory, one more than a decade and two theater troupes in the making. For an explanation, recall that way back in 1596, when the earlier manifestation of Shakespeare's company, the Lord Chamberlain's Men, was barely two years old, James Burbage purchased the refectory, or dining space, of Blackfriars, a sprawling monastic complex just southwest of St. Paul's Cathedral. The builder and owner of the Theatre in Shoreditch, and father of that company's great tragedian Richard Burbage, James was acting as speculator in hopes of creating for the Lord Chamberlain's Men a second, much more centrally located, and far more prestigious and profitable space to perform plays. The hall, where Dominicans used to take their meals, had fallen into neglect since 1538, a time when Henry VIII, in defiance of the pope, was dissolving many a Catholic religious house throughout the realm. Amid the dust and cobwebs, Burbage found there a rectangular space with great possibilities for a handsome indoor theater. That said, the dimensions, roughly two stories in height and 45 by 65 feet, would create a playing space far more intimate than the jutted stage and circular playhouse of the Theatre, where penny-paying, sometimes disruptive groundlings surrounded the performance. By comparison, the much higher ticket price of six pence would effectively ensure that no groundlings attended shows at Blackfriars. This was six times the cost of their typical penny admission price. Similarly, seating in this new theater would allow for seven hundred spectators at most, as opposed to the

Portrait of Henry VIII, ca. 1536–37 *(Hans Holbein the Younger)*

roughly three-thousand-person capacity for a show in an outdoor theater.

James Burbage was envisioning a more exclusive event, a new kind of commercial theater in London, but there was one problem: he had chosen a location amid a very exclusive urban neighborhood. On each side of the complex, lining the Thames shore like jewels, were the great houses named after powerful families—Leicester House,

Arundel House, Essex House, Somerset House. In Blackfriars itself, Parliament had met there in the past, the Holy Roman Emperor Charles V had stayed there as a guest, and at present, noblemen were residing there. (In fact, Burbage was counting on this new space to resemble the sort of noble manor-house hall where dramatic performances were traditionally held.) And shortly, this fashionable area would attract Shakespeare's fellow writer Ben Jonson and the great seventeenth-century court painter Van Dyck. In short, the location proved to be *too* exclusive. The neighbors, when they heard of this enterprising plan for a disreputable Shoreditch playing company to begin performances in *their* neighborhood, would have none of it. Soon they enlisted the help of the City aldermen to prohibit Burbage's plan.

Actually, we might sympathize with these residents for a moment. To do so, first Google "Civitas Londinium" ("city of London" in Latin) or the "Agas Map of London." Hit the link that allows you to download a jpeg file, which provides you a map of the densely populated, highly built-up Renaissance city, sitting within its outer walls like a sideways crescent along the northern shore of the Thames. Now, zoom in a few times toward the city's western side, and you will see just to the right of the wall, in between Water Lane and St. Andrew's Hill, and south of the port of Puddle Dock, the words "Black Fryers" scripted among the waves. The words were not that far from the opposite shore of the Thames, where nearby the phrase "Paris Garden" marked one of the few developed settings in the suburb of Bankside. A few small houses were clustered around the stairs and dock leading from river to south shore. The Agas map shows a couple of wooden fences, and very soon the tellingly named Gravel Lane, tree- and shrub-lined, extends southward. On each side, cattle graze in pastures. A little to the east of Paris Garden, behind the single row of

buildings facing the river, were gardens followed by two small, circular theaters—not for the acting of great tragedies, but for bull and bear baiting, respectively (not that those theaters were met with any more approval by the neighbors).

Now *this*, whether here in Bankside or north of the city in Shoreditch, where Burbage already owned a theater, was the suburban neighborhood of the playhouses. Later, on Wenceslaus Hallar's map of 1647, the phrases' proximity remained the same, except that the phrase "The Globe" has replaced "Paris Garden"—a sign of the landmark status by then of Shakespeare's and his theater company's home. So, these pairs of place names were adjacent on these maps, but in reality, the two places were social universes apart. For example, just downriver from Blackfriars stood Baynard Castle, rebuilt after a fire in 1428 by Humphrey Duke of Gloucester, immortalized in Shakespeare's early history plays, *1* and *2 Henry VI*. Likewise, Richard Duke of Gloucester, famous as the villain-king in *Richard III*, accepted the crown, as the play has it, "in the court of Baynard's Castle." The area for Shakespeare was full of English myth and history, the haunt of great men, and, as Shakespeare's contemporary John Stow wrote in the magisterial *Survey of London*, "The castle now belongeth to the Earl of Pembroke." Unsurprisingly, then, professionals, gentlemen, and even noblemen such as Pembroke who resided in the mansions and castles around Blackfriars fought fiercely to keep out Burbage, the Lord Chamberlain's Men, and their common audiences. Let the suburbs, they argued, continue to house unsavory, rowdy activities such as bear-baiting and stage plays. The only upwardly mobile commoners they wished to encounter were those characters mocked on stage in plays such as Jonson's *Volpone*.

To be clear, this should not suggest that Londoners of the professional classes and higher gen-

Portrait of Richard III from the sixteenth century, probably based on an earlier work. *(Artist unknown)*

precincts. The Puritans despised the theaters because they were condemned as ungodly; the upper classes' animosity derived from social snobbery. Thus, Burbage in 1596 had to give up his dream of opening an indoor commercial theater and hosting a classier sort of customer in the heart of the city. It would be a radical expansion for the highly contested social practice of public theater, and London's respectable sort were not ready for it. At least not for the time being. James Burbage died one year later, and the unusable property became his actor son's problem.

Richard Burbage quickly arrived at a makeshift solution—he leased the Blackfriars hall to the shrewd Welsh lawyer Hugh Evans. Teaming up with the choirmaster of the Chapel Royal, Evans soon became the landlord at Blackfriars for a revived children's theater company consisting of the queen's choirboys. How did Evans manage to get away with these theatrical performances, if the elder Burbage's efforts to establish a public theater had been dashed? The status of private theater made all the difference: Evans claimed he did not care to hold formal performances at Blackfriars, but that it was merely a convenient space for the boy company to rehearse, in case Queen Elizabeth called on them with little or no notice. Once this activity was approved, Evans was slyly able to allow certain "privileged" onlookers to pay to see one of these "rehearsals." Like I said, Evans was shrewd, and had an eye for opportunity. However dubious this plan sounded, there was actually precedent: a similar children's theater troupe had performed in the same space from 1576 onward, but in the late 1580s their

try never ventured to the public theaters in those down-market neighborhoods of the city. Alfred Harbage once argued that public-theater audiences largely comprised apprentices and artisans, but Jennalie Cook, in *The Privileged Playgoers of Shakespeare's London*, has argued otherwise, envisioning an unusually mixed social presence there. These privileged playgoers may not have minded deigning to take part in that mixed assembly, but they certainly did not want that sort of atmosphere in their more exclusive home

shows became entangled with the political and ecclesiastical controversies at the heart of the Martin Marprelate pamphlet war, and the boys' company was shut down. Fortunately for Shakespeare and his fellow actors, this fate would prove to be something of a pattern.

Originally, the Chapel Royal's singers had combined with the boys' choir at St. Paul's Cathedral, but now, in 1597, the Blackfriars Theatre housed only the Children of the Chapel Royal, while St. Paul's Boys, performing in a private house near the cathedral, became intense competitors. This rivalry, and a general shift in Elizabethan literary culture toward a more caustic, satirical comedy, swiftly led to a renewal of edgy performances by these companies—critical of the rival company and, in an effort to attract playgoers at the other company's expense, willing to be outrageous in speech and politically daring. Each company retained a house playwright—Ben Jonson at Blackfriars and John Marston at St. Paul's—and both could be devastatingly effective when writing in the trendy vein of satire. These two authors commenced to attacking each other, the rival companies, and the less elite, less fashionable public-theater companies: this was the "Poets' War" or "War of the Theatres" discussed earlier. Shakespeare as playwright and company man certainly contributed at least to a counteroffensive against the children's companies, along with Thomas Dekker, another playwright for his troupe. Yet it was another controversy a half decade later that caused such a stir and significant change within the theater landscape.

The Chapel Royal boys and their managers doomed their company when, in March 1608, they staged George Chapman's play entitled *The Conspiracy and Tragedy of Charles, Duke of Byron*. The politically sensitive content so outraged the French Ambassador that he appealed to King James to abolish the theater company responsible. To add insult to injury, the children's company also attacked Scotland, mocked James I as a drunkard, and made fun of his royal habit of hunting. Outraged, the king swiftly shut down the company, and so by mid-March, the Children of the Queen's Revels was disbanded. The children likely had been performing Ben Jonson's latest play, *Epicoene*, but henceforth they would never act again, King James fulminated, even if they had to beg for their bread. Hugh Evans, the company's manager, now had no choice but to surrender the lease back to Richard Burbage. Shakespeare's colleague Burbage was suddenly faced with a lack of tenant for the Blackfriars property, but quite possibly he also sensed the amazing opportunity that was at hand. No doubt anxious, excited conversations took place among company members throughout the spring and summer of 1608. On August 9, a lease was executed that conveyed the Blackfriars Theatre to seven principal sharers, or lessees, or "housekeepers," five of which were members of the King's Men—including Shakespeare, of course, and his fellow actors Burbage, Heminges, Condell, and Sly. This last actor died a week later, thereby increasing the other six investors' stake in the new theater.

The elder Burbage's commercial dream for his company and for London theater in general had now been fulfilled. The King's Men had now taken legal possession of the Blackfriars Theatre. James and Richard, father and son, had correctly predicted a new theatergoing public in seventeenth-century London—a more literate, sophisticated, and demanding audience who preferred the "great hall" type of theater to the vulgar rudeness of an outdoor, circular bear-baiting pit. The company, in securing the playhouse for its own repertory's performances, also leaned in its orientation toward the audiences, values, and aesthetics of the court, as opposed to the city. It is as if the King's Men had some slight premonition of the tumultuous years to come, later in the century, when the English nation would be split by civil war, and London's rulers, consisting at that time of a Puritan majority, would shut down for good the public theaters of the Renaissance. Aesthetically, this shift involved the ascension of a new, hybrid genre of play, tragicomedy; a greater influence on music and spectacle, borrowed from that highly popular form of court drama, the masque; and more attention within plays to emotional subtlety and intimacy, as opposed to the sheer passion and grand proclamations and soliloquies often heard in the open-air, public theaters. These changes in literary fashion and dramatic values would soon affect Shakespeare's writing practices and the last plays he produced.

OBSTACLES IN LONDON, LOSSES IN STRATFORD

Despite the excitement that the King's Men must have felt at finally securing, in the men's fourteenth year of existence as a London theater company, the private indoor theater of Blackfriars, they could not immediately begin producing shows there. Moreover, at the very moment of this success and promise of expansion, their livelihoods—and their very lives, in fact—stood under clouds of uncertainty. First, the very occasion that led to the Children of the Queen's Revels' dissolution and opened a door for the King's Men ironically threatened the prospects for the entire profession of theater in London. James I may have been developing his reputation as the "wisest fool in Christendom," but he was politically shrewd, and his high, absolutist sense of his royal office explains his harsh responses to scurrilous and politically questionable plays. He knew that plays were popular, and shows mocking the king reduced his stature among his citizens. Thus he initially closed down, in March 1608, not just the children's company, but *all* theater companies

in London, and there was a very real sense that this might be a permanent royal proscription. Now that the King's Men had access to Blackfriars, would they ever be able to perform plays there, or even in their longstanding, still crucial Globe Theatre?

James's edict was not permanent, fortunately, but there soon arose a second and even more dire problem: the plague was once again raging through London. The bill of mortality for the week when the Blackfriars lease was signed shows that fifty people died of the plague, and the numbers remained high for nearly a year and a half, till December 1609. Although records no longer exist to verify this, it is very likely that the King's Men were unable to stage productions, at either their outdoor or indoor theater, for a great deal of this terrible season of the plague.

Back home, with his Stratford family, Shakespeare had to endure painful news as well. His mother, best remembered today by her maiden name, Mary Arden, lived as a widow for seven years following the death of John Shakespeare. She died shortly after her son William became an investor in the Blackfriars Theatre. For September 9, 1608, the Stratford register lists the burial of "Mayry Shaxspere, widow."

The fate of another of Shakespeare's family members gave a new occasion for sadness. At some point William's brother Edmund also became an actor and followed his older sibling into London's theater world. Edmund was the youngest child of John and Mary Shakespeare. Much less is known about his professional life, and he did not seem to have any direct involvement with his established brother's theater companies. Whereas William found great prosperity in London, for the younger Edmund, the city proved to be lethal: he died in December 1607, at the age of twenty-seven.

(continues on page 196)

SHAKESPEARE'S COLLABORATIONS

Playwriting and the entire business of staging plays are by their nature communal enterprises. It was true in Renaissance London and is just as true today. For any writer, the solitary act of composition is a necessary but not sufficient step—publishing lies ahead, and the reaching of an audience. Yet writers of plays are dependent on audiences to a greater degree, and the work it takes to reach those audiences is more complicated, and therefore must involve far more people. The playwright produces no ultimately finished product, but only a script that must be given further life, embodied and enacted, by a range of persons—a producer willing to cover the costs, a director with a vision for staging words on a page, a cast of actors who make the script's characters three-dimensional, and costume and sound designers, technical directors, stage managers, and so on. All of these people contribute to a performance of a written work, which is given and then gone. That is the magic and the sadness of the theater. Then and only then, after an opening night and (hopefully) a long run of shows with audiences keen to attend and experience, is a script fully realized. With this end in mind, the very thought of a play written but never produced, perhaps stored in a desk drawer, is a little sad.

So in this sense, playwriting is always collaborative, inasmuch as it requires many different artists to make an author's story a reality in the theater. This shared effort, spread among so many people, can be inspiring and collegial, or else unpredictable and exasperating. With the writing itself, however, today's playwright tends to be a solitary sovereign over his work. In Shakespeare's day, amid the market-driven bustle of the professional theater world, this single arrangement was not always the case. In some ways, in fact, an author such as Shakespeare—known, respected, and usually solely responsible for composing his own plays—was quite an exception. Collaboration so permeated the world of English Renaissance theater that even Shakespeare was not completely unfamiliar with it.

Shakespeare's first efforts at writing plays may have been collaborative. At least for a long time (though less so today), it was thought that he was merely one contributor to *Titus Andronicus*, with significant sections written by the likes of George Peele or Christopher Marlowe. Other writers, including Shakespeare's early attacker in print Robert Greene, were connected with the *Henry VI* plays, which are now almost always attributed to the Bard. Many current scholars believe he also wrote passages for *Edward III*, another history play from the 1590s.

His most important act of collaboration, and the example most interesting for readers and historians, was likely his contribution of three folio pages to a manuscript known as *The Book of Sir Thomas More*. The presumed history of this play reveals strikingly the committee-like nature of playwriting in Shakespeare's day. The script was begun by Anthony Munday and Henry Chettle, but the Master of the Revels (the official censor) and the theater company had problems with it and demanded improvements. Therefore some passages were deleted, others were rearranged, and additional writers were brought in to write specific parts to be included. For example, Thomas Dekker wrote apprentice scenes, full of London street language, and Thomas Heywood seems to have been a co-writer as well. (Elsewhere Heywood boasts of being involved in literally hundreds of plays, having, in his words, his full hand in some of them and only a finger in others—that is, he was the single author of some and a collaborator on others.) Shakespeare contributed a scene in which a rebellion is defused, and these priceless manuscript pages are likely the only ones we have, or may ever have, of his own handwriting recorded as he was in the process of completing a scene.

Later in his career, Shakespeare became a little more receptive to collaborative writing. The second half of the play *Pericles* (1608) is now thought to be by Shakespeare, with the first half attributed to a frankly dubious partner, a writer and brothel owner named George Wilkins. Shakespeare's last two plays also appear to be the works of collaboration. *Henry VIII* and *The Two Noble Kinsmen* feature scenes by both Shakespeare and a younger playwright, John Fletcher. How did this literary relationship develop? Maybe Shakespeare was keen to work as a kind of mentor figure to Fletcher, who would be his eventual successor as house playwright for Shakespeare's playing company (known as the King's Men by that time). Or maybe, later in his career, Shakespeare's well-known industry and facility as a writer were flagging, as his mind began to think more about his pending retirement back to Stratford and away from London's theaters. Perhaps he worked off the younger author's fresh energy and more current writing style.

There are arguably other kinds of collaboration, if the word is taken more broadly. There is no evidence that Shakespeare ever worked with Thomas Nashe, who did, it seems, collaborate on an early play of Christopher Marlowe's (both were at Cambridge University) and may have contributed the comic scenes to Marlowe's greatest play, *Doctor Faustus*. Nashe's feisty, streetwise prose definitely influenced Shakespeare, most memorably and profitably in the scenes in the Eastcheap tavern in *Henry IV*. Can direct influence be considered a kind of collaboration? Or what about Shakespeare's first editors, his fellow actors Heminges and Condell, who collected the writer's manuscripts and presumably made difficult editorial decisions about what to publish, in what order, and so on? Or how about those later writers who revised Shakespeare's plays, often making them dramatically different? Or today's editors who modernize Shakespeare's early-modern language and suggest clear meanings to facilitate for students their reading experiences today? All of these questions suggest one thing, at least: collaboration is a complicated business, especially in the world of the theater.

SEE ALSO:

Muir, Kenneth. *Shakespeare As Collaborator*. London: Methuen, 1960.

Schoenbaum, Samuel. *William Shakespeare: A Compact Documentary Life*. New York: Oxford University Press, 1977.

Stern, Tiffany. "Repatching the Play," *From Script to Stage in Early Modern England*, ed. Peter Holland and Stephen Orgel, New York, N.Y.: Palgrave Macmillan, 2004.

Stern, Tiffany and Simon Palfrey. *Shakespeare in Parts*. New York: Oxford University Press, 2007.

Vickers, Brian. *Shakespeare, Co-Author: A Historical Study of the Five Collaborative Plays*. Oxford, U.K.: Oxford University Press, 2004.

Seventeenth-century portrait of John Fletcher by an unknown artist

(continued from page 193)

A few months earlier, in August, a presumably illegitimate son of Edmund's also perished. The register at the church of St. Giles Cripplegate reads for August 12, "Edward, son of Edmund Shackspeere, player, base-born." That final phrase is jarring—a social condemnation of a young man who remained, despite the profession's increasing stature, in the disrespected world of acting. Only William's abilities, as an actor and writer, and his good fortune, and specifically his growing fortune as a theater owner, allowed him to secure that gentleman's coat of arms, and thus avoid the kind of social stigma heard in the phrase "base-born." William's brother Edmund was laid to rest just to the east of the Globe, at St. Saviour's, otherwise called St. Mary Overy (meaning "over the river"), the cathedral church in Bankside, quite near London Bridge. A sexton's note in the church burial register indicates that Edmund, listed here simply as a "player" or actor, was "buried in the Church with a forenoon knell of the great bell." A cost of twenty shillings, a substantial amount, is also listed, suggesting that Edmund received a handsome, solemn burial, one unusual for a young, poor actor. Almost certainly his successful older brother William was the one who paid the expenses. Samuel Schoenbaum, one of Shakespeare's greatest modern biographers, suggests that a "forenoon" tolling of the bells was specified so that Shakespeare and his fellow actors and playwrights could attend the ceremony, and yet be returned to the theater for afternoon performances.

In addition to this grief from family deaths, public records show that Shakespeare during this time remained prone to legal grievances with fellow Stratford citizens. We have seen how Shakespeare sued his neighbor Philip Rogers, an apothecary who had purchased, but not entirely paid for, twenty bushels of malt. He returned to court in August 1608, this time suing and seeking to recover £6 plus damages from John Addenbrooke. The case dragged on till June of the following year. Eventually the jury sided with Shakespeare, but it remains unknown if he ever collected the money legally due to him. Another Stratford public document, in which Shakespeare is one of the "orators" complaining to Lord Chancellor Thomas Ellesmere about others' failure to pay on Shakespeare's and others' share of holdings from the Stratford tithes, may also date from this time, or more precisely, it may be as early as 1609. This all may seem like aggressive business practice, but litigation was quite common during Shakespeare's era, and besides, with London's theaters closed due to royal suppression and outbreak of the plague, Shakespeare the Stratfordian may have been in need of any money currently owed him. The date suggests that Shakespeare the family man may have had increased financial demands at this time. As discussed in the last chapter, Shakespeare's older daughter, Susanna, married in June 1607, and by this time she was thriving—her husband was an upstanding town physician, and she gave birth to a first child, a daughter, in February 1608. To support the new family, grandpa William bestowed upon them one hundred and five acres of his land in Old Stratford, a very significant dowry.

TWO LAST TRAGEDIES: *ANTONY AND CLEOPATRA* AND *CORIOLANUS*

During these busy years of family marriages, births, and deaths, Shakespeare remained highly active as a playwright. He may already have been hard at work on the late plays that would signal a surprising, enchanting new phase of development in his professional life as a writer and imaginer of great theater. Indeed, certain moments in these plays, traditionally grouped together as the

"Romances," from their bold, dazzling uses of spectacle to their new depths of feeling involving forgiveness and reconciliation, sometimes seem to partake in Renaissance drama's version of the miraculous. While these final plays glowed and simmered in Shakespeare's brain or in his first manuscript drafts, however, two late tragedies were staged between 1606 and 1608. These two plays, along with *Timon of Athens* presented in the last chapter, are hard to catalog: either half-finished or like nothing else Shakespeare produced (in the case of *Timon*), or, in the cases of *Antony and Cleopatra* and *Coriolanus*, looking both backward and forward at the same time. That is, they are recognizably like previous plays by Shakespeare, and yet are clearly written later, and particularly after those great few years of writing tragedies. Their tone and tenor is more mature, more seasoned: more sophisticated in narration and pacing in *Antony and Cleopatra*, sterner in theme and spirit in *Coriolanus*, and in both, more various and nuanced in poetic rhythm and dramatic voicing.

For example, Shakespeare in 1605–06 returned once again to the subgenre of Roman tragedy and built into this next effort, *Antony and Cleopatra*, something like a grand, pre-operatic flavor. What resulted was one of his most all-around consummate plays, featuring in Cleopatra one of his greatest creations of female character. In short, this play stands as far beyond *Julius Caesar* in its proud heights and depth of spirit as *Caesar* stood, in its own time at the turn of the century, beyond the bloody Roman revenge play *Titus Andronicus*. On the other hand, it would be misleading to suggest that *Antony and Cleopatra* was composed as or treated as a wholly new form of drama. It may at first seem like a departure from the preceding great tragedies, but recall that Shakespeare found his sources for *King Lear* and *Macbeth* in a historical work, Holinshed's *Chron-*

icles, and just so, the playwright was again finding new subject matter by tilling the fertile fields of history—in this instance, his trusty, probably by now well-read and well-thumbed copy of Plutarch's *Lives of the Noble Grecians and Romans*, full of biographies of ancient kings, generals, and statesmen. Shakespeare knew full well that the particular story of one highly accomplished, very fashionable Egyptian queen, and her revolving dramas of Roman imperial lovers, was easily one of the most mesmerizing stories in the bunch. He also sought inspiration from contemporary plays on Cleopatra and Antony by Samuel Daniel and the Countess of Pembroke, but again Plutarch proved to be his clear go-to source.

Antony, the first of the play's title characters, is rendered here with convincing complexity, displaying far more internal conflict and personal capriciousness than Shakespeare's prior Roman heroes. That said, make no mistake: Cleopatra is undoubtedly the major figure of this play. The allure is hers, the beautiful poetry is hers, or is dedicated to describing her, and the climactic death will be hers as well. Taken together, the story of this sensuous queen and this grand Roman general explains how Shakespeare's play seems to exhibit such range—vast in scale, as it moves back and forth from Rome to Egypt, and yet highly domestic, too. We see here, more than in any other Shakespeare play, characters' closed-door lives, inconsistencies, and oddities. Of course, as a historical personage, Cleopatra was as fascinating to Shakespeare and his fellow Renaissance Englishmen as she is today. Just recently, award-winning biographer Stacy Schiff retold Cleopatra's story for a twenty-first-century readership, one of five such works to appear in the last five years. In Schiff's Pulitzer Prize winner, the queen appears as glamorous, and as savvy, as ever. Persuasive, famed for her wit, speaking nine languages, this Cleopatra resembles today's female executive. Shakespeare's dramatic rendering of Cleopatra, needless to say, had lent much to this legacy and reputation:

> The barge she sat in, like a
>   burnish'd throne,
> Burn'd on the water: the poop was beaten
>   gold;
> Purple the sails, and so perfumed that
>   The winds were love-sick with them; the
>   oars were silver,
> Which to the tune of flutes kept stroke, and
>   made
> The water which they beat to follow faster,
> As amorous of their strokes. For her own
>   person,
> It beggar'd all description: she did lie
> In her pavilion--cloth-of-gold of tissue--
> O'er-picturing that Venus where we see
> The fancy outwork nature: on each side her
> Stood pretty dimpled boys, like smiling
>   Cupids,
> With divers-colour'd fans, whose wind did
>   seem
> To glow the delicate cheeks which they did
>   cool,
> And what they undid did.

Thus Enobarbus reports Cleopatra's first meeting with Antony on the river Cydnus. Note especially here the rich imagery and the Baroque attention to refining details, a verbal parallel to the pageantry and splendor of the event itself. It is a lushly descriptive passage, for centuries famous for exemplifying Shakespeare's lyrical sublimity, and for influencing later verse descriptions in, for example, T. S. Eliot's *The Waste Land*.

Plutarch speaks of the queen's "charms and sorceries," and as the play opens, Antony is clearly entranced in this way, enthralled by the good life of Egypt. Yet he remains haunted by his unfulfilled heroic destiny: resisting appeals to return to Rome, he feels that he is a "shadow" of his former self. News of the death of Antony's wife, Fulvia, finally urges upon him a return to Rome. Soon Antony agrees to marry Octavian's (that is, the future Caesar Augustus's) sister, "holy, cold, and still" Octavia, who is the far less interesting female character in this play. At the play's midpoint, we see Cleopatra's rantings and ravings at the news of Antony's betrothal, and soon enough, Antony's disgraceful return to Egypt. Infuriated, Octavian goes on the attack, and Antony, strategizing with his lover, lacks a good general's discernment: he ignores the advice of counselors, and eventually suffers a ruinous naval defeat at the Battle of Actium.

For all of its verbal and visual glories, *Antony and Cleopatra* seems most of all to be a stunningly revealing play about middle-aged love, and about middle-aged lovers' spats, peevishness, and floundering. Rarely can characters seem so exalted and yet so capable of foolishness, of acting against their own best interests. Additionally, there is always present here the pain of past pleasures. Cleopatra speaks to Charmian of "My salad days, / When I was green in judgment, cold in blood," when recalling her past affair with Julius Caesar, while Antony, brooding on uncertainty, instability, and mortality in this world, reflects how "Sometime we see a cloud that's dragonish," which mocks our eyes with air.

Disgraced and defeated, the couple implodes. Antony blames Cleopatra for their defeat at sea. She soon sends feigned news of her suicide, which leads to his suicide attempt in response. He asks to be carried off, and to see his lover one final time. "I am dying, Egypt, dying," Antony soon declares, whose death here takes longer and is more awkward than nearly any other figure in Shakespeare's dramatic universe. Like the matters of the heart and his political and personal relationships throughout the play, Antony manages his own suicide less than well, hence his prolonged gasping at the edge of death. "The crown o' the earth doth melt," laments Cleopatra, adding later, "And there is nothing left remarkable / Beneath the visiting moon." Eventually Cleopatra faces her own reduced, cornered circumstances, far beneath a hero or a queen. In one memorable scene, she disdains being marched captive through the streets of Rome (and her imagined fate is quite in keeping with the fate of criminals or prisoners in London). She hates the thought of "squeaking Cleopatras" (or boy actors) that "boy my greatness"—that is, imitating and making a mockery of her and her life, presenting her as a whore. The use of "boy" as a verb here is a characteristically strong, specific flash of language, and this reference to the English Renaissance acting conventions of boys or young men playing the female roles becomes an interesting inclusion here: maybe Shakespeare had a particular young actor in mind, and perhaps that actor played the role of Cleopatra and thus said these very lines warning him, as it were, against himself. The same young man may have also played the role of Lady Macbeth. Shakespeare, it seems, had a knack for recognizing acting talent in his company, and then writing parts that would take advantage of a certain actor's unique strengths. He likely noticed with pleasure a similarly talented young actor a few years earlier, when creating the unparalleled pair of female comic characters, Viola from *Twelfth Night* and Rosalind from *As You Like It*. Cleopatra's "boy" reference therefore may be an inside joke between young actor and old writer, or a winking occasion of "meta-theater"—hearing this speech in the audience, playgoers would well know that the character of Cleopatra was enduring already the fate she most feared. We see here, in Shakespeare's language choice and shrewd theatrical awareness, how a great playwright works magic upon a simple historical statement: the historian Livy records that Cleopatra said simply, in a letter to Octavian, "I will not be led in triumph." Finding no other options, no solutions, imagining only outcomes beneath her royal dignity and passionate history, Cleopatra, like her lover Antony, chooses death. "I have immortal longings in me," she says, managing at once to sound sultry, needful of sexual relief ("riggish," to use Shakespeare's word for it), and nobly tragic, unflinching in the face of her pending death. "Husband, I come," she says. Her resulting suicide, done by applying secretly gathered poisonous asps to her bosom and arm, represents a satisfying occasion of Cleopatra's trickery at the young, efficient Octavian's expense. (Schiff, one of the queen's latest biographers, doubts the historical accuracy of the asp detail, but it makes great theater.) At least in Shakespeare's play, Rome's new emperor destroys but does not defeat Cleopatra, who in the poet's hand becomes ever beautiful and intriguing, and ever fresh and timely, in her "infinite variety."

Like *Coriolanus*, different claims have been made about the staging of *Antony and Cleopatra*. Its sense of geographical vastness and swift, scenic shifts would seem to invite the bare stage of the Globe, the outdoor public theater, and yet the play's intimate settings and lack of crowd scenes would play well in the indoor confines of Blackfriars. The King's Men likely performed the play in both theaters. A listing for *Antony and Cleopatra* in the May 1608 Stationers' Register suggests plans for quarto publication, as well as a previous season of performances, but no printed version appeared till the 1623 First Folio. *Coriolanus*, too, did not appear in print till being included in the First Folio, although historical allusions to the "great frost" of 1607–08 and the Midlands food riots in the early summer of 1607 support dating the play close to *Timon of Athens* and *Antony and Cleopatra*. (Shakespeare, likely spending time in Stratford then, may have known of these riots firsthand.) That said, it may have reached the stage as late as 1609–10. Like *Julius Caesar* before it, *Coriolanus* takes its audiences to the very streets of Rome, whose robust language and certain fashions (Stuart bonnets, for instance!) seem very much like Renaissance London's crowded, sometimes disorderly lanes. As opposed to the increasingly swift changes of setting in *Antony and Cleopatra*, in *Coriolanus* the Romans find themselves under siege, the city walls surrounded by the enemy Volscians. Despite these differences of scenic effect, however, Shakespeare was once again consulting Plutarch's *Lives* for this latest play idea.

The play begins with famished citizens in a state of near revolt: they form a mob and intend to attack Caius Marcius, a despised patrician politician. The senator Menenius Agrippa confronts the mob and temporarily calms it down, employing the metaphor of the "body politic" to justify the better-off patrician class's easier access to food.

> The senators of Rome are this good belly,
> And you the mutinous members; for
>   examine
> Their counsels and their cares, digest things
>   rightly
> Touching the weal o' the common, you shall
>   find
> No public benefit which you receive
> But it proceeds or comes from them to you
> And no way from yourselves. What do you
>   think,
> You, the great toe of this assembly?

Menenius clearly feels neither affection nor respect for the plebians, but he at least slightly conceals his class snobbery, and attempts some explanation for the circumstances outraging the commoners. When a citizen asks why he is the big toe, Menenius continues,

> For that, being one o' the lowest, basest,
>   poorest,
> Of this most wise rebellion, thou go'st
>   foremost:
> Thou rascal, that art worst in blood to run,
> Lead'st first to win some vantage.
> But make you ready your stiff bats and
>   clubs:
> Rome and her rats are at the point of battle;
> The one side must have bale.

Unfortunately, just as the mob is appeased, their target, Caius Marcius, appears before them, and immediately he incites the commoners afresh: the mob should be hanged, he says dismissively. Soon, though, Caius Marcius's strength and valor are needed to combat the approaching Volscians, led by Tullius Aufidius, who throughout the play will reveal an ambivalent relation to and reflection of the play's title character. Speaking of which, how does Caius Marcius become known as Coriolanus? By his heroism in battle: he leads the Roman troops forward, and soon occupies Corioles. His new name, then, is a military honorific. Coriolanus reenters Rome in triumph, causing two tribunes to fear his political ascendancy over the city. The Senate nominates their military savior as consul, which requires Coriolanus to address the common citizens and seek their votes.

To better understand the title character's singular, and ultimately disastrous, inability to figuratively bend his knee toward the commoners, we must introduce another character, his mother, Volumnia. Speaking of her son Caius Marcius, her "man-child," she says she "was pleased to let him seek danger where he was like to find fame," even when he was youthful, "tender-bodied," and therefore vulnerable. Nevertheless, she happily sends him forth into a "cruel war," and he soon returns crowned with the victor's oak branch. What if he had perished there, she is asked? Her reply—"Then his good report should have been my son"—is admirably direct, and an admirable valuing of Roman honor. Yet, for a mother commenting upon her son, there is something a little heartless in the statement, too, as there is when she thanks the gods upon hearing that her son has been wounded in his battle with the Volscians. She revels in the soldier's glory that the injury will bring him, along with a possible augmentation of his power in the city. There is little visible love between mother and son in the steel-cold personality of Volumnia, but then again, Coriolanus himself seems hardly loveable. Arrogance characterizes both mother and son, and both despise the commoners whose approval Coriolanus needs. Volumnia inadvertently sets in motion her son's destruction when she encourages him to disguise his true feelings and appeal to those plebian citizens. He tries, but his own great pride prevents his continued self-abasement, as he sees it, "Lest I surcease to honour mine own truth[.]" He can only remain aloof. As the critic Jonathan Crew argues, the ambivalence surrounding the play stems from our simultaneous admiration for Coriolanus's convictions and growing realization that such personal rigidity often generates a tragic outcome.

Temporarily Coriolanus believes he has received the necessary votes, but his adversarial tribunes Brutus and Sicinius have swayed the citizens against him. They have withdrawn their support, which leads to Coriolanus's embittered tirades against commoners and tribunes alike. After Coriolanus is banished, he immediately visits the Volscians in Antium and, by joining forces with his erstwhile enemy Aufidius, plans revenge against a Rome that does not deserve him. Aufidius remains ever the opponent, though, and indicates that as soon as Rome is sacked, he will betray his new ally. Romans repeatedly attempt to dissuade Coriolanus from his revengeful march,

Coriolanus's mother, wife, and son beg him not invade Rome in Act 5, Scene 3 of *Coriolanus*. This painting is from 1652–53 *(Nicolas Poussin)*

but to no avail. Only his mother, wife, and son, little Marcius, succeed in making him relent, and while the city celebrates, Coriolanus ponders the more ominous outcome that his change of heart will mean:

> O mother, mother!
> What have you done? Behold, the heavens
>   do ope,
> The gods look down, and this unnatural
>   scene
> They laugh at. O my mother, mother! O!
> You have won a happy victory to Rome;
> But, for your son,—believe it, O, believe it,
> Most dangerously you have with him
>   prevail'd,
> If not most mortal to him. But, let it come.
> Aufidius, though I cannot make true wars,
> I'll frame convenient peace.

His mortal premonition proves correct: the Volscians soon declare him a traitor, and they stab and trample the alienated Roman. "Cut me to pieces," he has said defiantly, and they do. *Coriolanus* ends with Aufidius, who comes to recognize in the namesake character a worthy foe, shedding tears for the fallen anti-hero, and commanding his honorable burial.

Shakespeare's final tragedy is lean in its language and fierce in tone. In its unforgiving atmosphere and relationships, and its haughty protagonist's brutal reversal of fortune, it becomes the Shakespeare play that most resembles a Greek tragedy. "Its characteristic style seems to be carved out of granite," writes the critic Stanley Wells, as if Shakespeare were chiseling his lines into a marble tablet in the Roman Forum. It is a fitting kind of style for a highly intellectual, less passionate and humane tragedy. *Coriolanus* has never been a widely popular play, but then again, it has always had its adherents. For example, the actor Ralph Fiennes has been devoted to the play

since playing Coriolanus in a London production, and he is overseeing a forthcoming film version also starring Vanessa Redgrave and Gerard Butler.

PERICLES AND A TIME OF TRANSITION

One final play, *Pericles*, similarly inhabits a transitional space in the progress of Shakespeare's writing style and theatrical artistry, although it does so in ways differing from the Roman tragedies *Antony and Cleopatra* and *Coriolanus*. First of all, while it is hard to say exactly what sort of play *Pericles* is, it is definitely not tragedy. Most critics position it as the first of the Romances, briefly introduced above, all of which are characterized by supernatural elements; unapologetically improbable plots, including tales of shipwreck and fabricated deaths and intense suffering followed by intensely moving reunions; an increasing use of spectacle, music, and stage machinery (reflecting both the influence of court masques and the exciting new possibilities of staging now available to Shakespeare and his company at Blackfriars); and frequently disorienting shifts across exotic settings and long stretches of time. (This last quality irritated later authors bent on more Neoclassical dictates, including a "unity of time and place" in dramatic representation deriving from Aristotle's *Poetics*.) In short, Shakespeare in these late plays seems almost to set for himself various dramatic challenges of yoking extremes of circumstance and character and confrontation into a marvelously cohesive dramatic whole. These plays also feature some version of recovery, redemption. "Seemingly tragic events," explains David Scott Kastan, "are seen to participate in a divine comedy." This achievement often culminates in these romances in a crystallized action, sometimes a reanimation, sometimes a renunciation, and, on a couple of striking occasions,

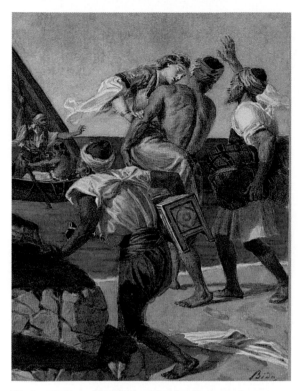

Pirates kidnapping Marina in this nineteenth-century illustration of Act 4, Scene 1 of *Pericles*. *(Alexandre Bida)*

with the sudden appearance of a pagan deity. (For instance, the goddess Diana appears in *Pericles*.)

In these respects, *Pericles* solidly stands as the transitional harbinger of a new kind of Shakespearean play, but certain unresolved tensions nevertheless surround the work. First, if *Pericles* introduced a new king of indoor-theater sophistication, then it also seems to have been widely popular with Jacobean audiences. Furthermore, its 1609 title page presents the play as "diverse and sundry times acted by his Majesties' Servants, at the Globe on the Banck-side." French and Venetian ambassadors even attended a 1608 performance. This action-packed story—of storms, catastrophe, pirates, jousting kidnapping, the sex trade, incest, a magic formula, a murderous attack, a drowning, a revival, and a most unlikely

reunion—was in fact an ancient one, deriving from the Greek story of Apollonius of Tyre, and, more recently and natively, from a tale found in the less-than-fashionable fourteenth-century English poet (and Chaucer's contemporary) John Gower's *Confessio Amantis* ("The Lover's Confession"). Ben Jonson, fellow playwright and impatient classicist, apparently attacked *Pericles* as a "mouldy tale." Shakespeare's new, experimental style of play was much out of step with the popular dramatic genres of the day, including satirical drama and city comedies. Of course, Jonson was probably envious of Shakespeare and resentful of his competitor's success. Jonson's sneer notwithstanding, instead of trying to conceal his medieval source, Shakespeare instead chose to foreground his borrowing in dramatic terms—he made the author Gower himself address the audience as the play's Chorus. It was a shrewd decision on Shakespeare's part, as if to reassure his spectators that he, too, knew just how outlandish this story was; he more than anyone else was acknowledging the play's identity—as a tale. "To sing a song that old was sung / From ashes ancient Gower is come," says the choric narrator in jaunty iambic tetrameter couplets. He also presides over scene-connecting dumb shows, which hearken back to a simpler, more primitive type of drama in England. And later, in Act four, "Imagine Pericles arrived at Tyre," Gower says, giving the audience narrative details and encouraging his viewers toward their own flights of fancy to complement what occurs on stage. Incidentally, Shakespeare, while attending his brother Edmund's funeral at the end of 1607, very likely took note of the poet John Gower's grave and handsome memorial effigy, located in nearby Southwark Cathedral. A second tension associated with *Pericles* involves the impressions, in places, of dubious composition and the related question marks regarding its publication. Shakespeare, for reasons unknown,

TWO COLLABORATORS:
GEORGE WILKINS AND JOHN FLETCHER

The prior special feature, "Shakespeare's Collaborations," explored the complex practices of composition and collaboration among English Renaissance playwrights. Now we are poised to take a special look at two such collaborators whom we know worked with William Shakespeare in the later stages of his career.

The first, George Wilkins, is a dubious fellow, and as we shall see, scholars today are understandably troubled that Shakespeare may have had any dealing with Wilkins at all, much less worked with him as a collaborator. Allegedly these two men were co-writers of *Pericles*, a highly respected late play, if one with a complicated compositional and textual history. Its first quarto publication clearly depended on an imperfect manuscript copy, and it was one of only two plays by Shakespeare that his editors left out of the First Folio of 1623. *Pericles* did not appear among Shakespeare's works till the third printing of the Folio later in the century, and several other plays now thought not to have been by Shakespeare appeared then as well.

Wilkins was a known playwright before becoming co-author of *Pericles*. His play *The Misery of Enforced Marriage*, a tragedy based on a case of domestic murder, was in repertorial rotation in 1607, and he soon published a prose narrative, *The Painful Adventures of Pericles Prince of Tyre*, which borrows from a much earlier English version of this story, a version that was also a source for the Shakespearean play. Moreover, Wilkins's prose fiction borrows passages from the play as well; the two works were clearly connected to each other, and because the first quarto publication of *Pericles* is imper-

fect, some editors go so far as to claim that some of Wilkins's prose passages feature more authentic lines than Shakespeare's play.

So the textual circumstances for this play are complicated, but this is not the most problematic aspect of Shakespeare's collaboration with Wilkins. Scholars and general admirers of Shakespeare must accept the fact that, in the case of Wilkins, the famous author—whom we like to think of as thoughtful, reserved, and morally sensitive—was working with a real, well, bad guy. Wilkins resided in the London neighborhood of St. Giles Cripplegate, and for a while he seemed to busy himself with siring children and writing. Unfortunately, as Charles Nicholls's careful research of court records has shown, Wilkins was regularly in trouble with the law. Sometimes he is listed as a witness on behalf of someone else equally suspicious, but more frequently he is being arraigned for theft (he stole a cape and hat once), for threatening fellow citizens or assaulting them, or for involvements with prostitutes.

The two major threads of transgression throughout these court records are violence and prostitution, suggesting that Wilkins may have been a pimp. In one notorious case, Wilkins was accused of kicking a pregnant woman in the stomach. This dark context makes *Pericles*'s own dramatization of Marina's vulnerable encounters with the sex industry even more uncomfortable. Readers, too, may grow uncomfortable as they ponder the world of writing in Renaissance London. It is one more rough-and-tumble than we often imagine, if an outrageous figure such as Wilkins could not only write

seems to have collaborated with a co-author straight out of the dark, sinister underworld that serves as the greater setting for this play. In addition to a play for the King's Men, *The Miseries of Enforced Marriage*, George Wilkins wrote a

novella, *The Painful Adventures of Pericles Prince of Tyre* (1608), that likely borrows material from his and Shakespeare's play of the year before. The play itself was published in 1609, in what is obviously an imperfect copy. Perhaps the printers did

successfully, but also work with English literature's greatest writer. That said, scholars typically see a clear divide in quality between the first two acts of *Pericles* and its remaining three acts. For some, this suggests that the two authors did not work closely together. It is even possible that Shakespeare was asked to revise parts of Wilkins's original effort.

John Fletcher, Shakespeare's best-known collaborator, cuts an altogether different figure. He was born into a well-to-do family, but later financial stresses drew him to the theater and stage-writing. Fletcher's first play, *The Faithful Shepherdess*, was no commercial success, but it did win the respect of more established playwrights such as Ben Jonson and gave the younger Fletcher an occasion to think about the new mixed genre of tragicomedy, which he discusses explicitly in the preface to the play's printed edition. Soon Fletcher teamed up with Francis Beaumont, a fellow writer with whom he will always be connected, and they produced the successful tragicomedy *Philaster* for the King's Men, around the same time as Shakespeare was completing his late romance *Cymbeline* (1609). The two plays share a number of things in common, and the pastoral elements of Beaumont's and Fletcher's play also feature striking parallels with Shakespeare's *The Winter's Tale*, another contemporary play. Afterward, the pair produced in short order well-received plays such as *A King and No King* and *The Maid's Tragedy*.

Perhaps this work convinced Shakespeare and the rest of the King's Men that the company would do well to depend on Fletcher as a source of future plays. Already the troupe was having to think about the unthinkable—how would the King's Men continue to perform plays when the career of Shakespeare, its most consistent, reliable, successful playwright, came to a close? Textual evidence suggests that Shakespeare groomed Fletcher to be the King's Men's principal dramatist when the former writer retired. The pair collaborated on *Cardenio*, now unfortunately lost, and, just before Shakespeare's apparent retirement in 1613, on *Henry VIII* and *The Two Noble Kinsmen*. As with *Pericles*, scholars today have pretty good ideas about which scenes were composed by each writer. Usually, Shakespeare's passages seem superior as poetry and even as a piece of staged, scenic dramatic writing. Saying so is hardly meant to insult the young apprentice writer Fletcher, who went on to enjoy a long career as a writer of plays. Is there any collaborator, when working with Shakespeare, for whom this imbalance of literary accomplishment would not be so?

SEE ALSO:

Bowers, Fredson ed. *The Dramatic Works in the Beaumont and Fletcher Canon*, 10 vols. Cambridge: Cambridge University Press, 1982.

Duncan-Jones, Katherine. *Ungentle Shakespeare: Scenes from His Life*. London: Arden Shakespeare, 2001.

Finkelpearl, Philip J. *Court and Country Politics in the Plays of Beaumont and Fletcher*. Princeton, N.J.: Princeton University Press, 1990.

Jackson, MacDonald P. *Defining Shakespeare: Pericles as Test Case*. New York: Oxford University Press, 2003.

Nicholl, Charles. *The Lodger Shakespeare: His Life on Silver Street*. New York: Viking, 2008.

Wells, Stanley. *Shakespeare and Co.: Christopher Marlowe, Thomas Dekker, Ben Jonson, Thomas Middleton, John Fletcher, and Other Players in His Story*. New York: Pantheon Books, 2006.

not have access to Shakespeare's more finished manuscript, or perhaps it was a pirated text, reliant on actors' reconstructions of memory. The unevenness of the play's writing and scenic construction has supported a general critical consensus that Wilkins is the likely author of the first two acts (or scenes one through nine in the quarto), whereas Shakespeare's familiar poetic skills become more discernable in the third through fifth acts. The play's conclusion, in particular, has struck nearly all readers as a scene of moving intensity. Despite these attributable strengths, Shakespeare's friends, fellow King's Men, and editors of the First Folio (1623) decided to leave it out of this major collection. Why was *Pericles* discounted? For being a collaboration, or one peculiarly unsatisfying to its deceased author? Were the editors dissatisfied with their lack of a manuscript? If they could not improve on the obviously marred quarto edition, now more than a decade old, maybe they felt it was better to exclude the play than to perpetuate the imperfections of the existing text.

The neglect of *Pericles* in the authoritative Folio text will make many readers grateful for the quarto copy, whatever its problems. Without it, Shakespeare's version of this story would be lost to us. Instead, we are invited to read Gower's explicitly framed tale in which Pericles's wife, Thaisa, is seemingly lost at sea, but only after her husband's daring exploits and escapes in Tyre, Tarsus, and Pentapolis. (She apparently dies in childbirth, and rattled sailors demand that her body be thrown overboard.) Soon the presumed widower Pericles leaves his newborn daughter, Marina, with Tarsus's governor and his wife, Dionyza. She becomes jealous of the lovely, growing girl, however, and Pericles's daughter avoids death only because she is abducted by pirates. When Pericles discovers her missing, he determines to spend his remaining life in mourning. Meanwhile, Marina is sold into sexual bondage in Mytilene, although her chaste perseverance confounds the brothel operator. When Pericles arrives in Mytilene, the governor asks Marina to visit the mourner and comfort him with her song. Pericles understandably does not expect to have his lost daughter restored to him so directly, and so at first he fails to recognize her, but the father's and daughter's emergent recognition is handled with wonderfully artful pacing, as both characters seem to undergo a rebirth, or renewal, as they slowly become known again by their loved one. Finally, Pericles can only exclaim to his loyal servant—

> O Helicanus, strike me, honour'd sir;
> Give me a gash, put me to present pain;
>   Lest this great sea of joys rushing upon
>   me
> O'erbear the shores of my mortality,
> And drown me with their sweetness. O,
>   come hither,
> Thou that beget'st him that did thee beget;
> Thou that wast born at sea, buried at
>   Tarsus,
> And found at sea again! O Helicanus,
> Down on thy knees, thank the holy gods as
>   loud
> As thunder threatens us: this is Marina.
> What was thy mother's name? tell me but
>   that,
> For truth can never be confirm'd enough,
> Though doubts did ever sleep.

As Inga-Stina Ewbank argues, Pericles's past losses and present limitations are suddenly unloosed in the person of Marina, in whom the father's own restoration is made material—a family mirroring of some greater, happier reality. In truth, these 150 lines, in which Shakespeare renders Pericles's budding discovery that he has indeed recovered his daughter, long ago lost at sea, constitute one of the most distinguished examples of poetic writing and dramatic timing throughout all of his plays. Even so, the ending magic of *Pericles* is not yet at its height: Pericles will still experience a vision of Diana, who directs him to Ephesus. There, Thaisa, not dead after all, and long ago washed ashore, is now a votary at Diana's temple. All is restored, and a reunited family is now reborn. However exceptional or parenthetical the rarely performed *Pericles* may sometimes feel, those parts that are most clearly

Shakespearean ought not to be neglected. These scenes and the dramatic poetry that bring them to life are glorious in themselves, but they also point the way to the magical, suffering, but consolatory worlds of Shakespeare's final plays. Many have suggested that the character of Marina, and other young heroines to be found in the Romances, drew upon Shakespeare's new granddaughter, born around this time. James Joyce, for example, in his twentieth-century masterpiece *Ulysses*, has his Quaker librarian in Dublin speak of "the spirit of reconciliation" that presides over the "plays of Shakespeare's later years." This framework occurs within an ongoing conversation that Stephen Daedalus listens to, and he takes in the message that will later in the book apply to him: "What softens the heart of a man, Shipwrecked in storms dire, Tried, like another Ulysses, Pericles, prince of Tyre?" An answer is proffered amid the group. "A child, a girl placed in his arms, Marina." This identification of Marina with Shakespeare's granddaughter may be so, but in the Romances' reunions, something more profound is at work: there, Shakespeare the aging author gets to enjoy, however vicariously, the magical comforts denied to him as a Stratford son and brother, one perhaps still haunted by recent family losses.

Sources and Further Reading

Berry, Herbert. *Shakespeare's Playhouses.* New York: AMS, 1987.

Cook, Jennalie. *The Privileged Playgoers of Shakespeare's London.* Princeton, N.J.: Princeton University Press, 1981.

Kernan, Alvin. *Shakespeare, The King's Playwright: Theater in the Stuart Court 1603-1613.* New Haven: Yale University Press, 1995.

Menzer, Paul. *Inside Shakespeare: Essays on the Blackfriars Stage.* Selinsgrove: Susquehanna University Press, 2006.

Schoenbaum, Samuel. *William Shakespeare: A Compact Documentary Life.* New York: Oxford University Press, 1977.

Smith, Irwin. *Shakespeare's Blackfriars Playhouse.* New York: New York University Press, 1964.

SHAKESPEARE'S SONNETS AND THE LATE PLAYS

Looking down on the central London neighborhood of Blackfriars from the dome of St. Paul's Cathedral nearby, it looks like any other modern section of the city: grey-stone and red-brick buildings densely packed together, with lanes like veins running through them. In addition to the Globe, which would experience its own devastations and renewals during the last year's of Shakespeare's playwriting career, the King's Men's indoor theater in this neighborhood was most associated with Shakespeare's final plays, written and performed during the years 1609–13. It is also where he made a significant property investment, the only kind of its sort outside of his hometown of Stratford-upon-Avon, or at least the only one known today. On the ground in Blackfriars, there remain at least a few traces of the neighborhood Shakespeare would have known. Just south of the cathedral, Carter Lane runs east to west, and a little plaque at the side of one modern building's entrance announces this as the spot where Shakespeare's townsman, Richard Quiney, wrote a letter

In this section of Claes Janz Visscher's 1616 engraving of London, entitled *Londinium Florentissima Britanniae Urbs*, the Globe Theatre is identified at the bottom, south of the river and east of what is labeled "The Bear Gardne," the arena for bear-baiting.

to our author, the single existing one addressed to him. The place then was the Bell Inn, the year 1598. Now it is a Benihana's restaurant. Around the corner, the Cockpit Pub proudly marks the spot of Shakespeare's purchased property, mentioned above, there at the edge of Ireland Yard. It is fitting, then, that one of the stores nearby features a quotation from the ancient philosopher Heraclitus: "All is flux, nothing stays still."

Down this alley, Playhouse Yard represents a verbal remnant of the King's Men's Blackfriars Theatre. Two gardens in this area give information on the huge medieval Dominican Priory that once stood here, in the remains of which Shakespeare's playing company established its new theater. Another plaque stands a little to the west, at the edge of Blackfriars Lane, and commemorates the site of the priory, founded in 1238. There

This section of Visscher's engraving shows London Bridge.

remain, too, a few signs of the closed-off exclusivity associated with the neighborhood—Cobb's Court and Carter Court, and the courtyard before the apothecaries' hall. These more private spaces help a modern visitor to understand the noblemen and gentlemen property owners' resistance to the theater company carrying out its work here. Its theater would, they were sure, be a social blight upon a respectable neighborhood, a "very great annoyance and trouble," as they spoke of in a residential petition to the Privy Council. They wished to keep out the actors and the "vagrant and lewd persons" drawn to their plays.

During these last years of his London theater career, Shakespeare would have been traveling often between this neighborhood on the north bank of the Thames and the Globe on Bankside to the south, hailing a ferryman from either Puddle Dock, where now a large, modern conference center sits, adjacent to the major rail line at Blackfriars Station, or from the wharf near St. Benet's. The river would have been "his primary means of transport" during these years, as Peter Ackroyd reminds us, and "one of the highways of his invention." Shakespeare likely stayed very busy, making sure that his new plays were performed suitably in both of these quite different theater environments. However, Shakespeare's critics and biographers still disagree on how much time he spent where during these final years. Nicholas Rowe, in his early biography, wrote that Shakespeare returned to Stratford during his last years, and enjoyed the "Ease, Retirement, and Conversation of his Friends." He reported that Shakespeare had a large home there (New Place, he means). Emphasizing again this writer's good social standing, and among the right sort of people, Rowe described again how Shakespeare enjoyed the "Friendship of the Gentlemen of Stratford." Shakespeare appears to have had a strong circle of friends in London, too, and to have been generally esteemed in his profession. Around this time, the minor play-wright William Barksted spoke of Shakespeare as "so deere lov'd a neighbor."

Traditionally, this relocation from London back to Stratford has been dated around 1613, thereby consisting of the last three years of Shakespeare's life. However, some place the full-time return to Stratford earlier, perhaps around 1611, when the author, it seems, ceased to write plays entirely by himself, turning instead to collaboration with John Fletcher, a younger writer for the King's Men. The last two plays we associate with Shakespeare were of this co-written sort, along with a third one now lost. Recently Jonathan Bate and a few other critics have argued for pushing this transition even farther ahead: Bate points to the plague years affecting London in 1607–10 (why wouldn't Shakespeare flee the infected city, Bate argues, since he so easily could?), and to his new interest around this time of the more country-themed genre of pastoral romance. While it is true that this genre was generally growing in popularity during this period, the sheep-shearing scene in *The Winter's Tale* and the wild setting of Wales in *Cymbeline* do seem distinctively rural, following upon the urban classicism of the final tragedies or the exotic, sea-based locales of *Pericles*. Bate declares that these two plays in particular, the next two to be discussed, have the "most distinctive air of having been written back home in Stratford." He points to the precisely described image of the cowslip in *Cymbeline*, or the kind of marigold in *The Winter's Tale* that is specifically from a cottage garden. Thus he can easily imagine Shakespeare having more time to tend flowers and vines at New Place's Great Garden, and that attention drifting into his in-progress plays. (New Place itself is long gone, and only its foundation remains to archeologists, but the Great Garden behind it remains one of the glories of Stratford today.)

Strictly speaking, this arrangement may have started anytime after 1604, when we last have some record of Shakespeare's London residence, although the demands upon the King's Men for court performances likely kept him in the city on a regular basis. Conversely, there is no reason why Shakespeare did not continue to make regular trips to and stays in London during even his final years. We simply do not know. Whether in London or Stratford, though, wherever Shakespeare was hard at work on his last series of plays, in 1609 a pair of mysteries surrounding the printings of his books arose very close by the Blackfriars neighborhood, just to the northeast, on the other side of St. Paul's Cathedral, among the booksellers' stalls in Paternoster Row.

TROILUS AND CRESSIDA AND THE SONNETS: TWO PRINT MYSTERIES

Traditionally, Shakespeare's *Troilus and Cressida* has been grouped with the plays treated earlier as the "problem comedies," and it is dated roughly to the time of *Hamlet*—that is, 1600 or 1601. An item in the Stationers' Register suggests someone attempted to print Shakespeare's play about unfaithful love amid the Trojans and Greeks in 1603, but it appears the King's Men blocked publication, thereby protecting their dramatic property. In 1609, a quarto edition did in fact appear, "As it was acted by the Kings Majesties servants at the Globe." Shortly afterward, a new title page deleted any mention of the play's performance, speaking only of the "famous historie" of Troilus and Cressida and "Excellently expressing the beginning of their loves, with the conceited wooing of Pandarus." This second issuing also featured an anonymous prefatory letter, titled "A never writer, to an ever reader. Newes," in which it claims, on the contrary, that *Troilus and Cressida* was a "new play, never staled with the Stage, never clapper-clawed with the palms of the vulgar, and yet passing full of the palm comical." The letter writer then expressly praises Shakespeare's comedies, "so framed to the life, that they serve for the most common commentaries, of all the actions of our lives." They contain such dexterity and wit that even those who do not typically enjoy plays do enjoy Shakespeare's comedies. Increasing his rhetoric, the author suggests the plays were born "in that sea that brought forth Venus." He seems to warn his potential buyers to buy now while this book is available, because when Shakespeare is gone "and his Comedies out of sale, you will scramble for them." He repeats his earlier claim that this is a more elite play, "not being sullied, with the smokey breath of the multitude." Perhaps *Troilus*, for whatever reason, had not been performed previously, or perhaps the author means, rather opportunistically, that it is a newly *printed* play, and has not yet been read by common readers.

The publication of *Shakespeares Sonnets* in the same year of 1609 not only signals a second print mystery, but this little volume of 154 sonnets and a longer poem, "A Lover's Complaint," also represents one of the most enigmatic books ever associated with Shakespeare. Thomas Thorpe was the publisher, one with a record of bringing out unauthorized texts. No preface by Shakespeare appears with the sonnets, which marks one key difference from his earlier poems *Venus and Adonis* and *The Rape of Lucrece*. Instead, Thorpe himself, as "T. T.," includes a mystifying dedication that has stumped and obsessed scholars for centuries: "To the only begetter of these ensuing sonnets Mr. W. H. all happiness and that eternity promised by our ever-living poet wisheth the well-wishing adventurer in setting forth. T. T." Who is this "begetter"? The person who inspired these sonnets? Or perhaps an unknown fellow who obtained Shakespeare's manuscript for Thorpe? Or Shakespeare himself, who as their creator could be considered their true "begetter"? Does "Mr. W. H." simply represent a typo, one with extremely poor timing and unfortunate placement, and should it instead indicate Shakespeare as a "Mr. W. S." or "Mr. W.

Title page of the 1609 edition of the *Sonnets*.

Sh."? Oscar Wilde argued coyly that the initials stood for Willie Hughes, a young Elizabethan actor, and someone has even suggested that "W. H." stands for "William Himself"!

If we read "begetter" in the first way, then we are faced with two main candidates for the dedicatee, and possibly the subject of at least some of the sonnets to the "man right fair." The first is Henry Wriothesley, the Earl of Southampton, to whom Shakespeare dedicated his earlier two narrative poems and with whom he seems to have enjoyed a patron-poet relationship, if not something more. The second is William Herbert, Earl of Pembroke, a younger nobleman (who thus becomes a problematic young man if Shakespeare's early sonnets date from the early 1590s), and associated with a patron of Shakespeare's theater company. (The First Folio, in 1623, would be dedicated to him and his brother.) Skeptics, however, point out that both earls would likely object strenuously to being addressed as a mere "Mr.," or "Master," a title used with gentlemen but not noblemen. Are there other possibilities? A poem published in 1594, *Willobie his Avisa*, features the innkeeper's wife, Avisa, who rejects many suitors, including another possible W. H., "Henry Willobego." (As with Southampton, his initials would thus be cleverly reversed, to conceal further his identity.) Willobego admits his heartbreak to his "familiar friend W. S." Is this our poet? Who knows? There is even ambiguity in the dedication's grammar: is it "W. H." or "T. T." who is doing the wishing?

These are only the first of a host of questions regarding *Shakespeares Sonnets*. Whoever is meant in the dedication, why does Shakespeare not identify himself more officially with the book? The sonnets within are some of the most accomplished and enduring poems in English literature, after all. If he wished to publish his collection of sonnets, and to some degree oversaw or at least permitted its publication in 1609, it is worth asking, why did he do so only then? It would have been a much more timely and commercially promising book had he published it in 1598, when Francis Meres first spoke of Shakespeare's "sugared sonnets" circulating among his friends, or after five of his sonnets were included in the anthology *The Passionate Pilgrim* in 1599. Shakespeare's fellow writer Thomas Heywood acknowledged, in an epistle attached to his *Apology for Actors* (1612), that two poems included in a reprint of that anthology, and attributed to Shakespeare, were his. He was irritated because he feared readers would think Heywood stole the poems from Shakespeare, whom he clearly admires, and Heywood adds that Shakespeare was "much offended" that the opportunistic pub-

lisher of the anthology had "presumed to make so bold with his name." More intriguingly, Heywood adds that Shakespeare, "to do himself right, hath since published them [his own poems] in his own name." This last comment could refer to the *Shakespeares Sonnets* volume of 1609, and seems to suggest that Shakespeare himself desired to have them published.

Some scholars believe he may have permitted their publication but then regretted doing so because of the signs of carelessness and haste found in the Thorpe volume. As sonnet 103 says, he "sold cheap what is most dear," and this could also indicate regret at having them printed at all, as in the cheapening of poems that were originally private, even intimate. The modern poet W. H. Auden said that only the sonnets, among all of Shakespeare's writings, were "directly personal." This general feeling that Shakespeare reveals more of himself in these short poems, even if they remain highly artful, sophisticated lyric writings, has led many to argue that Shakespeare could not have authorized their publication. By this logic, the poems are simply too revealing, too embarrassing, and that fact becomes heightened when we remember that the first 126 sonnets seem to be addressed to a young man, and the second sequence dramatize a painful, shameful, adulterous relationship with a "dark lady." For example, sonnet 138 announces at the outset the speaker's awareness of the double falsehood shared by his partner: "When my love swears that she is made of truth / I do believe her though I know she lies." These are not aggrandizing, idealizing poems, and the "dark lady" sequence possesses a strain of repulsion and self-loathing throughout. Even in the earlier, longer sequence to the young man, most readers have trouble accepting that these poems merely record a pure, decorous friendship between two extremely close but platonic male friends. The Scottish poet Don Patterson has recently rejected such claims by arguing that the sonnets repeatedly reveal a different kind of desire: "This is a crazy, all-consuming, feverish, and sweaty love; love, in all its uncut, full-strength intensity." It is an adolescent love, Patterson adds, that happens to be expressed "by a hyper-literate thirty-something."

At least three other aspects relate to the question of *Shakespeares Sonnets* being an authorized or pirated publication. If it were authorized, then it is far more likely that the ordering of the sonnet sequence is as Shakespeare intended. Certainly the major groupings have been long established, such as the opening seventeen "procreation" sonnets, those involving a rival poet, or the "dark lady" sequence that follows those to the young man. Likewise, smaller groups of poems have noticeable sequential connections, as with 40–42, 50–51, 64–65, or 67–68. Bolder claims for an authorial ordering of sonnets in the 1609 volume have usually been held in check, although recently at least two scholars have more confidently stated that the sequence appears in Thorpe's 1609 volume as Shakespeare intended. Connected with ordering is the question of dating the sonnets, a matter itself connected with theories about their true dedicatee. If the Earl of Southampton is preferred, then the poems are usually thought to be written early in Shakespeare's career, primarily in the 1590s. If the younger William Herbert is the preferred recipient, then the poems become later work of the early 1600s. Evidence will be found for both early and late arguments in certain sonnets such as 107, where "The mortal moon hath her eclipse endured" may refer to the Spanish Armada (1588), Elizabeth I's illness or a lunar eclipse (1595), or the queen's death (1603). More recently, a coalescing argument has begun to receive notice. It claims that readings for early or late sonnets, or one or the other nobleman, are *both* right. That is, we have in the *Sonnets* a collection that appears to be a single, integral sequence, but in fact is a collection of diverse poems writ-ten over decades for diverse occasions and for diverse subjects. Thus one poem may be written as early as Shakespeare's courtship of Anne Hathaway, and another may have been addressed to the "lovely boy" William Herbert just shortly before the sonnets were published. The third related and very obvious question involves fact and fiction in the context of literary art. No one would easily mistake the historical Shakespeare for his dramatic creations such as Romeo or Iago or King Henry V, and yet with the *Sonnets* many have felt inclined—have not been able to resist, really—making a sure association between the seemingly unguarded voice in the sonnets and Shakespeare's own. "With this key," wrote William Wordsworth about the sonnets, "Shakespeare unlocked his heart." The poems do often sound remarkably revealing, vividly spoken, as if we were overhearing a lover's quarrel not meant for anyone else. For the German Romantic critic August Wilhelm von Schlegel, the sonnets contained "remarkable confessions" of Shakespeare's "youthful errors." To be sure, though, sometimes scholarly prudence and close reading and plain common sense demand restraint. We must temper an understandable wish to claim discovery of desired biographical facts about Shakespeare after seizing upon supposed clues or codes in his lyric poems. For example, it has been claimed by more than a few readers that Shakespeare was lame, based on the opening lines of sonnet 37:

> As a decrepit father takes delight
> To see his active child do deeds of youth,
> So I, made lame by fortune's dearest spite,
> Take all my comfort of thy worth and
>   mirth.

First of all, the opening two lines consist of a simile, or comparison: the "I" of the poem, which may or may not be Shakespeare, and in one critical respect certainly is not, being a textual representation, takes comfort in the addressee *just as* that decrepit father is comforted by his active, healthy child. Furthermore, there is no actual proof that Shakespeare is speaking autobiographically as that "I" here; sonnets are not memoir, just as memoir is not a deposition given under oath. And even that oath given may not be the truth outright. Shakespeare may have, at one point, felt himself figuratively wounded or made lame by a worsening of his fortunes, but this sonnet does not—cannot and does not wish to—verify that fact. Likewise, some readers have inferred from sonnet 110's opening confession, "Alas, 'tis true, I have gone here and there / And made myself a motley to the view," evidence that Shakespeare was eventually ashamed of his theater life onstage, touring and putting himself garishly in the public eye. Again, there is no way, beyond the poem, to confirm this inference, just as characters such as Jacques' or Macbeth's negative comments about the world being a stage or how we are all strutting players do not necessarily inform us of Shakespeare's personal views on his chosen profession, at which he was very successful.

Shakespeare, if we haven't figured this out by now, is incredibly crafty. John Hollander has pointed out that Shakespeare's sequence differs from other Elizabethan sequences by foregoing ostentatious, often cleverly punning pseudonyms. To illustrate, consider Philip Sidney's sequence *Astrophil and Stella*, where his poetic persona is Astrophil and his beloved Stella, or, etymologically, "Star-lover" and "Star." Renaissance humanists found such learned wordplay very entertaining. Shakespeare, on the other hand, evacuates these fictional character markers from his sequence, giving the impression, at least, that he wishes to keep identities concealed because the characters and incidents are, in fact, real. Hollander rightfully points out that this may be simply one more level of artful fiction-making. There may be no Dark Lady, no Rival Poet, although

there has never been, nor will there likely ever be, a shortage of candidates, or of highly convinced readers to suggest them. One book, *The Rose of Shakespeare's Sonnets*, finds a new candidate for "W. H." in the "homoerotic court of King James," while a second recent study treats the entire sonnet sequence in terms of Christian mystical allegory. As a counter to that, it should also be added that, in fact, Shakespeare's actual name is unusual, and possibly unique, in being so clearly associated with his sonnet sequence. Its title, remember, is *Shakespeares Sonnets*. Similarly, some of the later poems, and some of the bawdiest sonnets in the collection, to boot, clearly seem to pun on their author's first name, as in sonnet 136: "Make but my name thy love, and love that still, / And then thou lov'st me for my name is Will." These moments, too, may be artful provocations rather than embarrassing slip-ups or over-revealing of information. Complementing Hollander, Stephen Greenblatt sees these authorial clues as well as "tantalizing invitations to biographical speculation[.]"

Katherine Duncan-Jones, in *Ungentle Shakespeare: Scenes from His Life*, argues that shared features make the close publication dates of these two books seem timely indeed. *Troilus and Cressida* and the later "dark lady" sonnets, in particular, feature a harsher tone, and seem frequently preoccupied with imagery of venereal disease and plague. Pandarus's aggressive epilogue to the audience—"Till then I'll sweat and seek about for eases, / And at that time bequeath you my diseases"—is in keeping with the dark world of *Troilus*, including Thersites's railing, Hector's grim realism, and Achilles's and Ulysses's want of heroism, but when we consider that 1609 was a severe plague year in London, Pandarus's curse of disease toward the audience is even more radically hostile. Similarly, in one of the final sonnets, we read of a "sad distempered guest" who desires relief from love's burning pains in a "seething bath." Duncan-Jones believes the image refers to treatments in sweating tubs sought out by men with syphilis, and even surmises that Shakespeare, "sick withal" as the poem puts it, may have contracted a venereal disease at this point in his life. Furthermore, she posits that the commercial failure of the *Sonnets* (unlike his earlier poems, these were neither reprinted nor widely quoted or imitated) was a "severe disappointment" to Shakespeare. On the other hand, this lack of traction may not have been terribly surprising since their publication in 1609 occurred nearly a decade after the sonnet-sequence craze that characterized 1590s Elizabethan literary culture. Indeed, Shakespeare may have instead been relieved by their comparative failure if he found their appearance in print embarrassing and had not authorized their publication. As with many aspects of the *Sonnets*, the details will forever remain a mystery. That said, they have a devoted following even today: the singer-songwriter Rufus Wainwright visited Yale's Elizabethan Club recently in order to see a first edition of *Shakespeares Sonnets*, resting there in the club vault four hundred years later. And with more certainty, we can agree with Duncan-Jones that both *Troilus* and the *Sonnets* are "deeply rooted in an awareness of death, and of the desperate struggle to make one's voice heard before the disease destroys[.]" Shakespeare was forty-five years old. Half of his writings to date had been published.

DEFINING THE LATE ROMANCES: CYMBELINE AND THE WINTER'S TALE

The publication of *Troilus and Cressida* and *Shakespeares Sonnets* in 1609 no doubt gave, for readers at least, a fresh gloss on some older works by Shakespeare. For the author himself, however, he was almost certainly far more preoccupied with new plays, in particular *Cymbeline* and

The Winter's Tale, both written and performed between 1609 and 1611. Along with the transitional *Pericles*, these plays marked a further departure from the late tragedies and recent plays with classical sources and settings. It was a time, late in his career, of great artistic experimentation for Shakespeare. There exists in these late plays a pioneering spirit, an improvisational confidence, a conscious renovation of long-proven methods of story telling, poetry writing, scene construction, and spectacular staging. So different are these plays that they now earn their own, final designation of genre—the romances. The word choice speaks nicely to the fairy-tale motifs in these plays; their settings in remote places, sometimes spanning many years; their increased attention to emblem, symbol, and myth; and their willingness to rely on highly improbable storylines and plot developments. More profoundly, the genre of romance also announces a fresh, looser, more expansive spirit in Shakespeare's later works, as if he had endured the fateful destructions of family and individual in his tragedies and now appeared again in a more humane light. The critic Edward Dowden coined the term "romances" in 1875: "The dramas have a grave beauty, a sweet serenity, which seem to render the name 'comedies' inappropriate." The late romances feature magical worlds of losses and suffering, to be sure, but also one where these trials lead to reunion and reconciliation. Lost children are recovered, and an emotional forgiveness is offered for past wrongs. Shakespeare presents the harms and hostilities more unflinchingly in these late plays, which explains why they are often identified as "tragicomedies"—betrayals, deaths, and other tragic aspects deeply imprint the dramatic world, but they do not preside over the play's end; a more settled, if not always expressly happy, ending always prevails. Sometimes these endings, with their sense of a grand or even cosmic or miraculous conclusion, are brought about by the awe-inspiring but ultimately benign appearance of a divinity, or someone thought dead. The romances often involve transcendence, and not just closure.

This final, epiphanic element often illustrates these plays' increasing commitment to and capacity for stage spectacle, including music, dance, and dream visions—for example, the appearance of Jove in *Cymbeline*, the apparent statue that comes to life in *The Winter's Tale*, the shipwreck and masque in *The Tempest*. In turning to tragicomedy, Shakespeare was keeping up with theatergoers' shifting tastes. In fact, both *Cymbeline* and *The Winter's Tale* either influenced or were influenced by Francis Beaumont's and John Fletcher's highly successful *Philaster*; the composition dates make it too close to tell. More generally influential were the prestige and popularity of court masques, which led to increased uses of stage machinery and music in Shakespeare's late plays. The timing was felicitous because Shakespeare could now pursue these more sophisticated effects within the masque-friendly indoor playing space of Blackfriars Theatre. Act divisions become more apparent since candles had to be replaced during breaks in performance, and the music prominent in the climactic scene of *The Winter's Tale* is a likely trace of an indoor staging convention. The masques were opulent in their set designs and costumes, and were meant to ravish onlookers with a visual feast. Ben Jonson's *Masque of Queens*, which he produced in collaboration with court architect Inigo Jones, cost a truly shocking £3000. King James, who would have been the single most important audience member at a court masque, and around whose viewing perspective the scenery was built and performance choreographed, sometimes enjoyed participating in these productions, as did other members of the royal family.

Shakespeare's company, the King's Men, naturally kept their close connections with the court—the troupe performed there thirteen times over the Christmas holiday in 1609—and this affiliation, too, would have influenced these late plays. Gary Schmidgall speaks of a "courtly aesthetic" in Shakespeare's late writing, and he sees the very late play *The Tempest* as making this elite aesthetic more public, even as it critiques that taste. The play's famous "revels" speech, for instance, represents the "power and vanity" of the courtly vision of art. A key bridging figure here is Shakespeare's fellow writer Ben Jonson, who was King James's most successful masque writer, and who also moved effortlessly from his previous work with the children's company at Blackfriars to plays written for the King's Men in the same space, including *The Alchemist* and *Epicoene*.

Cymbeline first appeared in print in the 1623 First Folio, where it was mistakenly listed among the "Tragedies." Indeed, it is a play that regularly puts demands on audiences and resists critics' interpretations. Valerie Wayne intends no tongue-in-cheek hot air when she describes this play as a "tragical-comical-historical-pastoral play." Shakespeare, with an experienced playwright's bravado, freely mixes genres and multiplies storylines in *Cymbeline*, just as he mixes locales and eras, which include ancient Britain and classical, as well as Renaissance, Rome. This mixture reflects his different sources: Holinshed's *Chronicles* (yet again), where he found a history of the reign of King Cunobelinus, and, for the domestic intrigues, namely the testing of a wife's fidelity and a husband's mistaken belief that she has been unfaithful, Boccaccio's *Decameron*. The play synthesizes even at its broadest levels, such as with belief systems: the king's reign coincides with the birth of Christ, and yet the pagan god Jove, astride an eagle, makes a dramatic entry toward the end.

The play begins with newlyweds in crisis: Posthumus Leonatus has married King Cymbeline's daughter, the virtuous Imogen (or "Innogen" in the sources, and in some modern editions), angering her father and the queen, her evil stepmother. The queen had wished Imogen to marry her son Cloten, "Too bad for bad report." Posthumus is soon banished and, exchanging vows of loyalty with his bride, he flees to Rome, where he quickly encounters the urbane, cunning Iachimo. The Italian host questions the chastity of British women, and assures Posthumus that he can seduce Imogen. Once in Britain, she gently turns away Iachimo, but he resourcefully convinces her to keep a large trunk of his. It is delivered to her chamber, and in one of the most captivating bedroom scenes in all of Shakespeare, once Imogen is asleep, Iachimo rises stealthily from the trunk, taking a bracelet from her arm and noting on "her left breast / A mole, cinque-spotted." Posthumus, who impulsively accepted Iachimo's challenge in the first place, is all too easily convinced by Iachimo's supposed evidence of the infidelity of Imogen, whom he had thought "as chaste as unsunned snow." Imogen now comes under siege: the queen attempts to poison her and the loyal servant Pisanio, but the doctor gives her only sleeping potion, and in a rage, Posthumus sends a letter to Pisanio demanding that he kill his harlot wife. Instead, Pisanio reveals the note to Imogen, who is devastated and wishes to die. She does abandon her home and identity, dressing as a young man, Fidelio ("the faithful one"), and fleeing to the woods of Wales. The rotten son Cloten pursues her, but makes the mistake of challenging two young brothers in the forest, Guiderius and Arviragus. They kill Cloten, but are quick to befriend and adopt the disguised Imogen. In fact, they *are* her brothers! No one knows yet that they were abducted as babes from Cymbeline's court, and so a joyous royal family reunion is in store at play's end. In the meantime, however, she has drunk the sleeping potion, and the brothers believe she has died. They mourn her with one of Shakespeare's most enchanting songs:

> Fear no more the heat' o' th' sun
> > Nor furious winter's rages;
> Thou thy worldly task hast done,
> > Home art gone, and ta'en thy wages.
> Golden lads and girls all must,
> > As chimney-sweepers, come to dust.

Meanwhile, back at court, Cymbeline has refused to pay tribute to Rome, which advances an invading army to Britain. The Roman general Lucius soon takes custody of Imogen, but only after, in a scene that typifies the "shock treatment"

Painting of Posthumus and Imogen from 1865 (*John Faed*)

of certain moments in the romances, she has awakened from her sleep to find Cloten's headless body dressed in Posthumus's clothes. The phrase above is M. C. Bradbrook's, who goes on to describe the violence and incongruity of this scene, in which Imogen embraces Cloten's corpse thinking it is Posthumus's, as a Jacobean version of the Theater of the Absurd. As if in counterpoint, Posthumus has discovered Iachimo's treacherous fraud, and in despair offers himself to the Romans and is soon captured by the British. In prison he receives an ancestral vision accompanied by a "solemn music," after which Jupiter appears, regally assuring that all will turn out well for the hero: "Be not with mortal accidents oppresst. / . . . / to make my gift, / The more delayed, delighted. Be content." Nearly executed, Posthumus instead is spared and delivered to Cymbeline's court. The king makes peace with Rome, husband and wife are reunited, and multiple other plot surprises are revealed. It is clear by now how much the action of *Cymbeline* can strain a modern audience's expectation of at least a modicum of realism, but Shakespeare has also created a world that helps viewers to suspend their disbelief. The result can be quite affecting. The Romantic critic William Hazlitt thought it one of the most delightful of Shakespeare's plays. Its pathos, he argued, is "of the most pleasing and amiable kind," and there exists between Posthumus and Imogen "the very religion of love." The charm and enchantment of *Cymbeline* can take over, as audiences come to adore one of Shakespeare's great heroines, whom actresses such as Peggy Ashcroft and Vanessa Redgrave have brought to life in modern times.

Written around the same time as *Cymbeline*, or just slightly later, *The Winter's Tale* represents Shakespeare's reshaping of a 1588 prose tragedy, *Pandosto*, written by Robert Greene, ironically. He was the jealous, angry writer who first attacked the young playwright as an "upstart crow," that is, an actor who was assuming for himself the feathers of educated playwrights. Shakespeare's changing of Greene's characters and key plot details seems to tease us about which kind of play we are about to experience. During Shakespeare's time, a "winter's tale" usually referred to a fantastical story, and so this play is, but there is also a darker reference in the title. Mamillius, the young son of the Sicilian king Leontes and queen Hermione, early in the play promises his mother a story, saying, "A sad tale's best for winter." Just so, this will be in part a very sad tale. She invites him to "fright me with your sprites," and indeed, spirits of jealousy, paranoia, and rage are already encircling the mind of her husband. The play opens with Leontes pleading with his childhood friend Polixenes, king of Bohemia, to remain longer in Sicily, though he has already been in residence nine months. The pregnant Hermione pleads as well, and her very success makes her husband suspect an affair between his wife and old friend. Leontes's jealousy is disturbing for being so sudden, and leading to such condemnation and heartache despite being unproven. The reasons for Leontes's reaction, and its extremeness, remain ultimately mysterious, and thus the character has regularly beckoned to renowned actors such as Antony Sher to plumb his dark depths. (The production featuring Sher has recently become available on DVD.)

Leontes takes his son away from Hermione, and says she will only be able to "sport herself / With that she's big with." That is, she thinks their unborn child is Polixenes's and hers. This severance, or severances, is more painful because of the beautiful poetry that has shown so winningly what "twinned lambs" the kings were as boys. Thus Leontes's animosity is shocking. Yet he is convinced that he is now facing the full, deceitful, unfaithful truth of his most important relationships. He has, he says in one of the play's most memorable images, "drunk and seen the spider" in the glass's bottom. The story only gets worse: Hermione is put on trial, humiliated, and declared guilty. News arrives from the oracle at Delphi that Hermione is chaste, but Leontes perversely rejects this authority. We soon hear word that the son, Mamillius, is dead, and the king orders his servant Antigonus to take Leontes's and Hermione's newborn child and abandon it to the elements. As one Shakespearean has nicely put it, "The play seems trapped in tragedy," yet is in the nature of these late romances to resist the fated outcome and present inspired if improbable resolutions.

Antigonus leaves the child in Bohemia. Called Perdita ("the lost one"), she is fortunately found and cared for by an Old Shepherd. He, too, thinks her circumstances are a sign of an illicit conception ("some behind-door-work," he says), but unlike Leontes, he does not hesitate to adopt the child despite this inference. The shepherd has met, he says, "with things new-born," and this deliverance of the child signals the play's turning fortunes and shifting action. The scene now turns to the pastoral world of Bohemia, and the play becomes more fantastical overall. For example, Antigonus flees the stage and is killed, illustrating one of the most colorful stage directions in all of Shakespeare's plays: "Exit pursued by bear." The show may just have included one of the live bears, such as Titan or Harry Hunks, from one of the bear-baiting rings just around the corner from the Globe. A shipwreck off the supposed sea coast of land-locked Bohemia famously earned Ben Jonson's dismissal, but truly, Shakespeare seems blissfully unconcerned about such niceties or precisions of fact. He certainly isn't worried about the influential writer Philip Sidney having mocked early stage romances for moving from setting to setting and covering vast stretches of time. Here, in *The Winter's Tale*, Shakespeare brings onstage at the beginning of act four the personified figure of Time, equipped with wings and an hourglass,

to explain and perhaps justify his own narrative's abrupt jumping ahead: "Impute it not a crime / To me or my swift passage that I slide / O'er sixteen years." No, Shakespeare seems too busy having fun. In this later time of the play, the disguised swain Florizel (Polixines's son, in fact) woos the now-grown Perdita.

Different kinds of stage spectacle mark the second half of *The Winter's Tale*. A sheep-shearing festival in Bohemia features songs and dances that call to mind court masques, but do so within an explicitly rustic setting. Yet the play's greatest, most daring display of art-making is reserved for the finale, which returns us to Leontes's court. Florizel, having to evade his own angry father, elopes with Perdita, and the kind counselor Camillo helps the couple make their way to Sicily. We will end where we began. We only hear in a speech of Leontes's reunion with his long-lost, once-banished daughter Perdita, but we do see him still grieving with "saint-like sorrow" for his wife, Hermione, whom he heard died shortly after her trial. Leontes now understands his error, but he must continue to live with the destruction wrought by his jealousy. Hermione's servant, Paulina, has promised a statue of Hermione as a small consolation. Shakespeare has set up his story to conclude with an incredible moment of theater. Revealed, the statue's resemblance to Hermione makes Leontes wide-eyed. It is warm, he remarks. "Be stone no more," Paulina suddenly calls out. "Strike all that look upon with marvel." Paulina, and Shakespeare, know that this climax must overcome our incredulity, but unswervingly they proceed: Hermione is in fact alive, no statue at all, and though undeserving, Leontes once again gets to see daughter and wife.

This magical ending symbolizes, in the words of Northrop Frye, "nature's power of renewal." It

(continues on page 222)

WAS SHAKESPEARE SOMEBODY ELSE?

"What's in a name?" Juliet asks from her balcony, thinking herself alone, in *Romeo and Juliet*. Considering the tragedy that she, Romeo, and their rival Montague and Capulet families soon face, there hardly could have been a more important question. This often seems to be the case, too, with readers and scholars who have intensely asked this question with respect to Shakespeare, and have fiercely debated possible answers. However hard to believe, they have done so for centuries. Equally hard to believe, they apparently did not do so immediately after Shakespeare's death in 1616, and not for a long time thereafter: the Shakespearean sub-industry known as "The Authorship Question" did not fully begin till the nineteenth century. They might alter the question slightly: "What's with Shakespeare's name?" That is, they and many of us wish to know, was the historical William Shakespeare from Stratford-upon-Avon who we think he was? Public records and other evidence suggest that such a person did indeed exist, but was he in fact the same person who wrote the thirty-eight plays, several of them among the supreme glories of world literature, that we now attribute to him? To put the question more precisely, how could this simply educated, fairly mysterious man from Stratford, who led a life that one critic has called "too little and too limited," be capable of the literary feats to be found in Shakespeare's plays?

First of all, the rise in the late eighteenth century of intense Shakespeare adulation, often known as Bardolatry and situated in the town of Stratford and in the person of the actor David Garrick, may have caused a critically minded pushback against these author-centered praises. If this is so, these extremely positive evaluations of Shakespeare the man, author, and English "native genius" may have ironically given rise to the growth of alternative-author scenarios. Largely due to the Internet, and to raised expectations among readers today for literary self-revelation, or autobiography in creative writing, these theories about someone other than William Shakespeare of Stratford writing "Shakespeare" have become more prevalent and culturally acceptable than ever before. Recent decades have seen featured treatments of the authorship controversy not only in academic journals, but also in national magazines such as *Life* and *The Atlantic Monthly*. In fact, as James Shapiro argues in his fine study *Contested Will: Who Wrote Shakespeare?*, academic scholars have perhaps been too quick to ignore with disdain the rival claims of their opponents (often passionate amateurs) for Shakespeare's plays' authorship. In considering the question or the very notion of literary fraud to be beneath them, or long ago settled, they concede the argumentative field to the naysayers, or "Anti-Stratfordians," so called because this skeptical group believes the William Shakespeare from Stratford was duped and had his name stolen. Or else he participated in a massive literary deceit for the advantage of his own reputation. As the American novelist Henry James once said, " I am . . . haunted by the conviction that the divine William is the biggest and most successful fraud ever practiced on a patient world."

For the record, Shapiro's study is the most updated, thorough, healthily revealing treatment of the authorship crisis in quite some time. He does not wish to add one more theory to the biographical assembly line, but instead is fascinated by the rise of this enduring question as to Shakespeare's true identity. While admitting that his identity as an academic will, for some, discount his study from the outset, he also says he understands why some of the theories across the centuries have been compelling, and he most of all wishes to explore not what these defenders of these theories have argued, but why they began to do so. Ultimately, understanding this phenomenon helps us to better appreciate how we read now, and what we demand from an author of uniquely accomplished writing such as Shakespeare's.

The central reasons for skepticism about Shakespeare's identity include a shortage of life documents (a critical time of his development as a young man is known as the "Lost Years"), along with a belief that his writing and intellectual abilities were at odds with his education and class status. Could these plays, with their sophisticated artistry, have been composed by a glover's son, a working-class provincial actor from Stratford? Many have detected an aristocratic attitude in Shakespeare's plays, but it should be said that this tone is often inferred when reading any text that is four hundred years old. It has also been argued that Shakespeare's plays were the work of a well-traveled Renaissance man, who had some knowledge of various trades, discipline, and ways of life—sailing, the law, court life, and so on. The celebrated American novelist John Updike has stood up for Shakespeare's

Portrait of Francis Bacon from the eighteenth century, probably copying an older portrait done in Bacon's lifetime *(John Vanderbank)*

ability as a playwright to create characters different from, and socially better than, himself: "I have never had any problem with the idea that a child of the middling provincial gentry . . . might enter the theatrical profession and spin a literary universe out of his dramatic flair, opportune learning, and country-bred street-smarts."

Other points inviting skepticism include the various spellings of Shakespeare's name (though this reflects varying Elizabethan spellings more than it suggests near illiteracy on Shakespeare's part), a lack of contemporary references in Stratford to its famous writer and native son, and a corresponding lack of elegies following Shakespeare's death. For example, countless eulogies were written upon the deaths of Shakespeare's fellow playwrights Beaumont and Fletcher; relatively few appeared for Shakespeare, and not till they were included in the First Folio. And then there's his will: why does it not mention various books and manuscripts? (As for his plays, technically they were the property of his theater company in London.) Yet formidable support for Shakespeare's writings being his remain: why did everyone seem to go along with this supposed ruse that Shakespeare was only a stand-in playwright? Why was there no reaction against the First Folio's attribution of the plays to Shakespeare? Why did his colleagues complete tributes to their fallen fellow actor and playwright? Finally, why did Stratford soon build a monument to its citizen and homeowner?

These alternate-author theories have regularly enjoyed some surprisingly prestigious adherents, including John Greenleaf Whittier, Mark Twain, Sigmund Freud, Helen Keller, Malcolm X, and Harry A. Blackmun, the last a Supreme Court Justice and thus equipped (one supposes) with some level of judiciousness. Actors, too, have thought Shakespeare other than what he seems, including Sir Jacob Jacobi, who is convinced "our playwright wasn't that fellow." He also insinuates that Shakespeare's identity as author of the plays may be a case of opportunism for town leaders

(continues)

(continued)

in Stratford. More recently, Mark Rylance, a star Shakespearean actor, the modern Globe Theatre's first artistic director, and winner of two Tony awards, has expressed similar skepticism.

However much these prominent doubters may suspect that "Shakespeare" was not indeed the man from Stratford we think of, they rarely are the ones who devise intricate counter-possibilities. Early theorists felt that Shakespeare was in fact the great Renaissance law man and intellectual Francis Bacon, a view made popular by the American eccentric Delia Bacon in the nineteenth century, and carried on since then by Edwin Durning-Lawrence's *Bacon is Shake-Speare* and others. The other main claimant is Edward de Vere, the earl of Oxford, who has the noble background and worldly experience that many demand in their more believable version of Shakespeare. Unfortunately, he died in 1604, so supporters must do some creative work with the dating of Shakespeare's life events and plays. The schoolmaster Thomas Looney proposed this candidate in 1920, and many since then have followed, including Mark Anderson in his recent *Shakespeare by Another Name*. Calvin Hoffman in his *The Murder of the Man Who Was "Shakespeare"* (1956) developed a theory that Shakespeare's peer Christopher Marlowe had not been killed in a tavern brawl in 1593, but instead had fled to Italy, where in secret he wrote all of Shakespeare's plays. This theory has continued in some form in Rodney Bolt's recent *History Play: The Lives and Afterlife of Christopher Marlowe*, and in the fact that a new stained-glass memorial to Marlowe in Poets' Corner, Westminster Abbey, in London, gives his death date as "?1593," a gesture toward these views that Marlowe continued writing after his purported death. Many other candidates have not been excluded from consideration for being highly improbable: Lord Derby and other noblemen, the noblewoman Mary Sidney (see Robin Williams's *Sweet Swan of Avon*), nearly any fellow author living during Shakespeare's time, and the monarchs Elizabeth I and James I themselves.

Recently cognitive studies and computerized analyses of writing style have been adapted to offer usually contested evidence of the author question, but there is no sign today of the controversy subsiding. Even as James Shapiro's *Contested Will* was receiving attention and appearing on bookstore shelves, so was the latest book in favor of de Vere—Charles Beauclerk's *Shakespeare's Lost Kingdom: The True Story of Shakespeare and Elizabeth*. The identity of Shakespeare long ago became a "detective story," as Shapiro calls it, and our interest in this story seems inexhaustible. Othello's words begin to sound hauntingly applicable to his author, when we think of these conflicting cases: "Speak of me as I am; nothing extenuate, / Nor set down aught in malice."

SEE ALSO:

Beauclerk, Charles. *Shakespeare's Lost Kingdom: The True History of Shakespeare and Elizabeth*. New York: Grove Press, 2011.

Craig, Hugh and Arthur F. Kinney, eds. *Shakespeare, Computers, and the Mystery of Authorship*. New York: Cambridge University Press, 2009.

"Looking for Shakespeare: Two Partisans Explain and Debate the Authorship Question," *The Atlantic Monthly* 268, no. 4 (1991): 43-65.

Shapiro, James. *Contested Will: Who Wrote Shakespeare?* New York: Simon & Schuster, 2010.

Updike, John. "On Literary Biography." In *More Matter*. New York: Knopf, 1999.

(continued from page 219)

is the world we want, he adds. Against his sources and his own prior writing, Shakespeare is bent on presenting a play that ends with joyous wonder. In Greene's *Pandosto*, the Hermione character does not remain alive, and so in some ways Shakespeare's departure is a reversed example of his own manipulation of his source for *King Lear*.

In that earlier version, Cordelia lives and marries Albany, rather than appears onstage lifeless in her father's arms. The conclusion of *The Winter's Tale* also rewrites *Romeo and Juliet*. There, young lovers could not reconcile their warring families, but instead are doomed by the strife. Here, Perdita and Florizel help to reestablish amity between their parents of Sicily and Bohemia. As the critic Catherine Belsey admits in *Why Shakespeare?*, despite the far-flung settings, swiftly passing years, and eyebrow-raising outcomes, "Somehow, the stories stick." Another critic, Roger Warren, reviewing recent productions of the romances, has commented that "the one thing that has emerged above all others . . . would unquestionably be the sense of central characters going on spiritual journeys, voyages of discovery and self-discovery." We can certainly see how this observation applies to *Cymbeline* and *The Winter's Tale*, which both end with a gesture of resurrection and characters, Posthumus and Leontes, who are repentant of their deeply destructive delusions held in the first half of their respective plays. Typically, the main characters, and the audiences with them, experience a sense of restoration, transcendence, and, in Posthumus's and Cymbeline's case, a divinely given reclamation of identity and a promise of peace and prosperity. However, in the hands of a daring director, this impression of happy amplitude need not always apply. For example, in Declan Donnellan's bold 1997 production, Hermione was too scarred by Leontes's jealous abandonment and too reduced by her sixteen years of isolation to participate genuinely in the reunion and reconciliation signaled in the text.

Shakespeare achieved a great deal with this pair of plays, but his decreasing writing pace—roughly a play per year—is also noticeable during this time. It should be remembered, however, that during this time the theaters were repeatedly forced to shut down for stretches of varying length due to outbreaks of plague. This may have influenced his productivity, since at times he may have had no audience for which to write. Simultaneously, Shakespeare's earlier plays, it must be remembered, remained in heavy repertory circulation. To cite one example, the Prince of Württemberg records that he saw a performance of *Othello* at the Globe in April 1610. The fascinating, dodgy astrologer Simon Foreman remains the best-known playgoer during this period. Fortunately for theater historians, he kept a diary in which he recorded his impressions of a handful of Shakespeare plays. He saw *Macbeth* at the Globe on April 20, 1611, and *The Winter's Tale* on May 15. (The King's Men later performed the latter

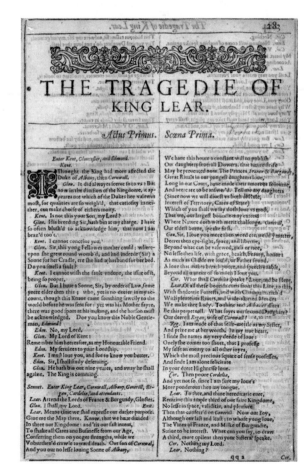

Title page of the First Folio edition of *King Lear*, published in 1623.

play at court in November.) Sometimes it is surprising to see what Foreman finds most memorable, and what he fails to mention. He makes no comment, for example, on Hermione's sudden coming to life at the end of *The Winter's Tale*, but focuses instead on the dubious peddler Autolycus. Recalling *Cymbeline*, he narrates Iachimo's appearance in Imogen's bed chamber and his taking of her bracelet while she sleeps. Peter Holland has emphasized that much of Shakespeare's time in his late career may have been spent revising and rewriting existing plays. Simply considering the very different quarto and folio versions of *Hamlet* or *King Lear* suggests the labor spent on plays after they were initially staged. [These texts, some preserved by print in quarto and folio versions, may be only two "snapshots" in an ongoing process of updating plays for new tastes or altering roles for specific actors.]

THE TEMPEST: THE CULMINATION OF SHAKESPEARE'S ART

This or that modern author has occasionally offered conjectures that William Shakespeare contributed to or even wrote large portions of the King James Bible (1611), which has recently enjoyed many 400th-anniversary commemorations. However fanciful, this theory has an understandable attractiveness: like Shakespeare's plays, the Jacobean translation of the Bible is one of the enduring monuments of the English language, and so connecting an obviously talented writer such as Shakespeare to the project helps to explain that translation's majestical prose rhythms and felicitous word choices. Rudyard Kipling in his story "Proofs of Holy Writ" (1934) imagines Shakespeare and his theater rival Ben Jonson hard at work on revising earlier English translations. "The glory of God has risen up upon me," reads Jonson from the Book of Isaiah, and Shakespeare gently chides him, "Up-pup-up!" The English novelist Anthony Burgess, too, has a story along these imagined lines,

"Will and Testament," although Burgess is best known for his fictional account of Shakespeare's amorous life, *Nothing Like the Sun*. However enjoyable it is to imagine England's great national writer polishing the English Bible toward fuller literary brightness, it is a far-fetched hypothesis. The King James Bible was produced by several committees of learned divines, and even if Shakespeare had showed interest in assisting (there is no reason to think he did), there is little chance that church authorities would have scandalized themselves and their work by having a mere playwright participate. However, we can with certainty connect Shakespeare to one major writing project of 1611: *The Tempest*, which was performed before the king in November of that year.

The Tempest is one of Shakespeare's most wildly original plays, and it rounds out the four works traditionally grouped as the late romances. The play has no source for its main narrative, involving a magic-aided confrontation between a deposed duke of Milan, Prospero, and his usurping brother, Antonio. The meeting is made possible by the tempest of the play's title, a shipwreck, and those on board washing up on an exotic island. All of this action opens the play on a highly dramatic note. (The acclaimed Canadian television series *Slings and Arrows*, about a Shakespearean troupe, takes advantage of this big opening by beginning its first episode with a rehearsal of this shipwreck.) Having noted the play's originality, we do catch glimpses in some of the settings and passages of what Shakespeare may have been reading, and which current events he may have found of great interest. The avuncular counselor Gonzalo gives a glowing speech about an idealized commonwealth, which echoes very closely a passage from the French writer Montaigne's *Essays*. And the exotic sea setting draws upon recent voyages to and pamphlets about the Bermudas—Prospero's spirit-servant Ariel speaks of the "still-vexed Bermoothes." And unsurprisingly, there are traces of one of Shakespeare's enduringly favorite books, Ovid's *Metamorphoses*. *The Tempest* is frequently hailed as belonging in the first tier of Shakespeare's greatest plays, and as one of the great masterpieces of literature. Here he seemed determined, late in his career, to produce something truly new and surprising.

Till the very end, he imagined and wrote at the highest of artistic levels. That said, he also achieves a satisfying artistic synthesis in this play: he continues the evolution of poetic sound effect and the boldness of story and staging found in the prior romances, yet he also, as critics have observed, seems intent on recapturing the "old mastery" of his earlier accomplishments, if with the new skins of this late play, the last one traditionally thought to be written by him alone. This new control is most obviously noticed in Shakespeare's strict adherence, in *The Tempest* as in no other work, to the unity of time and place required by classical authorities, and expected again in the neo-classical era following Shakespeare's time. That is to say, the play's action takes place in a single setting, the remote island ruled by Prospero, and the action requires only three hours, or about as much time as is actually passing by as the audience experiences the drama. This unusual simultaneity of play's action and playgoers' viewing time reflects in merely one way *The Tempest's* freshly self-conscious treatment of narrative, spectacle, and the creation of art generally. The greatest example of this self-consciousness resides in the doppelgänger figure of the magician protagonist, Prospero, himself. Despite warnings against treating Prospero too autobiographically, and thus reading this complex character as a mainly a mouthpiece of the author's, there is nevertheless a long, rich tradition of seeing in the consummate magician a figure for the image-making, character-raising playwright, now at the height, and nearly at the very end, of his powers. Prospero's "art" equates

all too easily with Shakespeare's own illusory arts in the theater.

Now to briefly summarize the action: Prospero's daughter, Miranda, witnesses the shipwreck from the island's shore, but is soon reassured by her father that "There is no harm done." It is the first of multiple occasions where the worst that might have happened is avoided, creating a sense of an ultimately reassuring world. This impression is in part, however, due to Prospero's intense overseeing of events about to unfold on the island. "The hour's now come," he says, to inform his daughter of their family history in the "dark backward and abysm of time." In this long series of speeches, by which Miranda comically finds herself distracted at times, much to the father's grumpy dismay, he explains to her how Antonio seized the dukedom in Milan, and how Prospero was, he admits, perhaps too preoccupied with his private studies rather than public rule: "my library / was dukedom large enough." Now, Prospero has intercepted his brother as he passed by on a ship with his ally Alonso King of Naples, who is joined by his brother, Sebastian, and son, Ferdinand. Also on board is the old counselor Gonzalo and a few lower characters, including Stephano the drunken servant and Trinculo the jester. This royal retinue was traveling back from the wedding of Alonso's daughter, Claribel, to the King of Tunis. During the shipwreck, father and son, Alonso and Ferdinand, have been separated, and each fears the other has perished at sea.

We soon meet as well characters that make Prospero's life in exile more interesting and complicated than might have been supposed. The spirit Ariel serves him, but pines for freedom, and Prospero keeps the spirit in his service by promising, and then deferring, Ariel's release. Prospero became Ariel's master when the magician freed the spirit from a tree, after being bound there by the more savage witch Sycorax. The witch has since died, and so Prospero has adopted her son,

Miranda offers to help Ferdinand move logs while Prospero looks on in Act 3, Scene 1 of *The Tempest*. This painting is from 1782 *(Angelica Kauffmann)*

the earthy man-monster Caliban, whose name suggests "cannibal." Originally, Caliban showed Prospero the island's resources, and it is he who speaks most reverently of the land's "Sounds and sweet airs that give delight and hurt not." However, there is a brute side to Caliban, too, thus Prospero has kept the native island dweller in subjugation ever since he attempted to rape Miranda. In the twentieth century, this relationship took on a special "post-colonial" resonance, and various rewritings (such as the one by Aimé Césaire) cast Prospero in the role of a harsh colonizer, and Caliban as the colonized whose rage is, at least to

some extent, justified. Shakespeare, too, seems able at times to sympathize with the oppressed's anger, inescapable in a dominion such as Prospero's: "You taught me language," says Caliban, "and my profit on't / Is I know now to curse."

Three plots unwind toward a climax of confrontation and reunion. First, Ariel leads the king's son Ferdinand to Prospero's and Miranda's habitation, and the spirit does so with one of Shakespeare's most haunting songs: "Full fathom five thy father lies, / Of his bones are coral made, / Those are pearls that were his eyes." Miranda is immediately taken with Ferdinand's "brave form."

Prospero encourages this first hint of love, but also demands that Ferdinand prove his worth by serving them. He quickly obliges. Second, Ariel next approaches a second band on the island, namely Alonso the king, his brother Sebastian, Antonio, and Gonzalo. The spirit's "solemn air" soon puts the king and counselor asleep, and now more immediate political treachery occurs, as Antonio urges Sebastian to slay his brother while he sleeps, thereby making himself King of Naples. Prospero, foreseeing the danger from afar, sends Ariel again, and the possible regicide is interrupted. And third, Caliban, hauling wood for his master, encounters Trinculo and Stephano, and soon the group is planning a drunken uprising against Prospero: "Remember / First to possess his books," advises Caliban, "for without them / He's but a sot[.]" Next Prospero appears before his brother-usurper, the king of Naples, and his brother (the "three men of sin"), conjuring a banquet that Ariel, in the appearance of a harpy, soon disrupts.

In one of the play's most memorable scenes, Prospero entertains the young couple with what Ferdinand calls a "most majestical vision." The ensuing masque features the goddesses Ceres, Iris, and Juno, as well as Naiads and "sunburnt sicklemen" (or reapers) who begin dancing. Prospero is enchanted by his own art before abruptly breaking off, aware suddenly of Caliban's conspiracy against him. Art's delights are nourishing, but must be temporary, and not at the expense of the world's demands upon us, our practical duties. Prospero explains as much to Ferdinand in one of the play's most celebrated speeches:

> Our revels now are ended. These our actors,
> As I foretold you, were all spirits and
> Are melted into air, into thin air:
> And, like the baseless fabric of this vision,
> The cloud-capp'd towers, the gorgeous palaces,
> The solemn temples, the great globe itself,

Ye all which it inherit, shall dissolve
And, like this insubstantial pageant faded,
Leave not a rack behind. We are such stuff
As dreams are made on, and our little life
Is rounded with a sleep.

Shakespeare may be describing a dissolving scene akin to the Globe or the decorated scenic space of an indoor theater such as Blackfriars, and many critics have glimpsed in this speech something more personal and valedictory. Notice he speaks of the "globe" dissolving, and Cynthia Marshall has identified this in terms of both Shakespeare's personal retirement from the Globe and his London writing life, as well as in apocalyptic terms, as Prospero envisions the whole world and the "insubstantial pageant" of our lives vanishing. It may be the first of Shakespeare's farewells to the stage in *The Tempest*, but it is not the most famous.

Caliban and his drunken mates arrive, but are soon driven out by spirits in the shape of hounds. Prospero appears in the last scene in his magic robes, and with Ariel's gentle urging, he resolves to bring his "project" to a close. Again, we encounter a great speech of resignation or retirement, as Prospero distances himself from his white magic, his "so potent art":

> But this rough magic
> I here abjure, and, when I have required
> Some heavenly music, which even now I do,
> To work mine end upon their senses that
> This airy charm is for, I'll break my staff,
> Bury it certain fathoms in the earth,
> And deeper than did ever plummet sound
> I'll drown my book.

Arthur Kinney has written powerfully about Prospero's power and knowledge requiring this self-abnegating act, this "consequential need to surrender." We see here, as Kinney puts it, that "Time catches up with Shakespeare in these last plays, catches up with his art in these last plays." The conclusion to *The Tempest* is at hand. Prospero, with Ariel's help, gathers all those remaining on the island, and confronts, and then forgives, his brother Antonio. The king of Naples and his brother are pardoned also. Moreover, Prospero orders Ariel to prepare good weather for a return voyage to Naples, for the wedding of Miranda and Ferdinand. After this task, we're told, the spirit will obtain his liberty. Near the play's end, Ferdinand speaks of receiving a "second life," and so it will be for all the characters, Prospero most of all. He is renouncing his magical power, but is also giving up the world of mastery and exile, and will return to Milan, with Caliban in tow. (One wonders a little nervously how that transition will go.) The characters enter into new stages of life. Nothing is ever guaranteed.

A final valedictory gesture occurs at the very end, in the play's "Epilogue," when Prospero reappears, half in character and half out, to announce that his charms are overthrown and his strength "most faint." He begs the audience for the applause that will, Ariel-like, release him: "But release me from my bands / With the help of your good hands." Otherwise "my project fails, / Which was to please." Who is speaking here? Prospero, or his creator Shakespeare? The shift is suggested further by a final claim—his ending will be despairing unless the audience relieves him (again, whom?) with prayers. "Let your indulgence set me free," this Prospero-actor-author-figure asks. Again we sense how the presence of the author hovers over this play. These moments of farewell outlined above have struck many through the centuries as a sort of Shakespearean goodbye to his own art, and the London theater that had given its stage to his spell-binding powers for more than twenty years. The playwright was forty-seven years old.

Writers have imagined and scholars have inquired about Shakespeare's work as an artist more with *The Tempest* than with any other work. The great modernist Virginia Woolf, after visiting Shakespeare's Stratford home, New Place, in May 1934, recorded her thoughts in her diary: "to think of writing *The Tempest* looking out on that garden; what a rage & storm of thought to have gone over any mind; no doubt the solidity of the place was comfortable." With similar attention, the director Sam Mendes recently staged a *Tempest*, as a part of the Bridge Project in London and New York, whose main subject is, as one reviewer said, "the world of the imagination"—Prospero's, Shakespeare's, our own.

Many others have found the play amenable to rewriting, revising, and reenvisioning in other arts and media. W. H. Auden wrote a dramatic commentary on the play and art in general in his long poem *The Sea and the Mirror*, and the novelist and memoirist Frederick Buechner recalls a World War II film that applied Caliban's line to the bombs, sirens, and anti-aircraft weaponry of the Blitz: "Be not a'fear'd: this isle is full of noises." And for a completely different treatment, there's the silly sci-fi film *Forbidden Planet*. More recently, Peter Greenaway's film *Prospero's Books* featured the great Shakespearean actor John Gielgud as the magician in an interesting, artsy take on Shakespeare's late tale, while Dexter Palmer's novel *The Dream of Perpetual Motion* sets its narrator on an air-ship shared with a cryogenically frozen corpse named Prospero and a mysterious voice of one Miranda speaking over the intercom.

More commonly, various Shakespeareans have explored precisely why the lyrical sounds of Shakespeare's late poetry feels both bare and magisterial, peculiar and yet with an authority ringing through it. Russ McDonald, in *Shakespeare's Late Style*, singles out several aural effects, including tendencies toward compression of thought or speech, increasingly enjambed lines and extrametrical endings, and metrical variety overall. Shakespeare's late versifying can seem so "utterly insouciant," McDonald claims, as to seem "almost random." Nevertheless, the sensitive ear will increasingly hear a subtle but still recognizable music here, one that grows more characteristic as we become more attentive to the speeches' short phrases, frequent pauses, reversed metrical feet, and feminine line endings. And against this willfully unpredictable formal practice, what McDonald calls the thought within the plays, their sentences' "semantic energies," pulse and move outward. The language seems more conversational, yet moves from clause to clause using, as McDonald calls it, syntax that is "suspended" and "divagated." Here is the paradox of late Shakespeare: the characters sound at times deeply easy in their natural speech, and at other times mysterious and bewitching in the movements of mind and tongue. Likewise, the critic Nicholas Delbanco, in *Lastingness: The Art of Old Age*, has recently argued that Shakespeare makes his last plays "less sequence-bound or yoked to plausibility. It is as though the peerless artificer has had enough of artifice." True, except when he has not had enough, as is frequently the case in the highly artful, masque- and spectacle-ridden romances. And all the while, Shakespeare, sometimes with-out our noticing, was achieving new kinds of stylized description and symbolic action.

Sources and Further Reading

Bearman, Robert. *Shakespeare in the Stratford Records*. Stroud: Sutton, 2006.

Cook, Judith. *Roaring Boys: Shakespeare's Rat Pack*. Stroud: Sutton, 2004.

Duncan-Jones, Katherine. *Ungentle Shakespeare: Scenes from His Life*. London: Arden Shakespeare, 2001.

Heylin, Clinton. *So Long as Men Can Breathe: The Untold Story of Shakespeare's Sonnets*. Philadelphia, Penn.: Da Capo Press, 2009.

Hopkins, D. J. *City / Stage / Globe: Performance and Space in Shakespeare's London*. New York: Routledge, 2008.

Lesser, Wendy. "Late Shakespeare," *Nothing Remains the Same: Rereading and Remembering*. Boston : Houghton Mifflin, 2002.

Lyne, Raphael. *Shakespeare's Late Work*. New York: Oxford University Press, 2007.

McDonald, Russ. *Shakespeare's Late Style*. New York: Cambridge University Press, 2006.

Warren, Roger. *Staging Shakespeare's Late Plays*. New York: Oxford University Press, 1990.

SHAKESPEARE'S LAST DAYS
IN LONDON AND STRATFORD

It is worth noting that Shakespeare's last plays have never been regarded, and are still not so, with universal acclaim. One of Shakespeare's greatest critics, Samuel Johnson, found the "unresisting imbecility" of *Cymbeline*'s endless disguises and revelations exasperating, and during Shakespeare's own time, Ben Jonson, never slow with criticism, seems to have a certain late romance in mind when he scornfully speaks of "tales, tempests, and such drolleries" in his Induction to *Bartholomew Fair*. Yet there were some who could comprehend early on what Shakespeare had accomplished with his three dozen plays. The young poet John Milton understood it when he contributed a sonnet in Shakespeare's praise for the Second Folio of 1630: "Thou in our wonder and astonishment / Hast built thyself a live-long Monument." Shakespeare was soon to enjoy a particular show of success and royal approval shortly after he completed *The Tempest*.

First, he had to endure more family sadness and loss at home in Stratford. His brother Gilbert died and was buried in Stratford on February 3, 1612, and his last remaining brother, Richard, died almost exactly a year later. A neighbor in Henley Street, the vintner and innkeeper Robert Johnson, also died around this time. He held a lease on a barn at the back of the Shakespeare family home on Henley Street, where now only the poet's sister Joan lived with her hat-maker husband, William Hart, and their children. William and Joan were the last two of John and Mary Shakespeare's eight children. The siblings' father had probably built that barn, and it was

still standing when Shakespeare's granddaughter Elizabeth made her will in 1670. We learn from it that another Johnson, presumably a relation of Robert's, was renting the space. In William and Anne Shakespeare's present home of New Place, their daughter Judith still lived there, and one Thomas Greene had been staying at the large property in 1609–10, if not longer. He brought with him his wife and two young children, and the family may have arranged for an annual lease. Stratford's town clerk, Greene had studied law at London's Middle Temple and was identified as a "cousin" of Shakespeare's. Even if not terribly eventful by most standards, various town affairs during these years kept Shakespeare involved in Stratford life, even at the time when he was busy preparing *The Tempest* for a November 11, 1611, court performance. Aldermen prepared on September 11 a list of seventy-one town residents who had donated "towards the charge of prosecuting the bill in Parliament for the better repair of the highways." Stratford officials was basically asking the national government to provide funds for upkeep. Nothing came of it, but Thomas Greene's name appears on the list, as does Shakespeare's at the very top, but added at the right. It is enjoyable to think that he had not been signed up initially because he had been in London then, casting and rehearsing *The Tempest*.

Back in London the following late spring, Shakespeare gave his deposition in the *Belott v. Mountjoy* case, discussed earlier. We therefore know where he was on May 12, 1612, although officially he stated that he could not recall details from eight years ago related to this dowry squabble. Shakespeare, listed as a gentleman of the age of forty-eight "or thereaboutes" and of Stratford-upon-Avon, was scheduled to testify again the following month, but appears not to have done so. He was probably glad to put this earlier tenancy on Silver Street, when he had been surrounded by domestic drama, well behind him. The rest of the year saw two deaths that shook all of England. In that same month of May, Robert Cecil died. He was a most shrewd counselor, had been James I's favorite, and had been one of the most powerful, informed men of the realm. More shockingly, later that fall the country reeled from the sudden death of Prince Henry, a martially minded young man in whom all the Stuart hopes of smooth succession had been placed. Funeral obsequies and tearful elegies flowed forth. The royal daughter, Elizabeth Stuart, had her planned wedding postponed because of this loss, and the next son, the less impressive Charles, began to be groomed for the crown. Princess Elizabeth finally married Prince Frederick, the Elector Palatine, in February 1613, for which extravagant celebrations were held at the palace at Whitehall. The event was marked by an astounding fourteen performances by the King's Men—a sure sign of the company's continuing dominance. Older plays such as *Much Ado About Nothing* and *Othello* were performed, as well as the more recent *The Winter's Tale* and *The Tempest*. It is possible that the nuptial masque in act four of *The Tempest*, beginning with "Soft music" and the entrance of Iris, was a festive addition to the play for this royal occasion specifically—"Some vanity of mine art," Prospero fittingly calls it. Around this time, Shakespeare also earned forty-four shillings for designing the *impresa*, or emblem and motto, to adorn the Earl of Rutland's shield in a theatrical jousting tournament before the king. The playwright was paid in gold, and his fellow King's Man Richard Burbage

was compensated as well for painting it. Burbage was apparently a talented visual artist as well as the finest actor of his age. Clearly these were good times professionally, and as Germaine Greer justly declares, the forty-eight-year-old Shakespeare was "in the prime of life and at the zenith of his career" during the first half of 1613.

SPECIAL PLACES IN LONDON, AND DEBATED OCCASIONAL VERSES

Shakespeare may well have used his portion of the handsome payment the company received for the wedding performances to make his final real-estate investment. He paid one hundred and forty pounds for a "dwelling house or tenement" above "a great gate" in the Blackfriars neighborhood. The property was adjacent to the King's Wardrobe. It may have been merely a rental property, since a John Robinson was residing there in 1616, but the nearness to the King's Men's indoor theater means it would have been a convenient working and living space for the senior company playwright. He paid eighty pounds in cash and took a mortgage on the remaining amount, for which he had three "co-purchasers," or trustees: his fellow actor John Heminges; William Johnson, a "common vintner" and proprietor of the famed Mermaid Tavern; and John Jackson, who may have been a friend related to a brewer on Puddle Dock Hill, quite close to Shakespeare's new property. The mortgage deed still exists in the British Library. Some biographers have made much of this financial arrangement, for in effect it would have prevented Shakespeare's wife, Anne, if widowed, from claiming a third of the property by dower right. Indeed, in 1618, the property was signed over to his daughter Susanna. We will soon see similar tensions debated with respect to Shakespeare's will. Those suspecting that Shakespeare was a Catholic have argued that the gatehouse, with its "places for secret conveyance," was a haven for priests. As a property owner in Blackfriars, Shakespeare was also involved in some low-level litigation on behalf of a neighbor in 1615. It appears that the gatehouse was knocked down in the late eighteenth century for the sake of erecting a new bridge.

We have now met William Johnson and heard of his Mermaid Tavern, and it ought to be said that Shakespeare for a long time has been sentimentally associated with the "bards of passion and of mirth" (the phrase is Keats's) who supposedly kept good company there. The proprietor Johnson once fell into legal trouble for serving meat instead of fish on Fridays. The tavern was on Bread Street, just east of St. Paul's Cathedral, and so would have been easily reachable for Shakespeare, arriving from either the Globe or Blackfriars. It was the very street where John Milton was born in 1608, and where John Donne lived at one point. Donne, along with poets such as Jonson, Walter Ralegh, and Francis Beaumont, traditionally make up Shakespeare's jolly circle of writers. It makes a fine oil painting, at least. Such a pleasant thought does not make it true, but it makes the legend of literary good cheer resilient, and that is just as well. It is easy to associate this social setting, or one smaller but similar to it in Stratford, with some of the epigrams, epitaphs, or other short lyric poems that have been ascribed to Shakespeare. None ever appeared in a contemporary publication authored by or otherwise connected with Shakespeare. Transcriptions begin to appear in seventeenth-century commonplace books.

Shakespeare is the purported author of two epitaphs on a Dugdale family tomb, and he is also said to have written a funeral verse for the Stratford moneylender John Combe. Upon his death in 1614, Combe left gifts for Stratford's poor and for Shakespeare, too. A single manuscript at the Bodleian Library, Oxford University, prints a more respectful epitaph that it says Shakespeare composed in response to this good deed. The original one for Combe is rather satirical, and is similar in spirit to a reported exchange over drinks between Shakespeare and Ben Jonson. "Here is Ben Jonson / That was once one," wrote the latter poet, which Shakespeare then completed: "Who while he lived was a slow thing, / And now, being dead, is nothing." A final, more serious epitaph attributed to Shakespeare exists, in the memory of that brewer, Elias James, mentioned above. Other competent but not remarkable verses exist: a ditty supposedly written for a Stratford schoolmaster to announce wittily a gift of gloves, and a short elegiac poem claiming to be by Shakespeare in the 1616 edition

This famous 1851 painting, entitled *Shakespeare and His Friends at the Mermaid Tavern*, envisions Shakespeare carousing with his writer friends. Sir Walter Raleigh, Ben Jonson, John Donne, Francis Bacon, John Fletcher, Francis Beaumont, and several others are all depicted. *(John Faed)*

of James I's *Works*. Finally, scholars occasionally debate whether or not this or that short or lengthy Renaissance lyric poem, usually found in a verse miscellany and often anonymous, is Shakespeare's. Examples have included the short lyric "Shall I die?" and the nearly six-hundred-line poem *A Funeral Elegy* by "W. S." Neither has met with widespread acceptance.

COLLABORATIONS WITH JOHN FLETCHER

There is no question that Shakespeare's most important relationship with another writer during this time was his collaborative partnership with John Fletcher. He certainly knew of the younger playwright and his dear friend and roommate Francis Beaumont. The pair already had experience collaborating on productions for Blackfriars audiences. True, none of their plays had yet enjoyed breakout success, but they were respectable works, including the parodying *Knight of the Burning Pestle* and *The Faithful Shepherdess*. Soon their fortunes turned, however, and plays such as *Philaster* and *The Maid's Tragedy* must have made the older Shakespeare take more notice. He may have also noted approvingly that Fletcher, with his "overflowing" wit, could write solidly and also quickly. It is possible that Fletcher in 1611 strove for Shakespeare's attention with a rather risky play, again in a parodying, even irreverent vein—*The Woman's Prize; or, The Tamer Tamed*, a sequel to Shakespeare's still popular *Taming of the Shrew*. In it, Katherine has died and Petruchio remarries. With his "Petruccio," Fletcher seeks to make "amends for ladies," and soon his new bride Maria is taming him—mainly by denying him sex. (Here Fletcher is cleverly looking back to Aristophanes's ancient comedy *Lysistrata*.) If this effort offended Shakespeare and his fellow company men, they must have gotten over it: in 1633, the King's Men presented the two plays consecutively, and in the past decade the Royal Shakespeare Company has done the same thing. Gordon McMullan has spoken of this "uncannily modern, even proto-feminist, play."

Much more immediately, Fletcher and Shakespeare appear to have begun working with each other rather swiftly, likely dividing scenes between them on at least three plays between 1612 and 1614—the lost *Cardenio*, *Henry VIII* (also known as *All Is True*), and *The Two Noble Kinsmen*. Far from going gentle into the night of retirement, Shakespeare, albeit in a less demanding co-author's role, seems to have intensified his projects at the very end of his writing life. As Rowe and others have affirmed, he may have been residing primarily in Stratford during the final three years of his life, but he clearly continued to visit London for work or pleasure, or both. For example, in 1614, his cousin and tenant Thomas Greene records, while in London, that Shakespeare "coming yesterday to town I went to see him how he did."

Perhaps, as one biographer has suggested, Shakespeare was like a repeatedly retiring professional athlete today: he couldn't stop saying goodbye to an urban theater world that had embraced him for two decades. He must have also reflected from time to time on how different the landscape of playwriting was late in his career, compared with his apprentice days in the late 1580s or early 1590s. Then, the plays had been staged in inn yards or in new public theaters, also outdoors, for any penny stinker who would pay to enter. Now, the increasingly refined, sophisticated shows took place at court, or in indoor theaters in fashionable central London, and for largely courtly and professional audiences. Then, Shakespeare numbered himself among a rogues' gallery of playwrights, many of whom would die young—Christopher Marlowe, Robert Greene, George Peele, Thomas Nashe, and so on. Now, he was working with

John Fletcher, who along with Beaumont brought a new social prestige to the theater world. Beaumont trained at Oxford and the Inner Temple, and was from an ancient, distinguished Leicestershire family, while Fletcher was the son of London's Lord Bishop and had studied at Cambridge. There remained theater sites for the masses, such as the Red Bull and the Fortune, but the King's Men's authors were increasingly writing for a more privileged clientele.

The now-lost play *Cardenio* derived from an episode in Cervantes's great Spanish work *Don Quixote*, which had just been translated into a masterful English version by Thomas Shelton in 1612. The King's Men performed this play at the court at Whitehall during the Christmas season of 1612–13, and again the following June at Greenwich. The tale involves an episode from Cervantes's sprawling novel, about the title character and crazed hero, betrayed by a friend, and his lost love Lucinda. It very much fitted the tragicomic genre for which Fletcher was quickly becoming known, and forty years later a publisher advertised the play as by "Fletcher and Shakespeare." If it was printed then, no early edition currently exists. The play resurfaced in the eighteenth century, when the Shakespeare editor Lewis Theobald "revised" the original play, from a manuscript he claimed to have had, into *Double Falsehood; or The Distressed Lovers* (1728). Lately Theobald's play, at least, has gained international attention, as critics and journalists have attempted to identify echoes of Shakespeare's voice in light of a recent publication, in the authoritative Arden series, of *The Double Falsehood*. Some welcome the newly accessible and publicized play with its genuine-sounding Shakespearean passages, while others have dismissed the publication as an effort for a publisher to "extend the brand." The Royal Shakespeare Company director Gregory Doran staged *Cardenio* in 2011, and for his production

he pragmatically worked to establish a full script based upon a combination of both Theobald's revision and pertinent passages in Shelton's early modern translation of *Don Quixote*.

The last play Shakespeare seems to have worked on with Fletcher was *The Two Noble Kinsmen*, likely completed by them in the second half of 1613. This play was eventually printed, but not till 1634, when it was assigned to "the memorable worthies of their time, Mr. John Fletcher and Mr. William Shakespeare, Gent." The comment suggests that the play was more Fletcher's than Shakespeare's, and readers keen to read the sections most likely by Shakespeare usually focus on acts one and five, and the opening scenes of acts two and three. Various critics have estimated that Shakespeare produced some of his greatest poetry in this last play, but perhaps because of the quantity of his involvement compared with Fletcher, Shakespeare's fellow actors decided to exclude *Two Noble Kinsmen* from the First Folio in 1623. (*Pericles*, another collaborative work, was also left out.) It was not expressly connected with Shakespeare until the mid-nineteenth century, when an editor included it in a volume of *Doubtful Plays*. The Prologue announces the immediate source, "Chaucer (of all admir'd) the Story gives," and specifically this narrative of love and war, warring friends, chivalry and tragedy comes from Chaucer's "The Knight's Tale," the first story told in his *Canterbury Tales*. (He himself borrowed this tale from Boccaccio's *Teseida*.) Plutarch's "Life of Theseus" and Philip Sidney's *Arcadia* are other likely sources. The play begins with three queens begging pity from Theseus and Hippolyta, rulers of Athens whom Shakespeare had already brought onstage in *A Midsummer Night's Dream*. A Morris dance organized by the schoolmaster in the middle of the play also looks back to the rude mechanicals' "Pyramus and Thisbe" performance in the earlier play, and the dance itself was taken from Francis Beaumont's anti-masque prepared for the royal wedding festivities in February 1613.

The queens lament the deaths of their husbands: they have fallen in battle to Theban Creon, who refuses to permit his dead foes' proper burial. Theseus thus attacks Thebes, and soon two of Creon's men, Arcite and Palamon, are taken prisoner. The play's dramatic focus will be on these two friends. Both fall in love with Emilia, whom they see through their prison window, and a rivalry erupts. Arcite is released but returns to Athens in disguise to attend on Emilia. Meanwhile, the Jailer's daughter falls for Palamon and helps him escape. Her character remains a highly entertaining one in modern productions, in part because of her frankness in her attraction for Palamon and the poignancy of her infatuation—he is like a poster-boy; she has no chance. In her eventual madness she resembles *Hamlet*'s Ophelia. Arcite soon encounters Palamon in a forest, and although their rivalry resumes, he shows Palamon courtesy by supplying food and armor in order to ensure an equal fight between them. Theseus arrests and condemns both lovers, but soon agrees to sanction a public joust between them: the winner will gain Emilia's hand, the loser will be executed. Beforehand, Arcite prays to Mars, and wins the battle. Palamon, in contrast, prays to Venus to win Emilia, and when the victorious Arcite is thrown from his horse and dies, Palamon's prayer is answered, too. Yet he is shaken by the loss of his friend, exclaiming, "O miserable end to our alliance!" In the end, though, the survivor weds his love.

HENRY VIII AND THE BURNING OF THE GLOBE

I have reserved Shakespeare's and Fletcher's likely middle play, *Henry VIII*, for last because it is associated with an event that effectively brings the Globe's golden age to a close, and shuts down the Shakespearean era of English Renaissance drama.

The writers were probably at work on the play in the spring of 1613, and it may even have been the show about Henry VIII scheduled for the royal wedding celebrations in February. Unfortunately, it was delayed then in favor of a masque. The subject matter, including Henry VIII's break from the Roman Catholic Church, his marriage to Anne Boleyn, and the birth of their daughter Elizabeth, marked a striking return to the genre of history play, which Shakespeare had not attempted for the past decade. He was again bringing the grand personalities of English history to the stage, though this was more recent history about the Tudor monarchy and the Reformation, rather than about medieval kings and the Wars of the Roses. That said, in another respect this curious late play must have felt less recent, insofar as it structurally looks back well beyond the history plays in the first half of Shakespeare's career. There is a medieval wheel-of-fortune shape to the subsequent rise and fall of those competing forces around Henry VIII—first the nobleman Buckingham, then the king's first wife, Katherine of Aragon, and finally Cardinal Wolsey, his counselor who could not obtain a papal annulment of this first marriage. The doomed Wolsey expresses this descent well: "I have touched the highest point of all my greatness; And, from that full meridian of my glory, I haste now to my setting." Archbishop Thomas Cranmer emerges into a position of power at the end of the play, and he is the one to give a long speech at Elizabeth's baptism, both praising the princess and prophesying her long, prosperous rule and that of her successor, the current king, James I. In this way, Shakespeare extends his royal treatments in his histories all the way through the Tudor monarchs and triumphantly, and flatteringly, into the current Stuart reign.

Henry VIII is memorable today for a few reasons. First, there is its surprisingly sympathetic,

THE FIRST FOLIO'S PRAISING POETS

The most important event in Shakespeare's writing career may arguably have been, as odd as this will sound, something that occurred a full seven years after the playwright's death. Shakespeare's First Folio appeared in print in 1623, thanks to the efforts of Shakespeare's fellow actors and King's Men John Heminges and Henry Condell. Its importance to the subsequent assessment of Shakespeare and the growth of his reputation cannot be overestimated: this collection of his plays, featuring all but two of those thirty-eight plays we have today, contained no fewer than eighteen plays that had never before been published. Can you imagine if half of the Shakespeare plays we now know suddenly vanished? We might know *of* them, and know them by their titles, but without the First Follo, we would not have the plays themselves. These plays, "new" for publication, constituted half of the works collected in the Folio. It was a felicitous development for the other half of Shakespeare's plays to appear here, too, for in many cases Heminges and Condell seem to have been working from Shakespeare's personal papers, or at least company copies of the plays that were often more authoritative than the early quarto versions previously available in print (and sometimes almost certainly pirated).

The First Folio, then, is one of the most important books in all of literary history, and it was also the first folio-sized publication (that is to say, large and expensive) dedicated exclusively to dramatic works. This, too, was a sign of Shakespeare's unique status as a valued English author. Merely to read some of the prefatory matter—those dedications, introductions, and poems that appear before Shakespeare's plays themselves—is to hear again and again the high notes of praise for a much missed fellow theater worker who was increasingly becoming a singular English author. Now, it should also be added that a literary convention existed during the Renaissance to include effusive, even flattering poems in support of an author's published work. It served a validating function for a nervous writer, and in some cases, it also became a kind of literary protection against those critics intent on trashing a writer's printed offerings. It should also be added that some literary publications, such as Edmund Spenser's epic poem *The Faerie Queene*, appeared with far more numerous dedicatory poems in praise of the author. Nevertheless, the apparatus surrounding Shakespeare's plays makes it clear that the publication of the First Folio was a literary event, and indeed it remains a cultural watershed for English letters. Playgoers had never before seen the likes of Shakespeare, and they never would again. Fortunately, readers could now revisit and reexperience his plays in secure, textual form.

Shakespeare's great stage rival Ben Jonson contributed two verses to the Folio. The first, "To the Reader," is meant to accompany the engraved portrait of the author on the title page. Jonson acknowledges "This Figure," or the engraver's image of the man, but laments that he could not render "his wit." Had he managed to capture Shakespeare's wit, then his work would "surpasse / All, that was ever writ in brasse." Jonson ends this short poem on a note of con-

ennobling characterization of the Catholic Katherine, Henry's rejected queen. "No friends, no hope, no kindred weep for me," she says plaintively, and soon she receives a vision of a half-dozen spirits in white, which dance above her and present her with a garland. Susan Frye has suggested that Katherine may be an oblique portrait of James I's queen, Anne of Denmark. Second, the play was originally, and has continued to be, a convenient vehicle for opulent displays of scenery and costume during called-for occasions of ceremonial spectacle, such as Anne Boleyn's coronation and Elizabeth's baptism. Long processions of richly appointed courtiers or church-

solation. Since the engraver cannot do this with Shakespeare's image, Readers at least can look "Not on his Picture, but his Booke." After the editors' dedication to William and Philip Herbert and their justly famous prefatory epistle, "To the great Variety of Readers" (discussed within the present chapter), Jonson again receives pride of place with his far more lengthy verse encomium to his fellow playwright, entitled: "To the memory of my beloved, The Author Mr. William Shakespeare And what he hath left us." Jonson begins by confessing (because he is a rival author?) that Shakespeare's writings "be such / As neither Man, nor Muse, can praise too much." However begrudging he could sometimes be, Ben Jonson deserves credit for penning some of the most famous epithets associated with Shakespeare: "Soule of the Age! / The applause! delight! the wonder of our Stage!" He towers, professes Jonson, over previous English authors such as Chaucer and Spenser, and his book will live as long as "we have wits to read, and praise to give." Shakespeare's truest company is found among the classical tragedians—Aeschylus, Euripides, Sophocles. Coming from a classicist such as Jonson, this comparison with the greatest of Greek stage writers is high praise indeed. He also compares Shakespeare as a comic writer with the Roman playwrights Terence and Plautus. Jonson praises his subject's natural facility, but also his artistic technique, an aspect that later praisers of Shakespeare would tend to overlook in favor of their cherished myths of his "native genius." No, for Jonson, Shakespeare worked hard to create "well turned, and true filed lines." Jonson concludes his praise poem by addressing the "Sweet Swan of Avon!" He next imagines him in mythological terms, ascending to become a constellation in the heavens: "Shine forth, thou Starre of Poets . . . "

Other, similar poems appear after Jonson's, though none is close to matching Jonson's length, scale, and achievement. Hugh Holland praises this "Famous Scenicke Poet," and one "I. M." declares that "this thy printed worth" means that Shakespeare will never truly die; he merely went forth "To enter with applause," as if the afterlife were just one more successive stage for which to create memorable characters and beautiful poetry. Leonard Digges offers a twenty-two-line poem, most interesting today because it mentions the well-known bust of Shakespeare, his "Stratford Moniment" or monument. Digges imagines that stone bust dissolving eventually under Time's ravages, but again, Shakespeare's printed works will never perish. Digges also published another praise poem in a later 1640 edition of Shakespeare's poems.

Apparently these various praises of the deceased writer had their desired effects: the volume was a success, so much so that a second edition was prepared and published in 1632.

SEE ALSO:

Blayney, Peter W. M. *The First Folio of Shakespeare*. Washington, D.C.: Folger Library Publications, 1991.

The First Folio of Shakespeare: The Norton Facsimile, ed. Charlton Hinman. New York: W. W. Norton, 1968.

Massai, Sonia. *Shakespeare and the Rise of the Editor*. New York: Cambridge University Press, 2007.

men repeatedly enter and exit the stage, and the play was likely performed at the Globe in order to exploit its large, bare stage for these crowded scenes. These processions also involved the shooting of ordnance from a small cannon, and this proved to be a fateful component. On June 29, 1613, the gunners fired their chambers as drums and trumpets played. This time, however, the tinder and gunpowder ignited the thatched roof of the theater. We are lucky to have a vivid account from Henry Wotton, the former ambassador to Venice, about this particular performance of this play, which he called *All Is True*. (Is the subtitle Shakespeare's tongue-in-cheek choice for a

Katherine begs for justice from the king in this nineteenth-century painting of Act 2, Scene 4 of *Henry VIII*. *(Henry Nelson O'Neil)*

history play? Or is it a boast, a promise that the costumes and stage effects will make the historical action seem utterly true?) Wotton describes precisely when the fire broke out:

> Now, King Henry making a masque at Cardinal Wolsey's house, and certain chambers being shot off at his entry, some of the paper or other stuff wherewith one of them was stopped did light on the thatch, where being thought at first but an idle smoke, and their eyes more attentive to the show, it kindled inwardly and ran round like a train, consuming within less than an hour the whole house to the very grounds.

Fortunately everyone was able to exit the theater, and only a "few forsaken cloaks" were lost in the flames. One man "had his breeches set on fire," but a "provident wit," Wotten concludes, "put it out with a bottle of ale." As difficult as it is to face this fact, far more might have been lost that day when the Globe burnt to the ground: in addition to the cloaks, many of the King's Men's costumes and stage properties may have been destroyed in the fire. More tantalizingly, what about plays in manuscript and prompt-books stored there? It is quite likely that many materials invaluable to theater historians were lost forever, never to be known. If some of Shakespeare's writings perished in the flames on that day, at least it appears that not all of them did, since there were still authoritative manuscripts to draw upon for the First Folio a decade later.

Puritans inferred from the Globe's destruction God's harsh judgment upon the actors and their profane plays. At least one contemporary street ballad about the fire has survived:

This fearful fire began above,
A wonder strange and true,
And to the stage-house did remove
As round as tailor's clew,
And burned down both bean and snag
And did not spare the silken flag.
Oh sorrow, pitiful sorrow,
And yet all this is true.

Although it is an unsentimental view, Shakespeare may have thought it was time for the King's Men to detach itself from an outdoor playhouse, and concentrate instead on indoor performances at Blackfriars. This was theater's future in England, and he may have intuited that. Instead, it was decided that the Globe would rise again, requiring of its leaseholders significant new investments of capital. Instead of suffering this financial setback, Shakespeare may have been ready to sell his share. He was, after all, a shrewd businessman till the end. At some point, he also must have sold his stake in Blackfriars, since his will contained no reference to assets involving shares in theaters. More certainly, despite the swift rebuilding of the Globe by its co-owners and its reopening within a year, a cultural epoch had ended. The second Globe, with a safer tile roof, would showcase plays for another thirty years, till the Puritans came to power and shut down all of London's theaters in 1642. They would be closed for nearly two decades.

FINAL DAYS AND DEATH IN STRATFORD

The eventful burning of the Globe may have hastened Shakespeare's ultimate retirement. If, afterward, he were residing at greater length or even full time in Stratford, existing records of his final years suggest he would have had much to keep him busy. Some of what he dealt with was far from pleasant. One thing that surely pleased him was the marriage of his daughter Susanna to Dr. John Hall. Their young daughter, Elizabeth, was thriving, and her husband was repeatedly enjoying professional success. His casebook of cures, *Select Observations on English Bodies*, received critical acclaim, and was translated into Latin (for a wider, more learned readership) decades after his death. In 1607, the Hall family was financially comfortable enough to purchase a timber house near her parents' home of New Place. Hall also gave a new pulpit to the Stratford church, and served as a warden there. He was an upright, respectable, possibly severe man, and he seems to have earned his father-in-law's trust. The couple did face one crisis of reputation in Stratford in July 1613, when one John Lane, twenty-three years old, accused Susanna of adultery, and of having gonorrhea. She promptly sued him for slander in ecclesiastical court, and won. It was the sort of sudden calumny that so often drove the plot forward in her father's plays.

In the spring of 1614, the town council provided a visiting preacher with wine and sack, and he found accommodation at New Place. He was probably there to preach a scheduled sermon before the council in the Gild Chapel, conveniently across the street from Shakespeare's spacious home. A few months later, on July 9, 1614, a fire spread through Stratford and destroyed more than fifty homes. Shakespeare's properties were not damaged, and it may not have even upset him terribly: this was the third such serious fire to affect Stratford in his lifetime. Another threat to his property arose later that fall—not to his homes in Stratford, but to his lands outside of town that he had purchased as an investment, and from which he drew tithe income. William

NEW PLACE,

From a Drawing in the Margin of an Ancient SURVEY, made by Order of SIR GEORGE CAREW, (afterwards BARON CAREW of Clopton, and EARL of TOTNESS) and found at Clopton near Stratford upon Avon, in 1786.

Illustration of New Place, published by J. Rivington & Partners in 1790. It is based on a drawing from the margin of an ancient survey made by order of Sir George Carew. *(J. Jordan)*

Combe, whose father had sold Shakespeare acreage in Old Stratford, was now wishing to enclose land in Welcombe, and he could boast powerful allies in his cause. The plan was to convert tillable farmland into more profitable pastureland, but it would mean eliminating farming jobs and would have an adverse affect on Shakespeare's and others' investments. Shakespeare wasted no time obtaining an assurance of compensation "for all such loss, detriment, and hindrance," although he ultimately did not believe the plan would succeed, or at worst felt the effects would be minimal. It seems that he tried to assure his cousin Thomas Greene, a much more nervous investor, of that fact. Greene writes that Shakespeare said "they mean to enclose no further than to Gospel Bush." The enclosures actually began, but were resisted and held up by townsmen, still reeling from the recent fire. Eventually Combe gave up and turned to other ventures. The modern playwright Edward Bond has written a play about Shakespeare and the Welcombe enclosures, *Bingo: Scenes of money and death*, and in 1997 Peter Whelan's play *The Herbal Bed* reached the stage, dramatizing the stories of John and Susanna Hall and the charge of adultery against her. The years that are traditionally thought to be Shakespeare's quiet time of peaceful retirement in Stratford have proven surprisingly ripe dramatically. And yet another such family incident was about to occur.

Shakespeare made his first will in January in either 1615 or 1616—the numbering on this venerated legal document is unclear. It is signed "in perfect health and memory," which may have been true. On the other hand, it was a conventional statement when preparing a will. Various biographers have suspected that the author was ill by this time, and the terseness of phrase and the shaky handwriting make this a more likely fact when Shakespeare called upon his lawyer, Francis Collins, to incorporate and notarize revisions on March 25, 1616. Shakespeare was less than a month away from his death. As for the first version of the will, it is more likely that Shakespeare drafted it in January 1616, having been spurred to set his estate in order in light of the pending wedding of his second daughter, Judith, on February 10. Shortly beforehand, on February 1, King James had granted a life pension to Ben Jonson, making him, with this royal support, the de facto poet laureate, if not yet so in name. What did Shakespeare make of this news? Happiness for his friend and main playwriting rival, or envy possibly? Truly, he probably had little time to reflect on it, with his daughter's wedding fast approaching. It is more certain that this wedding, and the misfortunes surrounding it, led to those determined, steely-eyed revisions to his will shortly before his death.

Judith's marriage to Thomas Quiney promised to be another happy Shakespeare family development, as her sister Susanna's marriage to John Hall was proving to be. Sadly, it was to be otherwise. Judith was thirty-one years old, increasingly beyond the marrying age for young women, and so the match may have been a pleasant surprise. Thomas was almost twenty-seven. Furthermore, the Quineys were family friends— it was Thomas's father, Richard, who wrote to Shakespeare to ask for a loan when he visited London in 1598. The newlyweds soon set up house on the corner of High Street, which Thomas, a vintner by trade, converted into a tavern. His mother lived next door. Unfortunately, the marriage was almost immediately a disaster; in fact, the very wedding itself caused problems for the couple. The ceremony occurred during the Lenten season prior to Easter, and so Thomas and Judith were required to obtain a special license from the bishop. (Judith's parents had had to scramble for a similar license many years ago.) They did not do this, and so were ordered to appear before the consistory court in Worcester Cathedral. Thomas did not show up, and so was excommunicated. Judith may have been as well. All seems to have been forgiven fairly soon, though, since a year later Thomas and Judith had a child baptized at Stratford's church. Greater problems followed. When Thomas married Judith in February, another woman, Margaret Wheeler, was about to deliver his child. Mother and infant died during childbirth, and both burials are listed in the parish register for March 15. The ecclesiastical court, popularly called "bawdy court" because it often dealt in such cases of fornication, called Thomas for a hearing. The newlywed confessed to unmarried sex with Wheeler on March 25. He was ordered to perform open penance in a white sheet in front of the church, but instead paid a fine of five shillings to close the case. A year later, the Quineys' first child died in infancy.

Shakespeare and his family, prominent in a small town, must have been terribly embarrassed by Thomas's social disgrace, and relations with the Quiney family were possibly strained, at least for a while. Shakespeare, probably feeling great displeasure toward his son-in-law and perhaps skeptical of his daughter Judith's judgment, was determined to alter his will in light of these regrettable events. The document as we now have it is three pages—the first page was made anew, and the second and third preexisting pages are full of corrections, additions, and items added in margins or between lines. Shakespeare signed the bottom of each page—adding on the last page "By me"—and the signatures of the March revisions are less steady, appearing to be completed by a struggling, sickly hand. Among Shakespeare scholars and those generally fascinated with his life and marriage, the will remains a much discussed and debated piece of evidence. Even this formal legal statement of Shakespeare's intentions for his estate and legacy raises more questions than answers. In this way, it resembles most other materials relating to Shakespeare.

The father retained an inheritance for Judith but required that she give up other rights to her sister, Susanna. Regarding another source of income, Judith was only to receive the interest from it, with the principal left untouched, and only if her husband could match the amount in question. Shakespeare seems concerned with ensuring that Judith not misspend the family inheritance, and also seems to demand that she and her husband be solvent on their own, and not rely primarily on a family income. Shakespeare showed special attention to his sister Joan, who became a widow in the same month as Shakespeare's death. He left her money for clothes and ensured her continued residence in the Henley Street family home. As for his movables, or housewares, he left a silver and gilt bowl to Judith, a sword to yet another member of the Combe family, and the rest of the plate was to go to his granddaughter Elizabeth. No plays are mentioned, but this is because Shakespeare did not, as an early modern playwright, legally own his plays; they were the property of the King's Men. Some manuscripts may have been destroyed in the Globe fire, and others—and additional legal records—were likely lost during the great fire of 1666. As for his library,

no books are mentioned, but any in his possession would have likely been left with the Halls. Shakespeare also left ten pounds for charity to Stratford's poor, which for someone of his wealth was a noticeably small figure; his lawyer, Collins, received three pounds more than this total for his work with the estate. He also specified an amount for his neighbor and dear friend Hamlet Sadler to buy a mourning ring, and, of greater interest to us, he similarly makes an allowance of twenty-six shillings for his "fellowes" in the King's Men to buy such rings. Only three men are named, though—Burbage, Heminges, and Condell, the latter two of whom would handsomely repay Shakespeare's rather modest bequest by preparing in his absence, and in honor of his memory, the First Folio of his collected plays.

The presence, or lack thereof, of Shakespeare's wife, Anne, in the will usually draws the most scrutiny, dismay, and/or defensiveness from readers. She is mentioned in the single most famous, most mysterious line in the document: "Item I give unto my wife my second best bed with the furniture." Is this a heartless rejection? A sneer from beyond the grave? Possibly, but it may also be that the second-best bed was their marriage bed, with the best bed being reserved for guests. What sounds like a dismissal may in fact be sweetly sentimental, an inside joke between longtime lovers and spouses. The current poet laureate of Britain, Carol Ann Duffy, has written a poem, "Anne Hathaway," cleverly giving this maddeningly silent wife a voice to this effect. But generally, Shakespeare's silences have sounded bitter or scornful to some. Nowhere does he formally bequeath to Anne the dower rights of one-third of the estate, which would traditionally fall to her. Then again, if this were a given fact, perhaps Shakespeare felt no additional need to stipulate that arrangement. The primary beneficiary of Shakespeare's will was his daughter Susanna, whom the father seemed to approve of and to trust the most. She was to receive New Place and additional properties. Her daughter, Elizabeth, and possible future children are carefully provided for as well. In fact, Shakespeare named Susanna and her husband, John, as executors of his estate. Even so, there is no affectionate language directed to the person who was clearly his favorite daughter, or to anyone else. This is consistent throughout the will. Peter Holland, in his *Oxford Dictionary of National Biography* entry on Shakespeare, says that the lack of even conventional terms of endearment, specific and substantial bequests to Anne, or, at the very least, formal permission for her to continue to live in New Place "amounts to a striking silence." That may be so, but again, it is good to stay sensitive to context. It may be that Shakespeare was quite ill by the time he wrote his will, and especially when he revised it. He may have been in no mood, in his pain, to address his wife of many years and the mother of his children as "wellbeloved," as some of his fellow King's Men did in their wills. It need not change the fact that Shakespeare was generally regarded for his wit and gentleness—he was, for John Davies of Hereford, "good Will"—and though he may not sound like it in his own will, his daughter Susanna very likely remembered him in this fashion. Perhaps Anne did, too, but that relationship remains most obscure, and the will does nothing to change this fact.

"In Warwickshire I have true-hearted friends," declares the Earl of Warwick in *3 Henry VI*. It is worth remembering that this was the region where Shakespeare grew up and where he later retired and died. Some anecdotes exist, fortunately, that suggest he did not face only property controversies and family marriage scandals during his last years. In fact, an early story claims that Shakespeare's final illness was precipitated by his being too much of a jolly man of the tavern. John Ward, a churchman who lived in Stratford in the 1660s, records that "Shakspeare, Drayton, and Ben Jonson had a merry meeting, and it seems drank too hard, for Shakespeare died of a fever there contracted." These may have been some of the occasions of those celebrated "wit-combats" between Shakespeare and Jonson, with the lively former poet showing off, in Thomas Fuller's words, "the quickness of his Wit and Invention." Michael Drayton was a fellow Midlands man who shared Shakespeare's poetic talents and love of their native countryside. Tradition often places these two writers in each other's good company during these last years. Ward's remarks deserve to be taken seriously: a memorandum indicates an appointment between the vicar and "Mrs. Quiney," being Judith Quiney, who died in 1662. Ward may have also heard stories from Shakespeare's nephew Thomas Hart, eleven years old when his uncle died. Shakespeare's son-in-law, John Hall, treated Drayton's maladies, and presumably he would have been caring for Shakespeare, too, as he grew ill or upon suffering a sudden, final sickness. Richard Davies, a rector at Sapperton in the Cotswolds, left an enigmatic note in a manuscript in 1700, saying simply about Shakespeare that "He died a papist," that is, one of the Roman Catholic religion rather than the Church of England. If this were so, his burial suggests that this fact, if true, was not public knowledge. On the other hand, we usually must proceed on what was publically thought to be so. The records suggest that Shakespeare personally had no crisis of conscience about worshipping or taking sacraments in the Anglican church.

Whatever the circumstances, the cause of death, and the state of his mind at the point of death, William Shakespeare was an aged man by Renaissance standards. His fellow playwright Francis Beaumont died in March 1616, in his early thirties. The older master followed soon after. Shakespeare died on April 23, 1616. It was St. George's Day, and very nearly, if not exactly, the same day he was born in 1564. He had entered the world in Stratford, and left the world there as well. He had just completed his fifty-second year. His tomb in the church floor bears an epitaph that traditionally has been identified as his own composition:

> Good friend for Jesus sake forebeare,
> To dig the dust enclosed here.
> Blest be the man that spares these stones
> And curst be he that moves my bones.

An anecdote dating from the end of the seventeenth century says that Shakespeare's descendents wished to be interred in his tomb, but they made other arrangements because they feared disturbing his bones and bringing upon themselves the curse of the epitaph. If these lines are by Shakespeare, and they may or may not be, then his writing had its powerful effects upon people to the very end. The Shakespeare family tombs occupy a very prominent spot in the church, suggesting his good civic standing and social prominence in the community. Besides William and Anne, also in this location are the tombs of Susanna and her husband, John Hall, along with that of Thomas Nash, the first husband of Shakespeare's granddaughter Elizabeth. Judith, the second daughter, is not buried here, but was buried outside, and the precise site of her grave has been lost.

The monument that masses of people still visit today, on the north wall above the chancel of Stratford's Holy Trinity Church, was probably installed before Shakespeare's wife, Anne, died in August 1623. The English actor Michael Pennington has commented on the "singularly unhelpful" bust, which makes his fellow actor and poet seem like nothing so much as a bourgeois landowner. And so he was. There are no signs, Pennington says, of the man made "tired with his own restless argument." Anne Shakespeare did not live to see the far greater, less disappointing, more enduring monument to her husband that appeared later that same year—the First Folio, assembled by two of his fellow actors. Although this collection may be infinitely valuable to most literature lovers, it is not an infinite book: it has a set number of pages, and contains thirty-six plays. That said, the thought and feeling in the plays, and how they express them, have proven far more expansive—making Shakespeare ever accessible, adaptable, and inexhaustible. Declan Donnellan, one of today's most esteemed directors of Shakespeare and founder of the theater company Cheek by Jowl, says it as well as anyone: when discussing Shakespeare, "I don't think you ever get to the end." In other words, biographies of Shakespeare, such as this one, must come to a close, but as for Shakespeare's poetry and characters and their confiding intimacies and dramatic outcomes, whether happy endings or tragic ends—well, those never do.

Sources and Further Reading

Bearman, Robert. *Shakespeare in the Stratford Records*. Stroud, England: Alan Sutton, 2006.

Cook, Judith. *Roaring Boys: Shakespeare's Rat Pack*. Charleston, S.C.: The History Press, 2006.

Greer, Germaine. *Shakespeare* (Oxford Past Masters series), New York: Oxford University Press, 1986.

McMullan, Gordon. introduction to John Fletcher, *The Tamer Tamed*. London: Nick Hern Books, 2003.

INDEX